MULTILINGUAL EDUCATION AND SUSTAINABLE DIVERSITY WORK

"This very original, inspirational book globalises our understanding of languages in education and changes our understanding of bilingual and multilingual education from something mostly western to being truly transnational: it spotlights the small, celebrates African and Asian cases of multilingual classrooms and demonstrates that such education is universally successful."

Colin R. Baker, Pro Vice-Chancellor, Bangor University, Bangor, Wales, UK

"A norm-setting work on multilingual education, which combines theoretical perspectives with practical experience from different parts of the globe, this book demonstrates convincingly not only that multilingual education works, but also that, for most developing countries, there is no viable alternative."

Ayo Bamgbose, Professor Emeritus, University of Ibadan, Nigeria

"This excellent volume brings to light the fascinating lived experiences of multilingual education in linguistically rich but resource impoverished countries, and offers important lessons from which we can all learn."

Amy B. M. Tsui, Professor, Pro Vice-Chancellor & Vice President, The University of Hong Kong, Hong Kong

"This is a book of hope and inspiration. Documenting the significant shift that is taking place in countries around the world in the status and legitimacy of mother tongue-based multilingual education, it represents a giant step towards a 'tipping point' where mother tongue-based multilingual education will be normalized as the preferred and, in fact, common sense option for educating the children of the world."

Jim Cummins, The University of Toronto, Canada

"This important book challenges us to think about multilingual education from a different angle – this time putting the periphery at the center. The effect is one of destabilizing old visions and imagining new worlds where multilingual education provides the backdrop for generous understandings of all peoples."

Ofelia García, Program in Urban Education, Graduate Center/
The City University of New York, USA

"There are regrettably few detailed accounts of successful elementary school instruction in the pupils' home language, which makes this book with its surprising examples (especially Ethiopia and Nepal but other third world cases) so relevant. Students of language education policy will learn a great deal about the possibility of multilingual education from the chapters of this important book."

Bernard Spolsky, Professor Emeritus, Bar-Ilan University, Israel

"At least half of today's languages are marginalised and endangered and the attention of the world needs to be focused on these minor and minority languages together with the value of multilingualism. If the book succeeds in enhancing the consciousness of the world towards predicaments of the third world, then its efforts will have been amply rewarded."

Debi Prasanna Pattanayak, Former Director, Central Institute of
Indian Languages, India

Drawing on the most powerful and compelling research data to date and connecting this research to linguistic human rights, this book explores the conditions and practices of robust bilingual and multilingual educational innovations in both system-wide and minority settings and what it is that makes these viable. It demonstrates how, in countries where educational practices are inclusive of linguistic diversity and responsive to local conditions and community participation, implementation of bilingual education even within limited budgetary investment can be successful.

Tove Skutnabb-Kangas is Associate Professor (Retired), University of Roskilde, Denmark and Associate Professor, Åbo Akademi University, Finland.

Kathleen Heugh is Senior Lecturer, English Language, University of South Australia and Extraordinary Associate Professor of Linguistics, University of the Western Cape, South Africa.

MULTILINGUAL EDUCATION AND SUSTAINABLE DIVERSITY WORK

From Periphery to Center

*Edited by Tove Skutnabb-Kangas
and Kathleen Heugh*

Routledge
Taylor & Francis Group

NEW YORK AND LONDON

NOT FOR SALE IN INDIA, PAKISTAN, BANGLADESH, SRI LANKA,
NEPAL, BHUTAN, AND THE MALDIVES.

First published 2012
by Routledge
711 Third Avenue, New York, NY 10017

Simultaneously published in the UK
by Routledge
2 Park Square, Milton Park, Abingdon, Oxon OX14 4RN

Routledge is an imprint of the Taylor & Francis Group, an informa business

© 2012 Taylor & Francis

Library of Congress Cataloging in Publication Data
Skutnabb-Kangas, Tove
  Multilingual education and sustainable diversity work : from periphery
  to center / Tove Skutnabb-Kangas, Kathleen Heugh.
  p. cm.
  1. Education, Bilingual—Cross-cultural studies.
  2. Multilingualism—Cross-cultural studies.
  3. Multicultural education—Cross-cultural studies.
  I. Heugh, Kathleen. II. Title.
  LC3715.S58 2011
  370.117'5—dc23
  2011019110

ISBN13: 978–0–415–89366–4 (hbk)
ISBN13: 978–0–415–89367–1 (pbk)
ISBN13: 978–0–203–81589–2 (ebk)

Typeset in Bembo by Swales & Willis Ltd, Exeter, Devon
Printed and bound in the United States of America on
acid-free paper by IBT Global

CONTENTS

Foreword   *vii*
  Adama Ouane
'Who Am I?'   *xi*
  Dainess Maganda
Acknowledgements   *xiii*
Notes on Terminology   *xv*

    Introduction: Reclaiming Sustainable Linguistic Diversity
    and Multilingual Education   1
    Tove Skutnabb-Kangas and Kathleen Heugh

  1 Multilingual Education in Ethiopian Primary Schools   32
    Carol Benson, Kathleen Heugh, Berhanu Bogale and
    Mekonnen Alemu Gebre Yohannes

  2 Language Choice, Education Equity, and Mother Tongue
    Schooling: Comparing the Cases of Ethiopia and
    Native America   62
    Teresa L. McCarty

  3 Language and Culture in Education: Comparing Policies
    and Practices in Peru and Ethiopia   85
    Susanne Pérez Jacobsen and Lucy Trapnell Forero

4 A Critical Comparison of Language-in-Education Policy
and Practice in Four Southeast Asian Countries and Ethiopia 111
Carol Benson and Kimmo Kosonen

5 MLE and the Double Divide in Multilingual Societies:
Comparing Policy and Practice in India and Ethiopia 138
Ajit Mohanty

6 Enhancing Quality Education for All in Nepal through
Indigenised MLE: The Challenge to Teach in Over a
Hundred Languages 151
Iina Nurmela, Lava Deo Awasthi and Tove Skutnabb-Kangas

7 MLE from Ethiopia to Nepal: Refining a Success Story 178
Shelley K. Taylor

8 Setting a Tradition of Mother Tongue-Medium Education
in 'Francophone' Africa: The Case of Burkina Faso 197
Norbert Nikièma and Paul Taryam Ilboudo

9 'There is No Such Thing as "Keeping out of Politics"':
Arabisation and Amazigh/Berber Mother Tongue Education
in Morocco 216
Ahmed Kabel

10 Implications for Multilingual Education: Student
Achievement in Different Models of Education in Ethiopia 239
*Kathleen Heugh, Carol Benson, Mekonnen Alemu Gebre
Yohannes and Berhanu Bogale*

11 'Peripheries' Take Centre Stage: Reinterpreted
Multilingual Education Works 263
Kathleen Heugh and Tove Skutnabb-Kangas

About the Authors 284
Index 291

FOREWORD

Adama Ouane

Languages are the keystone to humanity's intangible heritage. They are markers of identity, the foundation shared by societies and indispensable tools for communication. They have variously been seen as the basis of thought; as the expression of the human spirit; as an instrument for representing the world; and as the reflection of the collective memory and identity of the speakers. As languages are an integral part of society, it follows that neither should be isolated from the other.

Education for All requires that we consider the many and varied cultural and linguistic contexts that characterise our societies today. It also requires us to cater for all learners. There is sufficient evidence to demonstrate that multilingual educational initiatives are both possible and viable means of enhancing Education for All and other goals, and that these go a long way towards accommodating diversity. However, what capture our attention in today's world are the enormous inequalities among the multitude of languages in existence, which can be a major barrier to any education, let alone quality education. Linguistically homogeneous countries, like Iceland, are rare, and the majority of the world's countries and regions boast a wealth of linguistic diversity. In some cases, the sheer range of languages is a complex issue in itself, as with Papua New Guinea, with over 800 languages, Indonesia, with more than 700 and Nigeria, with over 400.

Safeguarding cultural diversity today is one of our most urgent challenges. It is one that UNESCO has undertaken to address by committing to a number of normative instruments on education, such as the 1960 Convention against Discrimination in Education, the 2001 UNESCO Declaration on Cultural Diversity, the Convention on the Protection and Promotion of the Diversity of Cultural Expressions of 2005, as well as the Convention for the Safeguarding of the Intangible Cultural Heritage, which entered into force on 20 April 2006 and is currently attracting much attention as the subject of wide-ranging and passionate debate.

The challenge that education systems now face is to provide quality education that takes learners' needs into consideration, whilst at the same time balancing these with contemporary social, cultural and political demands. A multilingual educational approach, in which language is recognised as an integral part of a student's cultural identity, is an important factor for inclusion, participation and democracy. It promotes respect, tolerance and equality for others. Educating 'in and for diversity' teaches us how to live together. It also enables us to develop new ways of learning to do, learning to know and learning to be based on pluralism, mutual understanding and respect, democratic relationships and fundamentally human values. It is for these reasons that it should be recognised as a crucial part of all educational systems.

Most countries introduce an international language during the upper primary grades; few, however, allocate time to local languages. These policies not only undermine the preservation of linguistic diversity, but also reduce the positive effects of multilingualism, which can improve intellectual functioning and intercultural dialogue.

From 2003 to 2006, the Association for the Development of Education in Africa (ADEA) and the UNESCO Institute for Lifelong Learning (UIL) examined a range of approaches to mother tongue, and bilingual education in sub-Saharan Africa. An extensive report for ADEA and UNESCO in 2006 (Alidou et al. 2006) summed up the study by concluding that the most effective way of guaranteeing African children quality education and of achieving sustainable development was to provide strong models of bilingual education. The report furthermore indicated that the best educational models were those that integrated additional languages into programmes that continually fostered the development of children's mother tongues and mother-tongue literacy.

A collection of case studies (on Mali, Papua New Guinea, Peru and the USA) gathered by UNESCO in 2007 (Bühmann and Trudell 2008) again points to the benefits of mother tongue-based multilingual education. These indicate that mother tongue-based bilingual programmes are significantly more effective in enhancing learners' outcomes and academic achievements than their monolingual second-language counterparts. Four key lessons can be learned from these case studies. First, implementing initiatives like these is contingent on developing the capacities of a critical mass of professionals at all levels. Second, there is already a great deal of expertise available that can be shared and used. Third, the available evidence from research and practice suggests that the medium- and long-term benefits of effective mother tongue-based multilingual education programmes that link education to learners' lives far outweigh the costs of the reforms needed to implement such programmes. And last but not least, these initiatives are dependent on community support and empowerment.

In light of the above, *Multilingual Education Works* is a timely and highly significant work. The calibre of the contributing authors, their depth of expertise and experience, all add weight to the arguments they put forward and increase the value of this publication considerably. Furthermore, the volume's focus on the use of languages in multilingual settings and the role of multilingual education in language policies, and its core message – that the promotion and protection of languages in a national landscape is of the utmost importance – shed light on shared concerns that continue to gain ground in our rapidly changing world. The recent data this book explores point to the crucial benefits that inclusive multilingual education programmes centring on linguistic diversity offer developing countries.

A further distinctive factor of this volume is its attempt to provide the basis for international comparison by examining and analysing the experiences of one country in particular: Ethiopia. Does this country deserve such scrutiny, we might ask ourselves. Indeed, it does! Ethiopia is a multilingual country with a long and unique social and political history. In particular, Article five of its constitution – born after the fall of a repressive regime built on the ashes of an imperial nation – stipulates that all Ethiopian languages must enjoy state recognition. The pragmatic implementation of this decree has left the various regions free to implement programmes of education that go beyond merely recognising Amharic as the country's common national language and English as its international language. The richness and variety of the multilingual models and contexts found in Ethiopia create a strong empirical basis not only for assessing the situation in the country, but also for identifying lessons and experiences of relevance far beyond its national boundaries.

The Ethiopian study showcases many of the models of language education currently in place in African countries. Its multilingual education approach has become central to its educational policy as a whole. Initially, the main argument for adopting a mother-tongue educational approach was based on both constitutional and educational considerations. Since then, Ethiopia has proved that linguistic diversity can be managed efficiently by maintaining a balance between centralised and decentralised policies. However, it should be noted that the study also indicates that key decisions have sometimes post-dated the implementation of policies, thereby inevitably undermining their effectiveness, however progressive the policies in question. The study furthermore points to the not unambiguous role of donors/grants/agencies, and the unreliable evaluations and advice that have hampered decision-makers.

Crucially, this volume argues that voices from the margins make a valuable contribution to education – both on the margins and in the mainstream. These voices help to reposition the locus of expertise to Africa, South America and South-East Asia and to correct misleading historical preconceptions about Africa and the other so-called developing regions of the world. The book includes and validates the indigenous knowledge and expertise of those on the margins. In addition, it aims to identify the stakeholder interests that can hinder multilingual approaches, as well as those that can encourage these stakeholders to advocate for real and lasting change.

I was particularly pleased to see the inclusion of a selection of case studies that provide the basis for international comparison. In addition to the studies of language policies in India, Burkina Faso and Morocco, we can find the example of a language policy in Peru that establishes a powerful link between the right to be taught in languages other than Spanish and Indigenous people's struggle to see their cultural heritage and collective rights recognised and defended. A similar insight is provided in the analysis of the situation of the Navajo people in the US State of Arizona. A thorough exploration of multilingualism in the South-East Asian context adds weight to the case for increased 'South–South' cooperation and collaboration with regard to the status and promotion of non-dominant languages. All of these studies concur that 'while maintenance of linguistic diversity depends on a host of complex factors, use of languages in education is seen as a powerful force in survival and development of languages' (Mohanty, this volume).

Finally, and most importantly of all, this publication gains strength from the background of its two lead editors. The analytical insights and powerful arguments posited by Tove Skutnabb-Kangas and Kathleen Heugh paint a convincing portrait of the inestimable value of local languages in the educational setting. While Tove Skutnabb-Kangas offers a fully fledged theory of 'linguicide' (linguistic genocide) that makes an audacious and compelling case for guaranteeing the right to one's mother tongue, Kathleen Heugh boldly tackles the economic issues relating to local language use and does not flinch from confronting the 'clerics' of the economic orthodoxy with her findings. The conviction and complementarity of these two perspectives is the most compelling feature of this book.

I am honoured to contribute to this landmark publication in the field of multilingual education, and would like to conclude simply by quoting E. Wolff's eloquent tenet cited in the UIL/ADEA study: 'Language is not everything in education, but without language everything is nothing in education.'

References

Alidou, Hassana, Boly, Aliou, Brock-Utne, Birgit, Diallo, Yaya Satina, Heugh, Kathleen and Wolff, H. Ekkehard (2006). *Optimizing Learning and Education in Africa – the Language Factor*. A Stock-taking Research on Mother Tongue and Bilingual Education in Sub-Saharan Africa. Joint report, Association for the Development of Education in Africa (ADEA), UNESCO Institute for Education (UIE) and Deutsche Gesellschaft für Technische Zusammenarbeit (GTZ). UNESCO: Paris.

Bühmann, Dorthe and Trudell, Barbara (2008). *Mother Tongue Matters: Local Language as a Key to Effective Learning*. UNESCO: Paris.

Mohanty, Ajit K. (this volume). MLE and the Double Divide in Multilingual Societies: Comparing Policy and Practice in India and Ethiopia.

WHO AM I?

Dainess Maganda

I am a lost identity
I am a struggling soul
I am a shuttered mind
I am a mumbling mouth
I don't know who I am
I was born with a voice but lost it
I am told English is all that matters
I am told my identity doesn't matter
I am persuaded my voice is worthless
I am taught to learn what is popular
I am told to ignore who I am
I am told to forget what it means to be me
I am told to go with the flow
I am forced to mourn the loss of my essence
But, I don't know who I am and so, I don't think it matters
I am a lost soul, a lost voice, a lost identity, a lost value of humanity

The world tells me
Don't worry,
You don't need to learn in a language you understand
Because it is not the language of power
You don't need to comprehend what you learn
You don't need to be who you are in order to know what the world is
You don't need to be heard for the world to notice you
You only need to speak as the world does – what matters is what
you should do and not what you need to do.

Cry your heart out – the world cannot hear because it doesn't know your voice
Speak, the world won't mind because it doesn't understand your language
Sleep, the world won't notice because it can't feel your heart beat
Close your mind, because that is what the world wants you to do and
Close your heart, because that's what the world NEEDS you to do
BUT, I say
Let me speak, let me breathe,
Let me live.
My life makes Humanity
I matter.

ACKNOWLEDGEMENTS

This book is dedicated to children who struggle to attend and participate in school education in environments which are multilingual and in which they are members of Indigenous/tribal and minority communities, vulnerable or at risk. We also dedicate this book to our own (multilingual) children and grandchildren: Ilka, Kea, Uki, Caragh and Leila.

We would especially like to thank Robert and Anthony for their patience and encouragement as this was probably a more complex project than either of us had at first thought. Each of the contributors to this volume has brought unique insight and expertise and we should like to acknowledge their willingness to contribute to the volume and their children for allowing them the time to do so.

Several people have generously provided translations of 'multilingual education works' (or 'mother tongue education works') for the cover of the book. We would like to thank Berhanu Bogale and Mekonnen Alemu Gebre Yohannes for Amharic, Tigrinya and Afan Oromo (Ethiopia); Lava Deo Awasthi with Yogendra Yadava for Maithili (Nepal); Norbert Nikièma and Paul Taryam Ilboudo, with Jules Kinda, Gérard Kedrebeogo and Emmanuel Sawadogo for Mòoré (Burkina Faso); Ajit Mohanty with Lokanath Panda for Oriya, Kui and Saora (India); Susanne Pérez and Lucy Trapnell Forero with Nonato Rufino Chuquimamani Valer for Quechua (Peru); and Irene Silentman with Teresa McCarty for Navajo (USA). We thank Miranda Roccisano, and the Research Centre for Languages and Cultures at the University of South Australia, for assistance with the index.

Finally, we should like to acknowledge the courageous solid work, often accomplished under extremely difficult conditions, of scholars from the 'periphery' whose work offers so much experience, expertise and dignity for the 'centre'.

Likewise, we want to celebrate the creative teachers in these countries who work with few material resources, large classes, mostly inadequate formal training, and also parents and communities who find ways to build classrooms and support stable and sustainable learning environments.

Trønninge Mose and Adelaide (distance 15,286 km/9,498 miles; thanks Skype!)
Tove Skutnabb-Kangas and Kathleen Heugh

NOTES ON TERMINOLOGY

We use the following abbreviations throughout the book (additional abbreviations specific to each chapter will be defined or explained in the relevant chapters):

MLE	Mother Tongue-Based Multilingual Education
MOI or MoI	Medium of Instruction
MT	Mother Tongue
MTM	Mother Tongue Medium

We want to emphasise the following distinctions, because their importance is often overlooked:

Indigenous people/s vs indigenous populations/groups. Only 'a people', plural 'peoples', have the right to self-determination: 'populations' and 'groups' do not. 'Tribals' is an official term for Indigenous peoples in India. We use 'Indigenous peoples' in the book.

Indigenous vs minority. Minorities do not have the right to self-determination. They are not included in UNDRIP, the United Nations Declaration of the Rights of Indigenous Peoples. Indigenous peoples have all the rights that minorities have, plus additional rights. 'Linguistically diverse students' have no rights in international law; 'minority students' do.

MLE vs multilingual classrooms. Some people call a multilingual classroom with students who have different mother tongues, MLE. This is a misuse of the concept. MLE, mother tongue-based multilingual education, is based on strong development of the mother tongue (or language of the immediate community best known by the child), with the addition of at least one other language (often two or even three other languages). All will be used for teaching some subjects, in a carefully considered sequence, to achieve high levels of multilingualism and multiliteracy. Bilingual education is a subcategory under multilingual education.

Mother tongue as a subject vs mother tongue as a medium. Mother tongues can be taught as subjects in school while all other subjects are taught using another language as the medium for teaching and learning. This is not bilingual education. When the mother tongue is used as the teaching and learning language for mathematics, history, etc., it is the medium of education. Initially, it may be the only medium. For Indigenous peoples and minorities, a dominant language may later become a, or the, medium of education. UNESCO uses the term 'mother tongue education' for 'mother tongue-*medium* education'. Even if UNESCO, clarifies what is meant, the term itself may be ambiguous and (mis)understood to mean the teaching of the mother tongue as a subject only.

Submersion vs immersion. In *submersion programmes*, linguistic minority children with a low-status mother tongue are obliged to accept instruction through a foreign or second majority/official/dominant language, in classes in which the teacher does not understand the minoritised mother tongue, and in which the use of the dominant language constitutes a threat to the further development and use of the mother tongue. It runs the risk of being replaced; a *subtractive* language learning situation. In another variant, stigmatised majority children (or groups of minority children in a country with no decisive numerical and/or power majorities) are obliged or coerced (through dominant discourses of power) to accept instruction through the medium of a foreign or second (often former colonial) high-status language (because mother tongue-medium education does not exist). In classical *immersion programmes*, parents of linguistic majority children with a high-status mother tongue (e.g., Anglophones in Ontario, Canada) choose voluntarily to enrol their children in a programme in which instruction is conducted through the medium of a foreign/minority language. Most of the children in these classes are majority language children with the same mother tongue. Teachers are bilingual and well qualified; children can initially use their own language and still be understood. Children's mother tongue is not in danger of being replaced by the language of instruction; it is an *additive* language learning context. Although children enrolled in French immersion programmes in Canada initially represented a largely homogeneous Anglophone population, increasingly, children whose mother tongue is neither English nor French are enrolling in these programmes. Even when the medium of instruction is initially a language foreign to the children in both submersion and immersion, the contexts and results are completely different.

Revitalisation immersion programmes for Indigenous peoples or minorities are for dominated-group children who have partially or completely lost their ancestral language; they or their (grand)parents have been forcibly assimilated linguistically. They choose voluntarily, among existing alternatives, to be instructed through the medium of the Indigenous/minority language, in classes with children with the same goal and target language, in which the teacher is bilingual so that children can initially use their dominant language, and in contexts in which the dominant language is not in danger of being replaced by the Indigenous/minority language; also an a*dditiv*e language learning context.

Subtractive vs additive language learning. In subtractive learning (some of) the dominant language is learned at the cost of the mother tongue (which does not develop up to a high formal level). Literacy (sustainable literacy for everyday purposes, and academic literacy) is often not achieved. In additive learning a dominant language and other languages are learned in addition to the mother tongue and the goal is to develop a high level of literacy and communicative and cognitive competence in each of them.

Editorial note on the use of terminology. We deliberately make use of terminology in this volume that has most widespread and current use. Most sociolinguists problematise the use of terminology in general, and some specifically in relation to language in education. We do this too (see, e.g., Skutnabb-Kangas and McCarty's article on definitions, 2008). But we make a distinction between the application of terminology which is currently in use both in research literature and in the broader context of society, and some of the contemporary debates on this terminology in sociolinguistics. There are a number of terms in common and frequent use, most especially the term 'mother tongue' which draw considerable debate. The philosophical deconstruction of vocabulary and concepts, for example, whether or not 'languages' per se and concepts like 'mother tongue' are imagined or invented, is undoubtedly a valuable philosophical activity in exploratory debates in the academic field. We acknowledge all of the debates here and the extensive literature on these. Nevertheless, ordinary people in most parts of the world use the term 'mother tongue' in its broad figurative sense – which often includes several varieties or languages – rather than in a narrow, literal and monolingual sense. The practical realities of what to teach and how to teach children to read and write so that they have tangible access to a curriculum that will equip them for contemporary and globalised society require pragmatism based on sound, evidence-based principles. Thus we work with practical notions of what languages are and how they function inside educational institutions and how they may be used to facilitate the best possible access to quality education.

INTRODUCTION

Reclaiming Sustainable Linguistic Diversity and Multilingual Education

Tove Skutnabb-Kangas and Kathleen Heugh

I.1 Why this Book?

The mirage of a homogenous globalised world imagined during the latter decades of the 20th century is dissolving. Globalisation, coinciding with a revolution in information technology, at first appeared to point to a gravitational pull towards international languages of wider communication, especially English. Simultaneously, new patterns of migration arising out of a complex mix of sociopolitical and economic tensions, have brought about unprecedented changes which increase linguistic, cultural and faith-based diversity in urban and educational settings. At this time, it has become evident that there are apparent contradictions between the reality of diversity and an aspiration towards homogeneity. These have significant implications for the provision of education if the needs of diverse students for participatory citizenship are to be met. In the South, where diversity has long been acknowledged, there are numerous examples of productive engagement with multilingualism and sustainable development. It is towards some of these examples that this volume turns when the challenges of the UNESCO Decade for Sustainable Development in Education (2005–14) are still before us. The authors in this book illustrate successful advances in, and implementation of, mother tongue-based bi/multilingual education (MLE) despite limited resources in contexts which are spatially dislocated from, or at significant distance from, those which are positioned as at the centre. The purpose of this book is to demonstrate that expertise in the management of sustainable models of education in the so-called 'peripheries' offers valuable insights into bilingual and multilingual theory, decentralisation and cost-efficient resourcing of education systems which are sensitive to widely varying student needs.

I.1.1 MLE and the Year 2050

The world's future depends on how well the youth is educated, today and tomorrow. The languages that are used to teach various subjects in school are decisive for the outcome of the education that children get. Everywhere in the world people need several languages for participation in local, regional, national and sometimes international activities. High levels of bi/multilingualism have to be a fundamental goal in schools, alongside content-related and attitudinal goals. Bilingualism is the minimal requirement for people in the 21st century.

Nobel laureate Amartya Sen (e.g. 1985; Dreze and Sen 2002) states that poverty is not only about economic conditions and growth. Expansion of human capabilities is a more basic locus when analysing poverty alleviation, and it should be a more basic objective of development (e.g. Misra and Mohanty 2000a, b; Mohanty 2000).

Dominant-language medium education for Indigenous, tribal and minority (ITM) children, the type of education that most receive if they attend school at all, often curtails the development of children's capabilities. Thus it perpetuates poverty. The questions, then, are: what can be done and is being done to ensure that all children receive a formal education that enhances their capabilities? And what is the role of the medium of education in this challenge?

Today's education in most of those countries that will be most populous, and have the largest percentage of children and youth in 2050 (see below) is a veritable disaster for all but a small elite. The United Nations Millennium Development Goal 2 is: 'Ensure that, by 2015, children everywhere, boys and girls alike, will be able to complete a full course of primary schooling' (see http://www.un.org/millenniumgoals). Even a cursory look at the World Bank's online Atlas of Goal 2 shows that most of Africa south of Sahara still has fewer than 50% of school-going students complete primary education. Pakistan is the only country in other parts of the world with equally low completion rates (see http://devdata.worldbank.org/atlas-mdg/).[1]

Most of the world's Indigenous and tribal peoples and most of the world's minorities live in Africa, Asia, Latin America and the Pacific. That is also where most of the world's languages are. What about the year 2050?

Between 2010 and 2050, virtually all population growth will take place in the countries classified as 'less developed'[2] (LDCs) by the United Nations. In many 'more developed countries' (MDCs), most growth will likely be due to immigration from LDCs. While the population in LDCs is projected to increase from 5.6 billion in 2009 to 8.1 billion in 2050, it is projected to grow from 1.2 billion to just 1.3 billion in the MDCs (http://www.prb.org/Publications/Datasheets/2009/2009wpds.aspx).

What is the significance of these statistics for this book? The education system fails the majority of students in those countries that will be most populous in 2050, for many reasons explored in this book.

According to the Population Reference Bureau (http://www.prb.org), 'about one in five people, over 1.2 billion people, are between the ages of 15 and 24'. The vast majority (almost 90%) of the world's youth, 1.1 billion, are in LDCs. Sub-Saharan Africa has the world's most youthful population and it is projected to stay that way for decades. Educational opportunities of the youth are vital for the world's future – and the medium of education plays a decisive role in this.

With the right investments in health, education, rural agricultural development, entrepreneurship, and training, a large youth population can be an opportunity for development and economic growth. However, without educational opportunities and a strong economy with healthy labour markets, the youth bulge can be problematic. The lack of job opportunities for youth in many countries breeds frustration. Some youth with few job prospects and little hope of future advancement may resort to antisocial and criminal activities or join in armed conflicts (Bremner *et al.* 2009: 6). To what extent can the youth develop their capabilities to the full through education? Chapters in this book show that, despite major challenges, there are solutions in the very countries where they are most needed. These solutions may also contribute towards challenges in 'MDC' countries.

In this section, we sketched some of the challenges for 2050 in relation to what mother tongue-based multilingual education (MLE), must achieve. Section I.1.2 presents the main ideas behind this book and section I.1.3 focuses on a few gaps and challenges in earlier research. In section I.2.1, the authors summarise their chapters in their own words, through their abstracts, in the same order as in the list of contents. In section I.2.2 we select a few issues related to the abstracts for a brief discussion; more follows in our concluding chapter. In I.3, the final section of the Introduction, we contextualise at a macro level the various countries' children of school-going age and their education, by presenting some statistical data about economic, social and health-related living conditions and school attendance. We also look at the extent to which international human rights instruments can be used to support (mother tongue-based) MLE.

I.1.2 The Background and Purpose of this Book

For the last century or more, the dominance of Western and Northern epistemological influence accompanied by considerable economic and human investment has been brought to bear on education in countries of the South/South-East (e.g. Skutnabb-Kangas 2000; Mazrui 2002; Wolff 2006; Phillipson 2009, amongst many others). While these have materialised in educational curricula programmes and textbooks largely modelled on those from North America and Europe, they have eschewed local and regional linguistic diversity and seldom borne fruit in Africa, South America, South and South-East Asia. Local, indigenous or organically developed educational practices have been largely overlooked or misunderstood from without and replaced with ones which do not meet the needs of communities on the margins.

As part of a five-point plan to reinvigorate education in Africa, Alamin Mazrui threw down a gauntlet to scholars in the South in 2002 to take their research and scholarship into the Western and Northern diaspora. This volume responds to that challenge. It also broadens it by including successful practices in education which foreground the systematic use of the mother tongue/local language alongside an international language of wider communication and, possibly, a third language with regional or national significance. The book is about the use of these languages, side by side, in programmes developed from within 'peripheried' contexts of both the South and the East, namely Africa, India, Nepal, South-East Asia and Latin America, as well as in North America. In these settings communities are not necessarily numerically in the minority, but peripheried as minority communities, nevertheless, through dominant discourses held in the North.[3]

The case studies here demonstrate current bilingual, multilingual and intercultural practices, valuable across the wider global stage. They identify what works, as well as the risks and vulnerabilities which offer both challenges and opportunities for their productive management.

The purpose of this book is to demonstrate that in low-income countries where educational practices are inclusive of linguistic diversity, and responsive to local conditions and community participation, recent compelling data show successful implementation of bilingual and multilingual education, even within limited budgetary investment. Authors from different parts of the world engage here with an earlier study (Heugh, Benson, Bogale and Gebre Yohannes 2007)[4] of the medium of instruction in Ethiopia where bi/multilingual models of education are implemented through different regional models (from subtractive to very late-exit transition). Each of these models has been the subject of scholarly debate for the last three decades. But this is the first occasion in which student achievement through each model can be compared across a whole system. Ethiopia thus offers an authentic 'laboratory' case study of comparative bilingual and multilingual education at an international level.

The Ethiopian case confirms decades of language acquisition, bi/multilingual theory of Baker, Cummins, Garçia, Lo Bianco, May, McCarty, Phillipson, Skutnabb-Kangas, Hornberger, and Spolsky, amongst other 'Western' researchers. It also confirms and goes much further than earlier research on mother tongue and bilingual education in South Africa (Malherbe 1946) and Bamgbose in Nigeria in the 1970s. It chimes with the work in other contexts, for example, of Pattanayak, Mohanty, Annamalai, and Agnihotri in India, and López in Bolivia. There are at least two reasons why the Ethiopian case is instructive. First, it demonstrates that a poor country can implement a linguistically diverse education system. Second, the student assessment chimes with that of large-scale studies of minority bilingual education gathered in a very different, richly resourced, USA (Thomas and Collier 2002 and later).

It is the significance of the Ethiopian study, for both low-income countries and dominant world powers exhibiting unprecedented (trans)migration, urbanisation and diversification, that gave rise to early discussions about this volume. Developments in bi/multilingual education, often together with intercultural education, occur in many other low-income contexts and have equally significant contributions to international knowledge of the field. Contemporary South–South reflexive debate and engagement with key educational concerns emerge in this book where innovative bi/multilingual programmes are examined in relation to the Ethiopian study to explore possibilities for transformative education through new lenses and for their relevance to both South and North.

1.1.3 Earlier Research and Gaps

The scientific literature on bilingual and multilingual education dates back at least as far as the late 1930s in South Africa. Students in dual medium education for the seven years of primary school achieved higher scores in school at the secondary school leaving examinations, had developed higher levels of bilingual achievement, and were socially more tolerant of difference than students in monolingual schools with the second language as a subject (Malherbe 1946).

Since that time, a considerable body of work has contributed to international discussions on bilingualism, from the work of Peal and Lambert in the 1960s and 1970s (particularly the identification of subtractive and additive bilingualism), to that of Cummins, Baker, García, Skutnabb-Kangas and Çenoz,[5] among others, from the 1970s onwards. Most of this work, however, has been conducted in settings where the majority population uses English, or where English occupies a position of dominance, or both. While significant contributions by Pattanayak, Agnihotri, Annamalai and Mohanty (writing in English), have filtered through to the debates in Europe and North America, this has not been the case for much of the work from Latin America, Africa and the Far East. This is a serious gap: both the context of education in these settings and the configuration of languages in use in society are entirely different from North America or Europe.

A second significant gap in the research, concerns second (and possibly also third) language acquisition, SLA (Jessner 2008), particularly in relation to a second (or foreign) language as medium of instruction. Watson-Gegeo and Nielsen (2003) suggest that a weakness in SLA theory has been an over-emphasis on the cognitive aspects of language learning with scant regard for the sociocultural and interactive contexts in which language is learnt (addressed by Pérez and Trapnell, and McCarty, in this volume). A further weakness has been that the studies have been conducted on small samples and often in rarefied laboratory-like settings (see Doughty and Long (2003) for a critique of this) rather than in the hurly-burly of (large) classroom settings, and particularly where resources are limited. Missing from the main body of research is SLA in situations where the L2 has an official/institutional function in a multilingual society (e.g. Kiswahili in Tanzania, Amharic in Ethiopia, Spanish in Peru, Hindi in India) or where the L2 is a minority language in the numerical sense (e.g. English in South Africa, French in Senegal, Portuguese in Mozambique) and where a majority of learners have (an)other language(s) as L1. Both situations apply to most countries in Africa, South and South-East Asia and Latin America.

The Association for the Development of Education in Africa (ADEA)-UNESCO Institute for Education (UIE) *Report on Mother Tongue and Bilingual Education in sub-Saharan Africa* (Alidou *et al.* 2006) identified a number of short-comings in the research on bilingual education progammes. Many are currently early-exit models, frequently accompanied by unreliable evaluations. In a nut-shell, one simply cannot tell if a new early literacy, mother tongue, or bilingual model is likely to have a lasting and positive effect on student learning without an accompanying longitudinal study in which students' progress is tracked over six years or more (cf. also Thomas and Collier 2002).

Missing also from the debates in the South has been a strong South–South conversation about MLE and an effective mechanism for sharing the information and learning from the experiences of others.

I.2 What Does this Book Bring?

I.2.1 Abstracts of the Chapters

In this section, the authors summarise their chapters in their own words, through their abstracts. Readers might want first to glance at the tables in section I.3, to make it easier to locate the countries under discussion. In section I.2.2 we select a few issues from the abstracts for a brief discussion; more follows in our conclud-ing chapter.

Carol Benson, Kathleen Heugh, Berhanu Bogale and Mekonnen Alemu Gebre Yohannes summarise their chapter, 'Multilingual Education in Ethiopian Primary Schools', in the following way:

> In 2006 the Ethiopian Ministry of Education commissioned a study to evaluate how a multilingual education policy had been implemented across the various regions of the country since 1994. This chapter summarises the study and its findings. The Ethiopian case is exemplary for many rea-sons, including the adoption of a national policy that is consistent with contemporary research supporting extended educational use of learners' first languages. The study illustrates decentralised educational policy imple-mentation across nine semi-autonomous regions and two city administra-tions. Differences in practice make Ethiopia something of a microcosm of different 'models' of bi/trilingual education, in terms of number of years of mother tongue-medium schooling (none, four, six, or eight). The sys-tem includes a 'national' language of wider communication (Amharic, as a second language) and English (as a foreign language, FL). The case also demonstrates how some years after the policy was first implemented, a later

misplaced focus on an FL, English, at higher levels of the system appears to compromise effective mother tongue practices. The Ethiopian experience, nevertheless, demonstrates that theoretically sound language policy can be implemented in poor schools, and that it can significantly improve learning outcomes for learners in multilingual settings.

Teresa L. McCarty writes the following about her chapter, 'Language Choice, Education Equity, and Mother Tongue Schooling: Comparing the Cases of Ethiopia and Native America':

Recent research on medium-of-instruction in Ethiopian primary schools provides compelling evidence that 'strong' models of bi-/multilingual schooling produce superior academic outcomes. These findings refute widespread policies and popular discourse that schools and learners must choose *either* mother tongue schooling *or* schooling in the language of wider communication. This chapter extends lessons from the Ethiopian study, drawing parallels and contrasts with language education for Indigenous students in the United States. The chapter focuses on two data sets, one from programmes in which the Indigenous/minoritised language is the primary language, and a second from programmes in which the Indigenous language is learned as a second language but is nonetheless the language of identity and community. The Native American findings show that the dominant tongue will be learned at high levels when a strong academic programme is provided through the Indigenous language, even when it is learned as a second language. The chapter concludes with a comparative analysis of Native American and Ethiopian cases, a response to cautionary findings from the Ethiopian study, and a summary of 'best knowledge' on effective and equitable language education practices and policies. Together, the cases argue against a 'one-size-fits-all' approach and for local, Indigenous control over curricular content and delivery.

Susanne Pérez Jacobsen and Lucy Trapnell Forero present their chapter, 'Language and Culture in Education: Comparing Policies and Practices in Peru and Ethiopia', as follows:

The study of Ethiopia highlights a number of issues that are relevant to a discussion regarding the way in which language and education are approached in multicultural and multilingual settings. This chapter focuses on the similarities and differences that exist between Peruvian and Ethiopian education policies and practices. It concentrates on three issues which help to establish comparisons at political and pedagogical levels and to introduce new elements for discussion about quality education: (1) the pedagogical and political agendas behind Peru's education policies; (2) language and culture in classroom practice; and (3) the approach to intercultural bilingual education (IBE) in regional education policies. Owing to the intimate relation between bilingual education and indigenous peoples' political organisation in Peru, this chapter includes language and education policies as part of a larger discussion about education, language, culture and power. The chapter is based on the experience of the two authors in the development of intercultural bilingual programmes in Peru, and research. Data sources include a literature review, personal observations in the field, and interviews with people involved in the development of IBE.

Carol Benson and Kimmo Kosonen write the following about their chapter, 'A Critical Comparison of Language-in-Education Policy and Practice in Four Southeast Asian Countries and Ethiopia':

> The case of Ethiopia raises a number of issues that are relevant to a discussion of language-in-education policy and practice in Southeast Asia. We begin with an introduction to the region and the four case study countries – Cambodia, Lao People's Democratic Republic (Laos), Thailand and Vietnam – each with an autochthonous national and/or official language as well as diverse ethnolinguistic minority groups. Next we compare and contrast their approaches toward improving educational offerings to ethnolinguistic minority learners. We then analyse language-in-education policies and subsequent practices from a Southeast Asian perspective with reference to three key issues which we have identified from the Ethiopian case: (1) adoption of a theoretically sound approach toward mother tongue-based education; (2) recognition of the negative effects on learners' languages when the dominant language is prioritised; and (3) the role of decentralisation in implementing a bi-/multilingual policy, particularly with regard to linguistically heterogeneous regions. Finally, we demonstrate how Southeast Asian countries and Ethiopia could learn from one another, providing insights for policy and practice in these and other parts of the world.

Ajit Mohanty summarises his chapter, 'MLE and the Double Divide in Multilingual Societies: Comparing Policy and Practice in India and Ethiopia', as follows:

> Aspects of language-in-education policy and experimental MLE programmes in India are discussed with comparative reflections on the Ethiopian issues and findings. A double divide – one between English and the major national language(s) and, the other, between the national and the dominated Indigenous/tribal and minority languages – characterises multilingualism in India and Ethiopia. The need to balance between English and the languages of national and regional identities is a major factor in

language-in-education policy and practice in both the countries. It is suggested that the preference for early English in Indian education needs to
be problematised in view of the Ethiopian finding that strengthening the
mother tongue (MT) is necessary for quality learning of English. MLE for
tribal mother tongue children in two states and an innovative *MLE Plus*
programme in India show some initial success. The early transitions from
mother tongue to other languages and to English in India might be better
than submersion education in a dominant language. Nevertheless, as the
Ethiopian findings show, late-exit multilingual education, which uses MT
as a language of teaching for at least six to eight years, would be the most
effective strategy for development of high levels of competence in other
languages, including English.

Iina Nurmela, Lava Deo Awasthi and Tove Skutnabb-Kangas sum up their
chapter, 'Enhancing Quality Education for All in Nepal through Indigenised
MLE: The Challenge to Teach in Over a Hundred Languages', as follows:

> Nepal is materially one of the poorest countries in the world, but linguisti-
> cally and culturally it is incredibly rich. In order to maintain that richness
> and to start granting all Nepalese children linguistic and cultural human
> rights and equal access to efficient quality education, detailed educational
> language planning is necessary – and it is going forward. About 50% of
> the population have other mother tongues; still Nepali was until recently
> the only medium of education in government schools. Today, the Con-
> stitution guarantees basic education through the medium of the various
> mother tongues. The policy is excellent, but the implementation processes
> are, understandably, challenging. In this chapter we present in some detail
> Nepal's planning and implementation processes for mother tongue-based
> multilingual education, MLE, starting from Nepal's international commit-
> ments and proceeding to national commitments, plans and developments,
> with all the various challenges. We are especially interested in the role of
> the various mother tongues in education. A recent Multilingual Education
> Programme (2006–2009) is presented and lessons from it are drawn and
> discussed.

Shelley K. Taylor writes in her abstract for 'MLE from Ethiopia to Nepal:
Refining a Success Story':

> This chapter presents the results of experiences with the implementation of
> a mother tongue-based multilingual education (MLE) project in Nepal. It
> begins by reviewing key concepts and practices related to MLE in West-
> ern settings, and then reviews how many of the assumptions on which
> these concepts and practices were based are inadequate for dealing with

the degree of linguistic heterogeneity and complexity found in Nepal. The author then discusses issues that arose when MLE was implemented in the field, including how to prepare teachers, teacher trainers and materials developers to understand key concepts of MLE, create linguistically/culturally responsive L1-based teaching materials and learn pedagogical practices to promote children's linguistic and academic development. The findings suggest that glitches occur when attempting to implement innovative programmes on a grand scale in complex situations, and that they should be fixed before the MLE model is cascaded nationwide. The author cautions that MLE is not synonymous with multilingual classrooms and provides examples of difficulties that arise for children when it is implemented as if it were. MLE has the potential to greatly benefit Indigenous and minority children. Therefore, pains should be taken to ensure conceptual clarity and eliminate implementation glitches.

Norbert Nikièma and Paul Taryam Ilboudo write about their chapter, 'Setting a Tradition of Mother Tongue-Medium Education in "Francophone" Africa: The Case of Burkina Faso' as follows:

> This chapter documents an extension of the teaching of the mother tongue (MT) in an early-exit transitional model of bilingual schools, known as *Écoles Bilingues*, into junior high school and pre-schools in Burkina Faso. The programme has extended the development and use of mother tongues from one (during the early years of implementation) to eight languages of the country. The establishment of pre-school centres (2003) presents an opportunity to begin MT education prior to the first grade, i.e. during the three years of pre-school. The extension of the use of MT into junior high schools opens up an opportunity to extend the teaching of the MT as a subject (not as a medium at this stage) from the fourth grade of primary into the fifth grade, which is in junior secondary. It is thus now possible to conceive of a nine-year span for the formal inclusion of local languages in school, which is a significant achievement in a francophone country. We describe the context of the development of the model before discussing achievements and efficiencies in pre-school, primary school and junior high school. We draw attention to the lessons learned, and the challenges that still have to be addressed.

Ahmed Kabel's summary of his chapter, '"There is No Such Thing as 'Keeping out of Politics'"': Arabisation and Amazigh/Berber Mother Tongue Education in Morocco', is as follows:

> Language planning and language-in-education policies are hardly purely technical areas of scholarly practice. Deliberations and decisions regarding

those issues are deeply ideological and are informed by political interest and rationalisation. Language and language-in-education policy in Morocco are no exception, more especially in the case of medium of instruction (Arabisation) and mother tongue instruction as a subject (Amazigh/Berber). The policy of Arabisation has been fundamentally a political affair, and its implementation a matter of political expediency. Arabisation formed an ideological mainstay and foundational creed for the postcolonial state of Morocco and a discursive regime for garnering legitimation for a (modern) nascent political entity. Its implementation in education and other domains smacks of parochial *realpoliticking*, ambivalence and inefficiency, issues which are equally of no less political significance. Ideology and politics have been likewise very much in evidence throughout the whole process of Amazigh education in terms of mother tongue planning, policy and teaching. This arena has been a privileged site for ideological contestation and the promotion of vested interest between the state and Amazigh/Berber elites. The overwhelmingly ideological and political nature of the Berber mother tongue instruction project has deeply, and perhaps irrevocably, affected its implementation.

Kathleen Heugh, Carol Benson, Mekonnen Alemu Gebre Yohannes and Berhanu Bogale write about their chapter, 'Implications for Multilingual Education: Student Achievement in Different Models of Education in Ethiopia':

This chapter focuses on student achievement across the nine regions and two city-states and in relation to different models of multilingual education. System-wide student assessment data gathered by the Ethiopian Ministry of Education in 2000 and 2004 are analysed in relation to the implementation of a mother tongue-based bi/trilingual policy from 1994 to about 2004. From this point onwards, an increasing emphasis towards English has exerted a downward pressure through the education system. Its effect had been anticipated during the study discussed in Chapter 1, but the speed and extent to which this occurred became evident only with the data emerging from the third system-wide assessment in 2008. The three sets of data collectively point towards the trends in achievement of students after eight, six, four or zero years of mother tongue-medium education (MTM). Student achievement appears to follow a sliding scale: higher with the longer period of MTM and lower with fewer years of MTM. The data also point towards positive differences in student achievement in relation to communities further from the capital and other large cities, and where community participation appears to be stronger. The data are also analysed in relation to the change of emphasis towards increasing use of English through the system from 2004 onwards and evident in the assessment data of 2008.

The Ethiopian case appears to offer contemporary findings on the relationship between the duration of mother tongue-medium MLE and student achievement on a scale which has never before been available to the scholarly field or to the educational community.

I.2.2 Reflecting on Linguistic Diversity, its Maintenance and Endangerment, and Multilingualism as an Educational Goal

Our set of tables in section I.3, gives some background data to make comparing the countries described and analysed in this book easier. Our first reflections are about the reliability and complexity about the number of languages and their relationship to educational achievements. Of course, all statistics about numbers of languages, 'living' or 'with no known speakers', categories that the *Ethnologue* (Lewis 2009) uses, are notoriously unreliable. Many of the statistics are based on data that are a decade or two old; still, situations change rapidly. In addition, there is the difficulty of defining what 'a language' is (and whether 'languages' as countable entities exist) and where the borders between 'languages' and 'dialects' are (see, for example, Skutnabb-Kangas 2000, chapter 1, for a discussion). In India, for instance, the 1961 census gave 1,652 'languages as mother tongues' whereas the *Ethnologue* gives 438 'living languages'.[6] Harmon and Loh state in their new Index of Linguistic Diversity (2010) that about 20% of the world's languages disappeared in just 35 years, between 1970 and 2005. Still, generally speaking, languages have been, and are being, maintained much better in poor South countries, especially in Africa, Southeast Asia and parts of the Pacific, than in Western relatively much richer countries. Some of the ideologies and strategies in place or being considered in language-in-education in countries where languages *have* been maintained, have aspects that are worth considering everywhere. Many of them are discussed in this volume.

All chapters show clearly the complexity of the challenges in highly multilingual states (see Table I.1 in section I.3). Of the 11 countries discussed in detail in this book, four have over 100 languages according to the *Ethnologue*; only two – Cambodia with 23 and Morocco with 9 – have fewer than 68. There is some kind of official acceptance of these languages (for instance, as 'national languages', see de Varennes 1996) in many South countries; thus the opportunities for MLE could be considerable.

In states with one autochthonous (domestic) official language only, and where this language is spoken by a very large percentage of the population (around half or more), it may be enough for Indigenous, tribal and minority children (ITM children)[7] to learn three languages well: the mother tongue, the dominant official language, and English. In Peru, it may be sufficient for an Indigenous Quechua-speaking child to learn Spanish and some English in addition to Quechua. In Ethiopia, an Amharic-speaking child living in an area with few speakers of other languages may be content with just two languages, Amharic and some English.

In Nepal, an Indigenous Tamang or Magar (demographically large groups of Indigenous peoples) child can often manage well if she learns three languages, the mother tongue, Nepali and English.

But even in Nepal, just as in many of the other countries in this book, Indigenous children from demographically very small language groups may also need to learn another Indigenous or minority language, if they live interspersed with a larger ITM group. In Thailand the same is true for speakers of all of the other 84 languages who do not have Thai as their mother tongue; they need minimally to learn three languages, but often four. In countries with several official languages, such as India, an ITM child mostly also needs four languages. For instance in Orissa, India, a tribal Kui, Santal, Juang, Kishal, Koya, Bondo, Munda, Oraon, Kuwi, or Saora child needs, in addition to her own language, to learn Oriya (the regional state language), Hindi, and English (Mishra 2006). In Assam, India, the tribal Bodo language (one of India's official languages) is used as a medium of teaching for 12 years, Assamese is taught as a second language from the third/fifth year onwards, and Hindi and English are introduced between the fourth and sixth years of school (Skutnabb-Kangas and Mohanty 2009: 46).

As several Indian researchers have often mentioned, a four-language formula is needed, and is being developed in that context. As compared to the European Union countries where learning two foreign languages in school (i.e. a weak three-language formula) is an official goal (COM(2008) 566 final 2008), the situation in the highly multilingual countries described here both forces and enables children to learn several languages, in and outside school. The situation of English, French and Portuguese, in former colonial African countries, may be an exception: in rural African contexts, the former colonial language is often heard only in school, and students experience great difficulty in learning this language where it has little functional use in civil society.

Multilingualism as a general educational goal is accepted in many parts of the world, with some good implementation and many challenges, whereas in other parts of the world it is a dream, and is sometimes seen as a nightmare. Even bilingualism is a reluctantly accepted goal, for instance in parts of the USA – but only for minorities and often only for first- and maybe second-generation immigrants; it is something to be shunned after that. Typically, bilingualism has been seen as a handicap not a resource, in this deficit theory. In the South, multilingualism is seen as normal and often desirable. Pattanayak, the first Director of the Central Institute of Indian Languages, has formulated it like this (1984: 82):

> The dominant monolingual orientation is cultivated in the developed world and consequently two languages are considered a nuisance, three languages uneconomic and many languages absurd. In multilingual countries, many languages are facts of life; any restriction in the choice of language is a nuisance; and one language is not only uneconomic, it is absurd.

Most of the languages discussed in this book face some degree of endangerment. The least endangered languages in the world are the languages of demographic linguistic majorities, with many speakers, whose language is an official language in the state in which they live. Examples are Mandarin Chinese in China or Italian in Italy.

The most endangered are Indigenous/tribal or minority languages with few speakers, with no official status, and spoken in one country only (e.g. most of the languages in Papua New Guinea). Many of the ITM languages in the countries described in the chapters in this book belong to this most endangered category. Nevertheless, a substantial number can also benefit from being spoken in one or even more neighbouring countries. This could also benefit education, through joint teacher training, exchange of materials, networking, etc., and we have examples of that. Because of the colonial legacy, state borders are not necessarily language borders in Africa, Southeast Asia and in some Latin American countries. This is true for many languages in Africa (e.g. Bamgbose 2000; Djité 2008). In Asia, for instance, Santhali is spoken in both India and Nepal. Likewise, some of the official dominant languages can often function as lingua francas[8] even between countries. In many contexts people draw on their repertoires of several regional lingua francas instead of, or in addition to, English.

In Africa, linguists point towards the continuum of languages, a characteristic of long-term multilingualism. Here, a lingua franca 'might best be envisaged not as a single language but as a multilayered and partially connected language chain that offers a choice of varieties and registers in the speaker's immediate environment, and a steadily diminishing set of options to be employed in more distant interactions' (Fardon and Furniss 1994: 4). They suggest that 'multilingualism is the African lingua franca'.

We need to contextualise contemporary debates about the term 'mother tongue'. The extensive literature variously suggests that the term is reductionist, anachronistic, sexist, essentialist, obsolete, etc. These debates are mostly confined to philosophical lexical discussions among linguists and sociolinguists rather than the communities who use the term, not in a literal and necessarily monolingual sense, but in a figurative and often multilingual sense. Whether one is in a village in India or Nepal; in a small town in Tanzania, Malawi, Senegal, Cameroon, Mozambique or Eritrea; in the Republic of Mari-El in the Russian Federation, or in Northern China or Sri Lanka, ordinary people use the term 'mother tongue' in its broad figurative sense. Sometimes it is meant in a singular form, sometimes in relation to several varieties or a continuum. As Pattanayak puts it: 'Places are not geographical concepts; they exist in people's consciousness. So does the concept of "mother tongue". It is not a language in the general sense of the word, neither is it a dialect. It is an identity signifier waiting to be explained' (1992).

In the realm of 'playful' socio- and applied linguistics, notions of 'language' and 'mother tongue' may be contested. In this volume, we engage with applied linguistics 'at work' in the education of children, mostly in vulnerable and marginalised settings, and we work with practical notions of what languages are, how they function inside educational institutions and how they may be used to facilitate the best possible access to quality education. Critics of the notion of MT or MTM have seldom rolled up their sleeves and got stuck into the jobs of: teaching a (large) group of children in a classroom how to read and write, in order to negotiate a globalised curriculum; how to train teachers or produce textbooks; or how to get all these things to fit together coherently. Once local languages are in the system, sensible people find creative solutions to make them work and articulate with, rather than against, community participation.

There is now substantial evidence from all over the world of the principal criteria necessary for successful education in multilingual contexts. These do differ from one place to another, but only in their contextualisation, not theoretically grounded principles. There are clear differences amongst the different initiatives taken in the country studies in this volume. Some are much further down the road of reaching additive bi/multilingual education than others. Some are near the beginning of the journey, and it will take many years before they are able to reach longer term or optimal levels of multilingual education. We include these initiatives in order to demonstrate the range, the journey, their potential, their successes and challenges. The contexts differ and the beginning and endpoints may also differ, but the essential principles of inclusivity of linguistic diversity remain the same. The goal is always equitable quality education through the only mechanism which is known to make this possible, namely bi/multilingual schooling, necessarily based on mother tongues.

Unfortunately, we need also to draw attention to a common misconception about MTM education, where its antagonists construct a false dichotomy of either the MT or the international language (see Skutnabb-Kangas (2009, 2010), for some of these misconceptions). This polarisation of two necessary components of productive linguistic repertoires emerges only from a clearly anachronistic monolingual position (see Heugh 2006; McCarty in this volume). We say this very firmly here: there are no serious proposals anywhere in the world which suggest that children at school in the 21st century can do without substantive access to a language of power, usually one of the big international languages. Equally firmly, in the absence of any viable alternatives (which have been shown to work as well or better), there is no choice other than to proceed with strong, additive mother tongue-based bilingual and multilingual options. And these can be realised despite serious economic and other restrictions and challenges, to which we turn next.

1.3 Contextualising Education – Human Development Index and Other Data

Formal education is, together with media, decisive for the future of the world's languages. The wrong medium of education has been, and is, killing languages at an accelerating pace, as Skutnabb-Kangas has shown in many books (see her home page, www.tove-skutnabb-kangas.org, for a list of her most recent books). When claiming that the medium of education, and especially the length of MTM education are among the most important factors in explaining results, we are of course aware of the many other factors which frame the situation in schools and families. In this section we contextualise this situation, by giving some socio-economic, political, legal and educational background data about the countries discussed in this book. We have also added our own countries of origin, South Africa and Finland, to relativise the figures: Finland as another rich country, in comparison to USA, and South Africa as the richest country in Africa. Likewise, we have added two geographically large and linguistically rich countries, one from Africa (Nigeria) and one from Latin America (Brazil). We also want to include Papua New Guinea (see Benson and Kosonen, this volume) because it is, despite the relatively low population figure (under 7 million) the country with the largest number of languages in the world, over 800. Table I.1 presents HDI indicators from the Human Development Index 2009 online country fact sheets (http://hdr.undp.org/en/statistics/) together with other relevant background data. The first figure in the first column is the country's rank in relation to other countries, the second the value of the HDI indicator.

The number of languages in a country does not correlate with population or geographical size. Compare the three countries in Table I.1 with similar population figures, all under 7 million: Laos, with 84 languages, has a land area of 236,800 sq. km and a population density of 28.2 per sq. km; Papua New Guinea, 830 languages, 462,840 sq. km, and a density of 12.8; and Finland, 12 languages, 337,030 and 15.6, respectively; all from 31 December 2008, http://www.mong-abay.com/igapo/world_statistics_by_area.htm). Rather, the number of languages reflects the geography (including relative isolation and the presence of mountains that prevent contact); the climate (rain, temperature); how many crops per year; how self-sufficient in food, medicine, building, clothing, etc. a group can be[9]); and several other factors.

These factors also influence the maintenance of languages. But a much more decisive factor for the maintenance of languages is the educational policy of the country, especially the medium of education. Thus originally multilingual countries where only one dominant language has been used in education for a long time have a large number of languages 'with no known speakers'. The speakers have been (forcibly) assimilated, and education through the medium of the dominant language has been decisive in this assimilation (Skutnabb-Kangas and Dunbar 2010). Urbanisation has also extinguished many languages, but, again, often because multilingual education has been seen as impossible in cities with large numbers of languages (see our discussion of this in our concluding chapter, section 11.2.4). The two most urbanised countries on our list, USA and Brazil, are also those with much the highest number of extinguished languages (see Table I.1 for population numbers, the degree of urbanisation, and the number of languages).

TABLE I.1 Comparison of countries by demographic, poverty, malnutrition, mortality and linguistic diversity statistics[10]

Countries with rank for HDI value, and the (HDI value) itself	Population, end of 2009, in thousands	Urban population as %age of total	Life expectancy at birth population	Percentage living below poverty line	Gross Nat. Income (GNI) per capita 2009 ranking (213 countries)		Child malnutrition, % of children under 5, based on height/weight	Infant mortality per 1,000 live births	Number of languages Ethnologue 16th ed.	
					Atlas	PPP			Living	No speakers
Burkina Faso 161. (0.305)	15,757	21	53	46.4	190	193	44.5/37.4	90.8	68	0
Cambodia 124. (0.494)	14,805	19	61	35.0	186	176	39.5/28.8	68.0	23	0
Ethiopia 157. (0.328)	82,825	17	55	44.2	205	200	50.7/34.6	67.1	85	5
India 119. (0.519)	1,155,348	64	64	28.6	164	154	47.9/43.5	50.3	438	14
Laos 122. (0.497)	6,320	30	65	33.0	178	167	47.6/31.6	52.9	84	0
Morocco 114. (0.567)	31,993	56	71	n.d	136	143	23.1/9.9	38.6	9	2
Nepal 138. (0.428)	29,331	17	67	30.9	196	192	49.3/38.8	48.1	124	2
Peru 63. (0.723)	29,165	71	73	53.1	115	109	29.8/5.4	25.5	92	12
Thailand 92. (0.654)	67,764	33	69	13.6	122	115	15.7/7.0	14.1	74	0
USA 4. (0.902)	307,007	80	78	n.d.	18	15	n.d./1.3	6.8	176	65
Vietnam 113. (0.572)	87,280	27	74	28.9	176	161	35.8/20.2	19.5	106	1
Papua New Guinea 137. (0.431)	6,732	13	61	37.5	164	166	43.9/18.1	54.3	830	11
Brazil 73. (0.699)	193,732	85	72	21.5	84	99	7.1/2.2	17.3	181	55
Finland 16. (0.871)	5,338	61	80	n.d.	19	35	n.d./n.d. (0)	2.5	12	0
Nigeria 142. (0.423)	154,728	48	48	34.1	161	170	n.d./27.2	85.8	514	11
South Africa 110. (0.597)	49,320	60	51	n.d.	97	100	n.d./n.d.	52.4	24	4

n.d. = no data available

Human Development Indexes (HDI) present measures that look beyond Gross Domestic Product (GDP) towards broader definitions of well-being and inequality. The HDI provides a composite measure of three dimensions of human development: living a long and healthy life (measured by life expectancy), having a decent standard of living (measured by purchasing power parity, PPP, income), and being formally educated (measured by adult literacy and gross enrolment in education) (*Human Development Report* 2009, hereafter HDR 2009). Table I.1 presents some of these indicators, from HDR 2009 and the World Bank statistics (see also Table I.2). We can get an idea of the living conditions of many of the people/s that this book is about, by looking at the indicators for both *life expectancy at birth* and the percentage in the 16 countries of people *below the poverty line* (which is obviously a relative measure, adjusted in each country) (http://hdrstats.undp.org/en/indicators/104.html). The USA and Finland do not provide any data, even though at least 20% of school children in the USA live below the poverty line.[11] Some indicators show inter-indicator differences, e.g. South Africa's low figure in relation to life expectancy as compared to relatively high figures on other indicators – explanations are the climate, the prevalence of HIV-AIDS, etc.

When comparing children's prerequisites/preparedness to receive formal education (if they receive it at all), their, and their mothers', nutritional state plays a very important role. Getting enough food is a basic prerequisite for well-being. Living above the poverty line is often necessary for being able to afford to send children (especially girls) to school, also because of school fees. Hungry children cannot concentrate, and severe malnutrition stunts many of the functions and capacities needed for learning. We have included two indicators directly reflecting this in Table I.1, infant mortality and malnutrition of under fives, based on children's height and weight.

Norway has the highest HDI value in the world for 2009 (0.938), and Zimbabwe the lowest (0.140). The HDI for Ethiopia is 0.328, which gives the country a rank of 157th out of 169 countries with data (sub-Saharan Africa has 0.389, South Asia 0.516). Japan has the highest life expectancy at birth, 83.2 years, Afghanistan the lowest (44.6); Ethiopia has 56.1 (sub-Saharan Africa 52.7, South Asia 65.1) Liechtenstein has the highest Gross National Income (GNI) per person (US$81,011, followed by Qatar, US$79,426), Zimbabwe the lowest (US$176), and Ethiopia US$992 (sub-Saharan Africa US$2,050, South Asia US$3,417).

To improve the index which did not include important indicators such as gender or income inequality nor more difficult-to-measure concepts such as respect for human rights and political freedoms the HDR 2010 has developed three new indexes: an Inequality-adjusted HDI (IHDI), a Gender Inequality Index (GII) and a Multidimensional Poverty Index (MPI) (HDR 2010: 87–100). Most of the world's multidimensional poor live in South Asia and sub-Saharan Africa (Figure 5.10 in HDR 2010: 98). Comparing the HDI with the IHDI shows the distribution of inequality *within* countries – if there was no intra-country inequality, they would be the same. Countries with low general HDIs also tend to have the highest IHDIs, i.e. the less general well-being, the more inequality within the country. Inequality shows especially in the dimensions of health and education. Both HDI and IHDI, as well as GII and MPI show the very large gaps in life chances and well-being in the world. Ethiopia is far below the general trend of countries in sub-Saharan Africa.

Table I.2 presents a few educational data.

The enrolment rates are clearly lowest in Africa, whereas the pupil/teacher ratios are more mixed. Some of the survival rates to grade 5 are low in Asia too. The differences between dropout rates and survival rates depend on different years for the data, unreliable data and different definitions. It is important to note that the transition rates from primary to secondary education in general programmes (at the age 11–12 in most countries) seem high, but then they are counted on the basis of those who survived until the last grade of primary school, not those who started school. In Africa, for more than 50% of children who begin school,

TABLE I.2 Educational statistics (all but Pupil/teacher ratio in percentages)[12]

Country	NER Primary educ.[a]	Pupil/ teacher ratio, primary school	Dropout rates all grades,% of primary school cohort	Survival rate to grade 5	Transition rate from primary to secondary	Literacy rates in %, adults (over 15) and youth (15–24)	
						Adults[b]	Youth
Burkina Faso	58	49.1	28.9	80	52	28.7 **(148)**	39.3
Cambodia	89	48.5	45.6	62	79	77.6 **(103)**	87.5
Ethiopia	71	59.3	59.7	64	89	35.9 **(145)**	49.9
India	89	40.2	34.2	66	84	62.8 **(120)**	81.1
Laos	86	30.5	33.2	61	78	72.7 **(110)**	83.9
Morocco	89	26.5	23.8	84	80	56.4 **(132)**	76.6
Nepal	80	37.8	38.4	62	81	57.9 **(130)**	80.8
Peru	96	20.9	17.0	93	98	89.6 **(74)**	97.4
Thailand	95	16.0	n.d.	n.d.	87	93.5 **(52)**	98.1
USA	92	13.7	1.5	95	n.d.	n.d.	n.d.
Vietnam	n.d.	19.9	7.9	92	93	90.39 **(69)**	96.8
Papua New Guinea	n.d.	35.8	n.d.	n.d.	n.d.	59.6 **(129)**	66.5
Brazil	93	23.0	24.4	n.d.	82	90.0 **(71)**	97.8
Finland	96	14.4	0.2	100	100	n.d.	n.d.
Nigeria	64	46.3	25.1	n.d.	49	60.1 **(112)**	71.5
South Africa	86	31.0	23.0	n.d.	94	89.0 **(80)**	96.8

Notes

a Net enrolment rate (NER). The number of pupils or students in the theoretical age group for a given level of education enrolled in that level, expressed as a percentage of the total population in that age group.

b Adult literacy also has the ranking of the country in brackets.

primary is terminal (with substantially lower secondary enrolment for girls, especially in Sudan and the Horn of Africa, owing to a high incidence of abductions and early marriage). In every country that provides the data, the youth literacy rates are much higher than the adult literacy rates. This is encouraging, to the extent that the data are reliable. It is also very much a question of what kind of literacy is meant.[13] In South Africa, however, as a consequence of the HIV-AIDS pandemic, literacy amongst girls is falling because many leave school early to care for ill parents or orphan siblings (Heugh 2007). Enrolment in low-income countries is a particular concern for the education of girls and matters of health and gender equity (e.g. Benson 2005). Although some figures suggest that 25% of secondary-school-going children do enrol in secondary school in Africa at present (33% at junior secondary level and 19% at upper secondary) (Lewin 2008: 92), many do not attend regularly and most of these do not remain to the end of secondary. Table I.3 (compiled from Lewin 2008) presents some regional comparisons.

The comparative statistics in Table I.3 show that this is particularly devastating in two of the countries in this book, Burkina Faso and Ethiopia. The gender gap is widest in those countries with lowest GER2 (Lewin 2008: 92). Lewin points towards several key reasons for prioritising increased access and throughput to secondary, including the positive effects of secondary education in relation to health education and arresting the devastation of the HIV-AIDS pandemic, social and political equity and development (ibid. 59–69). This has particular importance for girls and their vulnerability to continued cycles of poverty, ill-health and abuse in many countries (see Chapters 1 and 10 in this volume). We emphasise the data on low enrolment specifically in African countries because in predominantly rural and pastoralist societies children are frequently withdrawn from school during harvest time, thus literally every hour in school counts. Each hour needs to be gainfully spent by children and literacy developed as robustly as possible in the languages which facilitate this best of all, if literacy is to have any lasting effect for children in such circumstances.

TABLE I.3 Gross Enrolment in Secondary Education (GER2) in percentages: regional comparisons[14]

Sub-Saharan Africa	24.3
Ethiopia	18.5
Burkina Faso	10.6
Nigeria	36.4
South Africa	83.6
South and Southwest Asia	51.9
Arab States and North Africa	60.3
East Asia and Pacific	64.9
Latin America and Caribbean	82.5

Some industrialised countries do not collect adult literacy data – it is assumed that all adults are literate (this is certainly not true for the USA, regardless of how literacy is defined). One can get much more detailed data on the indicators and also build one's own tables based on the HDI 2010 at http://hdr.undp.org/en/statistics/data/. It is also clear that the relationship of the other indicators with the education index, Combined Gross Enrolment Ratio, is far from simple. Countries with high adult literacy do not always send the children to school to the same extent (compare Brazil and Vietnam); countries with similar enrolment percentages may have widely differing income levels, Gross Domestic Products (compare Morocco and Nepal); two African countries with similar life expectancies may have very different percentages of children in school (compare Burkina Faso and South Africa). Thus much more contextualisation would be needed just to understand to what extent children enrol in school – and stay on.

There are seldom statistics disaggregated by language or ethnicity or indigenousness, even though the United Nations Permanent Forum on Indigenous Issues (www.un.org/esa/socdev/unpfii/) has been recommending this for a long time. Indigenous and tribal peoples as groups, especially, live under much worse conditions than the rest of the population (with extremely few exceptions, including the Saami in Finland, Norway and Sweden). At the December 2010 launch of ECLAC's (Economic Commission for Latin America and the Caribbean) *Social Panorama of Latin America 2010* report, the authors stated that 'the education policies adopted by governments in the region have failed to reduce the learning gaps between children from poor and non-poor homes, rural and urban households, and Indigenous and non-indigenous families'. Their disaggregated data showed that, 'on average in the region, 49 percent of men and 55 percent of women aged 20–24 have completed secondary education, while in rural areas the figures are 26 percent of men and 31 percent of women, and 22 percent and 20 percent, respectively, among Indigenous people of that age.' They also stressed that 'education is one of the main factors that can undo inequalities of origin (family or territory based) and provide equal opportunities for lifetime well-being and productivity for society as a whole' (reported in the UN journal *Terraviva*, 2 December 2010).

If children under the harsh conditions described in this section face a foreign language when they enter school, the school certainly fails the child in even more serious ways than it fails children under otherwise similar life conditions but with their own language as the teaching/learning language.

The countries in this book include some of the poorest countries in the world. Many have high infant mortality, malnutrition, low figures for school enrolment and for adult literacy, and many people living on a shoestring. Still, some of them have developed educational models, strategies and theories on MLE from which the rich part of the world can learn.

Finally, we want to look at MLE as a human right (HR). Access to quality education is definitely an HR – see Skutnabb-Kangas and Dunbar (2010) for the argumentation and the relevant human rights instruments. If one sees the right to MTM education as a necessary prerequisite for access to education, then MTM education itself must also be seen as a human right (ibid.). Signing and ratifying those HRs instruments that contain these rights[15] can be seen as a signal of wanting to grant children these rights. Three of the most central HRs instruments for MLE are the CRC, ratified by all other countries in the world except Somalia and the USA; *ILO 169*, ratified by Nepal, Peru and Brazil but none of the other countries in our comparison tables; and the *UNDRIP*, where, of 'our' countries, Burkina Faso, Cambodia, India, Laos, Nepal, Peru, Thailand, Vietnam, Brazil, Finland and South Africa voted for it in the UN General Assembly, Ethiopia, Morocco and Papua New Guinea were absent, Nigeria abstained, and the USA voted against. Of course signing and ratifying a HRs instrument does not mean that its requirements are honoured; implementation is an altogether different issue (see section 11.2, Risks, in Chapter 11). In the same way, a right to MTM education can be in a country's constitution for decades, without implementation. South Africa is internationally regarded as having a model HRs-based constitution, supplemented with a mother tongue and additive bilingual education policy and accompanying legislation. Still, its national education system disregards all such policies and legislation. India is another example with a positive constitutional right to MTM education but little general implementation (Mohanty, this volume). On the other hand, the Ethiopian constitution of 1994 resulted in the immediate implementation of MLE across the entire country (see Chapters 1 and 10).

Still, it is important to clarify properly what HRs instruments, taken together, can offer; how they can be interpreted; and how they interact with the more linguistic, pedagogical, sociological and psychological insights in this book. Skutnabb-Kangas and Dunbar (2010) have discussed what HRs instruments can and cannot do, in relation to the right to mother tongue-medium education and MLE.

Katarina Tomaševski,[16] the former UN Special Rapporteur on the Right to Education, has illustrated how the State obligations in some of the most important HRs instruments for this book[17] contain four elements, namely *availability*, *accessibility*, *acceptability* and *adaptability*. She states that 'mere access to educational institutions, difficult as it may be to achieve in practice, does not amount to the right to education' (Tomaševski 2004: para. 57). 'Language of instruction' has been discussed by Tomaševski under the concept of '*Acceptability*' (2001: paras. 12–15, and 29–30), where respect for the parents' choice of language of instruction is seen as similar to respect of parents' religious convictions in education. Language of instruction belongs in Skutnabb-Kangas' and Dunbar's view mainly under the concept of '*Accessibility*' where one of the points is 'identification and elimination of discriminatory denials of access'.[18] Barriers to 'access' can be interpreted as: (1) *physical* (e.g. distance to school); (2) *financial* (e.g. school fees – not even primary education is free in 91 countries (Tomaševski 2004: para. 23), or the labour of girls being needed in the home). They can also be: (3) *administrative* (e.g. requirements of birth registration or residence certificate for school enrolment (Tomaševski, 2004: para. 4b), or school schedules (Tomaševski, 2001: para. 12)); or (4) *legal*. If the educational model chosen for a school (legally or administratively) does not mandate or even allow Indigenous or minority children to be educated mainly through the medium of a language that the child understands, then the child is effectively being denied access to education. If the teaching language is foreign to the child and the teacher is not properly trained to make input comprehensible in the foreign language, the child does not have access to education.[19] Likewise, the ITM child does not have equal access to education, if the language of instruction is neither the mother tongue/first language or minimally an extremely well-known second language of the child and if the teaching is planned and directed towards children who have the language of instruction as their mother tongue – that is, where the norm is a child who already knows the teaching language. Here we then have a *combination of linguistic, pedagogical and psychological barriers to 'access' to education.*

The *Committee on the Rights of the Child* held at their 34th Session (15 September–3 October 2003) a Day of General Discussion on the Rights of Indigenous Children. Their Recommendations on Education recommend 'that States parties ensure access for Indigenous children to appropriate and high quality education'.[20] Interpreting this access, they wrote:

> The Committee recommends that States parties, with the active participation of indigenous communities and children [. . .]
>
> b) implement indigenous children's right to be taught to read and write in their own indigenous language or in the language most commonly used by the group to which they belong, as well as the national language(s) of the country in which they live;[21]
>
> c) undertake measures to effectively address the comparatively higher drop-out rates among indigenous youth and ensure that indigenous children are adequately prepared for higher education, vocational training and their further economic, social and cultural aspirations;
>
> d) take effective measures to increase the number of teachers from indigenous communities or who speak indigenous languages, provide them with appropriate training, and ensure that they are not discriminated against in relation to other teachers;
>
> e) allocate sufficient financial, material and human resources to implement these programmes and policies effectively.

Recommendation (b) clearly indicates that bilingual education systems should be created by States working with Indigenous (or minority) communities, if the States are to 'ensure access for indigenous children to *appropriate* and high quality education' (emphasis added). Skutnabb-Kangas and Dunbar (2010) have demonstrated that this is a necessary prerequisite for high levels of multilingualism and for preparing the children for higher education.

The fewer speakers a language has, the more necessary it is for the children to become high-level multilinguals in order to be able to get access to the basic necessities needed for survival. The language/s which people know and use most in their immediate community, usually called the MTs, are needed for psychological, cognitive and spiritual survival – cultural rights. All the other languages, including an official language in the state where the children live, are needed for full participation in civil society, meaning for social, economic, political and civil rights. A child must be able to speak to parents, family and relatives; know who he/she is; and acquire skills of how to think, analyse and evaluate. The MTs are a fundamental part of the linguistic repertoire necessary for this for most people of the world. Further education, job prospects, and being able to participate in the wider society require high levels of proficiency in other languages, which cannot be achieved across education systems in the absence of strong MTM education. Thus, high levels of multilingualism must be one of the goals of adequate quality education. As mentioned earlier, the greatest population growth is expected in those parts of the world which have high levels of multilingualism. This book shows that the goal of high levels of multilingualism is possible to reach, even in countries with severe budgetary and other restrictions.

The editors and authors of this book recognise that enabling language-in-education policy may be established or followed by governments which are associated with both progressive and reactionary systems. We do not endorse or support any reactionary or discriminatory government or system in countries discussed in this volume. However, we do draw attention to language education policy which has the potential to enhance cognitive and academic development of the widest cross-section of the society, sometimes despite undemocratic governments.

Notes

1 All website addresses in this book were up-to-date when the book went to press; therefore, we do not include the dates for when they were accessed.
2 All countries are hopefully developing. If the terms 'less developed' or 'developing' are used of poorer or less industrialised countries whereas rich industrialised countries are called '(more) developed', the rich countries are implicitly posited as models for the others. 'This is the familiar evolutionist paradigm, where it is clear who constitutes the norm, and where it is only some who need to develop (to undergo structural adjustment programmes) because they are still deficient in relation to the norm' (Skutnabb-Kangas 2000: 661).
3 Many researchers have analysed and criticised this minoritisation, calling it scientific imperialism (e.g. Tuhiwai Smith 2004; Deloria 1988; Hancock 1991; several authors in Odora Hoppers, ed. 2002).
4 In Ethiopia, the conventions for naming authors are different from Western English-speaking contexts and two of these authors, Berhanu Bogale and Mekonnen Alemu Gebre Yohannes would normally be referred to as Berhanu and Mekonnen in citations

and references within Ethiopia. We have used the Western convention, aware of the power issues relating to this disjuncture between conventions, after lengthy consultations with the authors.

5　The work of Skutnabb-Kangas spans many different linguistic contexts where English is not dominant (e.g. with the Saami in the Nordic countries) and Jasone Çenoz is best known for her work with Basque in Spain and France.

6　An example of the complexity is India: Census returns for 'mother tongue' have given names of a language or regional or social variety, but also the name of a writing system, a cast, a religious sect, a place, a profession, a people, etc. (see Skutnabb-Kangas (2000: 11) for examples). Mohanty 2010 and Skutnabb-Kangas and Mohanty 2010 give more recent information about the 3,372 mother tongues (1,576 listed by name, 1,796 listed as 'other languages').

7　'*Indigenous peoples*. The International Labour Organisation's (ILO's) 1989 definition may be the strongest legally: peoples in independent countries who are regarded as Indigenous on account of their descent from the populations which inhabited the country, or a geographical region to which the country belongs, at the time of conquest or colonization or the establishment of present state boundaries and who, irrespective of their legal status, retain some or all of their own social, economic, cultural and political institutions' (Skutnabb-Kangas and McCarty 2008: 7).

　　Self-identification is included within the ILO definition 'as a fundamental criterion for determining the groups to which the provisions of this Convention apply' (http://www.unhchr.ch/html/menu3/b/62.htm)' (Skutnabb-Kangas and McCarty 2007: 7). 'Tribal' is an official term in several countries, including India, for indigenous peoples – see ILO 169 (http://www.ilo.org/indigenous/Conventions/no169/lang--en/index.htm).

　　'*Minorities* are defined similarly to ethnic groups (numbers, dominance, characteristics), and by a desire to maintain distinctive characteristics; there is often no common descent (e.g. women; gay, lesbian, bisexual, and transgendered persons; Deaf persons). Ethnic minorities can have national/autochthonous or immigrant origins. . . . "Being" a minority in the sense of having less power than some other group(s) (i.e. being minoritised) is a relationship rather than a characteristic; it presupposes that (an)other group(s) has/have been majoritised. In international law, the existence of a minority does not depend on a decision by the state but must be established by objective criteria. Minorities have some rights in education that are not accorded in international law to children under other labels (e.g. "linguistically diverse students," "English language learners"). In international law, minorities do not have a right to self-determination (e.g., independence), whereas Indigenous peoples do' (ibid., 10).

8　We use the term lingua franca to mean a language which is used for horizontal purposes between people for everyday communicative activities in a bilingual or multilingual situation. It may be a language or a language continuum which is understood in different ways depending upon the context. For historical reasons it may simultaneously be associated with political dominance of a former regime (e.g. Afrikaans in South Africa, Amharic in Ethiopia) and also as a de facto language of the informal economy. See also a critique of the concept lingua franca (Phillipson 2009: chapter 7).

9　The number of languages correlates with biodiversity (see www.terralingua.org, and Skutnabb-Kangas, Maffi and Harmon 2003). The more biodiversity, the more languages – biodiversity enables self-sufficiency for even very small groups. If a group is less self-sufficient, this necessitates more contact with other groups for trade; contact may (but does not need to) lead to languages merging, disappearing, etc. 'The more ecological space we leave for other species, the more economic space we leave for the marginalized sectors of society – peasants, women and children – and for future generations to meet their needs. Biodiversity is therefore not just an indicator of sustainability, it is also an indicator of justice' (Shiva 2000: 127).

10 Sources for Table I.1:
   Population data: http://web.worldbank.org/WBSITE/EXTERNAL/DATASTATIS
   TICS/0,,contentMDK:20399244~menuPK:1192694~pagePK:64133150~piPK:6413
   3175~theSitePK:239419~isCURL:Y,00.html
   Urban population: http://search.worldbank.org/data?qterm=urban+population
   &language=EN&format=html Malnutrition http://search.worldbank.org/data?qterm
   =malnutrition&language=EN&format=html
   Life expectancy: http://data.worldbank.org/indicator/SP.DYN.LE00.IN
   Population living below the poverty line: http://search.worldbank.org/data?qterm=Percentage
   +living+under+poverty+line&language=EN&format=html
   Sources and definitions of GNI, Atlas and PPP (Purchasing Power Parity), http://econ.
   worldbank.org/WBSITE/EXTERNAL/DATASTATISTICS/0,,contentMDK:203
   99244~menuPK:1192694~pagePK:64133150~piPK:64133175~theSitePK:239419~
   isCURL:Y,00.html
   Infant Mortality: http://web.worldbank.org/WBSITE/EXTERNAL/DATASTATIS
   TICS/0,,contentMDK:20485916~menuPK:1297819~pagePK:64133150~piPK:6413
   3175~theSitePK:239419,00.html
   Number of languages: The *Ethnologue,* 16th edition, http://www.ethnologue.com/
   country_index.asp.
11 See, for example, http://blogs.edweek.org/teachers/living-in-dialogue/2010/10/
   krashen_easy_money_for_schools.html; and, in general, Steven Krashen on poverty
   and education.
12 Sources for Table I.2. *Pupil/teacher ratio:* http://search.worldbank.org/data?qterm=Pu
   pil%2Fteacher+ratio&language=EN&format=html; *Literacy rates, adults* and *youth* are
   a combination of Table 15, Adult and youth literacy 2005–2007, pp. 188–193, *Global
   Education Digest 2009* (as are the country rankings for adult literacy), and http://search.
   worldbank.org/data?qterm=Adult%20literacy%20rates&language=EN&format=html;
   http://search.worldbank.org/data?qterm=Youth+literacy+rates&language=EN&for
   mat=html. The rest are from *Global Education Digest 2009.* The figures for *Net enrolment rates* are from Table 3, Primary education, Enrolment and teaching staff, pp.
   84–93 (except for Ethiopia and India which are from Table 13 in HDR 2010, as are
   all the figures for Dropout rates). *Survival rate to grade 5,* and *Transition rates from primary
   to secondary* (general education) are from Table 4, Primary education, Measures for
   progression and completion, pp. 94–103. The definitions of the indicators, can be
   found in ibid., p. 256. Some qualifications of the data, explained in Readers' guide
   (pp. 56–58) and Technical notes (pp. 59–61) have been left out. The data are from
   2005–2008, mostly 2007.
13 For instance, in Denmark where the literacy rate in terms of the technical skill of being
   able to decode easy text and write a simple sentence would be nearly 100% for youth,
   several studies assess that 15–20% of youth graduating from grade 9 cannot read and
   write well enough to continue their studies even in vocational education, something
   that the Minister of Education (December 2009) Bertel Haarder claims necessitates
   more national tests (e.g. http://www.information.dk/emne/bertel-haarder, 3 December 2009).
14 Sources for Table I.6 are Lewin (2008), Table 2.2, p. 75 and Table 2.1, pp. 71–72,
   based on data from the UNESCO Institute of Statistics 2005 of data valid in 2001.
15 Relevant education paragraphs from HRs instruments can be read online in chapter
   2 of Skutnabb-Kangas and Dunbar (2010), at http://www.e-pages.dk/grusweb/55/,
   source of this note and the discussion that follows. The most important ones are listed
   here. Paragraph 1 of Article 26 of the **Universal Declaration of Human Rights**
   (http://www.un.org/en/documents/udhr/, adopted on 10 December 1948 by the
   United Nations General Assembly), guarantees the right of everyone to education.
   Paragraph 2 provides that such education *shall be directed to the full development of the*

human personality, and *shall promote understanding, tolerance and friendship among all nations, racial and religious groups*. **The International Covenant on Economic, Social and Cultural Rights** (the 'ICESCR') of 1966 (http://www2.ohchr.org/english/law/cescr.htm), paragraphs 1, 2 and 3 of Article 13 recognise the right of everyone to education, add a reference to the sense of the dignity of the human personality, and add 'ethnic groups' to the list in the Universal Declaration (above) amongst which understanding etc. shall be promoted. It also notes that education shall *enable all persons to participate effectively in a free society*. The 1960 **Convention against Discrimination in Education** (http://www.unesco.org/education/pdf/DISCRI_E.PDF), Article 5, subparagraph 1 (a) provides that Education shall be directed to, amongst other things, the full development of the human personality. The United Nations' **Convention on the Rights of the Child** of 1989 is important (the 'CRC', http://www.hrweb.org/legal/child.html; see also http://www.unhchr.ch/tbs/doc.nsf/%28symbol%29/CRC.GC.2001.1.En?OpenDocument), Article 17, para. 4, Article 28, para. 1, Article 29, para. 3, and Article 30, para. 2. The basic right to education is set out in Article 28, paragraph 1, in which the States parties to the CRC recognise *the right of the child to education*. The paragraph also provides that with a view to achieving this right *progressively and on the basis of equal opportunity*, States will take a range of steps, including, in subparagraph (e), *measures to encourage regular attendance at schools and the reduction of drop-out rates*. Article 29, subparagraph (a) stipulates that education shall be directed to the *development of the child's personality, talents and mental and physical abilities to their fullest potential*. Article 29, subparagraph (d) stipulates that education should be directed to the development of *respect for the child's parents, his or her own cultural identity, language and values*. Article 30 provides: *In those States in which ethnic, religious or linguistic minorities or persons of indigenous origin exist, a child belonging to such a minority or who is indigenous shall not be denied the right, in community with other members of his or her own group, to enjoy his or her own culture, to profess and practice his or her own religion, **or to use his or her own language*** (emphasis added). The **International Covenant on Civil and Political Rights** (the 'ICCPR') of 1966 (http://www2.ohchr.org/english/law/ccpr.htm), Article 27, has the same famous 'minorities provision', except the CRC has added 'or is indigenous' and 'he or she'. **ILO Convention No.169 on Indigenous and Tribal Peoples** (http://www.ilo.org/public/english/region/ampro/mdtsanjose/indigenous/derecho.htm) Article 28, para. 1, asks States to *implement indigenous children's right to be taught to read and write in their own indigenous language, wherever practicable, or in the language most commonly used by the group to which they belong, as well as the national language(s) of the country in which they live.*

UNDRIP, the **United Nations Declaration on the Rights of Indigenous Peoples** (download from http://www.un.org/esa/socdev/unpfii/en/drip.html) provides in Articles 13 and 14:

> 13.1. Indigenous peoples have the right to revitalize, use, develop and transmit to future generations their histories, languages, oral traditions, philosophies, writing systems and literatures, and to designate and retain their own names for communities, places and persons.
> 13.2. States shall take effective measures to ensure that this right is protected and also to ensure that indigenous peoples can understand and be understood in political, legal and administrative proceedings, where necessary through the provision of interpretation or by other appropriate means.
> 14.1. Indigenous peoples have the right to establish and control their educational systems and institutions providing education in their own languages, in a manner appropriate to their cultural methods of teaching and learning.
> 14.2. Indigenous individuals, particularly children, have the right to all levels and forms of education of the State without discrimination.

14.3. States shall, in conjunction with indigenous peoples, take effective measures, in order for indigenous individuals, particularly children, including those living outside their communities, to have access, when possible, to an education in their own culture and provided in their own language.

16 See Tomaševski (2001); also at http://www.right-to-education.org/content/primers/_rte03.pdf. The 4-A model was 'adopted by the [UN] Committee on Economic, Social and Cultural Rights in General Comment No. 13' (Wilson 2004: 165). See also Tomaševski's Reports to the UN, E/CN.4/1999/49, paragraphs 51–74; E/CN.4/2000/6, paragraphs 32–65; E/CN.4/2001/52, paragraphs 64–65.
17 Article 13, paragraph 1 of the ICESCR and Article 28, para. 1 of the CRC.
18 Tomaševski (2004), paragraph 12; at paragraph 10, though, she warns, that 'access to education blurs the difference between education that is free and education accessible only after the payment of a fee'. In our discussion, 'accessible' refers to demands in addition to education being free.
19 The U.S. Supreme Court acknowledged this in *Lau v. Nichols* (1974) 414 US 563.
20 See E/C.19/2004/5/Add.11, Annex, p. 10.
21 This recommendation comes from ILO 169, Article 28, para. 1 which, however, has the addition 'wherever practicable'.

References

Alidou, Hassana, Boly, Aliou, Brock-Utne, Birgit, Diallo, Yaya Satina, Heugh, Kathleen and Wolff, H. Ekkehard (2006). *Optimizing Learning and Education in Africa – the Language Factor. A Stock-taking Research on Mother Tongue and Bilingual Education in Sub-Saharan Africa*. Association for the Development of Education in Africa (ADEA). (http://www.adeanet.org/adeaPortal/adea/biennial-2006/doc/document/B3_1_MTBLE_en.pdf).

Bamgbose, Ayo (2000). *Language and Exclusion: the consequences of language policies in Africa*. Münster, Hamburg and London: Lit Verlag.

Benson, Carol (2005). *Girls, Educational Equity and Mother Tongue-based Teaching*. Bangkok: UNESCO. (http://www.ungei.org/infobycountry/files/unesco_Girls_Edu_mother_tongue.pdf).

Bremner, Jason, Haub, Carl, Lee, Marlene, Mather, Mark and Zuehlke, Eric (2009). World Population Highlights: Key Findings from PRB's 2009 World Population Data Sheet. *Population Bulletin* 64:3, September 2009. (http://www.prb.org/Publications/PopulationBulletins/2009/worldpopulationhighlights2009.aspx).

COM(2008) 566 final (2008). Multilingualism: an asset for Europe and a shared commitment. Communication from the Commission to the European Parliament, the Council, the European Economic and Social Committee and the Committee of the Regions. Brussels: Commission of the European Communities.

Deloria, Vine, Jr (1988). *Custer Died for Your Sins: an Indian manifesto*. Norman: University of Oklahoma Press.

de Varennes, Fernand (1996). *Language, Minorities and Human Rights*. The Hague, Boston, London: Martinus Nijhoff.

Djité, Paulin (2008). *The Sociolinguistics of Development in Africa*. Bristol: Multilingual Matters.

Doughty, Catherine and Long, Michael (2003). The Scope of Inquiry and Goals of SLA. In Doughty, Catherine and Long, Michael (eds), *The Handbook of Second Language Acquisition*. Malden, MA and Oxford, UK: Blackwell, 3–16.

Dreze, Jean and Sen, Amartya (2002). *India: development and participation*. New Delhi: Oxford University Press.

Fardon, Richard and Furniss, Graham (eds) (1994). *African Languages, Development and the State*. London and New York: Routledge.

Global Education Digest 2009. Comparing Education Statistics Across the World. Montreal: UNESCO Institute of Statistics.

2008 EFA Global Monitoring Report. Education for All by 2015: will we make it? Oxford and Paris: Oxford University Press and UNESCO.

2009 EFA Global Monitoring Report. Overcoming Inequality: why governance matters. Oxford and Paris: Oxford University Press and UNESCO.

2010 EFA Global Monitoring Report. Reaching the marginalized. Oxford and Paris: Oxford University Press and UNESCO. http://www.unesco.org/en/efareport/reports/2010-marginalization/.

Hancock, Graham (1991). *Lords of Poverty. The free-wheeling lifestyles, power, prestige and corruption of the multi-billion dollar aid business*. London: Macmillan.

Harmon, David and Loh, Jonathan (2010). The Index of Linguistic Diversity: a new quantitative measure of trends in the status of the world's languages. *Language Documentation & Conservation* 4, 97–151. Can be downloaded from http://nflrc.hawaii.edu/ldc/2010/.

Haub, Carl and Kent, Mary Mederios (2009). *2009 World Population Data Sheet*. Washington, DC: Population Reference Bureau. (http://www.prb.org/Publications/Datasheets/2009/2009wpds.aspx).

HDR 2010 – see United Nations

Heugh, Kathleen (2006). Theory and Practice – Language Education Models in Africa: research, design, decision-making, and outcomes. In Alidou *et al.*, 56–84.

Heugh, Kathleen (2007). Language and Literacy Issues in South Africa. In Rassool, Naz (ed.), *Global Issues in Language, Education, and Development: perspectives from postcolonial countries*. Clevedon: Multilingual Matters, 187–218.

Heugh, Kathleen, Benson, Carol, Bogale, Berhanu and Gebre Yohannes, Mekonnen Alemu (2007). *Final Report: Study on Medium of Instruction in Primary Schools in Ethiopia*. Research report commissioned by the Ministry of Education, Addis Ababa, September to December 2006. (http://www.hsrc.ac.za/research/output/outputDocuments/4379_Heugh_Studyonmediumofinstruction.pdf).

Jessner, Ulrike (2008). Teaching Third Languages: findings, trends and challenges. *Language Teaching*, 41:1, 15–56.

Lewin, Keith (2008). *Strategies for Sustainable Financing of Secondary Education in Sub-Saharan Africa*. World Bank Working Paper No. 136. Africa Human Development Series. Washington, DC: World Bank.

Lewis, M. Paul (ed.) 2009. *Ethnologue: Languages of the World*, 16th edition. Dallas, TX: SIL International. (http://www.ethnologue.com/).

Malherbe, E. G. (1946). *The Bilingual School: a study of bilingualism in South Africa*. London: Longmans.

Mazrui, Alamin M. (2002). The English Language in African Education: dependency and decolonization. In Tollefson, James W. (ed.), *Language Policies in Education. Critical issues*. Mahwah, NJ: Lawrence Erlbaum, 267–281.

Mishra, Mahendra Kumar (2006). *Report of the 2nd multilingual education workshop on development of materials on tribal languages*. Bhubaneshwar, India: OPEPA. Manuscript.

Misra, Girishwar and Mohanty, Ajit K. (2000a). Consequences of Poverty and Disadvantage: a review of Indian studies. In Mohanty, Ajit K. and Misra, Girishwar (eds), *Psychology of Poverty and Disadvantage*. New Delhi: Concept Publishing Company, 121–148.

Misra, Girishwar and Mohanty, Ajit K. (2000b). Poverty and Disadvantage: issues in retrospect. In Mohanty, Ajit K. and Misra, Girishwar (eds), *Psychology of Poverty and Disadvantage*. New Delhi: Concept Publishing Company, 261–284.

Mohanty, Ajit K. (2000). Perpetuating Inequality: the disadvantage of language, minority mother tongues and related issues. In Mohanty, Ajit K. and Misra, Girishwar (eds), *Psychology of Poverty and Disadvantage*. New Delhi: Concept Publishing Company, 104–117.

Mohanty, Ajit K. (2010). Language Policy and Practice in Education: negotiating the double divide in multilingual societies. In Heugh, Kathleen and Skutnabb-Kangas, Tove (eds), *Multilingual Education Works. From the periphery to the centre*. Hyderabad: Orient BlackSwan, 164–175.

Odora Hoppers, Catherine A. (ed.) (2002). *Indigenous Knowledge and the Integration of Knowledge Systems. Towards a philosophy of articulation*. Claremont, RSA: New Africa Books.

Pattanayak, Debi Prasanna (1984). Language Policies in Multilingual States. In Gonzales, A. (ed.), *Panagani. Language planning, implementation and evaluation*. Manila: Linguistic Society of the Philippines.

Pattanayak, Debi Prasanna (1992). Mothertongue Awareness. Lecture given at Cambridge University, UK, September (1992). Manuscript.

Phillipson, Robert (2009). *Linguistic Imperialism Continued*. New York: Routledge/Taylor & Francis. Also Delhi: Orient Blackswan.

Sen, Amartya (1985). *Commodities and Capabilities*. Amsterdam: North Holland.

Shiva, Vandana (2000). *Tomorrow's Biodiversity*. London: Thames and Hudson.

Skutnabb-Kangas, Tove (2000). *Linguistic Genocide in Education – Or Worldwide Diversity and Human Rights?* Mahwah, NJ: Lawrence Erlbaum. Slightly updated version, 2008, New Delhi: Orient Longman.

Skutnabb-Kangas, Tove (2009). MLE for Global Justice: issues, approaches, opportunities. In Skutnabb-Kangas, Tove, Phillipson, Robert, Mohanty, Ajit and Panda, Minati (eds), *Social Justice through Multilingual Education*. Bristol: Multilingual Matters, 36–62.

Skutnabb-Kangas, Tove (2010). Crimes against humanity in education, and applied linguistics – corporate globalisation or geopolitical knowledge glocalisation? Plenary at BAAL (British Association for Applied Linguistics). 9–11 September 2010, Aberdeen, Scotland. http://www.tove-skutnabb-kangas.org/en/lectures_events.html.

Skutnabb-Kangas, Tove and Dunbar, Robert (2010). *Indigenous Children's Education as Linguistic Genocide and a Crime Against Humanity? A Global View. Gáldu Čála. Journal of Indigenous Peoples' Rights* No 1, 2010. Guovdageaidnu/Kautokeino: Galdu, Resource Centre for the Rights of Indigenous Peoples (http://www.galdu.org). As an e-book, free of charge, at http://www.e-pages.dk/grusweb/55/.

Skutnabb-Kangas, Tove, Maffi, Luisa and Harmon, Dave (2003). *Sharing a World of Difference. The Earth's linguistic, cultural, and biological diversity*. Paris: UNESCO Publishing. UNESCO, Terralingua, and World Wide Fund for Nature. (www.terralingua. org/).

Skutnabb-Kangas, Tove and McCarty, Teresa (2008). Clarification, Ideological/Epistemological Underpinnings and Implications of Some Concepts in Bilingual Education. In *Encyclopedia of Language and Education*, 2nd edition. Volume 5. Cummins, Jim and Hornberger, Nancy H. (eds), *Bilingual Education*. New York: Springer, 3–17.

Skutnabb-Kangas, Tove and Mohanty, Ajit (2009). *Policy and Strategy for MLE in Nepal.*

Report by Tove Skutnabb-Kangas and Ajit Mohanty. Consultancy visit 4–14 March 2009. Sanothimi, Bhaktapur, Nepal: Multilingual Education Program for All Non-Nepali Speaking Students of Primary Schools of Nepal. Ministry of Education, Department of Education, Inclusive Section. (http://www.tove-skutnabb-kangas.org/en/articles_for_downloading.html).

Skutnabb-Kangas, Tove and Mohanty, Ajit (2010). MLE as an Economic Equaliser in India and Nepal: mother tongue based multilingual education fights poverty through capability development and identity support. In Henrard, Kristin (ed.), *Socio Economic Participation of Minorities in Relation to their Right to (Respect for) Identity.* Studies in International Minority and Group Rights, Volume 2. Leiden and Boston, MA: Brill/Martinus Nijhoff Publishers.

Smith Tuhiwai, Linda (2004). Seventh impression [1999]. *Decolonizing Methodologies. Research and Indigenous Peoples.* London & Dunedin: Zed Press & University of Otago Press.

Thomas, Wayne P. and Collier, Virginia P. (2002). *A National Study of School Effectiveness for Language Minority Students' Long Term Academic Achievement.* George Mason University, CREDE (Center for Research on Education, Diversity & Excellence). (http://www.crede.ucsc.edu/research/llaa/1.1_final.html; see also http://www.thomasandcollier.com/Research%20Links.htm).

Tomaševski, Katarina (2001). *Human Rights Obligations: making education available, accessible, acceptable and adaptable.* Right to Education Primers 3. Lund & Stockholm: Raoul Wallenberg Institute of Human Rights and Humanitarian Law & Sida (Swedish International Development Cooperation Agency).

Tomaševski, Katarina (2004). *Economic, Social and Cultural Rights. The right to education. Report submitted by the Special Rapporteur Katarina Tomaševski.* Economic and Social Council, Commission on Human Rights, 60th session, Item 10 on the provisional agenda. E/CN.4/2004/45. 26 December 2003.

Unicef (2009). *Tracking Progress on Child and Maternal Nutrition. A survival and development priority.* November 2009. New York: United Nations Children's Fund.

United Nations Development Programme (2010). *Human Development Report 2010. 20th Anniversary Edition. The Real Wealth of Nations: pathways to human development.* New York: United Nations Development Programme. (http://hdr.undp.org/en/reports/global/hdr2010/chapters/en/).

Watson-Gegeo, Karen and Nielsen, Sarah (2003). Language Socialization in SLA. In Doughty, Catherine and Long, Michael (eds), *The Handbook of Second* Language Acquisition. Malden, MA and Oxford, UK: Blackwell, 155–177.

Wilson, Duncan (2004). Report: A critical evaluation of the first results of the monitoring of the Framework Convention on the issue of minority rights in, to and through education (1998–2003). In Filling the Frame. Five years of monitoring the Framework Convention for the Protection of National Minorities. Proceedings of the conference held in Strasbourg, 30–31 October 2003. Strasbourg: Council of Europe Publishing, pp. 163–233.

Wolff, H. Ekkehard (2006). Background and History – Language Politics and Planning in Africa. In Alidou *et al.*, 26–55. (http://www.adeanet.org/adeaPortal/adea/biennial-2006/doc/document/B3_1_MTBLE_en.pdf).

1

MULTILINGUAL EDUCATION IN ETHIOPIAN PRIMARY SCHOOLS

Carol Benson, Kathleen Heugh, Berhanu Bogale and Mekonnen Alemu Gebre Yohannes

1.1 Introduction

Ethiopia, with a population of 73.9 million of mostly subsistence farmers, is one of the poorest countries of the world (Population Census Commission/PCC 2008).[1] The 'working language of government', also known as the national language, is Amharic, which is spoken as a mother tongue by approximately 27% of the population and as a second language/lingua franca by an additional 9.9% according to the 1994 census (Central Statistical Agency of Ethiopia/CSA 2007). The *Ethnologue* (Lewis 2009) lists another 84 indigenous languages known as 'nationality' languages, including Afan Oromo/Oromifa representing 34.5% of the population and Tigrinya and Somali at about 6% each (confirmed by PCC 2008). Though it has few first language (L1) speakers, English is considered the 'most widely spoken foreign language' at 0.3% of the population (CSA 2007; Wagaw 1999).[2]

In 1994 Ethiopia adopted a multilingual national Education and Training Policy (Ministry of Education/MoE 1994), which calls for the use of learners' mother tongues for literacy and learning through the full eight years of primary schooling. This policy includes the teaching of Amharic (beginning in grades 3 or 5) to the 73% of students with other home languages. English is introduced as a subject starting in grade 1 and is the official medium of instruction (MoI) from grade 9 onwards (in secondary and higher education). The policy is bilingual for L1 speakers of Amharic and trilingual for speakers of other languages (L1 + Amharic + English).

Ethiopia's national policy has been implemented to differing degrees by its nine semi-autonomous regional states and two city administrations. In 2006 the Ministry of Education commissioned the authors of this chapter to evaluate implementation of the language policy in primary schools. A wide range of quantitative and qualitative data was collected in eight of the nine regions and one city-state, Addis Ababa. The findings informed evidenced-based recommendations for future policy and practice.[3]

This chapter presents an abridged version of the report, *Study on Medium of Instruction in Primary Schools in Ethiopia* (Heugh, Benson, Bogale and Gebre Yohannes 2007) along with updated information on changes to policy implementation through 2010.[4] This chapter demonstrates that where the political will is present, a national system even in a low-income country can initiate and implement mother tongue-based multilingual education (MLE) policy within a relatively short time frame (six to ten years, in this case). In Chapter 10 (Heugh, Benson, Gebre Yohannes and Bogale, this volume) we focus on the implications of the system-wide assessment of student achievement in the different models of bilingual and trilingual education practised between 2000 and 2008. This quantitative data helps draw attention to correlations between student achievement, the number of years of mother tongue-medium education (MTM education, hereafter MTM), and more recent emphasis on English since 2004.

The case of Ethiopia is likely to be of interest to international audiences for a number of reasons. First, the national policy for primary schooling is consistent with contemporary research supporting extended educational use of the mother tongue and the addition of other languages through bi- or trilingual approaches (e.g. Alidou *et al.* 2006). Next, it appears that decentralised educational decision-making has made it possible for the semi-autonomous regional states to choose regional and/or local languages and develop the materials needed to implement national policy, albeit to varying degrees and with greater challenges in more linguistically diverse regions. Uneven implementation makes Ethiopia something of a microcosm of the different models of bi/multilingual education currently on offer internationally. The Heugh *et al.* (2007) study provides clear evidence that particular learning outcomes are associated with the extent to which mother tongues are used in education (see also Chapter 10 here). Most importantly, the Ethiopian experience demonstrates that theoretically sound multilingual education (MLE) can be offered even in challenging, resource-scarce conditions, and that this type of education can dramatically enhance school results for all learners.

The study also revealed some inconsistencies in the national policy. There is a tension between the implementation of a mother tongue-based MLE system and aspirational pressure towards English as a perceived language of access to the world. This has resulted in the early introduction of English as a subject from grade 1 and its use as medium of instruction (MoI) for secondary and further education. We found evidence that overly ambitious aspirations for English compromise the teaching and learning of academic content and put undue pressure on effective MLE, which sounds a warning for other countries with such aspirations. The under-utilised educational potential of Ethiopia's national language, Amharic, may also have implications for other multilingual contexts.

1.2 The Context of Ethiopian Multilingual Education

1.2.1 Brief Sociolinguistic Overview

Four major ethnolinguistic groups – the Oromo, Amhara, Tigray and Somali – together comprise approximately 74% of the population (PCC 2008). The remaining 26% of the population belong to about 80 ethnolinguistic communities. Table 1.1 lists the Ethiopian languages that have at least one million speakers.

For historical and political reasons, Amharic was made the official working language of the Ethiopian government in the 1955 Constitution. Although the primacy of Amharic is contested, particularly among the more numerous Afan Oromo speakers, it nevertheless functions as a lingua franca of business and administration across the country.

English has been the most popular foreign language in Ethiopia since the British helped Ethiopia expel the Italians after their brief occupation during the Second World War (e.g. Negash 1990). However, English is used only by a small minority of urban educated economic and/or political elite. The practical diffusion of English in Ethiopia is limited to fewer functional domains than in many other African countries. A difference between other 'anglophone' countries and Ethiopia is that in the former, English was used in the administration, legislation and upper levels of education and the economy from the late 1800s, thus functioning as a second language for urban dwellers. English is a relatively foreign language across Ethiopia, a country never colonised by an English-speaking power.

1.2.2 History of Language in Education

The first 'western' school was established in Addis Ababa in 1908 for a small number of young men from privileged families who were to learn English,

TABLE 1.1 Major Ethiopian languages

Language/ethnic group	Number of speakers	% of population
Afan Oromo/Oromo	25,488,344	34.5
Amhara	19,867,817	26.9
Somali	4,581,793	6.2
Tigrinya/Tigray	4,483,776	6.1
Sidama	2,966,377	4.0
Gurage	1,867,350	2.5
Wolaita	1,707,074	2.3
Hadiya	1,284,366	1.7
Afar	1,276,372	1.7
Gamo	1,107,163	1.5

Source: adapted from PCC 2008, Table 2.2, p. 16; ethnic groups used as proxy for language

French and Italian (Negash 1990). Although English and Italian were used in the few schools that were established in the first part of the century, Amharic was used as the medium of instruction for primary schools from the mid-1950s onwards. Students were expected to switch to English medium in secondary school.[5] The use of Amharic, while welcomed by Amharic speakers, was resented by other ethnolinguistic groups, particularly the more numerous Oromo (or Oromifa). Many communities, therefore, kept their children out of school and enrolment was lower than in most African countries.

The overthrow of Haile Selassie in 1974 by the socialist Dergue gave Ethiopian 'nationalities' the right, in theory, to use their languages for educational and other regional sociopolitical purposes. The Dergue's literacy campaigns were established in 15 Ethiopian languages, but Amharic continued as the only language of primary education, even though research demonstrated that Amharic negatively affected school achievement for speakers of other languages (Negash 1990; Gebre Yohannes 2005).

Social and political change at the beginning of the 1990s resulted in the downfall of the Dergue and the independence of Eritrea. The Ethiopian People's Revolutionary Democratic Front (EPRDF), together with several opposition parties, formed the Transitional Government of Ethiopia (TGE).The right of every Ethiopian 'nation and nationality' to use and develop its languages and cultures was strengthened in the Ethiopian Constitution of 1994, and in the Education and Training Policy of the same year (MoE 1994). Ethiopia thus transformed from a single-party military political system to a self-proclaimed multi-party, multi-ethnic state; from a centrally controlled to a decentralised administrative system; and from a monolingual education system to a multilingual one.

The 1994 Education and Training Policy identifies the learner's mother tongue (L1) for primary schooling, Amharic as the national working language (L2 for about 73% of students) and English (L3/foreign language) as the language

TABLE 1.2 Language distribution according to the National Education and Training Policy

Language	Level of education	Function
L1: Mother tongues (nationality languages)	Primary (grades 1 to 8) only	Medium of instruction
L2: Amharic (countrywide use in oral and written communication)	In practice from grade 3 or 5 through secondary (starting point not specified)	Subject
L3: English (foreign language)	From grade 1 through university	Subject in primary; Medium of instruction from grade 9 upward (secondary and tertiary)

Source: adapted from Gebre Yohannes 2005

of secondary and tertiary education. Table 1.2 shows how each language is to be used and at what levels of education.

While this national policy serves as a guide, decentralisation of education administration to regional education bureaus (REBs) has allowed for some variation in implementation. The more linguistically diverse regions have understandably experienced most challenges, but over time increasing numbers of languages have been adopted in education (23 by 2006, 32 by 2010).

1.2.3 The Context of Ethiopian Education

Ethiopia is a low-income country and educational achievement generally is low. Throughput to secondary education is also low and there is significant gender disparity across the system. About 85% of the population lives in rural areas, making it difficult to expand educational and other services, particularly since the country's GDP per capita is estimated at US$ 636.[6] According to UNICEF (2008), net enrolment in primary schooling is 66% (69 for boys and 64 for girls), and net enrolment in secondary schooling is 32% (37 for boys and 26 for girls). Statistics are not consistent, however, and the World Bank offers a significantly lower rate for gross enrolment in secondary at 18.5%, based on UNESCO Institute of Statistics data in 2005 (Lewin 2008: 71). The pupil–teacher ratio is 72 : 1 in primary schooling. Both the positive outcomes of the 1994 policy and the challenges need to be understood in this context.

1.2.3.1 Improving Educational Quality, Access and Equity

In recent years the MoE has been concerned about the practical implementation of a workable language policy supporting *equitable* delivery of *quality* education to which all have *access*. Like other countries, Ethiopia undertook a commitment to Universal Primary Education (UPE) and the UNESCO Education for All Frameworks (EFA) at the Jomtien Conference of 1990. The goal of quality education is to facilitate optimal cognitive development of the pupil through schooling (UNESCO 2005), and research demonstrates many connections between quality and mother tongue-based schooling (MLE).

Concerned with delivery of quality education and with reducing gender disparities in enrolment and retention, the MoE engages in ongoing monitoring and evaluation of the system, including system-wide assessments of grade 4 and 8 students. In Chapter 10, we draw on some of the results from these to demonstrate how mother tongue-medium (MTM) education is working and where the risks lie.

1.2.3.2 Civil Society Perceptions of MTM Education

At the outset, public response to the 1994 policy was reportedly mixed. In the Oromiya region, where support for Afan Oromo has been strong and where the level of linguistic development is advanced, practice may have been ahead of policy. However, in other regions, reservations were expressed regarding the use of nationality languages in education. George (2002) reports that parents were concerned that focus on the L1 might negatively affect their children's ability to speak Amharic or English, which could cause them to fail the grade 8 examinations (for similar concerns in other contexts see Mohanty; Nikièma and Ilboudo, this volume). Some Ethiopian parents expressed misperceptions or fears similar to those elsewhere in Africa, including: that MTM education is too expensive, that mother tongues (MTs) may not be sufficiently developed for education or that this might delay access to English, or that mathematics and science can only be taught through a language like English (see also Gebre Yohannes 2005). These concerns occur where communities do not have access to reliable information regarding multilingual education, even though they are addressed in the research literature (e.g. Alidou *et al.* 2006). Many concerns can be successfully refuted with the data reported in our study (see below, and Chapter 10).

1.2.3.3 The Position of English

Contemporary use of English in school had its roots in Ethiopia's relationship with Britain during the Second World War, which led to adoption of curriculum and teaching materials based on British models. English has consistently been used as the medium of secondary education and teacher education, initially with a large number of the teaching corps being English-speaking 'ex-pats'. However, owing to limited use of English beyond school, students have not been able to develop the degree of proficiency in English required (see Hussein 2010). The number of English-speaking teachers declined during the Dergue regime, and researchers found that English presented serious barriers to effective teaching and learning (Negash 1990). Based on field surveys in the mid-1980s, a key advisor recommended that English should not be used as a MoI until later stages in the education system, and that government should:

> ensure that students and parents fully realize that . . . 'Later English means better English'! . . . 'Later English means better science, mathematics, geography . . .'
>
> *(Stoddart 1986: 19)*

As Table 1.2 above illustrates, the 1994 Education and Training Policy removed English as MoI from eight years of primary school but introduced it as a subject from grade 1. Unfortunately, teachers have never had the English language proficiency necessary to implement this policy. Until recently, the teaching of English in the 1st cycle of primary schooling (grades 1 to 4) was expected to be undertaken by classroom teachers who had received a one-year teacher-training certificate after a grade 10 school-exit examination. Teachers in the 2nd cycle (grades 5 to 8) were expected to be trained in three-year diploma programmes in which they specialised in languages or in science. By 2009 the teacher-training system changed, now requiring all teachers to complete three-year diploma courses taught through English. Besides threatening the quality of teacher education, this represents a serious threat to MLE, as we discuss in the findings section.

In response to expectations of high-level English proficiency in school-exit examinations (see below) and low English proficiency of teachers, the Ministry of Education (MoE) embarked on a costly English Language Improvement Programme (ELIP) in collaboration with the British Council in 2004. This involved training a core group of specialist English language trainers and the establishment of English Language Improvement Centres at colleges and universities from 2005. Between 2005 and 2006, 42% of the national teacher education budget was re-routed towards ELIP involving a cascade model in-service programme for every teacher in the Ethiopian school system, even those not teaching English or through English. This programme involved an intensive 120 contact-hour programme followed by 80 hours of distance education (see McLaughlin, Woubishet, Fite and Kasa 2005). A second English language improvement strategy was the installation in 2004 of (plasma generation) television monitors in every secondary classroom, and simultaneous beaming of programmes by the Ethiopian Educational Media Agency (EEMA). Programmes were commissioned from a foreign agency to teach the Ethiopian curriculum through the medium of (South African) English (e.g. Hussein 2008). Criticisms, including our own, identify the unrealistic pace of content delivery, the unfamiliar variety of English used, and the replacement of Ethiopian teachers with television teachers.

1.3 Methodology of the Study Medium of Instruction in Primary Schools in Ethiopia

Our 2006 study took into account recent evidence-based research on language education in multilingual contexts, including a report of the Association for the Development of Education in Africa (ADEA)-UNESCO Institute of Education (UIE) study on mother tongue and bilingual education in Africa (Alidou *et al.* 2006). This and prior work by members of the research team (in Ethiopian, African and other international contexts) provided the theoretical and practical basis for the investigation in Ethiopia. Our findings were related to current understandings of how students develop optimal language skills to facilitate quality, retention and educational throughput. The recommendations arising from the Ethiopian study, while considering practical issues, were grounded in current pedagogical and linguistic arguments, some of which for the sake of brevity are omitted from this summary.

1.3.1 Choice of Regions and Sites for Research

The original terms of reference for the study included five regions, which the team increased to eight regions (Afar, Amhara, Oromiya, Southern Nations and Nationalities Region/SNNPR, Tigray, Gambella, Harari, and Somali) plus Addis Ababa because the regional socio-economic and ethnolinguistic differences required contextualised data analysis. Dire Dawa city-state and Benishangul Gumuz region were not visited owing to time and logistical constraints, but some data were obtained on these areas from regional officials. Updates received between 2007 and 2010 are included here.

1.3.2 Data Collection and Reporting Instruments

Numerous qualitative data collection instruments were developed in consultation with the Ministry of Education (MoE) and a consortium of development agencies in Ethiopia. Instruments were designed to capture information from a wide range of stakeholders (community representatives, parents, students, teachers, teacher educators, linguists) and the various levels of the education system including federal, regional, zonal, and even woreda (local) staff. We utilised available records of data, including system-wide student assessment, curriculum planning documentation, policies and practices of materials development and publication, languages levels required for teaching and teacher education, etc. for purposes of triangulation with the field data and impressionistic data collected (see Appendices in Heugh *et al.* 2007).

While classroom observations focused on rural (including remote) schools, we included urban primary and secondary schools. Classroom observation instruments and questionnaires (translated into several Ethiopian languages) were developed, trialled and modified during the data collection period (October–December 2006). School visits permitted the collection of data on classroom conditions, classroom language practices, availability of learning materials and what student notebooks revealed about teaching and learning. We observed all grade levels, but depending on the regional policy we tried to focus on grade levels in which languages were introduced as subjects or where a shift in medium of instruction occurred.

A consultative workshop to discuss findings and verify data with regional representatives was held at the end of the data collection phase in December 2006. Representatives from all of the regions, the federal MoE and the development agency partners which supported the study participated, allowing us to check our work for omissions or inaccuracies as well as to present our analysis for discussion. The final report, including recommendations for further policy and implementation, followed. Our data and analysis are summarised next.

1.4 Findings and Analysis

We begin with a table (1.3) summarising the medium of instruction (MoI) practices in primary schooling and teacher training in each regional state or city administration. The regions are grouped according to degree of compliance with the national policy, and then each group is described and analysed based on the available data, including updates to 2010. We conclude with an overall analysis in which we identify strengths and weaknesses of existing policies and practices.

1.4.1 Regional Data

As mentioned above, different regions have implemented the national policy to varying degrees, depending on decision-making capacity, level of political will, degree of linguistic diversity, stage of development of the relevant languages and other factors. In Table 1.3 we group the regions by number of years of MTM education offered.

1.4.1.1 Regions with Eight Years of MTM Education (MTM 8) – Full or Near-full Compliance with National Mother Tongue Policy

While the policy calls for eight years of mother tongue-medium (MTM) primary education, and for teacher training to be given in 'the nationality language used in the area' (MoE 1994, 2002), only Oromiya region has been completely consistent. The regional majority language, Afan Oromo, is the MoI for all primary schooling and has been used for the training of both lower and upper primary teachers. Tigray and Somali regions have been consistent with policy in that they have used regional majority languages as MoI for eight years of primary schooling

TABLE 1.3 Language models represented by region

Region	Years of mother tongue medium	Grade in which there is a switch to English medium
Oromiya★ Tigray Somali Amhara (before 2006)	8	9
Amhara (since 2006) Harari	6 for maths and science; 8 for other subjects	7 for maths and science; 9 for other subjects
Addis Ababa Dire Dawa★★ SNNPR (until 2004)	6	7
SNNPR (since 2005/6) Gambella	4	5
Afar Benishangul Gumuz	0 (6 years – L2 Amharic)	7

★ Afan Oromo is also offered in Oromifa-speaking streams in other regions like Amhara where there are substantial numbers of speakers.
★★ One subject (Civics) is taught in MT for 8 years.

and for lower primary teacher training; however, both of these regions use English as MoI for upper primary teacher training even though these teachers will be using the L1. This may be a result of pressure to 'professionalise' teacher training, which threatens the use of the L1 even for lower primary teachers, as discussed further below.

Table 1.3 also shows that Oromiya and Somali regions offer Amharic-medium streams for those who do not speak the majority regional languages, which means that minority groups in these regions are not all getting MTM education. Tigray region deserves credit for attending to its minority languages: Saho was introduced as MoI starting with a grade 1 cohort of students in 2009, and the piloting of Kunama was scheduled for 2010.

The fact that only Oromiya systematically uses MTM education throughout teaching and training may be due to the dominance of Afan Oromo in the region. However, Afan Oromo-medium streams in Amhara region are also consistent with national policy, demonstrating serious commitment to the policy among speakers of Afan Oromo, even when they live outside Oromiya region.

Despite the teacher training issues, Oromiya, Tigray and Somali regions are reaping the benefits of offering eight years of primary education through major regional languages, recording superior levels of achievement in relation to other regions. This success is particularly well documented in the Grade 8 National Assessments (see Chapter 10).

1.4.1.2 Regions Implementing Six Years of MTM Education (MTM 6)

The two city-states, Addis Ababa and Dire Dawa, might be expected to follow national policy more closely since they are seats of decision-making. However, they are consistent with national policy only up to grade 6, along with Amhara (which changed from eight years of MTM to a mix of six and eight years of MTM in 2006) and Harari (with the same system).

In Addis Ababa, there is an assumption that all children speak Amharic, whereas approximately 50% of students are estimated to have other home languages. Also significant is the earlier introduction of English medium in grades 7–8. This trend coincides with a widespread myth that local languages are not suitable for abstract thought. In 2006, MTM was used in grades 7–8 for all subjects except mathematics and science in the Harari and Amhara regions, but only for Civics in Dire Dawa, and not at all in Addis. The MoI for teacher education in 2006 was clearly divided between lower primary (grades 1–4) in MT and upper primary (grades 5–8) in English, constituting a mismatch between the MoI of teacher training and classroom practice for upper primary school teachers.

The decisions, to cut MTM education short before the end of grade 8 and to train upper primary (and since 2006, increasingly lower primary) teachers through English, go against national policy and are contrary to what national assessment results indicate regarding how students learn most effectively. We believe they can best be explained by the negative effects of English-medium secondary schooling, as we will discuss further below – and as the situations in the remaining regions demonstrate even more acutely.

1.4.1.3 Regions with Four Years of MTM Education (MTM 4)

Two regions, Gambella and SNNPR (since 2006), have introduced English medium much earlier than the national policy calls for, i.e. at the beginning of upper primary (grade 5). Both regions are linguistically more diverse than other regions, and use local languages only at the lower primary level.

Gambella and SNNPR also face greater resourcing challenges in providing MTM education than other regions. In Gambella, despite offerings in Nuer and Anguak (and more recently Meshenger), students from other language backgrounds must learn through whichever of these is used in their local schools, or find a way to pay for private schooling in Amharic or English. SNNPR has made greater progress in offering 12 languages for four years of MTM and as subjects to the end of primary. At the time of our study, the MoI in teacher training matched MoI in the schools. Regional officials reported in 2006 that the region was to expand the number of languages taught in MTM in lower primary and also to extend the teaching of these languages as subjects to the end of primary.[7] According to our informants in 2009, there were pilot projects to teach Basketto, Korete and Shekacho as subjects, Me'enit was ready to be taught as a subject, and orthographies were being tested in five additional languages – Bench, Duizzi, Sheko, Bale and Suri. These developments are very encouraging and add another nine languages to the 12 which are already used in the school system. Unfortunately, changes in teacher education have taken a reverse trajectory, leading us to wonder if MLE will be threatened.

Throughout our travels, the research team was surprised by the degree to which the default language is English when instruction or materials are not available in local languages. Judging by the limited English language competence of the many primary teachers we met, and their generally much higher proficiency in Amharic, we would have expected Amharic to be more useful and used in teaching (discussed further below).

1.4.1.4 Regions with No MTM Education, but Six Years of Amharic Second Language/L2 Medium

Neither Afar nor Benishangul Gumuz offers MTM in formal primary education. In Afar region, Afar language is used in limited alternative basic education (three years of primary) designed to reach nomadic communities. Since 2009 Benishangul Gumuz has run pilot programmes in local languages. These regions offer learners six years of schooling through Amharic, learners' L2, before switching to English at grade 7.

Although Afar region is relatively linguistically homogeneous, its failure to provide MTM education is likely a result of geo–political and economic factors. Afar is an extremely poor desert region sparsely populated by pastoralist communities, and there is low school retention beyond grade 4. Benishangul Gumuz is more diverse, with six major languages and many others (PCC 2008). According to 2009 data, the latter region is piloting Gumuz, Bertha and Shinasha as MoI in grades 1 and 2. In both regions, Amharic (L2) appears to be the default MoI to the end of grade 6. While we were told that there are different teaching and learning materials and methods for Amharic L1 and L2, we did not see any Amharic L2 materials in any of our school observations in these or other regions.

1.4.2 Educational Use, Competence and Status of Languages

Throughout the system there are patterns of use of the first language/mother tongue (L1); the second language (L2), Amharic; and the foreign language, English. We discuss these below.

1.4.2.1 Mother Tongues (MTs) – The Most Promising Choice for MoI

Our classroom observation data showed that where the L1 is used as MoI, both spoken and written communication between teachers and learners are more likely to be effective. Even though teacher talk dominates in virtually all classrooms, the quality of classroom interaction is markedly higher where the MT is used, because teachers and students are able to engage in two-way communicative exchanges. Student talk in the L1 is characterised by extended answers to questions, more original responses and even unsolicited questions regarding lesson content.

Materials generally take an alphabetic/phonetic approach to beginning literacy, after which children are expected to read short texts and answer comprehension questions. At higher levels, much more complex texts are accompanied by some grammar-based exercises. We were concerned that literacy materials appeared to follow unrealistically high expectations of student achievement, yet neither observations nor interviews indicated that students had particular difficulty with MT literacy at any grade level.

Despite the efficiency of MTM compared with attempts to use English medium, we noted that many teachers, students and parents expressed pessimism regarding the role of L1 in education. Interview and survey data suggest that while few deny the effectiveness of the MTM, many people tend to equate access to English language skills with educational success.

Teachers in some regions told us that local languages lack terminologies and are insufficiently developed for MTM, especially for maths and sciences in upper primary. While it is true that some languages are in earlier phases of standardisation and development, especially in more heterogeneous regions like SNNPR

and Benishangul Gumuz, we believe that the real issue is teachers' own proficiency in educational discourse in these languages. In Tigray, for example, teacher
trainers who had learned through Amharic/English claimed that Tigrinya, spoken
by 4.5 million Ethiopians, with a literary tradition since the 1200s,[8] could not
be used to teach maths or science. Their colleagues who had learned through
Tigrinya disagreed, since they knew from experience it was possible. Amharic and
Afan Oromo have already been successfully used to express scientific concepts in
teacher training and other forms of higher education.

Some informants reported that local languages could not be used owing to the
lack of dictionaries and other reference materials. However, we noted that very
few reference materials were available in any language in the schools. Implementing MTM requires the work of curriculum developers, local language specialists
and linguists, along with the financial resources to support their work. We identified significant human resources, but additional economic resources are needed
for linguistic development and to retain qualified MT teachers. For example,
Gambella region reported having difficulty retaining qualified teachers who speak
Nuer and Anguak because they are poached by health, agriculture and other more
profitable service sectors. On the positive side, this is evidence of both supply of,
and demand for, professionals who are bi- and multiliterate.

Linguistic diversity within primary schools was sometimes offered as reason to
avoid MTM While this is a challenge in urban schools, we encountered a number
of creative practices that accommodated diverse L1s. In Harar region, parallel
MTM Harari, Amharic and Afan Oromo streams are provided in some schools,
while parallel Somali and Amharic streams co-exist in the Somali region. Another
practice is matching teacher recruitment and placement according to mother
tongue (Nuer, Anguak, Meshenger), which is being done in Gambella region.

1.4.2.2 Amharic – National Status, Yet Missed Opportunities

Overall, the teaching of Amharic to students with other mother tongues across
all regions appears to be consistent with the national policy. In Oromiya region
and in the Afan Oromo streams in Amhara region, Amharic (L2) is introduced
in grade 5; elsewhere it begins at grade 3. The main exception to policy is where
Amharic is used as MoI as if it were the mother tongue of all learners, in mixed
areas and urban schools where this is clearly not the case (notably in Addis Ababa).
A related concern is whether or not teachers are prepared and materials available
to teach Amharic L2 rather than Amharic L1.

While 73% of students must have three languages (L1, Amharic and English),
L1 speakers of Amharic are required to have only L1 plus English. Most respond-
ents did not see reasons why L1 speakers of Amharic should learn an additional
Ethiopian language, which is evidence of unequal relations between groups.

That Amharic is a widely spoken lingua franca in Ethiopia is apparent in all of
these situations, and many urban adults are highly competent L2 speakers. How-

ever, visits to rural schools revealed that Amharic is not well understood by many learners. The use of Amharic as MoI in heterogeneous language contexts, that is, where it is an L2 for students, has had mixed success. While teachers appear to have sufficient proficiency in Amharic, we did not observe many using appropriate L2 methodologies; the situation clearly places a strain on students who have not been exposed to Amharic in their communities.

In Harari and Somali regions, where both local mother tongues and Amharic are used in parallel MTM streams or in different shifts, some students have voluntarily opted for the Amharic MoI stream/shift. Parents and students offered three reasons for this, believing: one, that strong Amharic would offer portable language skills within the wider Ethiopian context; two, that teachers who use Amharic are better trained or more competent; and three, that learning resources are more plentiful in Amharic. It should be noted that only one of the three reasons has to do with language, and the others with educational quality.

We had anticipated that students learning two scripts might experience difficulties with reading and writing skills. Amharic and Tigrinya are written in Ethiopic script whereas most other Ethiopian languages use the Latin script. Since English (Latin script) is also taught, all students will need both Ethiopic and Latin scripts. To our surprise, we found that students appeared to learn both scripts in lower primary without great difficulty, and that they could keep the two writing systems separate. We did find that students in some regions experienced difficulty learning Amharic in general; for example, Nuer students in Gambella showed a marked preference for (and greater competence in) English over Amharic, and some teachers in Oromiya said their students found learning the Amharic script difficult. In the latter case, where Amharic study begins in grade 5 (later than in other regions), and where there is a lack of L2 methods and materials, there are clearly missed opportunities to cultivate Amharic second language competence.

There are also missed opportunities for Amharic beyond primary school. We asked informants about the feasibility of using the national language instead of English for secondary and higher education, since Amharic is much more widely spoken. This was perceived as more feasible in some regions than in others, probably owing to historical and political experiences. (Here we might draw some parallels with South Africa, where a language that is actually a widely spoken lingua franca, Afrikaans, is also associated with past injustices, and English may be preferred for its supposed neutrality.) Despite the politics, there is no question that Ethiopian teachers and students especially in urban areas have much more exposure to, and thus higher competence in, Amharic than they do in English, making Amharic (in the absence of the mother tongue) a more appropriate language for learning.

1.4.2.3 English – Misplaced Advocacy

The study of English as a subject begins at grade 1 in all regions, in line with federal policy. Nothing in the policy calls for English as MoI in primary schooling, yet apart from the Oromiya, Somali and Tigray regions, all other regions have adopted English as MoI at some point in upper primary schooling. As the regional summaries indicate, English has come into grades 7–8 as MoI for mathematics and the sciences in some regions, and increasingly for all subjects in other regions and the city-states. The regions least consistent with MoI policy are using English as MoI for all of upper primary schooling beginning at grade 5.

The use of English as MoI in the training of upper primary teachers has been problematic since 2006, particularly because it has not matched the MoI for upper primary teaching, at least not in all subjects. It now appears that the MoI in schools is adjusting towards MoI in teacher training rather than the reverse. At the time of our study, lower primary teacher training was still conducted through the appropriate languages in most regions, but by 2009 this was changing due to efforts to 'professionalise' teacher education, as mentioned above. Our study found no indication that teacher education given through English results in higher teacher proficiency in English; on the contrary, there was clear evidence that it hampers understanding. For example, the dean of a TTC in Tigray region told us that students were not able to express their practical experience through English: 'Last year the language of portfolios was English and they were very limited, with lots of copying. This year we changed the language of portfolio writing to Tigrinya, and they can express themselves without a problem' (see also Hussein 2010).

School managers and local education officials tended to overstate teachers' English language proficiency when researchers first arrived at schools. They often began by claiming that teachers had the necessary English language expertise to teach in English, referring to the participation of 140,000 teachers in the above-mentioned English Language Improvement Programme (ELIP) (McLaughlin *et al.* 2005). When probed, however, they admitted that any new language skills acquired through ELIP were not sustainable since there are limited opportunities for teachers to use English outside of the classroom. Teacher educators, REB officials and teachers in Harari and SNNPR informed us that ELIP had led them to believe that the objective was to improve the teachers' English for future employment or for entering university. Teachers also reported that their understanding of 'communicative language teaching' was that acceptable teaching practice included 'practising' their own 'broken English' on students in the classroom. The aim of the ELIP intervention seemed to have shifted from quality teaching and learning towards aspirational benefits for teachers.

Meanwhile, we found evidence of a large gap between the aspiration for English proficiency and reality. This is illustrated in interview data regarding English as MoI with five upper primary practicum teachers at a rural primary school in Tigray. Although teachers initiated the discussion in English, they experienced great difficulty understanding our questions and were unable to formulate comprehensible answers. When Gebre Yohannes of our research team switched to Tigrinya, these trainees were able to explain in fluent Tigrinya why English should be the medium of instruction: 'Because it is an international language!'

Our observations showed that as soon as English is introduced as the MoI, communication in the classroom is drastically reduced. With the exception of some urban schools in Gambella and Amhara regions, and a handful of older teachers, we found that teachers seldom had the necessary English language proficiency for teaching purposes. Teachers and students in many instances had built up a series of ritualised stock phrases which could be used and repeated over and over again (e.g. T: 'Is it clear?' Students: 'Yes'). This superficial discourse is indicative of low levels of cognitive engagement with lesson content. We observed a Gambella teacher struggling to teach a science subject through English, so much so that it was difficult to work out what the teacher wanted to say. We witnessed teachers in several regions become so flustered trying to teach through English that they switched to a completely different subject during observed lessons. In Somali region, a senior school management staff member stopped teaching altogether when members of the team asked to observe his class. Although many teachers attempted to use English consistently while we were present, as soon as we left the classroom we heard them revert to the local language. This happened consistently at the grade levels where transition to English medium occurred in that region, whether at grade 5, 7 or 9, and it was often done in the years subsequent to the change of medium. We learned that normal classroom teaching involves regular and unsystematic use of code switching between English and an Ethiopian language. While this is not necessarily a negative activity if it promotes understanding, it does indicate that English does not sit well as a MoI. Furthermore, if code switching is not recognised as a legitimate pedagogical process, it is unlikely to facilitate systematic learning (Heugh 2009).

Because of a system of 'self-contained classrooms', each lower primary teacher is expected to teach all subjects of the curriculum, including English as a subject. There are some exceptions to this, e.g. in Harari region where there is a ready supply of teachers. Here teachers who are English language specialists teach English as a subject in lower primary classrooms, thus relieving the pressure from the classroom teacher. In general, however, teachers with the least training (a one-year certificate programme following grade 10) are giving learners their early school experiences in English.

Interactive Radio is intended to support teachers with limited English language proficiency, but many teachers we observed had difficulty understanding the basic English of the radio broadcasts, made more difficult by electrostatic and other noise outside the classroom.

In some regions it is assumed that four years of English taught in this way will prepare students to use English as a medium of instruction. The results were clearly limited, as we found when we recorded grade 5 students in simple interaction with Bogale of our research team. They responded to basic questions in inappropriate ways, demonstrating lack of comprehension:

Researcher [to one student]:	Do you have a pen?
Student:	I am ten years.
Researcher [to another student]:	Do you have a pen?
Student:	Yes.
Researcher [to same student]:	Where is your pen?
Student:	No.

Materials for the teaching of English as a subject are prepared at the federal level. In most classes we observed, there were English language textbooks, even where other subjects (particularly those taught in the mother tongue) were in short supply.

In conclusion, while educators, learners and families aspire to high competence in English, current conditions even with a great deal of government input do not allow this exogenous language to be viable for instruction. The situation of English in education in Ethiopia is one of expensive advocacy in the face of all evidence of futility.

1.4.3 Strengths and Weaknesses of Existing Policies and Practices

We conclude this discussion with an analysis of the overall findings organised by strengths and weaknesses of existing policies and practices. We focus on three strengths: the MoE policy recommending eight years of mother tongue-based education; the degree to which decentralised decision-making favours implementation of MTM and the successful development of human and material resources through experience in MTM. We also point out three weaknesses: the mismatch of medium of instruction for teacher training versus primary teaching; the widespread assumptions and myths concerning language acquisition and learning; and the negative washback (or backwash) effects caused by use of English at secondary and tertiary levels of the Ethiopian education system.

1.4.3.1 The Strength of the MTM Education Policy

Eight years of MTM within a bi/multilingual system synchronises with international research and theory which support long-term development and maintenance of the first language as a foundation for MLE and access to meaningful education. As demonstrated in the most policy-consistent regions of Oromiya, Somali and Tigray, the positive effects include improved access to, and quality of, primary education, including high teacher and student language proficiency, improved classroom interaction and better student performance in all subjects (see Chapter 10). While there are still difficulties encountered in teaching Amharic and English as additional languages, the main question remaining in those regions is whether the L1 could be extended into higher levels of education to take advantage of its effectiveness and efficiency.

Compared with post-colonial African countries, the Ethiopian language education policy is especially progressive. Eritrea, a neighbouring country in the horn of Africa sharing several cross-border languages with Ethiopia, began work on a six-year MTM education policy in nine languages in 1991 but for reasons of political instability has not been as successful with implementation. Another example which demonstrated the benefits of extended use of MTM was the six-year Yoruba-medium experiment in Nigeria undertaken in the 1970s (e.g. Akinnaso 1991). Despite its positive effects, this approach was never implemented through the system. Somalia and Guinea Conakry are two other examples of MT development in primary schooling in the 1970s–80s. South Africa experienced the longest period of extended mother tongue education (eight years of MT for speakers of African languages) from 1955–1975, during which period student achievement showed marked increases in school-exit examinations across the curriculum (Heugh 1999, 2003). However, in each of these latter cases, educational decisions were reversed due to their negative political associations. For the most part, countries in Africa have been reluctant to implement MTM education for longer than three to four years prior to a switch to an international language.

Compared with other countries, Ethiopia's national MTM education policy of 1994 is currently the most progressive and best implemented, even considering the challenges described here. Although there is still progress to be made for smaller language communities, the number of languages in which MTM education has been developed should cater for up to 84% of students in the school system. This is a remarkable achievement for any country. However, there are risks posed by high aspirations for English, as we discuss further under weaknesses.

1.4.3.2 The Strength of Decentralised Decision-making

While we understand that there are still structural challenges to be addressed, particularly with appropriate distribution of scarce economic resources, the decentralised education system in Ethiopia appears to favour development of locally appropriate policies and practices that serve the language communities of each region. Countries with top-down decision-making tend to implement single educational models with little regard for diversity in terms of language attitudes and use, exposure to national and/or official languages, goals of schooling, and so on. In the Ethiopian case, the regional education bureaus have financial resources and have developed technical expertise which favour language development, with models and materials based on sound policy. Within the regions, more district administrative units, *woredas*; and local *kebele*, school clusters and even individual schools, were observed exercising some decision-making power.

We found decentralisation to be functioning well even at local levels. For example, in Harari region the REB had the resources to employ additional specialist language teachers for lower primary, thus supplementing regular classroom teachers' more fragile proficiency in English. We encountered a similar decision made at the school cluster level in Tigray region. At the *woreda* level, when there are insufficient numbers of textbooks, decisions are made so that all schools get materials in proportion to their numbers. We also found that *woreda* educators are often involved in linguistic development and elaboration of curricular materials in their local languages. Even at the school level, we found creative examples, for example in Harari and Somali regions where schools organised parallel language streams and/or morning/afternoon shifts to accommodate different language groups. In another example, a rural school principal in SNNPR gave us an account of a classical bilingual model of teaching in Gamo and English in his school. In another instance in Harari region, we found the multilingual resources of both teacher and students in Harari, Amharic and Afan Oromo being used to facilitate understanding of the lesson.

A significant strength of decentralisation is the local production of school books. Regional responsibility for learning materials development in local or regional languages has resulted in decentralisation of local and regional printing and publishing for primary school materials other than English as a subject. English materials and secondary school materials have been produced in Addis Ababa for the whole country, and international publishers have not until 2009 been given an opportunity to enter this market. Local publishing keeps book costs low and even if all students do not have all of the books they require, most school students do have access to some books which they are allowed to take home each day. In contrast, in South Africa where school books are produced on glossy paper and in colour, they are exorbitantly expensive. This means that most rural and poor children are not allowed to take books home and thus have limited reading opportunities after school hours. The beneficiaries there are the multinational publishers not the school pupils.

Although decentralisation appeared generally positive, we also recognised risks, one being that policy-makers at the regional or local levels may privilege other considerations above the pedagogical ones. Clear examples come from regions like Harari and Amhara that changed their policy from MTM 8 and introduced English earlier as MoI for grade 7–8 maths and sciences, along with plans to continue extending English MoI further down the system. These 'reverse planning' changes have come about because of the perceived benefits of preparing students for secondary schooling through English, as we discuss further below. Another risk with decentralisation is that budget limitations may delay materials' development. At most REBs we met curriculum specialists who were busy elaborating, publishing and distributing MT/L1 materials, but there were often printing delays owing to regional and/or federal delays in disbursing budgetary allocations timeously. Insufficient L1 materials signals inconsistent implementation of policy, but this could be addressed through more support to the regions from Addis Ababa especially if all Ethiopian languages are to be resourced. Thus there is a need for stronger leadership from the central level, and/or better incentives for implementation of the national policy.

1.4.3.3 The Strength of Increased Capacity Owing to Experience in MTM

We found evidence that the use of Ethiopian languages in education has built a strong foundation for further development, and that the 'stronger' language communities and regions have developed expertise that can contribute not only to their own expansion but also to others. At this time at least 23 languages have been well developed for primary school teaching (as languages and across the curriculum), provision of learning materials, and teacher training (Appendix E in Heugh *et al.* 2007). An additional 13 languages are being developed for piloting or use in early grades. Some regional bureaus and TTC educators told us they believed their languages could serve as MoI at higher levels of the education system as well.

We discovered an impressive range of governmental and non-governmental resources that support development of Ethiopian languages. These include the Ethiopian Languages Resource Centre (ELRC) based at Addis Ababa University (AAU) which works with less-developed languages and supports orthography development and dictionary compilation. The Linguistics Department at AAU has recently initiated BA and MA programmes in Applied Linguistics. There are NGO-supported language bodies which promote development of Harari, Afar and the languages of SNNPR, and several other languages in the regions.

The REB curriculum departments responsible for preparing materials in Ethiopian languages based on the national curriculum, are staffed with qualified people who are charged with the task of transforming national syllabi/frameworks into curricular materials written in regional languages. The overall level of competence at the regional level is impressive (Master's degrees, several years of experience, and commitment). Although several curriculum officers requested further training in textbook production and skills sequencing, we believe that they have contributed positively to effective teaching and learning.

Most educators we met at the REBs and TTCs had a sophisticated understanding of, and supported the pedagogical principles behind, MTM education. However, we encountered individuals who were less aware, notably less experienced REB heads. Experienced educators are generally very knowledgeable and can justify MLE to parents and community members, and many are frustrated with public misconceptions and the constant pressure towards English.

There is MTM expertise at the school level as well. Owing to decentralisation, teachers are likely to share the same languages and cultures of their students. In regions like Oromiya and Gambella, potential teachers are even recruited to TTCs on the basis of language affiliation. These conditions demonstrate a strong foundation of knowledge and experience that supports MLE.

1.4.3.4 The Weakness of Inconsistent MoI Decisions for Teacher Training

Until recently, teachers have been trained at certificate level (grade 10 plus one year of training, or 10+1) to teach in lower primary schools through the MT, except when teaching English as a subject. Teachers should be trained at diploma level (10+3) to teach in upper primary (grades 5–8), where according to policy they should be teaching in the MT, but where in reality the medium varies depending on regional policies and practices. In regions where the MT is used as MoI, the MoI of certificate (lower primary) training in almost all cases has been the same, creating a match between languages of instruction. At the time of this study, as the regional summaries demonstrate, there were a number of mismatches between upper primary training and school MoI, even in regions whose school policies are consistent with the national MT policy.

As specialists point out (cf. review in Stroud 2002), there are serious quality implications when the language used for training teachers is not the same as the language that teachers will use to teach children (cf. Gebre Yohannes 2005). The main difficulty from the teacher's point of view is the lack of access to technical and pedagogical vocabulary in the mother tongue, including specialised terms for teaching academic content (e.g. 'photosynthesis' and 'equation'), for talking about language (e.g. 'noun' and 'phrase'), and for giving classroom instructions. Other implications are both real and symbolic; for example, the message implicit in the use of English for post-secondary education is that Ethiopian languages do not belong there.

Whether intentional or not, this message is sent by federal and regional governments. As an illustration, we tried to trace the sequence of decisions which replaced Tigrinya with English at one TTC. Bureau officials were aware of the mismatch but reluctant to act on it. TTC educators claimed that although no one had specifically told them to teach through English, since the syllabi and curricular materials sent from Addis were in English, lack of time and money prevented translation into Tigrinya, a claim subsequently repeated elsewhere.

We found evidence that the use of English for teacher training negatively influences teachers' MT competence and makes them less likely to believe that local languages can be used in teaching, especially for mathematics and science. Yet, one TTC dean in the Amhara region was puzzled that trainers would prefer English for maths and sciences, saying:

> It's a paradox . . . [that] TTC trainers find it difficult to teach these subjects in Amharic, except those who learned in their own language – they have good mother tongue skills in their fields. [T]he mother tongue is more helpful. Since we changed to English, students find it very difficult to express themselves.

A trainer in the Tigray told us that TTC students have been uneasy about the MTM to grade 8 because they mistakenly believe that students from other regions, like Addis Ababa, may perform better at secondary level because of earlier use of English as MoI. Though we found only evidence to the contrary (see Chapter 10, this volume), this provides some insight into the pressures put on the system by use of English beyond primary schooling.

Our informants (in 2009–2010) give us further cause for concern. As mentioned above, the MoE is phasing out one-year certificate training, and all primary teachers will be expected to attend the three-year diploma course. Students in the diploma course will be required to specialise in: language/s (including regional languages, Amharic and English); sciences and mathematics; or aesthetics. Although the MoE claims to be favourably disposed towards MTM teacher education, only Oromiya region has consistently offered diploma-level training through the MT, whereas all other regions have switched or are switching to English. Teacher 'professionalisation' thus privileges English as academically important while threatening the viability of MTM because teachers are not receiving training in the linguistic and methodological tools they need. Specialisation poses additional risks: nationality languages will not be taught across the curriculum; only language teachers will learn appropriate methodology needed to implement MTM education; and language stream teachers will be overly concerned with attempting to teach English rather than through MTs. Teacher trainees also will have great difficulty understanding the content of their training.

1.4.3.5 The Weakness of Pervasive Myths about Language Learning

People at most levels of the education system and in civil society told us that English MoI helps students learn English and achievement across the curriculum. These informants referred to the pressure of secondary education in English and had similar (mis)understandings of the relationship between language and learning, e.g.:

- English is used as MoI from grade 9, and earlier introduction to English medium will equip students to cope with the pre-recorded plasma television lessons (even though these are delivered in non-Ethiopian English, spoken too quickly for foreign language learners).
- Students are expected to write the grade 10 and 12 examinations in English. Therefore, the earlier students learn through English, the better they will be prepared for public examinations.
- Since higher education is in English, students need to have English MoI as early as possible.
- Since reference and academic material required by students is available only in English, students should therefore learn through English earlier rather than through Ethiopian languages.

- English proficiency offers access to international travel and economic opportunities.

These 'hypotheses' were not shared across all regions. For example, primary teachers in Oromiya supported Afan Oromo as MoI and believed that students could develop a satisfactory proficiency in English taught as a subject. School principals and teachers in Somali and SNNPR, and even several senior staff in TTCs held similar views.

These beliefs are neither new nor peculiar to Ethiopia but they are surprisingly persistent given significant evidence that L1 development is more likely to improve achievement in additional languages and across the curriculum. International research indicates that children require at least six (and preferably eight) years of learning the L2 as a subject before they can effectively understand content instruction through this language, and children can require more time when the 'foreign' language (FL) is not used outside school. This is the situation in most parts of Ethiopia. We do know, from studies conducted in other African countries, that students can become proficient in English as a second language, taught as a subject, under certain conditions, that is, when taught by trained teachers with advanced English language proficiency (as in the Six-Year Yoruba medium Primary Project). We also know that where English is a foreign language to most students, and in under less ideal conditions (such as in South Africa between 1955 and 1975), students can become proficient in English by studying it as a subject while receiving primary education through the mother tongue for eight years (Heugh 2003).

In Ethiopia, English is a second language only for a very small educated elite and a FL for most others, since it is rarely or never heard or used in their homes or communities. There is no evidence that demonstrates that use of a FL (e.g. English) MoI improves the learning or use of that language when its use outside of the school is negligible. Our field research found strong evidence that lack of teachers' English proficiency (despite participation in ELIP) seriously erodes the quality of secondary and further education. Pressure to bring English MoI into lower levels of primary schooling threatens the entire system, as explained below.

1.4.3.6 The Negative Washback Effects of a Prioritisation of English

Our research suggests that Ethiopians aspire to an unrealistic proficiency in English, even though English is a FL used in few functional domains. There is a serious gap between the aspiration towards English and the socio-economic and educational realities of the country. This is not dissimilar to other African countries where proficiency in French, English or Portuguese is similarly prized. The difference between Ethiopia and other African countries is that the latter have longer histories of European language use due to colonial imprints on administration, legislation, higher education and the economy, with an accompanying diffusion of the European language as L1 or L2, at least amongst the elite. Ethiopia experienced only short periods of Italian occupation, but no sustained period of English language influence, thus the aspiration for English is difficult to explain. Certainly Ethiopia's historic connections with Britain have had an influence, but it is more likely that the spread of English as a 'global' language is behind current pressures. Aspiration towards English is unfortunately equated with adopting English-medium education, despite the fact that English is foreign to most Ethiopians, and high-level English language proficiency is simply unrealisable in the foreseeable future.

The pressure of English-medium secondary and further education seems to indicate a 'washback effect' (following Messick 1996) on practices at the primary and teacher training levels. Washback is usually understood in relation to the influence of assessment on teaching and learning. In this case, the high-stakes national examinations in English at grades 10 and 12, along with entrance requirements for English at teacher training college and university entrance, exert pressure on MoI decisions in secondary and then primary school. The decision to use English FL as MoI in the secondary and further education has had a markedly negative backlash on the MTM in primary education. We can trace this effect as an incremental process where decisions made at the top exert pressure all the way down to primary education.

A programme of English language support for first-year university students, known as 'Freshman English' and also as the 'Freshman Programme', was phased out between 2003 and 2004, mainly for budgetary reasons. This decision increased the high-stakes value of English language proficiency in the school-exit examinations at grade 12 for university entrance and grade 10 for entrance to teacher colleges. The prioritisation of English in higher education may seem understandable in relation to the globalisation of English. However, firstly, it does not have a functional role within horizontal patterns of communication and the linguistic ecology of Ethiopia. Secondly, English language proficiency among teachers, students and the general population does not support implementation of English-medium education across secondary and higher education at this time. Yet, two expensive and very damaging measures, with no possibility of success, have been adopted in an effort to make English fit the context: the (South African) English language TV programming of secondary education from 2004, at an undisclosed but clearly astronomical cost, and the system-wide cascade delivery of the English Language Improvement Programme from 2005, costing 42% of the teacher education budget.

There is now strong evidence of the failure of both measures, along with a great number of unintended and negative consequences. One such consequence identified in this section is misguided policy-change introducing English MoI earlier in primary education. Another is the replacement of Ethiopian languages as MoI with English medium in teacher education, escalating since 2006. There are less obvious consequences, such as the failure to retain female students in primary and secondary education.[9] However, the most dire consequence has been to convince civil society that English is more important than learning.

1.5 Conclusions and Implications

The purpose of the 2006 study was to explore the existing models and practices of language education in Ethiopia since 1994, and to determine which practices have been most effective, in order to make evidenced-based recommendations for further language education policy. We have discussed the findings according to region; we have analysed the educational use of Ethiopian languages (L1), Amharic as L2 and English as FL/L3; and we have discussed the strengths and weaknesses of current practices. In conclusion, we draw attention to the most significant findings.

1.5.1 Implementation of MTM Education is Possible, Across a System, in a Poor Country

The main findings of the study show that since 1994, the national MTM/MLE policy has been implemented across the country of nine regions and two city-states, albeit to varying degrees. In Oromiya region and for the Afan Oromo streams in Amhara region, the MTM 8 has been completely consistent across the whole of primary schooling and teacher education. Tigray and Somali regions have both implemented MTM 8 in primary schools. Addis Ababa, Dire Dawa, Harari region, and Amhara region for speakers of Amharic have implemented six years of MTM education in schools with varying degrees of English medium for grades 7 and 8. Finally, SNNPR and Gambella have implemented MTM education only to grade 4, but have made strides in their diverse language offerings, reaching 12 languages and three languages, respectively.

Amharic (L2) medium has been implemented in various regions as follows:

* in Benishangul Gumuz and Afar Regions for six years of primary;
* in SNNPR for minority linguistic communities which do not yet have MTM;
* in Addis Ababa along with the L1 speakers of Amharic.

The findings show that it has been possible to implement MTM education across most of a large, low-income, 'developing' country. They also show that in the absence of MTM education, it is possible to implement L2 education in another Ethiopian language, and that this is likely to be preferable to use of a FL, such as English. The findings also show that decentralisation of education management to the regions has positive effects, but also possible risks. On the positive side, this encourages development of teaching materials and MTM teacher education. It is easier for more linguistically homogeneous regions (e.g. Oromyia, Somali, Tigray and Amhara regions) to implement MTM education. Afar region, sparsely populated by poor, remote, pastoralist communities, is an exception. Even though more linguistically heterogeneous regions like SNNPR and Benishangul Gumuz have not yet reached the goal of MTM 8, they have nevertheless made significant progress by offering lower primary education through an increasing number of L1s. SNNPR, in fact, offered MTM education in eight languages to the end of grade 6 until recently, and now offers MTM 4 in 12 languages, with these continuing as subjects to the end of grade 8. Benishangul Gumuz is at the beginning of the process.

For MTM education to continue being successful in some regions, and for it to be extended throughout the country, the MoI for teacher training should match the MoI teachers use in the classroom. This is because teachers need to develop their MT skills, as well as the subject/domain-specific technical and pedagogical vocabulary and syntax. Teachers who had not been trained in MTM did not believe their languages could be used to express difficult concepts, particularly from upper primary onwards, while those who had learned through their languages knew that abstract thought could be expressed through them.

1.5.2 Teaching of Amharic as a Second Language

Whether the teaching of Amharic begins at grade 5 (in Oromiya and for Afan Oromo streams in Amhara region) or grade 3 (in other regions), all regions teach the national language as a subject. Since we only found Amharic L1 materials in classrooms, our concern was that L2 materials and methodology for Amharic are used where they are needed. This is especially relevant in regions where Amharic is used as the default MoI because local MTM has not been developed.

1.5.3 Teaching of English as a Foreign Language

The study of English as a subject begins at grade 1 in all regions. However, English medium is used at some point in upper primary schooling in all regions except for Oromiya, Somali and Tigray. Our research instruments indicate that there is considerable public pressure put on REBs for English MoI in primary school due to the widespread belief that English medium will help students gain the language proficiency necessary for secondary school. The decision to prioritise English language improvement for all teachers, followed by the way ELIP has been implemented across the system, has resulted in a de-emphasis on training in the L1s and an increased focus on training in English. The most recent threat to MTM education is the new 'professionalisation' policy which includes three years of teacher training through English, even though the MoE claims to be considering how to accommodate the mother tongues.

Teachers throughout the system were observed to have extremely limited competence in the English language, and extremely limited exposure to English outside the classroom. Few can cope with the demands of teaching English as a subject, and even fewer with the challenges of using English to convey curricular content. There is a large gap between aspiration for English and what is possible within the socio-economic and educational realities of the country. The team attributes this to what is known as a negative washback effect, where a cumulative knock-on effect of one policy decision generates a set of perceptions that make people question the use of their own languages and lose focus on what is best for promoting teaching and learning.

1.5.4 Recommendations and Implications in the Ethiopian Situation

From the perspective of this analysis, the current MoE policy of MTM 8 for primary school offers the best possible opportunity for successful education on the continent. The decentralised system favours adoption of appropriate models and practices, and there are significant human and linguistic resources in the regions that can be built upon to support MTM throughout primary and teacher education. A number of options would promote multilingualism and multiliteracy in Ethiopian education. The team proposed that a special department for the promotion, development and use of Ethiopian languages in education be established within the MoE to support the policy through curriculum development, teacher training and leadership in MLE. Sufficient resources need to be allocated to the REBs to support materials' development and teacher education in relevant languages; another possibility would be to form regional-level language planning bodies like language academies (Terefe 2010).

It was also recommended that Amharic L2 and English as international language, be taught by adequately qualified personnel using appropriate materials. Teachers of English in particular should be required to demonstrate appropriate (advanced) levels of competence through a system of standardised assessment.

The research team emphasised that the primary objective of quality education is the delivery of education which will best allow students to achieve high-level academic proficiency across the curriculum. The language education policy and practice should support this objective. High-level academic literacy and proficiency in the languages, which will be most useful to students in their lives beyond school, should be a secondary objective.

There is considerable evidence in Ethiopia that high level of investment in teaching and assessing students through English has a very low rate of return. Given the evidence from the international and other Ethiopian and recent African research, our team presented a strong argument that similar investment in MLE would be likely to produce a much greater positive return for teaching and learning, school performance and throughput. We need to emphasise here that other research (cf. in Alidou et al. 2006; Ouane and Glanz 2010) shows that these costs are unlikely to exceed current investment in English (or French and Portuguese in other African countries).

Through constructive interventions it might still be possible to reverse the washback effect of aspirations for English (See Chapter 10). In our original report, we strongly urged the Ministry of Education to take measures to reverse the negative impact of English throughout the Ethiopian system. Writing in 2011, four years later, we can now see that despite great progress made in many parts of the country to implement the sound MTM 8 policy, some of the risks we identified, and hoped would be countered, have begun to work against effective teaching and learning in Ethiopian languages. The most important point to be made is that students can only learn what they can understand, and full implementation of the eight-year MTM policy, evident in our data analysis (Chapter 10), is the most effective means for promoting quality education in Ethiopia.

Notes

1 Ethiopian Population and Housing Census data are based on ethnic affiliation rather than home language, however because there is a considerable degree of overlap between home language and ethnolingiustic identity, we use ethnic group membership as a proxy for speakers of languages.
2 We use data from the 1994 Population and Housing Census (CSA 2007, Wagaw 1999) where more recent 2006 census figures were not available.
3 At the time of writing, the 1994 education policy and legislation has not changed.
4 The authors are grateful to everyone who contributed to our data collection. We particularly wish to thank Mesfin Derash (formerly of the MoE) and Aija Katriina Ahlberg of SIL International for their detailed recent reports and updates.
5 During this period enrolment in school was minimal, restricted to a few urban areas and thus English has not had an opportunity for widespread diffusion in the predominantly rural country.
6 UNESCO/UIS statistics on Ethiopia (accessed 3 Nov. 2009 at http://stats.uis.unesco.org/unesco/TableViewer/document.aspx?ReportId=121&IF_Language=eng&BR_Country=2300&BR_Region=40540).
7 Until 2006 SNNPR had offered MTM education for six years in eight languages, so it was on a trajectory of expanding its linguistic base but limiting its use to the first four years of primary.
8 UCLA Language Materials Project http://www.lmp.ucla.edu/Profile.aspx?LangID=18&menu=004 (accessed 8 Oct. 2009); see also Lewis (2009).
9 The MoE/ICDR report on educational wastage (2002) shows the high incidence of absenteeism amongst rural girl students, and we know from other countries that the use of a foreign language like English, which girls are least likely to encounter outside of the classroom, significantly decreases the possibility that girls will succeed or remain in school (see Benson 2005). This in turn affects health and development issues in impoverished communities (Stromquist 2002).

References

Akinnaso, F. Niyi (1991). Toward the development of a multilingual language policy in Nigeria. *Applied Linguistics* 12:1, 29–61.
Alidou, Hassana, Boly, Aliou, Brock-Utne, Birgit, Diallo, Yaya Satina, Heugh, Kathleen and Wolff, H. Ekkehard (2006). *Optimizing Learning and Education in Africa – the Language Factor*. A Stock-taking Research on Mother Tongue and Bilingual Education in

Sub-Saharan Africa. Association for the Development of Education in Africa (ADEA). (http://www.adeanet.org/adeaPortal/adea/downloadcenter/Ouga/B3_1_MTBLE_en.pdf).

Benson, Carol (2005). *Girls, Educational Equity and Mother Tongue-based Teaching*. Bangkok: UNESCO. (http://www.ungei.org/resources/files/unesco_Girls_Edu_mother_tongue.pdf).

CSA (Central Statistical Agency of Ethiopia) (2007). Population and Housing Census of 1994 metadata and documentation. (http://www.csa.gov.et/surveys/Population%20and%20Housing%20Census%201994/survey0/index.html).

Federal Negarit Gazeta (1995). The Constitution of the Federal Democratic Republic of Ethiopia 1994. *Federal Negarit Gazeta* 1(1). Addis Ababa.

Gebre Yohannes, Mekonnen Alemu (2005). *Socio-cultural and educational implications of using mother tongues as languages of instruction in Ethiopia*. Unpublished Master's thesis, University of Oslo.

George, Eileen S. (2002). Reaching out to marginalized populations through curriculum reform: A discussion based on research and experiment in Southern Ethiopia. Paper presented at the annual conference of the Comparative and International Education Society, Orlando, Florida, 6–9 March.

Heugh, Kathleen (1999). Languages, Development and Reconstructing Education in South Africa. *International Journal of Educational Development* 19, 301–313.

Heugh, Kathleen (2003). A re-take on bilingual education in and for South Africa. In Fraurud, Kari and Hyltenstam, Kenneth (eds), *Multilingualism in Global and Local Perspectives. Selected papers from the 8th Nordic Conference on bilingualism, November 1–3, 2001*. Stockholm: Centre for Research on Bilingualism, Stockholm University and Rinkeby Institute of Multilingual Research, 47–62.

Heugh, Kathleen (2009). Contesting the monolingual practices of a bilingual to multilingual policy. *English Teaching: Practice and Critique*, 8.2, 96–113. (http://education.waikato.ac.nz/research/files/etpc/files/2009v8n2art5.pdf).

Heugh, Kathleen, Benson, Carol, Bogale, Berhanu and Gebre Yohannes, Mekonnen Alemu (2007). *Final Report: Study on Medium of Instruction in Primary Schools in Ethiopia*. Research report commissioned by the Ministry of Education, Addis Ababa, September to December 2006. (http://www.hsrc.ac.za/research/output/outputDocuments/4379_Heugh_Studyonmediumofinstruction.pdf).

Hussein, Jeylan Wolyie (2008). Educational jeopardy and its impact on inclusive education: A critical ethnographic account from a remote Ethiopian high school. *Journal of Negro Education* 77: 2, 104–116.

Hussein, Jeylan Wolyie (2010). English supremacy in Ethiopia – autoethnographic reflections. In Heugh, Kathleen and Skutnabb-Kangas, Tove (eds), *Multilingual Education Works: from the periphery to the centre*. New Delhi: Orient BlackSwan, 224–238.

Lewin, Keith (2008). *Strategies for Sustainable Financing of Secondary Education in Sub-Saharan Africa*. World Bank Working Paper No. 136. Africa Human Development Series. Washington: World Bank.

Lewis, M. Paul (ed.) (2009). *Ethnologue: Languages of the World*, Sixteenth edition. Dallas: SIL International. (http://www.ethnologue.com/).

McLaughlin, Pat, Woubishet, Belainesh, Fite, Teshome and Kasa, Mintesnot (2005). *Guidelines for English language enhancement in our teacher education institutions*. Addis Ababa: MoE/ELIP (English Language Improvement Programme).

Messick, Samuel (1996). Validity and washback in language testing. *Language Testing* 13: 3, 241–256.

MoE (Ministry of Education) (1994). *Education and Training Policy.* Addis Ababa: St. George Printing Press.

MoE (Ministry of Education) (2002). *The Education and Training Policy and its Implementation.* Addis Ababa: MoE.

MoE (Ministry of Education)/ICDR (Institute of Curriculum Development and Research) (2002). *Educational Wastage in Five Regions of Ethiopia.* Addis Ababa: MoE.

Negash, Tekeste (1990). *The Crisis of Ethiopian Education: Some Implications for Nation Building.* Uppsala Reports on Education no. 29. Uppsala: Uppsala University.

Ouane, Adama and Glanz, Christine (2010). *Why and how Africa should invest in African languages and multilingual education: An evidence-based and practice-based policy advocacy brief.* Hamburg: UNESCO Institute for Lifelong Learning and the Association for the Development of Education in Africa. (http://unesdoc.unesco.org/images/0018/001886/188642e.pdf).

PCC (Population Census Commission) (2008). *Summary and Statistical Report of the 2007 Population and Housing Census.* Federal Democratic Republic of Ethiopia. Addis Ababa: UNFPA. (http://www.csa.gov.et/pdf/Cen2007_firstdraft.pdf).

Stoddart, John (1986). *The Use and Study of English in Ethiopian Schools.* Report commissioned by the Ministry of Education, Addis Ababa: MoE.

Stromquist, Nelly (2002). Literacy and gender: When research and policy collide. In Melin, Mia (ed.), *Education – A Way Out of Poverty?* New Education Division Documents No. 12. Stockholm: SIDA.

Stroud, Christopher (2002). *Towards a Policy of Bilingual Education in Developing Countries.* New Education Division Documents No. 10. Stockholm: SIDA.

Terefe, Gemechu Dereje (2010). *The Implementation of a Multilingual Education Policy in Ethiopia: The case of Afaan Oromoo in primary schools of Oromia Regional State.* Ph.D. dissertation in Social and Public Policy. University of Jyväskylä, Finland.

UNESCO (2005). *Education For All. The Quality Imperative. EFA Global Monitoring Report 2005.* Paris: UNESCO. (http://portal.unesco.org/education/en/ev.php-URL_ID=35939&URL_DO=DO_TOPIC &URL_SECTION=201.html).

UNICEF (2008). *Education Statistics: Ethiopia.* New York: Division of Policy and Practice, Statistics and Monitoring Section. (www.childinfo.org/files/ESAR_Ethiopia.pdf).

Wagaw, Teshome (1999). Conflict of Ethnic Identity and the Language of Education Policy in Contemporary Ethiopia. *Northeast African Studies*, 6: 3 (New Series) 75–88. (http://muse.jhu.edu/journals/northeast_african_studies/v006/6.3wagaw.pdf).

2

LANGUAGE CHOICE, EDUCATION EQUITY, AND MOTHER TONGUE SCHOOLING

Comparing the Cases of Ethiopia and Native America

Teresa L. McCarty

2.1 Introduction

What can we learn about bi/multilingualism and mother tongue schooling by comparing the cases of Ethiopia and Native America? To be sure, these are two very distinct demographic, sociolinguistic, and national contexts. Ethiopia, as Benson and her coauthors (this volume) note, is the second most populous country on the African continent, with more than 70 million people – 21% of the US population – 40 million of whom are of one ethnic group, Oromo/Oromifa. In contrast, there are five million American Indians, Alaska Natives, and Native Hawaiians in the US, representing some 175 languages and 564 Indigenous sovereignties, and 1.2 million First Nations, Métis, and Inuit people in Canada, representing 50 to 60 language groups. As Fettes (1998: 120) points out with respect to Canada, the situation of Indigenous peoples in Native America north of Mexico is one of 'small numbers and great diversity.' Further, while Indigenous children in Ethiopia enter school as native speakers of the Indigenous language, Native American languages are being rapidly displaced by English.

With a few exceptions – Inuktitut in the Far North, for example – virtually all Native North American languages are highly endangered (Krauss 1998; McCarty 2008a). Thus, the goals of language planning and policy in Native North America and Ethiopia differ in an important respect – mother tongue maintenance in the Ethiopian case and language revitalization in the Native American case – although in both cases a high level of competence in the language(s) of wider communication (LWC) is also a key goal.

There are other important parallels between the language education policy situations in Ethiopia and Native North America. Indigenous peoples in both contexts have long histories of colonization, exclusion, exploitation, and genocide;

economic injustice, educational disparities, and English supremacy are major axes of social stratification. In both settings, the fight for language rights has been waged in tandem with battles for cultural survival, education equity, and self-determination. The right to choose the medium and content of instruction is integral to these struggles (McCarty 2006). Can educational language policy that fosters the *right to choose* mother tongue schooling disrupt long-standing social and linguistic inequities by valorizing Indigenous languages and knowledges as tools for learning and self-empowerment?

In Heugh *et al.*'s (2007) study of the implementation of the Ethiopian Education and Training Policy described in abbreviated form by Benson *et al.* (2010 and this volume), we have compelling new evidence demonstrating the promise of such an educational approach. As Benson and her coauthors (2010, this volume) describe, the decentralized system of policy implementation, while not without its problems, favors the adoption of appropriate education models and practices that build on local linguistic and human resources to support mother tongue-medium instruction throughout the primary grades. Reviewing grade 8 national achievement results from 2000 and 2004, these researchers show that such models and practices enable students to outperform those learning through English. On the other hand, where the transition to English occurs early (by fourth grade), students experience lower overall achievement across all subjects. Citing similar evidence from international studies, including the largest single study of early-versus late-exit bilingual education, by Thomas and Collier (1997) in the US, these researchers conclude that using English as the medium of instruction (MOI) 'does not facilitate the teaching and learning of *either* English *or* other subjects' (Heugh *et al.* 2007: 81; emphases added).

I have intentionally highlighted 'either-or' in the quote from the Ethiopian report, because there is a widespread belief, reflected in public opinion and public policy, that schools and children must choose *either* mother tongue schooling *or* schooling in the LWC – Amharic and English in Ethiopia, and increasingly, English (only) throughout the world. Minoritized peoples are often 'made to believe it is necessary to choose between . . . languages: either a nostalgic minority identity and no economic opportunity . . ., or economic opportunity and leaving the minority language behind' (McCarty, Skutnabb-Kangas and Magga 2008: 301). Indeed, the Ethiopian researchers report similar attitudes among those they surveyed: teachers who believe their mother tongue cannot be used to express scientific concepts, particularly at higher grade levels, and the reality of English as the language of access to higher education and economic opportunity – a language known and used only by a 'small minority of urban educated economic and/or political elite' (Benson *et al.* this volume).

In this chapter I underscore and extend the lessons from the Ethiopian study, drawing parallels and contrasts to language education for Indigenous communities in the US with whom I have worked for many years. I begin by situating the analysis geographically, demographically, culturally, linguistically, and politically. I then draw comparisons between the Ethiopian case and two data sets from Native American education: programs in which, similar to Ethiopia, the Indigenous/minoritized language is 'first tongue', and those in which it is 'second tongue' but nonetheless 'heritage tongue' – the language of ethnic identity and community (McCarty 2008a). These Native American examples also address the cautionary findings in the Ethiopian report – the obstacles to equitable and quality education 'to which all have access' (Heugh *et al.* 2007: 11). I conclude with a comparative analysis of Native American and Ethiopian cases, a summary of 'best knowledge' on effective and equitable language practices and policies, and the fundamental principle of Indigenous choice in formulating and implementing language education policy for Indigenous children and youth.

2.2 Native American Demo-linguistic Profile

In the US, the term Native American encompasses diverse American Indians, Alaska Natives, and Native Hawaiians. Like Ethiopia, Native America is characterized by a diversity of Indigenous ethnicities and languages, though in much smaller numbers and within a much different national economic and political environment. Native Americans reside in every US state and territory, representing 619 reservations and Alaska Native villages, and 62 Native Hawaiian home lands (Snipp 2002; US Census Bureau 2001: 9). As Table 2.1 shows, the most populous tribe is Cherokee, located in the central and southeastern US, with 729,533 members, of whom 281,069 report 'Cherokee heritage alone.' Navajo, with a population of more than 298,000, is the second most populous tribe and has the largest land base, with a reservation the size of Ireland spread over three

TABLE 2.1 Ten most populous American Indian/Alaska Native groups

Tribe/tribal grouping	No. reporting 'American Indian tribal grouping alone or in any combination'	No. reporting 'American Indian tribal grouping alone'
Cherokee	729,533	281,069
Navajo	298,197	269,202
Latin American Indian	180,940	104,354
Choctaw	158,774	87,349
Sioux (Lakota, Dakota)	153,360	108,272
Chippewa	149,669	105,907
Apache	96,833	57,060
Blackfeet	85,750	27,104
Iroquois	80,822	45,212
Pueblo (includes multiple Pueblos in Arizona and New Mexico)	74,085	59,533

Source: US Census Bureau 2002: 10

southwestern states (US Census Bureau 2002; see Table 2.1). Most American Indian and Alaska Native groups are smaller geographically and numerically.

As in Ethiopia, economic and educational disparities among Native American communities are profound. Approximately one-third of American Indians and Alaska Natives (AIs/ANs) are children under 18, and more than one-quarter live below the federally established poverty line – a figure double that of the US population as a whole (US Census Bureau 2006: 12). AI/AN students are as much as 237% more likely to drop out of school than their White counterparts (National Caucus of Native American State Legislators 2008: 14). Similar disparities are evident across virtually all measures of education attainment (DeVoe *et al.* 2008).

The status of Native American languages is also quite different from that of Indigenous African languages. Linguists recognize at least 62 classes of Native American languages, each as different as are Sino-Tibetan and Indo-European (Goddard 1996). Every one of these languages is in a serious state of decline. Of 300 languages indigenous to what is now the US and Canada, 210 are still spoken, but, according to Krauss – reporting more than a decade ago – 141 of these languages (67%) are spoken only by the grandparent generation and older (Krauss 1998). These figures are supported by census data, which indicates that 72% of AIs/ANs five years of age or older speak only English at home (US Census Bureau 2006: 7).

Figure 2.1 shows the distribution of Native American language speakers according to the most recent available census data. As can be seen, most speakers

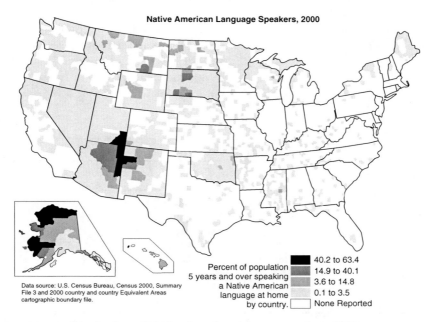

FIGURE 2.1   Distribution of Native American language speakers, 2000

reside in Alaska and the Southwest. Navajo, an Athabaskan language related to languages spoken from the circumpolar north to the US border with Mexico, has the most speakers (178,000 in the 2000 Census). As Table 2.2 shows, most Native American languages have many fewer speakers, and more than a third have just a handful of elderly speakers. Eyak, for instance, a language once spoken by people indigenous to what is now southern Alaska, lost its last native speaker, Marie Smith Jones, in 2008.

The root causes of Native American language loss lie in Anglo-European colonization and the physical, cultural, and linguistic genocide that ensued from the Western assault on the continent. Compulsory English-only schooling has been a primary tool for linguistic assimilation and Native language loss. As Benally and Viri (2005: 88–91) describe the assimilation process:

> In the late 19th century, boarding schools were devised as a systematic effort to assimilate large numbers of [American] Indian children. They were deliberately situated far from Indian reservations and communities . . . where [children] would not be under the influence of their parents and grandparents . . . Boarding school life was miserable . . . Added to physical punishment was the continual verbal assault and denigration of the home cultures and languages of the Indian children. . . . Many of these students, who later became parents, chose not to pass their tribal languages on to their children . . . they would emphatically insist that they did not want their children to endure the same social and academic hardships they did.

Thus, like language education in Imperial Ethiopia, Native American pupils were forced to learn a foreign language (English) from textbooks alien and disastrous to their own cultures (Heugh *et al.* 2007: 43). These historical causes are amplified by the modern forces of globalization and the growing hegemony of English, reflected in English-only policies enacted in more than half of the 50 US

TABLE 2.2 Native American languages with the greatest number of speakers

Language	No. speakers	Primary location of speakers
Navajo	178,000	Arizona, New Mexico, Utah
Western Ojibwe	35,000	Lake Superior, Montana, North Dakota
Dakota	20,355	Minnesota, Montana, Nebraska, North Dakota
Choctaw	17,890	Mississippi, Oklahoma
Western Apache	12,693	Arizona, New Mexico
Cherokee	11,905	Oklahoma, North Carolina
Tohono O'odham	11,819	Arizona
Central Yup'ik	10,000	Alaska
Eastern Ojibwe	8,000	Michigan
Zuni	6,413	New Mexico

Sources: Benally and Viri 2005; NCELA 2002

states, and federal laws that promote English at the expense of heritage/mother tongue schooling.

Further complicating Native American linguistic ecologies is the fact that Native American communities are traditionally oral societies. While grammars and practical writing systems exist for all Native American languages, it is the spoken word – oral tradition – that is the foundation of tribal societies (Sims 2005). This foundation is in danger of being lost. Thus, one cannot talk of 'best practices' or 'effective' language education policies for Native American children without considering how those practices and policies help restore health and vitality to endangered Indigenous mother tongues.

2.3 Tribal Sovereignty

Understanding the language education policy situation for Native Americans requires understanding their unique legal and political status. Unlike Ethiopia but similar to First Nations (Aboriginal) peoples in Canada, American Indians and Alaska Natives have a legally defined status as tribal sovereigns. Tribal sovereignty – the right to 'self-government, self-determination, and self-education' (Lomawaima and McCarty 2006: 10) – both predates and is recognized in the US Constitution. From their first encounters, American Indians and Europeans interacted on a government-to-government basis. The tribal–federal relationship was subsequently codified in treaties, judicial rulings, and federal law. In exchange for land, Native peoples entered into a trust relationship with the federal government in which it is obligated 'in perpetuity' to honor certain guarantees in education, health, and other social services. This legal–political relationship is unlike that of any other US ethnolinguistic group and unlike the political position of ethnic groups in Ethiopia. The tribal–federal trust relationship has profoundly influenced the present status of Native American languages, and, as discussed later in this chapter, it continues to shape the possibilities and constraints on Native American language education today.

I turn now to evidence from a cross-section of Native American school-community programs. Each case exemplifies locally relevant practices that enable students to achieve educational parity with their White mainstream peers in all content areas within five years of schooling – the defining criterion for 'academic success' in Thomas and Collier's (1997) study. Each of these programs also shares the goal of preparing Indigenous students for full participation in their home communities and as citizens of the world. The first data set derives from home language situations not dissimilar to Ethiopia, in which children enter school speaking the Indigenous language – a situation that is increasingly rare among Native American communities. Even in these cases (and unlike Ethiopia), the LWC (English) is prominent within local social-linguistic ecologies, such that a primary program aim is the intentional carving out of Indigenous-language-only pedagogical space. The second data set derives from settings that are much more common, in which children enter school with few or no apparent abilities in the heritage mother tongue. In these cases, the goal is heritage language revitalization alongside high levels of academic achievement and English proficiency. In both data sets, the heritage mother tongue is integral to the curriculum and used in its own right, not simply as a means to English-language ends (Holm and Holm 1995: 144). As will be seen, although the educational, cultural, and linguistic characteristics of the various programs differ, they share an overall additive approach similar to 'strong' mother tongue programs in Ethiopia and other parts of the world.

2.3.1 Data Set 1: Indigenous Language as First Language

2.3.1.1 The Rock Point Data

The community school at Rock Point, Arizona, within the Navajo Nation, has had a long-standing bilingual-bicultural education program in which 'rigorous, ongoing evaluation of student learning' has been a primary concern (Holm and Holm 1990: 178). In the early 1970s, the school began one of the first contemporary Indigenous literacy programs in the US. According to program cofounders Agnes and Wayne Holm, English at the time was a foreign language at Rock Point – much as it is for Indigenous children in Ethiopia – with nearly all students entering school dominant in Navajo. At the same time, Rock Point students scored near the bottom of all students in comparable Navajo Bureau of Indian Affairs (BIA) schools on English standardized tests (Holm and Holm 1990: 173).

Drawing on research from well-implemented bilingual-bicultural programs around the world, Rock Point based its program on the principle that children learn to read only once, most easily in the language they already speak (Rosier and Farella 1976). The design that emerged was called 'coordinate bilingual instruction', with separate but complementary time devoted to learning in each language. Navajo-language teachers (NLTs) taught and interacted entirely in Navajo, and English-language teachers (ELTs) taught and interacted only in English. Externally imposed status distinctions between credentialed (primarily non-Native) and non-credentialed (Navajo) teaching staff were dissolved, as NLTs and ELTs jointly planned, carried out, and evaluated instruction (Holm and Holm 1990: 176).

Using extant Navajo literacy materials and new ones developed locally, students learned to read first in Navajo, then English. They learned mathematics in both languages and studied science and social studies in Navajo, including Navajo clanship, history, social problems, government, and economic development. A secondary-level applied literacy program engaged students in locally relevant research that was published in a bilingual school newspaper and broadcast on a school television station (McLaughlin 1995).

Longitudinal data from Rock Point show that students not only outperformed comparable Navajo students in English-only programs, they surpassed their own previous annual growth rates and those of comparison-group students in BIA schools – and they did so by a greater margin each year (Holm and Holm 1990). As Rosier and Farella discuss these findings, students 'who spoke only limited English were able to express themselves more fully and [grasped] higher abstract concepts when the vernacular was used' (1976: 380) – the very same finding reported in the Ethiopian study that, 'Students who learn in their mother tongue can interact with the teacher, with each other and with the curricular content in ways that promote effective . . . learning' (Heugh *et al.* 2007: 6). In addition to learning English, of course, Navajo students, like those in Ethiopian mother tongue programs, had the benefit of additive bilingualism, becoming bilingual and biliterate in the mother tongue alongside the LWC.

In a 25-year retrospective analysis of the Rock Point program, Holm and Holm describe the 'four-fold empowerment' bilingual-bicultural education engendered: of the Navajo school board, who acquired increasing credibility with parents, staff, and students; of the Navajo staff, whose instructional expertise was validated within and outside the community; of parents, who played active roles in their children's schooling; and of the students, who 'came to value their Navajoness and to see themselves as capable of succeeding because of, not despite that Navajo-ness' (1990: 182–184). The significance of the Rock Point data, Holm and Holm conclude, is 'that they showed, contrary to the conventional wisdom, that being rural and speaking Navajo need not lead to doing poorly in school' (Holm and Holm 1990: 184; see also Holm 2006; Holm and Holm 1995).

2.3.1.2 The Rough Rock–KEEP Data

Located about 40 miles from Rock Point, the Rough Rock (Arizona) Community School, founded in 1966, is the first contemporary school to be controlled by an American Indian community. In 1983, anthropologists and reading specialists from the Hawai'i-based Kamehameha Early Education Program (KEEP) came to Rough Rock to learn whether the culturally compatible English reading strategies proven effective with Native Hawaiian children would work with Navajo students (Vogt and Au 1995; Vogt, Jordan and Tharp 1993). The Rough Rock–KEEP collaboration lasted five years, during which it was found that literacy pedagogies that had been successful with Native Hawaiian students needed to be significantly modified to produce successful outcomes with Navajo learners. By the end of the five-year period, the Rough Rock–KEEP partnership blossomed into a bilingual-bicultural, teacher-led initiative named the Rough Rock English-Navajo Language Arts Program (RRENLAP), which served approximately 200 students in grades K-6 (McCarty 2002: ch. 11).

Based on the principle that students are more successful if they are able to learn in ways that are socially, linguistically, and cognitively compatible with their natal culture, RRENLAP classrooms were organized around learning centers and small-group instruction in Navajo and English. Curriculum content was developed by local bilingual teachers and centered on local themes. Annual summer literature camps involved students, teachers, parents, and elders in field-based research on culturally relevant topics using Native storytelling, song, drama, and arts. Key to all of this was a strong professional development component in which bilingual teachers conducted their own classroom research and regularly collaborated to 'indigenize' the curriculum (Begay *et al.* 1995; McCarty and Dick 2003).

Longitudinal data from RRENLAP show that after four years in the program, the mean English reading comprehension scores of students in grades kindergarten through 3 (parallel to Primary I in Ethiopia) increased from 58% to 91%. On standardized English reading tests, RRENLAP students' scores initially declined, then rose steadily, in some cases approaching or exceeding national norms. When individual and grade cohort data were analyzed over five years, RRENLAP students demonstrated superior English reading, language arts, and mathematics performance compared to a matched peer group who did not participate in the program. In a similar fashion to Ethiopian Indigenous students receiving six to eight years of mother tongue-medium instruction(Benson *et al.* 2010: 55), Navajo students at Rough Rock had significantly higher mean achievement scores in all content areas than students who went through English-only schooling. Not surprisingly, RRENLAP students also were assessed as having stronger Navajo oral language and Navajo literacy abilities; they became stronger in both languages and had the benefit of additive bilingualism (McCarty 2002: ch. 11).

2.3.1.3 The Manokotak Data

In Alaska, two or more languages are spoken in many Native villages: the Native language as spoken by elders, the Native language modified by English, English modified by the Native language (called 'village English'), and 'standard' or 'schooled' English (Hartley and Johnson 1995). Situated along the southern coast of the Bering Sea in the Southwest Regional School District, Manokotak is one such village. In the 1990s, it remained an almost entirely Yup'ik-speaking community. Systemic problems within the local primary school, which was implementing an all-English curriculum, were evident in the high levels of student attrition, poor standardized test performance, student disinterest, and strained student–teacher and community–school relations. According to Elizabeth Hartley and Pam Johnson, educators who were close to the school, 'These stresses affected everyone in the village' (1995: 574).

Using international research on effective bilingual and English-as-a-second-language (ESL) approaches and data from a community survey, Manokotak established a Yup'ik immersion program with a strong ESL component, which started in kindergarten with four hours of instruction in Yup'ik and one in English, progressively increasing English instruction to 4.5 hours by the fifth and sixth grades. The program used a holistic approach to language arts, capitalizing on students' home-community experiences as content for literacy development. This approach enabled students to acquire 'Western' literacy skills in the context of their culture while retaining literacy in community-valued knowledge and skills. 'In this way,' Hartley and Johnson say, 'students' identity with their community was supported' (1995: 572). Ongoing staff and materials development and parent workshops were additional program components.

By the end of the program's second year, all student groups exceeded the district's expected means for their performance on standardized tests. Moreover, community feedback, student and family self-reports, student writing samples, behavior reports, and teachers' observations showed improved student self-esteem and school–community relations. As Hartley and Johnson describe these outcomes: 'Students reported feeling good about going to school and being interested in what they were doing. . . . Parents were able to discuss school with their children because they now had a common language' (1995: 581–582). In short, 'Vision, patience, and committed effort [were] the primary ingredients necessary to achieve needed improvements to enhance student success and community empowerment at the Manokotak site' (Hartley and Johnson 1995: 584).

Though smaller in scale and differing in the amount of government resources in support of their implementation, achievement outcomes from these Native American programs are akin to those in the Ethiopian study. The Native American data show that students who enter school speaking a language other than English perform significantly better on tests of cognitive ability and academic achievement when they have the benefit of sustained, systematic, well-implemented mother tongue-medium instruction – a finding that supports research on bilingual education and second language acquisition from around the world.

2.3.2 Data Set 2: Mother Tongue as Second Language

Cases of language revitalization for endangered Indigenous languages in the US offer an interesting and important counterpoint to studies of mother tongue schooling such as the Ethiopian case and the Native American cases just described. The situation of endangered languages requires an expanded view of mother tongue, typically thought of as the language one learns first and knows best, as in the UNESCO definition of mother tongue as 'the language which a person has acquired in early years and which normally has become his [sic] natural instrument of thought and communication' (cited in Fishman 1972: 689). By extension, under this definition mother tongue education is concerned with providing early instruction 'in a language children will understand and then adding a second [or third] language for wider communication' (Dutcher 2003: 1, 4). This is the situation for mother tongue-medium schooling in Ethiopia.

This concept of what constitutes a mother tongue only imperfectly fits the situation of most Native American communities today. Although the majority of

Native American languages are no longer acquired by children as first languages they are nonetheless languages of heritage and identity, and in this sense can be considered heritage mother tongues (McCarty 2008a). As Skutnabb-Kangas and McCarty (2008: 11) write, even if members of an Indigenous speech community do not know (much of) their ancestral language, it is properly considered a mother tongue on the basis of personal identification with it. Pedagogical data from endangered-language settings afford important insights into mother tongue-medium schooling. Three cases are examined here.

2.3.2.1 Nāwahīokalaniʻōpuʻu Laboratory School

The Hawaiian language is severely endangered, being spoken as a first language primarily by those born before 1920. In this context, Nāwahīokalaniʻōpuʻu Laboratory School (called Nāwahī for short), is making a difference for Native Americans while serving as the most fully developed model of Indigenous-language immersion in the US (McCarty 2008b; Wilson 2008). As Hinton (2001: 131) writes, 'Of all languages indigenous to what is now the United States, Hawaiian represents the flagship of language recovery, and serves as a model and a symbol of hope to other endangered languages.'

Nāwahī is a Hawaiian-medium, early childhood through high school affiliation of programs featuring a college preparatory curriculum rooted in Native Hawaiian language and culture. Named for a major 19th-century figure in Hawaiian-medium education, the school grows out of the 'Aha Pūnana Leo (Hawaiian 'language nest') movement that began in the 1980s. In 1983, a small group of parents and language educators established the Pūnana Leo non-profit organization and then its preschools, which enable children to interact with fluent speakers entirely in Hawaiian. The goal is to cultivate children's fluency and knowledge of Hawaiian language and culture, much as occurred in the home in earlier generations. The movement entered the public schools and added a grade a year, reaching intermediate school in 1994, when Nāwahī was founded (William H. Wilson, personal communication, November 23, 2008).

The school teaches all subjects through Hawaiian language and values. According to William H. Wilson, cofounder of the Pūnana Leo and Nāwahī School, English instruction begins in fifth grade with a standard English-language arts course; students enroll in such a course every semester through grade 12. Elementary students also study Japanese, and intermediate students study Latin – opportunities for contrastive linguistic analysis with Hawaiian and for building students' multilingual-multicultural skills. Students also study Hawaiian grammar, focusing on forms and usages that might be influenced by English. 'At Nāwahī,' Wilson states, 'we seek to give our immersion students the same, and even higher, metalinguistic knowledge of Hawaiian, as that of students who study Hawaiian as a second language in a strong high school program' (personal communication, September 8, 2008).

Some 2,000 Native Hawaiian students now attend a coordinated set of schools, beginning with Pūnana Leo preschools and moving through Hawaiian immersion elementary and secondary programs. The state of Hawai'i has established a Hawaiian Language College within the University of Hawai'i-Hilo to continue teaching through Hawaiian at the tertiary level. Among its several programs, the college includes an immersion teacher education certification program and a Ph.D. in Hawaiian and Indigenous language and culture revitalization. Nāwahī is the university's laboratory school. This educational system is further supported by widespread teaching of Hawaiian courses in English-medium high schools and colleges throughout the state (William H. Wilson, personal communication, November 23, 2008; see also Furman, Goldberg and Lusin 2007).

Although it has emphasized Hawaiian language and culture revitalization over (English-based) academic achievement, Hawaiian-medium schooling has yielded impressive academic results. Nāwahī students, 60% of whom come from high-poverty backgrounds that have tended to be among the most poorly performing students in Hawai'i schools, not only surpass their non-immersion peers on English standardized tests, they outperform the state average for all ethnic groups on high school graduation, college attendance, and academic honors. The school has a 100% high school graduation rate and a college attendance rate of 80% (Wilson and Kamanā, 2001; Wilson, Kamanā and Rawlins 2006). School leaders Kauanoe Kamanā and William Wilson (2001) attribute these outcomes to an academically challenging curriculum that is rooted in Hawaiian identity and culture. According to Wilson, the school has succeeded through its strong emphasis on achievement in Hawaiian language and culture 'and holding Hawaiian language and culture high through the hard work so highly valued by Hawaiian elders. . . . In today's world, that hard work means applying oneself in academics to outperform those in mainstream schools to move the Hawaiian people forward' (personal communication, July 23 and September 8, 2008).

2.3.2.2 Tséhootsooí Diné Bi'ólta' (Fort Defiance Navajo Immersion School)

One of the better-documented American Indian language immersion programs operates on the eastern border of the Navajo Nation, in the small town of Fort Defiance, Arizona. When the program began in 1986, fewer than one in 20 of all kindergarten and first grade students were considered 'reasonably fluent' speakers of Navajo; a third were judged to have passive knowledge of the language (Arviso and Holm 2001). At the same time, many Fort Defiance students were identified as 'limited English proficient'; they possessed conversational proficiency in English but struggled with the decontextualized academic English required by standardized tests (Arviso and Holm 2001).

In these circumstances, the school district opted for a voluntary Navajo immersion program similar to that developed for Hawaiian students and for the Māori in New Zealand. Starting with a kindergarten through fifth grade Navajo immersion track in an otherwise all-English public school, the program expanded into a full-immersion K-8 school, Tséhootsooí Diné Bi'ólta' (TDB, The Navajo School at the Meadow Between the Rocks, or the Fort Defiance Navajo Immersion School). In the lower grades, all instruction, including initial literacy, occurs in Navajo. English is introduced in second grade and gradually increased until a 50–50 distribution is attained by grade 6.

TDB's program affords maximum exposure to Navajo, incorporating tribal standards for Navajo language and culture and state (Arizona) content standards. According to the school's early leaders, TDB also emphasizes a 'Diné [Navajo] language and culture rich environment . . . including lunch room, playground, hallways and the bus' (Johnson and Legatz 2006: 30). Like Hawaiian immersion, a key program component is the involvement of parents and elders, who commit to spending time interacting with their children in Navajo after school.

Longitudinal data from TDB show that the benefits to Native-language revitalization have not come at the cost of children's acquisition of English or their academic achievement. Navajo immersion students consistently outperform their peers in English-only classrooms on local and state assessments of English reading, writing, and mathematics while also developing strong Navajo oral language and literacy skills. According to program cofounder Wayne Holm, there is another, less quantifiable but equally important benefit to this approach: 'What the children and their parents taught us was that Navajo immersion gave students Navajo pride' (2006: 33).

2.3.2.3 Puente de Hózhǫ́ Trilingual School

A final case in this data set comes from a trilingual K-5 school in northern Arizona. Called Puente de Hózhǫ́ (*Puente de* for the Spanish words 'bridge of', and *Hózhǫ́* for the Navajo 'beauty' or 'harmony'), the school's name means, literally, Bridge of Beauty. As school cofounder Michael Fillerup describes it, the name mirrors the school's vision 'to build bridges of beauty between the rich languages and cultures of the American Southwest' (2008: 1). In a school district in which 25% of the students are American Indian (mostly Navajo) and 20% are Latino, 'local educators were searching for innovative ways to bridge the seemingly unbridgeable gap between the academic achievement of language-minority and language-majority children' (Fillerup 2008: 2).

To do this, the school offers two parallel bilingual programs: a conventional dual immersion model in which native Spanish-speaking and native English-speaking students are taught jointly for a half-day in each language, and one-way Navajo immersion in which English-dominant Navajo students are taught in Navajo. In the latter program, kindergartners receive 90% of their instruction in Navajo, with English instructional time gradually increased to 80/20 in first grade and 60/40 by third grade, until a 50/50 balance is attained in grades four and five. All state standards are taught in Navajo and English or Spanish and English.

Many promising practices are evident at this school, but three are especially noteworthy. First, the school explicitly rejects the remedial labels historically associated with bilingual and American Indian education in the US. Rather than 'problems to be solved', students are considered an educational elite (Fillerup 2008: 2). For Navajo students, this means learning the language of the famous Native American Code Talkers that defied translation and speeded the Allied victory in World War II. Second, bilingual-bicultural-multicultural education is central, not auxiliary, to the curriculum; it is 'the reason the school exists' (Fillerup 2005: 16). Third, like Nāwahī and TDB, Puente de Hózhǫ has exceptionally high levels of parent involvement – a practice widely associated with enhanced student achievement but rarely ascribed to Indigenous families. (For more on the Puente de Hózhǫ case, see McCarty *et al.* (2011).)

Puente de Hózhǫ has consistently met state standards, with its students outperforming comparable peers in monolingual English programs by as much as seven points in English-language arts, ten points in mathematics, and 21 points in English reading. Equally important are less quantifiable but consequential program effects: enhanced student motivation and the 'smiles on the faces of parents, grandparents, and students as they communicate in the language of their ancestors' (Fillerup 2005: 16).

2.4 Best Knowledge, Sound Practice: Some Comparisons and Contrasts with the Ethiopian Case

What can be learned from these Native American cases, and how do they interface with the case of Ethiopia? Clearly the Native American and Ethiopian sociolinguistic contexts differ significantly (as do Native American programs and contexts among themselves). Unlike Ethiopia, English is pervasive within Native American linguistic ecologies. At the same time, like Ethiopia, access to 'academic English' and its perceived social, educational, and economic opportunities remains limited for Native American children, as it does for a majority of ethnolinguistic groups in Ethiopia. Also in contrast to Ethiopia, US language policies, historically and today, promote English monolingualism. In this political environment, despite their status as tribal sovereigns, Native Americans confront an ongoing history of linguistic and cultural repression and contests over federal versus tribal education control (i.e., choice).[2]

The first lesson of this comparative analysis, then, is that *context matters*; what is effective in one setting may be ineffectual, even deleterious, in another. Each of the Native American cases profiled here, like the Ethiopian examples in Heugh *et al.*'s (2007) report and the chapter herein by Benson *et al.*, arose in response to local needs, epistemologies, resources, and contingencies. A 'one-size-fits-all' approach – the hallmark of US language policy – is pedagogically unsound and morally corrupt. In this regard, the US has much to learn from Ethiopia's decentralized policy implementation strategy.

The Native American cases also reinforce findings from Ethiopia and the international literature on the efficacy and equity of 'strong' Native language and culture programs. As shown in Table 2.3, such programs are characterized by the use of the heritage mother tongue as the MOI for at least the first five years of schooling and, ideally, as in Ethiopia, the first eight years. In the US, long-term programs that begin with a solid foundation (90 to 100% of instructional time) in the heritage mother tongue and provide four to seven years of high-quality English instruction by the end of the program (which may entail as little as 20% of instructional time, as in the Hawaiian case), are most effective in promoting high levels of English achievement while supporting learning in and of the heritage language and culture.

The Native American data show that English will be learned 'even under circumstances where a strong academic program is provided through the "nationally weaker" language' (William H. Wilson, personal communication, September 8, 2008), a finding congruent with studies of French-English immersion in Canada and mother tongue-medium schooling in Ethiopia (see also Wilson 2008; Wilson and Kamanā 2006). Importantly, data from Native American education demonstrate that strong programs produce salutary academic outcomes for students who enter school as primary speakers of the Indigenous language (as is the situation in Ethiopia) and for children learning the heritage language as a second language – findings borne out in the large-scale study by Thomas and Collier (1997) cited previously, and by May, Hill, and Tiakiwai's (2004) national study of Māori-medium education in New Zealand and Hill and May's (2011) ethnographic research on Māori–English biliteracy development at Rakaumanga School (see also May and Hill 2008).

A factor not emphasized in Heugh *et al.*'s report, but central to strong Native American education programs, is the integration of Indigenous cultural acquisition with learning of the heritage mother tongue and academic content. This requires the active involvement of parents, elders, and community members in the entire education enterprise. In each case reported here, use of the Native language as the MOI is part of a more diffuse but explicit culturally based pedagogy. Premised on the theory that the most influential factor in students' school performance is 'how we teach and arrange social activity in schools' (Beaulieu 2006: 52), culturally based education (CBE, also called culturally responsive schooling or CRS) incorporates many of the promising practices described by Heugh *et al.* (2007) and Benson *et al.* (2010, this volume). In an exhaustive review of the CRS literature, Castagno and Brayboy state that CRS 'assumes that a "firm grounding in the heritage language and culture indigenous to a particular tribe is a . . . prerequisite for the development of culturally-healthy students and communities . . . and thus is an essential ingredient for . . . educators, curriculum and schools"' (2008: 941, citing the Assembly of Alaska Native Educators 1998). Beaulieu (2006) describes CBE as education that is both academically effective and locally meaningful, and argues that whole-school approaches that use the Native language as the MOI are more effective than 'add-on' programmatic interventions (see also Hermes 2005). Similarly, Demmert and Towner (2003), in a meta-analysis of the research on American Indian/Alaska Native student achievement, identify use of the Native language as the MOI (either as a first or second language) and strong Native community participation as 'critical elements' of effective CBE (see also Demmert, Grissmer and Towner 2006). Beyond improved performance on standardized tests, 'strong' CBE has been shown to improve attendance and college-going rates (e.g., Nāwahī), lower attrition (e.g., Nāwahī, Manokotak), and enhance teacher–student and school–community relations (e.g., Manokotak, RRENLAP, Puente de Hózhǫ).

Finally, the data from Native America provide models for teacher preparation and professional development – a limitation identified by Heugh et al. (2007) and Benson et al. (2010, this volume) in the implementation of Ethiopia's language policy. Virtually all Native American CBE programs have used a 'grow your own' approach in which local Native educators are positioned as language planners and supported in completing their teaching degrees. The most fully elaborated Native American model is Nāwahī and its affiliated college programs. Echoing the challenges to teacher preparation noted in the Ethiopian study, Wilson and Kawai'ae'a describe the formidable task of 'produc[ing] individuals who know the language, who can operate the structure through the language, and who have the psychological strength to use and expand the language under difficult circumstances' (2007: 41). To address these challenges, 'we needed a separate teacher education program in the medium of Hawaiian itself' (Wilson and Kawai'ae'a 2007: 42). What emerged was the Kahuawaiola Indigenous Teacher Education Program which requires, as prerequisites, eight full semesters of Hawaiian language, additional courses in Hawaiian culture, and a baccalaureate major in a content area recognized by the state for public school teachers. The three-semester Kahuawaiola program includes intensive immersion training at Nāwahī Laboratory School, a 'strong component in traditional lifestyles', and a full year of student teaching with master teachers in Hawaiian-medium schools. Closely related initiatives include the development of three Hawaiian-language-specific teacher licenses and Hawaiian education standards and a 'consortium relationship with . . . 'Aha Pūnana Leo' (Wilson and Kawai'ae'a 2007: 51). The transferable lesson to the Ethiopian case and beyond is Kahuawaiola's holistic approach in cultivating 'highly qualified teachers who are proficient in Hawaiian language and culture, native pedagogy and the necessary content knowledge and professional dispositions that nurture . . . well-being and wellness through education' (Wilson and Kawai'ae'a 2007: 51).

2.5 Indigenous Language Choice: Making Bi/multilingual Education Work

Though differing in the national and local contexts in which the programs have been implemented, data from Native American and Ethiopian language

TABLE 2.3 Typology of Native American/Indigenous language program models*

Program type	STRONG (additive or full bi-/multilingualism/multiculturalism)			WEAK (subtractive or limited bi-/multilingualism/multiculturalism)		
	Child's language status	Language of classroom	Program goals	Child's language status	Language of classroom	Program goals
Indigenous-Language and Culture Immersion	Indigenous/minority	Indigenous language	Indigenous-language maintenance/revitalization; full bilingualism, biculturalism, biliteracy**	N/A	N/A	N/A
Indigenous-Language and Culture Maintenance ("Language Shelter")	Indigenous/minority	Bilingual with emphasis on Indigenous language	Indigenous-language maintenance/revitalization; bilingualism, biculturalism, biliteracy	N/A	N/A	N/A
Two-Way Bilingual/Dual Language	Indigenous/minority and majority (50/50; 60/40, etc.)	Mixed Indigenous language/English (90%/10%; 50%/50%, etc.)	Indigenous-language maintenance/revitalization; bilingualism, biculturalism, biliteracy	N/A	N/A	N/A

Program						
Transitional	N/A	N/A	N/A	Indigenous/minority	Indigenous language used for first years of schooling, then replaced with English	Strong English dominance/ monolingualism; may include some Native-language and culture enrichment
Mainstream with Indigenous-Language and Culture Pull-Out Classes	N/A	N/A	N/A	Indigenous/minority	Indigenous language and English	Strong English dominance/ monolingualism, with some Native-language and culture enrichment
Mainstream with Foreign Language Instruction	N/A	N/A	N/A	Indigenous/minority and majority	English with Indigenous language taught as a 'foreign' language	Strong English dominance; limited bilingualism; little or no cultural emphasis
*Structured (English) Immersion***	N/A	N/A	N/A	Indigenous/minority	English only	English monolingualism/ monoculturalism (assimilation)

* Adapted from Baker (2006).

** A primary goal of some Indigenous-language programs is oral proficiency (not Native-language literacy).

*** Structured English immersion programs are best characterized as 'non-forms' of bilingual/multicultural education, also known as 'submersion' or 'sink-or-swim' (see Skutnabb-Kangas and McCarty 2008).

education show that strong mother tongue-medium schooling depends on the ability of Indigenous communities to exercise self-determination in the content and medium of their children's education. Indigenous communities 'need to be able to control curriculum content and its delivery as well as define achievement on their own terms', Māori educator Cath Rau writes (2005: 427). By definition, this entails choice – the placement of control over education decisions and approaches in local hands (Lomawaima and McCarty 2006; McCarty 2006).

Like Māori and Ethiopian mother tongue-medium schooling, strong Native American programs illustrate the possibilities inherent in Indigenous educational choice: *success* 'from the perception that one has succeeded through the Native language', *access* to 'cultural worlds denied mere monolinguals', and *meaning* through connections to one's people (Holm 2006: 41–42). 'Learning the language of one's people does not force you to live your life in one and only one way', Holm (2006: 41–42) points out:

> It keeps your options open. As a young adult, you can choose *whether* to use your language, *who* to use your language with, and *what* things you will talk about in your language. Children whose parents or schools deny them access to their language deprive the children of choice. . . . By the time a teenager . . . might choose to speak the language, for most, it is already too late.

Fortunately, it is not yet 'too late'. As the Native American and Ethiopian cases illustrate, there are many possibilities – multiple paths – out of and beyond the shortsighted dichotomy of mother tongue versus other tongue. Most importantly, these multiple pathways offer promise for education equity and the self-empowerment of Indigenous students and their communities.

Notes

1   Tribal sovereignty is complex, as political incorporation into the US has been different for American Indians, Alaska Natives, and Native Hawaiians, and among American Indian tribes themselves. The sovereignty of some tribes is recognized by states but not by the federal government; some tribes are not recognized either by states or the federal government. Native Hawaiians, whose internationally recognized sovereign kingdom was illegally overthrown by the US government in 1893 and who were officially incorporated into the US upon Hawaiian statehood in 1959, are still fighting for federal recognition, although the US Congress acknowledged the illegality of the takeover in the 1993 Hawaii Apology Act. The experience of Alaska Natives is different still. Nevertheless, all Native Americans share a distinct status as Indigenous peoples that entails sovereignty and a singular legal-political relationship with the US government.

2   On the positive side, two relatively recent federal policies – the 1990/1992 Native American Languages Act and the 2006 Esther Martinez Native American Languages Preservation Act – provide legal and (limited) financial support for Native American language education (Warhol 2009, 2010). However, as currently constituted, these

policies lack enforcement power, and school-based language programs remain subject to state and federal laws that privilege English (only). For a discussion, see McCarty (2009); Romero-Little *et al.* (2007).

References

Arviso, Marie and Holm, Wayne (2001). Tséhootsooídi Diné bizaad bíhoo'aah: A Navajo immersion program at Fort Defiance, Arizona. In Hinton, Leanne and Hale, Ken (eds), *The green book of language revitalization in practice*. San Diego, CA: Academic Press, 203–215.

Baker, Colin (2006). *Foundations of bilingual education and bilingualism* (4th edn). Clevedon, UK: Multilingual Matters.

Beaulieu, David (2006). A survey and assessment of culturally based programs for Native American students in the United States. *Journal of American Indian Education*, *45*(2), 50–61.

Begay, Sally, Dick, Galena S., Estell, Dan W., Estell, Juanita, McCarty, Teresa L. and Sells, Afton (1995). Change from the inside out: A story of transformation in a Navajo community school. *Bilingual Research Journal*, *19*(1), 121–139.

Benally, AnCita and Viri, Denis (2005). *Diné bizaad* (Navajo language) at a crossroads: Extinction or renewal? *Bilingual Research Journal*, *29*(1), 85–108.

Benson, Carol, Heugh, Kathleen, Bogale, Berhanu and Gebre Yohannes, Mekonnen Alemu (2010). The medium of instruction in the primary schools in Ethiopia: A study and its implications for multilingual education. In Heugh, Kathleen and Skutnabb-Kangas, Tove (eds), *Multilingual education works: From the periphery to the centre*. New Delhi: Orient BlackSwan, 40–83.

Castagno, Angelina and Brayboy, Bryan M. J. (2008). Culturally responsive schooling for Indigenous youth: A review of the literature. *Review of Educational Research*, *78*(4), 941–993.

DeVoe, Jill F., Darling-Churchill, Kristen E. and Snyder, Thomas D. (2008). *Status and trends in the education of American Indians and Alaska Natives: 2008*. Washington, DC: Institute of Education Sciences, National Center for Education Statistics, US Department of Education.

Demmert, William G. Jr. and Towner, John C. (2003). *A review of the research literature on the influences of culturally based education on the academic performance of Native American students*. Portland, OR: Northwest Regional Educational Laboratory.

Demmert, William G., Grissmer, David and Towner, John (2006). A review and analysis of the research on Native American students. *Journal of American Indian Education*, *45*(3), 5–23.

Dutcher, Nadine (2003). Promise and perils of mother tongue education. Retrieved 11 July 2011 from http://www.sil.org/asia/ldc/plenary_papers/nadine_dutcher.pdf/.

Fettes, Mark (1998). Life on the edge: Canada's Aboriginal languages under official bilingualism. In Ricento, Thomas and Burnaby, Barbara (eds), *Language and politics in the United States and Canada: Myths and realities*. Mahwah, NJ: Lawrence Erlbaum, 117–149.

Fillerup, Michael (2005, September/October). Keeping up with the Yazzies: The impact of high stakes testing on Indigenous language programs. *Language Learner*, 14–18.

Fillerup, Michael (2008). Building bridges of beauty between the rich languages and cultures of the American Southwest: Puente de Hózhó Trilingual Magnet School.

The Foreign Language Educator. Retrieved 11 July 2011 from http://puentedehozho.org/puenteschool.htm/.

Fishman, Joshua A. (ed.) (1972). The use of vernacular languages in education: The report of the UNESCO meeting of specialists, 1951. In Fishman, Joshua A. (ed.), *Readings in the sociology of language*. The Hague: Mouton, 688–716.

Furman, Nelly, Goldberg, David and Lusin, Natalia (2007). *Enrollments in languages other than English in United States institutions of higher education, Fall 2006*. New York: Modern Language Association. Retrieved 6 February 2011 from http://www.mla.org/2006_flenrollmentsurvey/.

Goddard, Ives (1996). Introduction. In Goddard, Ives and Sturtevant, William H. (eds), *Handbook of North American Indians vol. 17: Languages*. Washington, DC: Smithsonian Institution, 1–16.

Hartley, Elizabeth and Johnson, Pam (1995). Toward a community-based transition to Yup'ik first language (immersion) program with ESL component. *Bilingual Research Journal, 19*(3 & 4), 571–585.

Hermes, Mary (2005). 'Ma'iingan is just a misspelling of the word wolf': A case for teaching culture through language. *Anthropology and Education Quarterly, 36*(1), 43–56.

Heugh, Kathleen, Benson, Carol, Bogale, Berhanu, and Gebre Yohannes, Mekonnen Alemu (2007). *Final report. Study on medium of instruction in primary schools in Ethiopia*. Commissioned by the Ministry of Education. Addis Ababa: Ministry of Education of Ethiopia.

Hill, Richard and May, Stephen (2011). Exploring biliteracy in Māori-medium education: An ethnographic perspective. In McCarty, Teresa L. (ed.), *Ethnography and language policy*. New York: Routledge, 161–183.

Hinton, Leanne (2001). An introduction to the Hawaiian language. In Hinton, Leanne and Hale, Ken (eds), *The green book of language revitalization in practice*. San Diego, CA: Academic Press, 129–131.

Holm, Agnes and Holm, Wayne (1990). Rock Point, a Navajo way to go to school: A valediction. *The Annals of the American Academy of Philosophy and Social Science 508*, 170–184.

Holm, Agnes and Holm, Wayne (1995). Navajo language education: Retrospect and prospects. *Bilingual Research Journal, 19*(1), 141–167.

Holm, Wayne (2006). The 'goodness' of bilingual education for Native American children. In McCarty, Teresa L. and Zepeda, Ofelia (eds), *One voice, many voices – Recreating Indigenous language communities*. Tempe: Arizona State University Center for Indian Education, 1–46.

Johnson, Florian Tom and Legatz, Jennifer (2006). Tséhootsooí Diné Bi'ólta' [Fort Defiance Navajo Immersion School]. *Journal of American Indian Education, 45*(2), 26–33.

Krauss, Michael (1998). The condition of Native American languages: The need for realistic assessment and action. *International Journal of the Sociology of Language, 132*, 9–21.

Lomawaima, K. Tsianina and McCarty, Teresa L. (2006). *'To remain an Indian': Lessons in democracy from a century of Native American education*. New York: Teachers College Press.

May, Stephen and Hill, Richard (2008). Māori-medium education: Current issues and challenges. In Hornberger, Nancy H. (ed.), *Can schools save Indigenous languages? Policy and practice on four continents*. New York: Palgrave Macmillan, 66–98.

May, Stephen, Hill, Richard and Tiakiwai, Sarah (2004). *Bilingual/immersion education: Indicators of good practice*. Final Report to the Ministry of Education. Auckland, NZ: Ministry of Education.

McCarty, Teresa L. (2002). *A place to be Navajo – Rough Rock and the struggle for self-determination in Indigenous schooling.* Mahwah, NJ: Lawrence Erlbaum.

McCarty, Teresa L. (2006). Voice and choice in Indigenous language revitalization. *Journal of Language, Identity, and Education,* 5(4), 308–315.

McCarty, Teresa L. (2008a). Native American languages as heritage mother tongues. *Language, Culture and Curriculum,* 21(3), 201–225.

McCarty, Teresa L. (2008b). *State of the field: Native languages and cultures in American Indian, Alaska Native, and Native Hawaiian Student Achievement.* Policy paper commissioned by the US Department of Education, Office of Indian Education Programs. Spokane, WA: Kauffman Associates, Inc.

McCarty, Teresa L. (2009). The impact of high-stakes accountability policies on Native American learners: Evidence from research. *Teaching Education,* 20(1), 7–29.

McCarty, Teresa L. and Dick, Galena S. (2003). Telling the People's stories: Literacy practices and processes in a Navajo community school. In Willis, Arlette I., García, Georgia E., Barrera, Rosalinda B. and Harris, Violet J. (eds), *Multicultural issues in literacy research and practice.* Mahwah, NJ: Lawrence Erlbaum, 101–122.

McCarty, Teresa L., Skutnabb-Kangas, Tove and Magga, Ole Henrik (2008). Education for speakers of endangered languages. In Spolsky, Bernard and Hult, Francis (eds), *The handbook of educational linguistics.* Malden, MA: Blackwell, 297–312.

McCarty, Teresa L., Romero-Little, Mary Eunice, Warhol, Larisa and Zepeda, Ofelia (2011). Critical ethnography and Indigenous language survival: Some new directions in language policy research and praxis. In McCarty, Teresa L. (ed.), *Ethnography and language policy.* New York: Routledge, 31–51.

McLaughlin, Daniel (1995). Strategies for enabling bilingual program development in American Indian schools. *Bilingual Research Journal,* 19(1), 169–178.

National Caucus of Native American State Legislators (2008). *Striving to achieve: Helping Native American students succeed.* Denver, CO: National Conference of State Legislatures.

National Clearinghouse on English Language Acquisition (NCELA) (2002). *How many Indigenous American languages are spoken in the United States? By how many speakers?* Washington, DC: NCELA.

Rau, Cath (2005). Literacy acquisition, assessment, and achievement of year two students in total immersion Māori programmes. *International Journal of Bilingual Education and Bilingualism,* 8(5), 404–432.

Romero-Little, Mary Eunice, McCarty, Teresa L., Warhol, Larisa and Zepeda, Ofelia (2007). Language policies in practice: Preliminary findings from a large-scale study of Native American language shift. *TESOL Quarterly,* 41(3), 607–618.

Rosier, Paul and Farella, Merilyn (1976). Bilingual education at Rock Point – Some early results. *TESOL Quarterly,* 10(4), 379–388.

Sims, Christine (2005). Tribal languages and the challenges of revitalization. *Anthropology and Education Quarterly,* 36(1), 104–106.

Skutnabb-Kangas, Tove and McCarty, Teresa L. (2008). Key concepts in bilingual education: Ideological, historical, epistemological, and empirical foundations. In Cummins, Jim and Hornberger, Nancy H. (eds), *Encyclopedia of language and education vol. 5: Bilingual education.* New York: Springer, 3–17.

Snipp, C. Matthew (2002). *American Indian and Alaska Native children in the 2000 census.* Baltimore, MD and Washington, DC: The Annie E. Casey Foundation and the Population Reference Bureau.

Thomas, Wayne P. and Collier, Virginia (1997). *School effectiveness for language minority students.* Washington, DC: National Clearinghouse for Bilingual Education.

US Census Bureau (2000). *Native American language speakers, 2000. Census 2000 summary file 3 and 2000 county and county equivalent areas cartographic boundary file.* Washington, DC: US Department of Commerce, Economics and Statistics Administration.

US Census Bureau (2001). *The Native Hawaiian and Other Pacific Islander population: 2000. Census 2000 brief.* Washington, DC: US Department of Commerce, Economics and Statistics Administration.

US Census Bureau (2002). *The American Indian and Alaska Native population: 2000. Census 2000 brief.* Washington, DC: US Department of Commerce, Economics and Statistics Administration.

US Census Bureau (2006). *We the people: American Indians and Alaska Natives in the United States. Census 2000 special reports.* Washington, DC: US Department of Commerce, Economics and Statistics Administration.

US Office of Health and Human Services (2009). *Native Hawaiian and other Pacific Islanders profile.* Washington, DC: US Office of Health and Human Services, Office of Minority Health. Retrieved 7 February 2011 from http://minorityhealth.hhs.gov/templates/browse.aspx?lvl=2&lvlID=71/.

Vogt, Lynn A. and Au, Kathryn J. P. (1995). The role of teachers' guided reflection in effecting positive program change. *Bilingual Research Journal, 19*(1), 101–120.

Vogt, Lynn A., Jordan, Cathie and Tharp, Roland G. (1993). Explaining school failure, producing school success: Two cases. In Jacob, Evelyn and Jordan, Cathie (eds), *Minority education: Anthropological perspectives.* Norwood, NJ: Ablex, 53–65.

Warhol, Larisa (2009). *Native American language education as policy-in-practice: An interpretive policy analysis of the Native American Languages Act of 1990/1992.* Unpublished Ph.D. dissertation. Tempe: Arizona State University, Division of Educational Leadership and Policy Studies.

Warhol, Larisa (2010, June 14). Native American language education as policy-in-practice: An interpretive policy analysis of the Native American Languages Act of 1990/1992. *International Journal of Bilingual Education and Bilingualism,* 1747–7522, DOI: 10.1080/13670050.2010.486849.

Wilson, William H. (2008). Language fluency, accuracy, and revernacularization in different models of immersion. *NIEA News, 39*(2), 40–42.

Wilson, William H. and Kamanā, Kauanoe (2001). *'Mai loko mai o ka 'i'ini*: Proceeding from a dream'. The 'Aha Pūnana Leo connection in Hawaiian language revitalization. In Hinton, Leanne and Hale, Ken (eds), *The green book of language revitalization in practice.* San Diego, CA: Academic Press, 147–176.

Wilson, William H. and Kamanā, Kauanoe (2006). 'For the interest of the Hawaiians themselves': Reclaiming the benefits of Hawaiian-medium education. *Hūlili: Multidisciplinary Research on Hawaiian Well-Being, 3*(1), 153–181.

Wilson, William H., Kamanā, Kauanoe and Rawlins, Nāmaka (2006). Nāwahī Hawaiian Laboratory School. *Journal of American Indian Education, 45*(2), 42–44.

Wilson, William H. and Kawaiʻaeʻa, Keiki (2007). I kumu; I lālā: 'Let there be sources; Let there be branches': Teacher education in the College of Hawaiian Language. *Journal of American Indian Education, 46*(3), 37–53.

3

LANGUAGE AND CULTURE IN EDUCATION

Comparing Policies and Practices in Peru and Ethiopia

Susanne Pérez Jacobsen and Lucy Trapnell Forero

3.1 Introduction

The Ethiopian study offers a rich variety of new data regarding the benefits that children experience when they use their mother tongue (MT) as medium of instruction (MOI) throughout primary schooling. On the basis of comparative research of students' academic achievements with different language models in nine regions and two city administrations, the study concludes that the long-term use of the MT offers the best results regarding high-level academic proficiency throughout the curriculum. Based on these findings its authors offer a series of recommendations regarding language in education policies.

Their analysis of the consistency between national policy and regional implementation highlights a series of circumstances and attitudes that hinder the use of the MT as MOI throughout primary schooling. In this chapter we shall draw attention to some similarities and differences with Peru, a South American country which has, together with Mexico, Guatemala, Ecuador and Bolivia, the largest population of Indigenous peoples in Latin America. However, the intimate relation between bilingual education and Indigenous peoples' political organisation throughout this region makes it difficult to separate language and education policies from other aspects of the struggle that have developed during the last decades for the recognition of their collective rights. Among these are the right to self-determination, territory and the demand for new forms of schooling aimed to respond to a long history of colonisation and subjugation. Given this situation, we consider it necessary to approach language and education policies as part of a larger discussion regarding the relation between education, language, culture and power. We believe that this debate can offer new insights regarding how to approach the development of quality education in multilingual and multicultural contexts.

This chapter will focus on our experience in indigenous contexts; language-in-education policies in Peru have been exclusively oriented towards Indigenous peoples. We first introduce Peru's sociolinguistic context, followed by a brief historical review of Peru's language-in-education policies. Then we discuss four issues regarding classroom practice in indigenous contexts, to help comparisons with the Ethiopian case and to introduce new elements for discussions about quality education: the state of affairs regarding bilingual schools and teachers; the use of Indigenous MTs as MOI; the teaching of Spanish as a second language (L2) and the way in which Indigenous cultures are approached in formal schooling. Subsequently, we analyse recent tendencies in intercultural bilingual education (IBE) in the light of the regionalisation and democratisation of education policy initiated in Peru during the last decade. We conclude with a discussion about today's challenges regarding IBE in Peru and summarise the basic comparisons with Ethiopia made throughout the chapter.

3.2 Sociolinguistic Context

3.2.1 A Brief Presentation of Peru

Peru, as many of its South American neighbours, is a pluriethnic, pluricultural and plurilingual country with a surface area of 1,285,216 sq. km. The Cordillera de los Andes mountainous chain that runs parallel to the Pacific Ocean from Cape Horn to Panama, crosses Peru from north to south. The Cordillera determines Peru's configuration in three distinct regions: the Coast, the Andes and the Amazon, with different altitudinal levels, differentiated climates, varied types of soil and an impressive biodiversity.

According to the 2007 Census, Peru's population is 28,220,764. It is difficult to identify the percentage of the Indigenous population: information about ethnic identity was not included in this or in the 1993 Census.

3.2.2 Situation of the Indigenous Languages

Forty-two Indigenous languages are spoken in Peru, in addition to Spanish and other European and Asian immigrant languages. However, this section focuses on the relation between Indigenous languages and Spanish: most bi/multilingual contexts are associated with them, and language-in-education policies have been exclusively oriented to speakers of Indigenous languages.

Peru's linguistic situation has undergone dramatic changes during recent decades. The percentage of Indigenous language speakers has diminished considerably relative to the country's total population. Furthermore, various Amazonian languages, as well as two Aymara dialects are on the verge of extinction.

The 1993 and 2007 Censuses provide data regarding the number of speakers over five years with an Indigenous language as an MT. However, this information is incomplete since neither offers information regarding the number of bilingual speakers or those with some degree of socialisation in these languages (Chirinos 2001).

In the 1940s, 50% of the country's population spoke Quechua (Chirinos n.d.), the second most spoken language after Spanish. Quechua was spoken in all the Peruvian Andes since pre-Inca times and used as lingua franca by missionaries for evangelisation purposes. The percentage of both Quechua and Aymara speakers has diminished considerably during the last 60 years in relation to Peru's total population (Table 3.1).

In the Amazonian region 40 Indigenous languages are spoken by 42 Indigenous peoples (Figure 3.1). These languages, with some exceptions (e.g. Ashaninka) are included in both censuses as 'other native languages'. Amazonian Indigenous population has been severely decimated throughout the last five centuries due to enslavement, epidemics and genocide (Chirif 1991), even though they had less direct contact with Spanish colonisers than the Andeans and were less exposed to the servitude at the hands of powerful landowners after Peru's independence. As a result of this process, only four Indigenous peoples (Ashaninka, Shipibo, Kichwa and Awajun) number over 15,000, while the population for 16 Indigenous peoples is fewer than 500.

A significant difference also exists regarding the situation of Amazonian Indigenous languages. Children are still socialised into the majority of them. Nonetheless, during recent decades increasing contact with colonisers and the introduction of school education in Spanish has led to the displacement of some. In many cases the Amazonian languages are only spoken by parents and/or grandparents. Thus, the number of Indigenous-language speakers in Peru is dramatically lower than in Ethiopia, where 18 languages have over 230,000 speakers, and seven have over a million.

Another important difference, basic for the implementation of language-in-education policies is the distribution of Indigenous-language speakers within each country, and their levels of bilingualism. In Peru, Indigenous languages can be found throughout the country. According to the 2007 Census, Quechua is present in Peru's 25 regions and it is the MT of the majority of persons over five in Andean regions such as Apurímac (71.5%), Ayacucho (63.9%), Huancavelica (64.5%) and Cusco (52.0%). Furthermore, people who have Aymara as their MT

TABLE 3.1 Speakers (5 years or older) with Indigenous languages as mother tongues

Indigenous languages	1993 Census Absolute	%	2007 Census Absolute	%	Intercensus % variation
Quechua	3,177,938	16.6	3,261,750	13.2	−3.4
Aymara	440,380	2.3	434,370	1.8	−0.5
Other Amazonian languages	132,174	0.7	223,194	0.9	0.2

Source: National Institute of Statistics and Computing. National 1993 and 2007 Censuses.

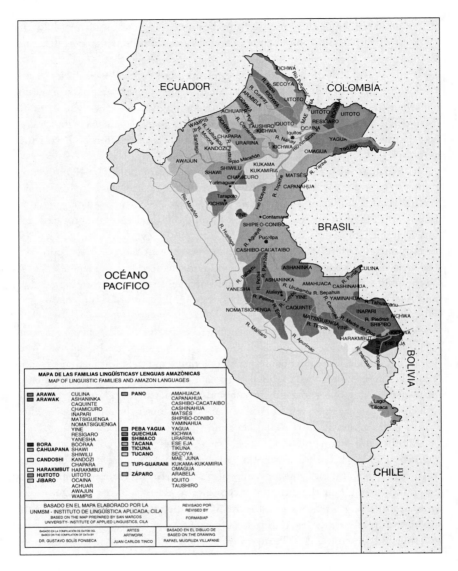

FIGURE 3.1 Linguistic map of Amazonian Indigenous languages in Peru

Source: Adapted from Landolt, Gredna. In El Ojo Verde. Cosmovisiones Amazónicas, p. 37. Programa de Formación de Maestros Bilingües. AIDESEP. Fundación Telefónica.

live in 17 regions, an increase of seven regions in comparison with the 1993 Census (National Institute of Statistics and Data Processing/INEI 2007).

In contrast with Quechua and Aymara, Amazonian Indigenous languages are basically spoken in their own communities. Yet, since the 1990s, there is a small but gradual expansion of Kukama-Kukamiria, Shipibo, Ashaninka, Uitoto, Shawi and Awajun families towards cities and towns near their communities. Moreover, according to the 2007 Census, speakers with Amazonian MTs can be found in 20 regions.

The monolingualism or incipient bilingualism which characterised many Andean and Amazonian rural areas during the 1970s is gradually diminishing in favour of greater levels of bilingualism. The expansion of formal schooling, the significant growth in Indigenous peoples' access to radio and television, increase of extractive activities (oil, lumber, gold, etc.) and the spread of colonisers who settle in the vicinity of newly constructed roads and highways in the Amazon region or rent lands inside native communities, are leading to massive expansion of Spanish use in everyday life. This dynamic and complex sociolinguistic context has generated a new situation where children – in contrast with 20–30 years ago – are competent in two languages before starting school, even though they are usually more fluent in one of them. In these cases the traditional divide between an MT and an L2 with which bilingual programmes have worked is no longer useful. This has given rise to the use of a new concept: 'the language of predominant use'.

The variety of multilingual contexts is usually ignored in the development of bilingual programmes in Peru and its Andean neighbours. Their proposals are usually based on the use of one Indigenous language and Spanish (see Hornberger and López 1998).

In section 3.3 we offer an overview of today's situation regarding IBE and highlight some of the historical processes that have led to it.

3.3 The Pedagogic and Political Agendas behind Language-in-education Policies and Practices

In the 1930s and 40s, owing to the strong indigenist current prevailing at that time, Quechua and Aymara were introduced as MOI during the initial year of primary school in some communities in the Andean areas. Nevertheless, this bilingual model aimed to assimilate Indigenous peoples into the nation (López and Küper 2000: 26–27).

Around the same time as the influential 1953 UNESCO report, *The Use of Vernacular Languages in Education* was published, the Summer Institute of Linguistics (SIL), a North American protestant organisation introduced bilingual education in Peru's Amazonian Indigenous communities (Trapnell and Neira 2006: 255).

SIL followed an early-exit-transitional bilingual model which ultimately aimed towards children's exclusive use of Spanish. The use of the MT as MOI was often restricted to three years at the very most (Trapnell 1985: 126). SIL held the monopoly on Indigenous education in Peru for almost two decades.

In 1968 Juan Velasco Alvarado's revolutionary government implemented various social, political and economic reforms. This government developed an educational reform that included the first National Bilingual Education Policy (1972) for speakers of Indigenous languages. It recognised the existence of a great diversity of sociolinguistic situations and gave teachers the liberty to make their own decisions regarding language use in education.

The 1972 policy was accompanied by other laws and measures in favour of Indigenous peoples' rights. This and the active role played by Amazonian Indigenous organisations and their allies heralded the beginning of a move away from the early-exit-transitional model towards the development of a maintenance-cum-development model. This model promoted the use of Indigenous languages as MOI and as subjects throughout the six grades of primary school.

During the mid-1980s, Amazonian Indigenous leaders and their allies questioned the practice of bilingual education: translating Western knowledge into Indigenous languages, while paying no heed to their cultural heritage. Like other Latin American countries, they began to use the concept *intercultural* bilingual education (IBE), in order to stress the need for a new type of education which would recognise their knowledges and values. The first definitions of IBE emphasised education based on Indigenous cultures, and an introduction of elements and contents based on other cultural horizons (Pozzi-Escot, Zúñiga and López 1991). In theory, the language and cultural traditions of different ethnic groups were to form the basic structure and content of formal educational processes. All the thematic areas from the majority-culture curriculum that the Indigenous child required would be aggregated gradually, in a non-conflictive and non-substitutive manner. Consequently, student achievement would not only be measured with the official curriculum as a norm, but in the language of, and according to the contents defined by, Indigenous peoples.

Since 1989 IBE has been part of two education policies and the General Education Law (GEL) from 2003 (Ministry of Education 1989, 1991 and 2003). In all three, IBE is only considered relevant for children with Indigenous mother tongues (Trapnell and Neira 2006: 268). The GEL affirms that IBE is to promote the appreciation and enrichment of one's own culture, respect towards cultural diversity, intercultural dialogue and consciousness of both Indigenous peoples' rights and those of other national and international communities, and the incorporation of Indigenous peoples' history, knowledge, technologies, value systems and social and economic aspirations.

The law guarantees Indigenous children's right to develop their Indigenous MTs from preschool to secondary school. It also recognises their right to learn Spanish as an L2 and also to learn other foreign languages.

The law includes a series of regulations on the implementation of IBE. Teachers working in bilingual schools must know the Indigenous language of their students, as well as Spanish. Indigenous peoples should play an active role in the development of IBE: '[IBE] . . . guarantees the participation of representatives for indigenous peoples in the formulation and implementation of education programs; they should form teams that are capable of progressively taking over the administration of these programs' (Ministry of Education 2003: Art. 20). Moreover, it attributes IBE an active role in the preservation and promotion of Indigenous languages. However, in contrast with Ethiopian policy which considers the need for teachers to be trained in the MT of their students, the GEL does not include any provision regarding teacher training.

The 2003 law's incorporation of a series of collective indigenous rights can be considered a consequence of Indigenous peoples' political mobilisation. This had led to Peru's 1993 ratification of the International Labour Organisation's (ILO) 169 Convention.[1] The active lobbying by anthropologists, linguists and educators involved in IBE programmes also played an important role in this process.

Both the 1991 policy and the 2003 GEL contain a distinction between Intercultural Education for all Peruvian students and IBE for bilingual ones (Trapnell and Neira 2006: 268). The GEL considers interculturalism to be the national education system's principal guideline; intercultural education is a means for the promotion of general understanding about the country's ethnic, cultural and linguistic diversity and for harmonious coexistence and interchange among the cultures of the world.

In our comparison with Ethiopia, we observe two central differences in language-in-education policies. The first is about criteria and arguments used to advocate MT use in education. Ethiopian policy was driven by arguments based on both the constitutional concern for linguistic equity, and learning theory.

> All Ethiopian languages shall enjoy equal recognition.
> *(Constitution of the Federal Democratic Republic of*
> *Ethiopia 1994, cited in Heugh et al. 2007: 50)*

> Cognizant of the pedagogical advantage of the child in learning in mother tongue and the rights of nationalities to promote the use of their languages, primary education will be given in nationality languages.
> *(Education and Training Policy 1994,*
> *cited in Heugh et al. 2007: 50)*

In contrast, the right to be taught in languages other than Spanish in Peru is closely linked to Indigenous peoples' struggle for the recognition and defence of their cultural heritage and their collective rights. Secondly, Peruvian policies give priority to the cultural dimension, which has been a central issue in Indigenous peoples' educational demands. Therefore, in contrast with Ethiopia, the concept of interculturalism, more than bilingualism plays today an important role in overall state policy. However, it must be said that the introduction of intercultural issues in Peru – as in many other Latin American countries – was closely linked to education in bilingual contexts. This is very different to what has happened in North America and Europe where interculturalism has been approached in such a way that it has often excluded bilingual or multilingual education. Here the Peruvian example may contribute significantly to the international debates on bi/multilingual education.

However, we have to agree with Tubino (2004) who affirms that the state's appropriation of the intercultural discourse has diluted its initial critical and liberatory potential and reduced it to a technical and instrumental function.

Even if IBE has a relatively secure legal base, the state has demonstrated little political will in its implementation. This is still mainly dependent on participation by Indigenous organisations and local and international NGOs, and on political pressure exerted by both. However, what happens in schools depends on the individual teacher's decisions. The problems confronted in the implementation of IBE as well as some of the lessons learnt in this process are elaborated in section 3.4.

3.4 Culture and Language in Educational Practice

3.4.1 Bilingual Schools and Bilingual Teachers

In Peru very little statistical information exists about bilingual schools, students and teachers. Furthermore, no official data exist on how many students should be included in IBE. The only available figures refer to the number of officially registered primary bilingual schools: 3,109 in the Andes and 788 in the Amazon region. According to Zavala (2007a), IBE only benefits 11% of primary school students in rural Indigenous areas and 18% of the schools located in them.

However, these figures must be taken with caution, since the name 'bilingual' is given to all the schools that have Indigenous students and have been officially registered as such. This does not necessarily mean that they have bilingual teachers for every grade or that their students have their MT as MOI and/or learn Spanish as L2, as IBE policies presuppose. In fact, most of these schools only have one teacher, who usually works with first and second grade students; some have two. There are very few cases where the whole staff is bilingual.[2]

Furthermore, all Indigenous teachers are considered 'bilingual'. One can find 'bilingual' teachers with receptive competence only in their language. In a more common situation a 'bilingual' teacher has serious limitations producing texts in their Indigenous language (see Vigil n.d.). Moreover, just as in Nepal, teachers are not always placed in schools according to their MTs. Therefore, some bilingual schools have 'bilingual' teachers who speak a language different from the MT of their pupils. Finally, there are also 'bilingual' teachers who are fully competent in the Indigenous language but only use it to comply with two weekly hours of Indigenous language as a subject or to reinforce some themes they have previously presented in Spanish.

3.4.2 *The Use of the Indigenous Mother Tongues as Mediums of Instruction*

Official language policies in Peru formally adhere to the maintenance bilingual education model whose goal is to preserve the native language while adding an L2. In this model students should learn to read and write in their MT, and later in L2. Instructional time in both languages should be included in accordance with the pupils' skills in each. Unlike Ethiopia, there are no clear guidelines regarding the use of the MT as MOI. The intensity of its use has been left to each teacher's decision. In theory this should be based on socio- and psycholinguistic diagnoses that IBE teachers learn to implement during their training. However, as we shall explain, many other factors influence their language-in-education strategies.

Our supervision experience of bilingual schools tells us that the existence of bilingual teachers does not guarantee the use of the Indigenous language as MOI, or even as a subject, throughout the six primary grades. In fact, we only know of one documented experiment where teachers currently use the Indigenous MT as the sole MOI beyond first grade. It is being developed in the Molle Molle community (Cusco) with support of the Asociación Pukllasunchis IBE programme. Here teachers use Quechua as the MOI during all primary schooling (from first to sixth grade) and introduce Spanish as a subject from grade 1. The experiment began in 2005 and Pukllasunchis plans to continue supporting it for another three years, in order to guarantee long-term results regarding student achievements.

We have witnessed that teachers use both Spanish and the Indigenous language as MOI from second grade onwards and sometimes even in first grade, without taking into consideration data drawn from their sociolinguistic and psycholinguistic baseline/diagnosis. They usually explain the lesson in Spanish and interpret it into their students' MT. A lot of mixing of languages or code switching occurs throughout the class. However, writing is usually only done in Spanish.

Teachers develop this language-in-education strategy for reasons related to their beliefs, attitudes and skills, public pressure, lack of teaching materials in the Indigenous MT and the composition of the teaching staff.

Most bilingual teachers believe that schools are places where children should primarily learn Spanish and Western knowledge. In accordance with parents' and community members' beliefs, Spanish is considered a basic tool in which Indigenous peoples defend their rights and prevent future marginalisation. They also give priority to Spanish since they consider that students' constant exposure to this language will prepare them better for secondary education in Spanish. Behind this practice is the common belief that using Spanish as MOI in different subjects, with some support of the Indigenous language, will help pupils to learn it gradually, as it happens in everyday life. This belief leads Indigenous teachers to use concurrent approaches, rather than resorting to the language separation strategies in which they were trained (see López 2008). Teachers, furthermore, respond to students' urgent desire to learn Spanish more than the need to teach them in a language they know, as Serrano (2003: 218) explains regarding his experience in Colombia.

Unlike Ethiopia, where teachers are aware of the problems that students encounter in understanding content in a language that is not their MT, most Peruvian teachers are unaware of these problems or tend to minimise their impact on learning. Especially in areas where children are exposed to Spanish in everyday community life, teachers usually justify their extensive use of Spanish as MOI by claiming that their students 'know Spanish'. In areas where students' only exposure to Spanish is in the classroom, teachers are generally more aware of the communication difficulties. However, most teachers believe that such problems can be solved through the simultaneous use of both languages in class.

Bilingual teachers also believe that mathematics and science cannot be taught in Indigenous languages. This is very much related to the characteristics of their training. Unlike Ethiopia where Ministry of Education policy determines that primary school teachers should have their training in the MOI of their students, no such policy exists in Peru. As Spanish is the only MOI in almost every teacher training college in the country, teachers do not have any opportunity of developing competence in using their MT languages as MOI. Consequently, in contrast with Ethiopian teachers, Peruvian bilingual teachers have not developed their technical and pedagogical MT vocabulary and structures needed to convey concepts in subject areas. However, this is slowly changing in some of the 15 teacher training colleges that offer IBE as a specialty. In a few Andean colleges a small number of teachers have begun to use Quechua as the MOI of some subjects (see Zavala 2007a: 178). The introduction of Indigenous languages as MOI is more difficult in Amazonian IBE colleges where students often speak a variety of languages. Nonetheless, some have begun to approach this challenge, as Trapnell (2008a: 27–28) explains in her analysis of the new proposals and strategies of the teacher training programme Programa de Formación de Maestros Bilingües de la Amazonía Peruana (FORMABIAP).

The use of the Indigenous language as MOI in primary school is also prevented by lack of learning materials in most Indigenous languages. Unlike Ethiopia where there are some materials for various subjects in the MTs at lower primary for 23 languages (Heugh et al. 2007 and Benson et al. in this volume), in Peru this is not the case. With a few notable exceptions, texts in Indigenous languages have been basically produced for the development of literacy skills. Moreover, nowadays learning materials are only available in some Indigenous languages.

Until the 1970s SIL was responsible for the provision of mimeographed texts for all bilingual schools. These consisted of basic materials for learning reading and writing skills and for the development of some specific contents of certain academic subjects. During the 1980s IBE programmes run by different NGOs designed textbooks in Quechua, Aymara, Amazonian Kichwa and Ashaninka. Nevertheless, only the Quechua and Aymara programmes developed materials for different academic subjects; the others focused on the production of books for the development of reading skills. During the 1990s the FORMABIAP teacher training programme, developed by an indigenous confederation and a teacher training college, started to produce books in 15 Indigenous languages. They were also basically oriented to the development of literacy skills. In this same decade the National Directorate for Bilingual and Intercultural Education promoted the design of texts for the Integral Communication and Mathematics academic areas in Quechua, Aymara and eight Amazonian Indigenous languages. Seven of these already had some materials designed by FORMABIAP. All those bilingual schools in which other languages are used only have materials in Spanish. Just a few have remnants of the SIL textbooks designed during the 1970s.

The composition of the teaching staff also has an important influence on the language strategies which bilingual teachers use. Those who work with first and second grade students with an Indigenous MT usually accelerate their learning of Spanish when the third or fourth grade teacher is monolingual in Spanish. This also happens with third and fourth grade teachers when their fifth and sixth grade colleagues ignore the Indigenous language.

Another frequently used argument to justify the use of Spanish as MOI is the existence of multilingual classrooms where students have different MTs. The most usual case is a class where the majority of children have an Indigenous MT and a minority have Spanish. However, trilingual situations (students with different Indigenous MTs plus Spanish MT-speakers) are also found in some Amazonian communities.

Last but not least, Indigenous parents have a crucial role in deciding the MOI in schools. Parents consider that schools should help their children develop oral and written skills in Spanish. They believe that these competencies will allow them to have better possibilities of communicating with Spanish speakers and give them better opportunities (López 2003: 43). In many regions parents reject the use of the Indigenous language by stating that their children already know it. Furthermore, they are against the written use of their languages in higher grades, since they believe that this will take time away from the development of written skills in Spanish. Bilingual teachers frequently justify their decisions regarding language use by referring to these attitudes (Vigil n.d.).

However, as Serrano (2003: 219) highlights, drawing from his experience in Colombia, parents' attitudes regarding the use of Indigenous languages in schools are not homogeneous, but usually related to the type of contact they have with national society; communities with frequent contact with colonisers are those who show more resistance to the use of the Indigenous language in education. Drawing from our experience, we would add that in Peru even these communities have begun to develop a more positive approach to this issue during the last decade due to better school achievement reported by bilingual teachers, affirmation by Indigenous organisations relating identity to language issues, and the creation of new educational opportunities, such as scholarships and university programmes which value the knowledge of Indigenous languages.

All these factors could help to explain poor levels of literacy, mathematics and science achievement and high rates of 'dropout' and repetition found among Indigenous primary school students. However, in contrast with Ethiopia where student assessment can help to demonstrate the relation between exposure to MTM education and student achievement, in Peru no systematic studies of this kind exist.

3.4.3 The Teaching of Spanish

The description of IBE teachers' approach to language makes it clear that Spanish is basically learnt through submersion in most IBE schools. It is extremely rare to find teachers who offer more than three hours a week to develop Spanish as L2 or who follow the methodology designed by the Ministry of Education (MoE) or IBE programmes. However, it would not be fair to consider that this is solely a result of the pressure which parents exert upon teachers, or of their personal options. Other factors, briefly described below are also involved.

Our experience, and studies in this field (López 2003) show general problems related to teachers' need for more understanding of the factors involved in learning an L2, their limited proficiency in Spanish and the lack of adequate methods and materials.

IBE teachers have learnt Spanish through submersion; they have never experienced learning it as an L2 subject. This makes it difficult for them to understand a crucial aspect on which IBE language teaching models are based: the similarities and differences between learning Spanish as an MT and as an L2. In the best of cases these teachers only learn about these differences theoretically. However, most IBE teachers have only 5–7-day IBE workshops (developed by the MoE or different NGOs), where L2 issues are one of many themes. Thus they have had no opportunity of understanding the theories that L2 teaching is based on; they have lacked the necessary time to learn about L2 methodology and to overcome their own problems in oral and written Spanish. However, in recent years some NGOs have decided to prioritise the time assigned to Spanish as an L2 in their IBE training programmes. This includes strategies such as preparing L2 classes in workshops, observing each others' classes on video or in school, and visiting pilot schools where teachers had received more training in L2 teaching and have tried out teaching models that fit rural multigrade schools' realities.

Most L2 models used in IBE programmes have been designed for children with no knowledge, or an incipient knowledge, of Spanish. As López (2003: 65–66) and Vigil (n.d.) observe, these models give little attention to the variety of sociolinguistic situations in which IBE programmes are implemented.

Teachers who have studied in IBE colleges are more aware of the theoretical and methodological issues involved in L2 teaching and have made remarkable progress in their oral and written skills in Spanish. However, this does not necessarily mean that they have acquired the proficiency they need to teach it as an L2.

In summary, IBE teachers in Peru, as in many other countries in the Andean region, are not specialised language teachers. They have been taught to use models that they do not always fully understand. Furthermore, they frequently lack the proficiency needed to teach Spanish. For all these reasons, many teachers with formal training in IBE also tend to apply the submersion model used when they learnt Spanish; consequently, they teach Spanish as if it were their students' MT.

However, Indigenous teachers are not the only ones who teach Spanish in IBE schools. They share this task with other teachers, usually responsible for children after grades 1–3. Unlike IBE teachers, they usually have no knowledge whatsoever of what it means to teach Spanish as an L2. The majority of them have only learnt how to teach Spanish as an MT and their training has been oriented to normative and grammatical aspects.

3.4.4 Culture in Education

As previously mentioned, during the early 1980s Indigenous peoples began to question the assimilatory agenda of education. They started to negotiate new forms of schooling aimed to respond to a long history of colonisation and subjugation. For the past 20 years, they have framed their educational agendas on the affirmation of their collective rights. Moreover, they have seen formal education as a key arena for the assertion of their identity and the revitalisation of their culture and language (Aikman 1999).

Most Indigenous education programmes have adopted the maintenance oriented model in theory. However, their approach to intercultural education has been quite diverse. From the late 1980s, they have focused on the need to make Indigenous knowledge visible in formal educational sites through its inclusion in formal curricula or in teachers' didactic plans. Many of them were based on what Stairs (1988) has called a 'culture-inclusion approach' to educational development, which treats culture as a static and bounded phenomenon for inclusion in an otherwise entirely majority-culture curriculum. Others approached Indigenous peoples' cultural heritage from a more inclusive and dynamic perspective and tried to incorporate some major changes in the official curricula through the use of diversification procedures. Some programmes, based on indigenous self-determination, with efforts to introduce Indigenous knowledge and values in school curricula, have acknowledged limitations in the ways in which they have approached this issue (see Trapnell 2008a).

A basic drawback in their approach to curriculum construction and diversification processes has been that the particular ways in which Indigenous people represent their social experience and their relation with nature have been ignored or marginalised when indigenous knowledge has been included in the conceptual framework of Western scientific disciplines (see Trapnell 2008a, 2008b). This critical evaluation has led some IBE programmes to design alternative curricula that incorporate Indigenous peoples' interpretative categories. Their aim of these programmes is to encourage the inclusion of their knowledge and narratives into national education, by promoting an approach to knowledge as a social and cultural construction (Trapnell 2006).

This reflection about different ways of reading the world has also made those working with IBE programmes aware that their focus on curricular content has left aside a central discussion about the ways in which people construct, transmit and transform knowledge. This has led to a critical evaluation of the cultural bias present in their pedagogical discourse and methodologies.

Drawing on these experiences, some IBE teacher training colleges try to include a more reflective approach to analysis of their practice. They endeavour to help pre-service teachers explain the presuppositions behind opting for certain strategies. These processes have allowed them to identify some social and cultural traits implicit in their work. These include approaches to discipline and control, and the ways in which they communicate with their pupils and evaluate their learning process. However, this reflection is still absent in most teacher training programmes. Experience demonstrates that it is very difficult for teacher trainers to critically distance themselves from hegemonic pedagogical discourse.

3.5 Regional Education Policies: New Opportunities for Intercultural Bilingual Education

3.5.1 Decentralisation Policies in Peru

A crucial element in Ethiopian language-in-education policies is the balance between centralised and decentralised policies and the level of freedom given to regional governments for the adoption of appropriate models and practices. In linguistically, culturally and geographically diverse countries, such as Ethiopia and Peru, decentralised decision-making is important for creating education models that respond to local conditions and needs.

This section focuses on how education and particularly IBE is administered in Peru. It includes an analysis of the opportunities and obstacles for IBE as a result of decentralization.

In the 1960s, Peru's MoE initiated its decentralisation process in order to assure the adaptation of national norms to the regional and local level (Díaz and Valdivia 2007: 27). Today, the MoE includes four administrative levels: the MoE, the Regional Education Office (REO), the Local Administration Unit (LAU) and the schools.

In the 1990s, the World Bank and the Interamerican Development Bank obliged many Latin American countries to carry out drastic reforms aimed towards an open market economy and a reduction or privatisation of the public sector (Oliart and Vásquez 2007: 6–7). Peru initiated this process in 1994 under the Fujimori regime. Even though Fujimori adhered to neoliberal ideas, he was quite reluctant to involve civil society in educational administration, in coherence with the World Bank model (Oliart and Vásquez 2007: 24). However, his government supported other Bank initiatives, such as offering teachers the possibility to adapt the national curriculum to regional and local contexts (Díaz and Valdivia 2007: 27).

In 2002, the Toledo government initiated a general public administration reform intended to transfer responsibilities to regional and local governments (Díaz and Valdivia 2007: 27). In this 'regionalisation' process (Trapnell and Neira 2006: 275), central government transferred responsibilities to its regional counterparts. Diversification of the national curriculum, regulation and supervision of regional education, teacher training, construction of educational infrastructure and strengthening school networks were included among these responsibilities (Díaz and Valdivia 2007: 28). In addition to administrative decentralisation, there was a political one, embodied in so-called Regional Educational Projects (REPs), meant to define regional education policies established through dialogue between civil society, regional political parties and public administration. REPs have the double aim of being the connecting link between national education policies and school policies, and of connecting education policies with the overall policies and visions for the development of the region (Salazar and Andrade 2006: 18). Various REPs include a variety of contents, which could offer Indigenous peoples the possibility to strengthen their and IBE's positions at regional and local levels. Before offering a brief analysis of the role assigned to IBE in four of these regional policies, we shall briefly outline IBE's position in the existing administrative structure.

3.5.2 IBE in the Existing Administrative Structure

IBE's position in the MoE administrative structure has varied since the first IBE Unit was created during the early 1980s (as a section of the General Directorate for Primary Education), because:

> different governments have created units or directorates depending on their vision about the place IBE should occupy within the Ministry and of the political message they wanted to transmit to indigenous organizations and international agencies.
>
> *(Trapnell 2008c: 5)*

In 2003 the two units responsible for IBE, and rural education, respectively, were merged into a single one. This act, which could be considered advantageous as most rural schools have de facto bilingual pupils, led to IBE's subordination to rural education and to the re-introduction of monolingual and monocultural policies and practices. Not only were bilingual children measured with monolingual tests, but also the training of IBE teachers has practically stopped since 2007 (Zavala 2008).

Furthermore, the IBE unit lacks a normative power:

> It cannot name or assign teachers; it cannot approve an alternative curriculum for the development of IBE at the different levels of the education system; and it has to limit itself to the strict conditions the MoE has established regarding curriculum diversification procedures, referring to the terms outlined by different offices that are responsible for basic and superior education.
>
> *(Trapnell 2008c: 6)*

The marginal position of IBE is the same at other levels. Regional education offices have in the best case one or two specialists working exclusively with IBE issues, even in regions where the majority of their schools are located in Indigenous bilingual communities. Furthermore, local MoE authorities in predominantly bilingual areas do not necessarily favour contracting bilingual teachers.

Due to lack of political will, a solid and well thought-through integration of IBE in the administrative structure of the MoE has not yet been achieved in Peru. Unlike Ethiopia where regional education bureaus have developed the competence to implement MTM education on a regional basis (see Benson *et al.* in this volume), this is not the case in Peru where the educational system maintains a monolingual and monocultural organisational structure and approach. In fact, most national, regional and local educational authorities conceive IBE as a compensatory programme for a small percentage of Indigenous people. Thus, no effort has been made to guarantee the training of the personnel that regional and local MoE offices need to respond to the demands and challenges of IBE.

3.5.3 Intercultural Bilingual Education in Four Regional Education Projects (REPs)

The recently implemented REPs define regional education policies, priorities and implementation strategies for the next decade and offer new opportunities for the implementation of IBE.

In this section we shall analyse the Amazonas, Loreto, Cusco and Ayacucho REPs (referred to from now on as: AMREP, LOREP, CUREP and AYREP) in order to compare how each REP approaches vital issues for the development of IBE, such as language policies, teacher qualifications, curriculum content and community participation. Amazonas and Loreto represent regions with Amazonian Indigenous peoples and languages, and Ayacucho and Cusco are among the five regions with most Quechua speakers (Trapnell and Neira 2006: 258–262).

General language policies: The REPs for all four regions present information about their regions' linguistic and cultural diversity and Indigenous peoples' living conditions. Only the Cusco REP mentions the number of speakers of each language and its actual situation. The LOREP uses the general term 'Indigenous peoples' to refer to the region's 20 Indigenous languages. All four REPs acknowledge the lack of information about Indigenous languages, cultural praxis and cosmologies and have included some policies aimed to strengthen research in these areas.

Language policies outside the education sector are vital for the revitalisation of Indigenous languages and their acceptance in society. Through different measures that address the valorisation of Indigenous languages, their speakers will regain confidence and their cultural and linguistic identity (Meliá 2003: 26). However, this aspect is absolutely ignored in LOREP. It only includes language policies for the education sector, even when this is the region with the most endangered languages. In contrast, AYREP and AMREP do propose policies for the use of Indigenous languages in the media as well as strategies to promote reading and writing in Indigenous languages (Ayacucho Regional Government 2006: 60, and Amazonas Regional Government 2007: 43; hereafter, Regional Government is shortened to RG). Cusco and Ayacucho also propose the use of Indigenous languages in public and private institutions and consider them official languages in their regions (Cusco RG 2007: 69; Ayacucho RG 2006: 60).

Language-in-education policies: IBE is central in all four REPs. Nevertheless, they do not suggest the number of years that should be devoted to learning in the MT; neither do they indicate the grade in which the L2 will be introduced.

The only REP that explicitly includes IBE for urban areas is Ayacucho; LOREP only refers to it in relation to rural areas. CUREP does not specify this issue, but in May 2008 the region's government made Quechua an obligatory subject at all educational levels and modalities (Cusco RG 2008).

Teacher training is acknowledged as an important asset in the implementation of quality IBE programmes by the four REPs; they consider the construction of regional IBE teacher training curricula (Amazonas RG 2007: 42; Cusco RG 2007: 51) or present general formulations about guaranteeing IBE teacher training (Ayacucho RG 2006: 59). However, none offer regulations on languages which teacher training institutions should use as MOI.

The cultural inadequacy of existing *educational materials*, teaching methods, and curriculum content have been criticised for decades. Recognising this, all four REPs formulate clearly the need to design curricula, materials, methods and evaluation strategies that are coherent with Indigenous cosmologies (Ayacucho RG 2006: 59–60; Amazonas RG 2007: 43; Loreto RG 2005: 27, 30, 50 and 57; Cusco RG 2007: 70).

Regarding the *curricula*, some regions propose the diversification of the existing national curriculum (Amazonas RG 2007: 43) or the production of curricular guidelines (Cusco RG 2007: 70), while others propose the construction of one regional curriculum (Ayacucho RG 2006: 59–60) or even an appropriate curriculum for each and every Indigenous people in the region (Loreto RG 2005: 57).

They also include proposals on curriculum *content* and education materials; AYREP and AMREP use almost identical formulations here. They propose the need to develop competencies and contents that are community-based and integrate Indigenous peoples' cultural and linguistic characteristics to strengthen collective ethnic identities and to recoup cultural diversity (Amazonas RG 2007: 43; Ayacucho RG 2006: 59–61).

CUREP and, particularly, LOREP offer detailed accounts on some curriculum contents related to Indigenous peoples' cultural heritage. CUREP proposes to 'integrate the history of the people, their knowledge, religiosity, science, technologies, value systems, philosophies, social and economic aspirations' (Cusco RG 2007: 70) in the construction of intercultural education. LOREP proposes materials with themes related to the reality of the region, for example, Amazonian history, geography and ecology (Loreto RG 2005: 49), and themes related to intercultural education, for example 'intercultural relations; mestizo cultural richness; existing indigenous peoples; indigenous cultural products; myths and legends; customs; fables and moral stories; typical characters' (Loreto RG 2005: 50). Furthermore, it proposes to 'incorporate the Indigenous peoples' cultural richness as curricular content in all stages, levels and modalities of the education system' (Loreto RG 2005: 54).

Community participation should be expected to be central to educational policies which aim at breaking with colonial structures. Nevertheless, only the LOREP gives this theme a central place throughout the document. It considers the local school the major force in what it calls 'decentralisation for development' (Loreto RG 2005: 72). In the other REPs community participation is not mentioned explicitly, despite some formulations about participatory strategies. The REPs represent their authors' views on the educational system. The desire for change is central to them. The possibility for communities to participate in the construction of new curricula, policy formulations and to decide about the education they need is unique. IBE is present in all four REPs and their policies are more ambitious than the legal framework. Three of the four REPs express an explicit desire to recover and develop Indigenous languages. Most importantly, they acknowledge the need to change the vertical approach that has characterised the relationship between the dominant mestizo population and Indigenous peoples.

Despite certain unclarified issues, it would appear that the ongoing regionalisation will be positive for Indigenous peoples. Regional education policies are in favour of IBE and show willingness to implement educational models that offer opportunities for the entire population. However, experience makes us sceptical. As we have explained throughout this chapter, little has been advanced in IBE during the past 30 years, even though many policies and laws have been designed.

The fear we share with other colleagues who have worked in IBE during recent decades is that, once again, many good ideas and intentions will not transcend the level of discourse.

3.6 Contrasts and Challenges

Peru and Ethiopia are multicultural and multilingual countries. Both have developed education and language policies aimed to offer quality education to students who speak a diversity of languages. However, considerable differences exist regarding the conceptions and motivations that have guided each country's language-in-education policy. Significant contrasts are also found regarding their implementation. In this section we shall focus on these two aspects and on the lessons that can be learnt from them.

Ethiopia's main argument for the use of MTE was based on both constitutional and educational considerations. The latter coincide with the UNESCO recommendations for optimal cognitive development of the pupil (UNESCO 2005, cited in Heugh *et al.* 2007: 11). In contrast, in Peru, as in many other Latin American countries, Indigenous peoples' political mobilisation has been vital for the development of education policies sensitive to the country's diversity. Thus, the recognition, in education policies, of language has been inextricably related to Indigenous peoples' demands and defence of their collective rights. Consequently, educational debate about quality education has not only included language issues, but also cultural aspects. This has led to critical discussions about the colonial underpinnings of school education.

In Ethiopia multilingual education has become a central issue in the country's educational policy. The Ethiopian state attempted to develop a coherent and systemic language-in-education policy, although the regions have interpreted it in different ways. The intended policy, implemented fully in three regions, includes essential features of MTE. Among these are the adoption of L1-based teaching and learning strategies for the entire eight years of primary schooling and the inclusion of L2 and L3 as subjects; teacher training in the students' MT; design of school texts in different languages; location of teachers in areas where they speak students' MT; and student assessment. Although not all regions have implemented this policy fully, there is MTE for at least four years for most children, and between six and eight years in eight out of 11 regions. In Peru, a series of historical processes have led to the adoption of an IBE approach which integrates language and culture issues. However, even though the Peruvian state recognises IBE, and several policies guarantee its implementation, IBE is rather peripheral to overall education practice. In fact, many regional and local educational authorities simply ignore the implementation of vital norms, such as the employment of bilingual teachers. Thus, the Peruvian situation is very different from that of Ethiopia where the state has been committed to the implementation of MTE, even if not for eight years in all regions. If IBE currently exists in Peru it is mostly because of the work of Indigenous organisations, local NGOs and international funding agencies and of the pressures they have exerted to guarantee the design of laws and policies which recognise Indigenous peoples' rights.

Clear evidence of the state's lack of commitment to IBE is that it is basically limited to primary schools in rural areas and that it applies to no more than 18% of the schools in Indigenous communities, even though more than 30 years have passed since the first national bilingual policy was adopted. Another important indication is that only 15 teacher training colleges – among more than 300 – offer IBE specialisation, and this is basically focused on the training of primary school teachers. Furthermore, existing policies regarding admission in these colleges have prevented Indigenous students from passing the entrance examinations over the last few years.

An important lesson of this comparative analysis is that a coherent state policy adjusted to different sociolinguistic contexts can offer convincing results on the effects of MT-based education in a relatively short time, as Heugh et al.'s 2007 study clearly demonstrates. Thus, since the implementation of the 1994 Education Policy, Ethiopia has produced an extraordinary number of resources for the development of bilingual education. Furthermore, Ethiopia's research-based evidence is an important referent of the possibilities regarding MT-based teaching and learning, and can help to break down some negative myths. Heugh et al.'s study demonstrates that any MT can be used to express science, mathematics and abstract thought. This is an issue that many teachers and educational authorities in Peru do not accept and which they use to justify Spanish-based education. It also questions the widely held assumption that using the dominant language as MOI will help students gain the competencies they need to deal successfully with secondary school in this language.

In Peru, it is absolutely necessary to give priority to the development of student assessment studies which can offer evidence on the benefits of IBE. In this case, the linguistic component should be complemented with culture-related aspects which should be identified by Indigenous people. This could strengthen their participation in the ongoing regionalisation process and be an essential factor in the monitoring of the implementation of the Regional Education Projects. In more than 30 years of bilingual education, very few such studies have emerged, even though Indigenous organisations and NGOs are developing important programmes in different Andean and Amazonian regions (see Zavala 2007b).

It is also necessary to pay more attention to the different ways in which Indigenous teachers approach language learning. Their claim that their use of Spanish as MOI allows their students to learn this language naturally and to use it spontaneously cannot be simply disregarded. Even if it is true that many teachers tend to sacrifice the understanding of content for the sake of learning Spanish, it is necessary to engage them in a more thorough reflection about this issue. Instead of insisting on the sole use of the MT as MOI, it would be extremely useful to promote their participation in action research processes which could help them to analyse their actual strategies and try out new alternatives. One of these could be to complement what they are learning in Spanish as MOI through the development of Spanish classes in which they could reinforce the contents which they have studied, as López (2003: 67) suggests. Research on these issues could also help teachers to identify the differences between Basic Interpersonal Communication Skills (BICS) and Cognitive Academic Language Proficiency (CALP), suggested by Cummins (1994) and to prepare Spanish language classes aimed to aid them in the understanding of academic texts. This kind of research, complemented with student assessment, would help teachers develop new ways of using the Indigenous languages and Spanish, suitable for the particular sociolinguistic contexts in which they work.

The Ethiopian example demonstrates that the development of research-based evidence is vital in any process aimed to change widely held beliefs or misperceptions about language use. Studies of this kind would help Peruvian educational authorities, teachers and parents to understand that high levels of investment in teaching Indigenous students through the medium of Spanish offers a very low rate of return to the system. Additionally, action research could offer important insights regarding new alternatives for IBE. However, this effort should not only include teachers but also educational authorities and parents, since research evidence shows that teachers' practice is highly influenced by the multiple contexts in which they work (see McLaughlin 2001; Fink and Stoll 2001). Owing to the colonial ideology which underpins widely held beliefs about the superiority of Spanish, this evidence should be complemented with critical reflection. It would be important to include an analysis of the factors that have led to the subalternisation of Indigenous languages and cultures.

Ethiopia's main advances in MT as MOI are based on the translation of the official curriculum. In Peru this approach has been questioned and there is ongoing debate regarding the need to include Indigenous ways of producing and transmitting knowledge. This discussion has led to critical reflection regarding the concept of educational quality. Contrary to what many educators are inclined to believe, this concept is not universal or neutral. Rather, it is highly influenced by social and historical perspectives related to the notions that one may have about the person, society, life and education, as Edwards (1991) accurately highlights. Therefore, the inclusion of cultural issues in education is an important consideration where Peru and other Latin American countries can contribute to related developments in countries such as Ethiopia, a multicultural and multilingual country with more than 80 ethnic groups with distinct languages and/or dialects and cultural features.

The authors of the Ethiopian report do not discuss intercultural aspects of education in relation to bi/multilingual education; this may point towards limited concern for intercultural considerations in Ethiopia. The authors discuss educational practices in terms of socio-, psycho- and applied linguistics (Heugh *et al.* 2007: 26). In our view this may point towards a weakness in the Ethiopian situation. In the Peruvian case, apart from the above-mentioned disciplines, pedagogy and anthropology have also offered substantial contributions to the development of IBE (Ames 2001: 373). Anthropologists and educators have offered important methodological observations about Indigenous ways of learning and teaching (Trapnell 2005; García 2007). Sociolinguists working on indigenous approaches to literacy have used multidisciplinary perspectives, identifying a diversity of literacy practices and underscoring the need to approach reading and writing from a cultural and social perspective (Zavala 2002). These and other studies have supported Indigenous peoples in their claim for curricular contents that include different aspects of their cultural heritage.

Finally, even though serious limitations exist regarding the implementation of IBE in Peru, it has, without doubt, become an important platform to discuss and influence other issues in Peruvian society, such as the role of the State, democracy, citizenship, coloniality, and the role of Indigenous peoples in society. Ongoing discussions about interculturalism in Peru and other Latin American countries highlight the need for a critical analysis of the way in which the State and different social and political actors approach this concept. They stress the need for it to acknowledge the profound asymmetries that characterise Latin American social, economic and political systems and transcend the 'cultural dialogue' perspective (Fornet Betancourt 2000). Based on this approach, Tubino (2004) and Trapnell and Neira (2006) also stress the need for intercultural perspectives to go beyond the educational system and to pervade the entire state apparatus.

Notes

1 The ILO 169 Convention (http://www.ilo.org/ilolex/cgi-lex/convde.pl?C169).
2 In multigrade schools teachers attend to more than one grade; they comprise an important part of the Peruvian educational system. According to official statistics, Peru has approximately 23,419 primary multigrade schools; 96% of them are located in rural areas. 90% of rural primary schools are multigrade (Ames 2004).

References

Aikman, Sheila (1999). *Intercultural Education and Literacy*. Amsterdam/Philadelphia: John Benjamins.
Amazonas Regional Government (2007). *Proyecto Educativo Regional Amazonas 2007–2021* [Amazonas Regional Education Project 2007–2021] (AMREP). Chachapoyas: Amazonas Regional Government.
Ames, Patricia (2001). ¿La escuela es progreso? Antropología y educación en el Perú [Is school progress? Anthropology and education in Peru]. In Degregori, Carlos Iván (ed.), *No hay país más diverso. Compendio de antropología peruana*. Lima: Red para el desarrollo de las Ciencias Sociales en el Perú, 356–391.
Ames, Patricia (2004). *Las escuelas multigrado en el contexto educativo actual: desafíos y posibilidades* [Multigrade schools in the current educational context: challenges and possibilities]. Lima: GTZ-PROEDUCA.

Ayacucho Regional Government (2006). *Proyecto Educativo Regional Ayacucho: 2006–2021* [Ayacucho Regional Education Project: 2006–2021] (AYREP). Ayacucho: Ayacucho Regional Government. Regional Directorate of Education.

Chirif, Alberto (1991). Contexto y características de la educación oficial en sociedades indígenas [Context and characteristics of official education in indigenous societies]. In Zúñiga, Madelaine, Pozzi-Escot, Ines and López, Luis Enrique (eds), *Educación Bilingüe Intercultural Reflexiones y desafíos*. Lima: FOMCIENCIAS, 27–70.

Chirinos, Andrés (2001). *Atlas Lingüístico del Perú* [Linguistic Map of Peru]. Cusco: Ministerio de Educación-Centro Bartolomé de las Casas.

Chirinos, Andrés (n.d.). *Las lenguas indígenas peruanas mas allá del 2000. Una panorámica histórica* [Peruvian indigenous languages beyond 2000. An historical overview]. Cusco: Centro Bartolomé de Las Casas.

Cummins, Jim (1994). Primary language instruction and the education of language minority students. In Leyba, C. F. (ed.), *Schooling and Language Minority Students. A Theoretical Framework*. Second edition. Los Angeles: Evaluation, Dissemination and Assessment Center, School of Education, California State University, 3–46.

Cusco Regional Government (2007). *Proyecto Educativo Regional Cusco al 2021* [Cusco Regional Education Project towards 2021] (CUREP). Cusco: Participative Regional Education Council.

Cusco Regional Government (2008). *Ordenanza Regional No. 025–2007-CR/GRC. CUSCO*. Lima: El Peruano 09.05.2008.

Díaz, Hugo and Valdivia, Néstor (2007). Descentralización educativa y niveles intermedios: algunos temas pendientes sobre el rol de las UGEL [Educational decentralisation and the intermediate levels: some unsolved issues regarding the role of Local Administration Units]. In *Revista Foro Educativo. Descentralización educativa: Transfiriendo competencias a los gobiernos regionales* Año IV No. 12. Lima: Foro Educativo, 26–35.

Edwards, Verónica (1991). *El concepto de calidad en la educación.* [The concept of quality in education]. Santiago de Chile: UNESCO OREALC.

Fornet Betancourt, Raúl (2000). *Interculturalidad y globalización.* [Interculturalism and globalisation]. San José de Costa Rica: Editorial DEI.

Fink, Dean and Stoll, Louise (2001). Educational change: easier said than done. In Hargreaves, Andy, Lieberman, Ann, Fullan, Michael and Hopkins, David (eds), *International Handbook of Educational Change*. Dordrecht: Kluwer Academic Publishers, 297–321.

Fuller, Norma (ed.) (2003). *Interculturalidad y política. Desafíos y posibilidades* [Interculturalism and politics. Challenges and possibilities]. Lima: Red para el desarrollo de las ciencias sociales en el Perú.

García, Fernando (2007). *Runa hina kay. La educación familiar y comunitaria orientada al respeto en una comunidad quechua* [Runa hina kay. Family and community education oriented towards respect in a Quechua community]. D Phil. Thesis. México: Departamento de Investigación Educativa del Centro de Investigación y Estudios Avanzados del Instituto Politécnico Nacional.

Heugh, Kathleen, Benson, Carol, Bogale, Berhanu and Gebre Yohannes, Mekonnen Alemu (2007). *Final Report. Study on medium of instruction in primary schools in Ethiopia*. Addis Ababa: Ministry of Education.

Hornberger, Nancy and López, Luis Enrique (1998). Policy, possibility and paradox: indigenous multilingualism and education in Peru and Bolivia. In Cenoz, Jasone and Genesee, Fred (eds), *Beyond Bilingualism: multilingualism and multilingual education*. Clevedon: Multilingual Matters, 206–242.

López, Luis Enrique (2003). ¿Dónde estamos con la enseñanza del castellano como segunda lengua en América Latina? [How far have we advanced with the teaching of Spanish as a second language in Latin America?]. In Jung, Ingrid and López, Luis Enrique (eds), *Abriendo la escuela Lingüística aplicada a la enseñanza de Lenguas*. Madrid: PROEIB Andes, InWent Ediciones Morata, 39–71.

López, Luis Enrique (2008). Indigenous contributions to an ecology of language learning in Latin America. In Creese, Angela, Martin, Peter and Hornberger, Nancy (eds), *Encyclopedia of Language and Education*. 2nd edition. New York: Springer Science and Business Media LLC, 141–155.

López, Luis Enrique and Küper, Wolfgang (2000). *Intercultural Bilingual Education in Latin America: Balance and Perspectives*. (http://www2.gtz.de/dokumente/bib/00-1510.pdf).

López, Luis Enrique and Rojas, Carlos (eds) (2006). *La EIB en América Latina bajo examen* [IBE in Latin America Under Scrutiny]. La Paz, Bolivia: Plural Editores.

Loreto Regional Government (2005). *Proyecto Educativo Regional. Lineamientos para su construcción* [Regional Education Project. Formulation guidelines] (LOREP). Iquitos: Loreto Regional Government.

McLaughlin, Milbrey Wallin (2001). Listening and learning from the field: tales of policy implementation and situated practice. In Hargreaves, Andy, Lieberman, Ann, Fullan, Michael and Hopkins, David. *International Handbook of Educational Change*. Dordrecht: Kluwer Academic Publishers, 70–84.

Meliá, Bartolomeu (2003). El silencio de las lenguas y la palabra recuperada [The silence of languages and the recovered word]. In Solis Fonseca, Gustavo (ed.), *Cuestiones de Lingüística Amerindia*. Lima: CILA-PROEIB ANDES GTZ, Universidad Agraria La Molina, 21–36.

Ministry of Education (1972). *Política Nacional de Educación Bilingüe* [National Policy of Bilingual Education]. Lima: Ministry of Education.

Ministry of Education (1989). *Política de Educación Bilingüe Intercultural* [Policy of Bilingual Intercultural Education]. Lima: Ministry of Education.

Ministry of Education (1991). *Política Nacional de Educación Intercultural y Educación Bilingüe Intercultural* [National Policy of Intercultural Education and Bilingual Intercultural Education]. Lima: Ministry of Education.

Ministry of Education (2003). *Ley General de Educación No. 28044* [General Law of Education]. Lima: Ministry of Education.

Ministry of Education (2004). Decreto Supremo 013 [Supreme Decree 013]. Lima: Ministry of Education.

National Institute of Statistics and Data Processing (INEI) (2007). National 2007 Census. (http://censos.inei.gob.pe/censos2007/).

Oliart, Patricia and Vásquez Luque, Tania (2007). La descentralización educativa 1996–2001: la versión real de la reforma en tres departamentos andinos [Educational decentralisation 1996–2001: the real version of the reform in three Andean departments]. In *Colección Mínima 60*. Lima. Instituto de Estudios Peruanos.

Pozzi-Escot, Ines, Zúñiga, Madelaine and López, Luis Enrique (1991). *Educación Intercultural Bilingüe: Reflexiones y Desafíos* [Intercultural bilingual education: Reflections and challenges]. Lima: FOMCIENCIAS.

Salazar, Luis and Andrade, Patricia (2006). Guia para la formulación concertada del Proyecto Educativo Regional. [Guide to an agreed formulation of the Regional Education Project]. Lima: Programa de Educación Básica de la Cooperación Alemana al Desarrollo PROEDUCA-GTZ.

Serrano, Javier (2003). La enseñanza de y en lengua indígena en el marco de la educación indígena en Colombia [The teaching of and through an indigenous language in the context of indigenous education in Colombia]. In Jung, Ingrid and López, Luis Enrique (eds), *Abriendo la escuela Lingüística aplicada a la enseñanza de Lenguas*. Madrid: PROEIB Andes, InWent Ediciones Morata 213–226.

Stairs, Arlene (1988). Beyond cultural inclusion: An Inuit example of indigenous educational development. In Skutnabb-Kangas, Tove and Cummins, Jim (eds), *Minority Education: From Shame to Struggle*. Clevedon: Multilingual Matters, 308–327.

Trapnell, Lucy (1985). Veinticinco años de educación bilingüe en la Amazonía peruana [Twenty-five years of bilingual education in the Peruvian Amazon]. In Gasche, Jürg and Arroyo, José María (eds), *Balances Amazónicos. Enfoques Antropológicos*. Iquitos: CIAAP-UNAP, 121–145.

Trapnell, Lucy (2005). Alcances y retos de la educación intercultural en el nivel de inicial [Achievements and challenges for intercultural education at pre-school level]. Paper presented to the IV National Congress of Anthropological Research. Pontificia Universidad Católica del Peru. Lima.

Trapnell, Lucy (2006). Descolonizar el saber: un reto para la educación intercultural bilingüe [Decolonising knowledge: a challenge for intercultural bilingual education]. Paper presented to the VII National Intercultural Bilingual Education Congress. Chiclayo.

Trapnell, Lucy (2008a). Los retos de la formación docente intercultural bilingüe: la experiencia de FORMABIAP [Challenges of intercultural bilingual teacher training: the FORMABIAP experience]. In *Docencia y Contextos Multiculturales*. Lima: Tarea.

Trapnell, Lucy (2008b). Addressing Knowledge and Power Issues in Intercultural Education. MA Dissertation. Bath: University of Bath.

Trapnell, Lucy (2008c). La educación intercultural bilingüe en el Perú: situación actual y desafíos [Intercultural bilingual education in Peru: actual situation and challenges]. En Molina, Fidel (ed.), *Alternativas en educación intercultural. El caso de América Latina: la educación intercultural y bilingüe*. LLeida: *De Paris edicions*, Centre de Cooperació Internacional de la Universitat de Lleida, 96–122.

Trapnell, Lucy and Neira, Eloy (2006). La EIB en el Perú [IBE in Peru]. In López, Luis Enrique and Rojas, Carlos (eds), *La EIB en América Latina bajo examen*. La Paz, Bolivia: Plural Editores, 253–355.

Tubino, Fidel (2004). El interculturalismo latinoamericano y los Estados Nacionales [The Latin American interculturalism and the National States]. Paper presented to the *Foro Latinoamericano sobre Interculturalidad, Ciudadanía y Educación* [Latin American Forum on Interculturalism, Citizenship and Education]. Mexico: FLAPE.

Vigil, Nila (n.d.). *El uso asistemático de las lenguas en las mal llamadas escuelas EIB del Perú* [The unsystematic use of languages in the so called IBE schools in Peru]. Lima: unpublished manuscript.

Zavala, Virginia (2002). *(Des)encuentros con la escritura. Escuela y Comunidad en los Andes Peruanos* [(Dis)encounters with writing. School and community in the Peruvian Andes]. Lima: Pontificia Universidad Católica del Peru. Universidad del Pacífico. IEP.

Zavala, Virginia (2007a). Situación de la formación docente para la educación intercultural y bilingüe en la zona andina del Perú [The situation of teacher training for intercultural and bilingual education in the Peruvian Andean region]. In Cuenca, Ricardo, Nucinkis, Nicole and Zavala, Virginia (eds), *Nuevos Maestros para América Latina*. Madrid: Morata, GTZ and InWent.

Zavala, Virginia (2007b). Avances y desafíos de la educación intercultural bilingüe en Bolivia, Ecuador y Perú: estudio de casos [Achievements and challenges in intercultural bilingual education in Bolivia, Ecuador and Peru]. Lima: CARE and IBIS Peru.

Zavala, Virginia (2008). Derecho a la diferencia [The right to difference]. In *El Comercio*, 7.12.2008, 4–5. (http://www.elcomercio.com.pe/edicionimpresa/Html/2008-12-07/derecho-diferencia.html).

4

A CRITICAL COMPARISON OF LANGUAGE-IN-EDUCATION POLICY AND PRACTICE IN FOUR SOUTHEAST ASIAN COUNTRIES AND ETHIOPIA

Carol Benson and Kimmo Kosonen[1]

4.1 Introduction

The case of Ethiopia raises a number of issues that are relevant to a discussion of language-in-education policy and practice in Southeast Asia. Meanwhile, special circumstances in Southeast Asian countries may provide new insights for Ethiopia or other multilingual contexts. This chapter examines issues that are of interest in the Ethiopian context and in four countries of Mainland Southeast Asia – Cambodia, Lao People's Democratic Republic (Laos), Thailand and Vietnam – which share many characteristics in terms of geography, history, culture, religion and languages. Each has a majority population and an autochthonous national and/or official language, as well as diverse ethnolinguistic minority groups living within its borders, some of which have linguistic and cultural connections with majority groups in neighbouring countries.

For the purposes of this discussion, we use the term *ethnic* (or *ethnolinguistic*) *minority* to refer to a group of people who: (a) share a culture, ethnicity and/or language that distinguishes them from others; and (b) are either fewer in terms of number or less prestigious in terms of power than the predominant group(s) in the given state. Although the term may be considered problematic internationally, it is widely used in Southeast Asian contexts, where the socio-economically and politically dominant groups are easily identified, having played a role comparable to that of colonial and neo-colonial elite in other parts of the world. The term ethnolinguistic minority thus covers all those who are ethnically and linguistically different from dominant groups. Our intent is not to hide the size of these groups, many of which number in the hundreds of thousands or even millions. Dominant groups are not necessarily numerical majorities; in Laos, for example, there is evidence that the dominant group, who are ethnic Lao, make up less than half of the population (Chazée 1999; Kosonen 2007), though the government claims that 55% are ethnic Lao (Lao PDR 2007).

We use the term *non-dominant languages* (abbreviated as NDLs) to refer to the languages or language varieties spoken in a given state that are not considered prominent in terms of number, prestige or official use by the government and/or the education system. In contrast, the *dominant language* (DL) is the language of the state, spoken by the dominant group.

Finally, we use the term *first language* or L1 to refer to a language spoken as a mother tongue, vernacular, native language or home language. This term can also be problematised, since bi- or multilingual people may consider several languages their mother tongues. According to Skutnabb-Kangas (2000: 105–108), the mother tongue can be a language that a speaker: (a) has learned first; (b) identifies with or is identified with by others;[2] (c) knows best; or (d) uses most (see also UNESCO 2003: 15). In order to discuss appropriate languages for education, we would like to add: (e) a language that one speaks and understands competently enough to learn age-appropriate academic content.

We begin by introducing the region and the four country cases, going on to discuss similarities and differences in their approaches toward improving education for minority learners. We then analyse language-in-education policies and subsequent practices from a Southeast Asian perspective with reference to three key issues identified from the Ethiopian case: (1) adoption of a theoretically sound educational approach toward developing learners' first languages; (2) recognition of the negative effects on learners' languages when the dominant language is prioritised; and (3) the role of educational decentralisation in implementing L1-based education, particularly with regard to linguistically heterogeneous regions. The discussion aims to stimulate bidirectional learning between contexts to gain insights for policy and practice.

The analysis draws on both authors' experiences in language policy and practice in Southeast Asia and beyond. Kosonen, a resident of Thailand since 1998, has worked as a university teacher, researcher and consultant in multilingual education (MLE) policy and practice, and has contributed to research and informational documents for UNESCO, UNICEF and SEAMEO (Southeast Asian Ministers of Education Organization). Benson, also a contributor to UNESCO publications, has worked in teacher training, curriculum development, research and evaluation of mother tongue-based MLE in African, Latin American and Asian contexts, and recently served as technical advisor to bilingual education projects in Vietnam and Cambodia. Our data sources for this chapter include literature, policy and project documents, interviews with key informants on language-in-education issues, our own observations in the field, and information from recent conferences on multilingual education and language policies.

4.2 Language Policy and Practice in Education in Mainland Southeast Asia

Education systems in Southeast Asia tend to favour dominant ethnic groups, their cultures and their languages, and NDLs tend to be seen as a problem rather than a resource. Consequently, speakers of these languages experience inequities in access, quality, attainment and achievement in education (Kosonen 2007, 2008; Kosonen, Young and Malone 2007; Kosonen and Young 2009; UNESCO 2005, 2007a, 2008b). While educational inequity is being addressed by all four of the countries highlighted here, their approaches vary according to their unique national histories, characteristics and conditions, and they do not necessarily see development of minority languages as desirable or feasible. Another challenge in the region is that policies supportive of NDLs in education and society may exist on paper, but programme implementation is weak. The discrepancy between rhetoric and reality creates a huge challenge for educators. For that reason, we attend to both policy implementation and educational practice in this chapter.

4.2.1 Language and Ethnic Classification

Cambodia, Laos, Thailand and Vietnam all have linguistic diversity, but there are significant differences in how they perceive languages and education. Cambodia and Thailand are less centralised than the other two, and their governments are less interested in controlling the identification of ethnolinguistic groups, so their descriptions are relatively straightforward. In *Cambodia*, where 25 languages are spoken, Khmer is the most widely spoken, by approximately 90% of the population (Lewis 2009). In *Thailand*, where 85 languages are spoken, Standard Thai (based on Central Thai as spoken in the capital, Bangkok) is the de facto national and official language (ibid.). Although an estimated 50% speak Standard Thai as their first language, there is no reliable data on the extent of people's bilingualism (Kosonen 2008, 2009). Members of the dominant group tend to assume that most people speak the standard, and they often incorrectly consider Thai-related languages to be dialects or non-standard varieties of Standard Thai.

In highly centralised Laos and Vietnam, identification of ethnolinguistic groups has been less straightforward due to political ideology. In the case of *Laos*, with 49 officially recognised ethnic groups (Lao PDR 2007), there is controversy concerning the number of languages spoken (Kingsada 2003; Kosonen 2007, 2009). Lewis (2009) has estimated that there are 89 languages, while linguists and anthropologists have identified over 100 (e.g. Chazée 1999; Schliesinger 2003). These differences of opinion can be explained by the lack of comprehensive language mapping in Laos, and the fact that the government has followed a Soviet-influenced approach to the classification of ethnic groups (see e.g. Barnes 1974; Bradley 2005; Pholsena 2006) that is not necessarily based on the languages people speak.[3] Such classification involves interpretations of reality to serve political purposes, thus population data collected by governmental and non-governmental agencies do not always match.

Issues of language and ethnic classification are similar in *Vietnam*, where the government officially recognises only 53 ethnic minority groups plus the Vietnamese-speaking Kinh majority. Officials claim that Vietnamese is spoken as a first or second language by an estimated 90% of the population; meanwhile, approximately 108 languages are reported in unofficial estimates and linguistic surveys (Bui and Bui 2009; Lewis 2009; Kosonen 2004, 2009; Vu 2008; World Bank 2009), and there is evidence that many lack exposure to the Vietnamese language (Aikman and Pridmore 2001; Kosonen 2004; Trần Kiều 2002: 51–52; World Bank 2009).

The legacy of Soviet-style, top-down language planning present today in Asian countries such as China, Laos and Vietnam requires a bit of elaboration here. Whereas diverse national groups of the Soviet Union under Lenin in the 1920s were encouraged to use their own languages to learn literacy and their civic duties under socialism, Stalin saw this as a threat to collectivisation in the republics; he therefore promoted Russian as a lingua franca, withdrew support for national ethnic languages, and identified ethnic groups as needed for specific administrative purposes (Barnes 1974; Pholsena 2006; Spolsky 2004; Stalin 1950; World Bank 2009). Beginning in the 1930s there was massive development of writing systems for previously unwritten languages in the Soviet Union (Stites 1999), and by the 1950s this model had spread to China and Vietnam. However, in all three Asian nations that adopted a Marxist-Leninist ideology,[4] the Soviet approach to language planning materialised in two forms: one of clumping related languages together to form larger 'official' ethnic groups, or one of splitting up single groups into multiple ones, sometimes quite arbitrarily (Barnes 1974; Bradley 2005, 2008; Bradley and Bradley 2002; Pholsena 2006; Stites 1999; Stalin 1950; World Bank 2009).

Ethnic group classification in centralised states is relevant to this discussion because it is difficult to make effective educational decisions if language is not the basis of the classification. In areas where several languages are clumped together under one officially recognised ethnicity with a designated language – which is often the most prominent 'dialect' – learners who speak other languages are not likely to benefit from what the government calls mother tongue-based education. While all non-dominant groups may suffer from such practices, the most rural and isolated (who rarely have access to other languages) urgently require recognition of their true language proficiency so that they can benefit from educational programmes. In the case of Vietnam, for example, many members of larger and more urbanised ethnic groups such as Hoa, Muong and Tay speak Vietnamese competently, and some have even lost their heritage languages. Studies show that enrolment of these minority groups in primary education is on a par with or even higher than that of the dominant Kinh (Kosonen 2006: 244–245), and there is evidence that even educational achievement may be comparable to that of the Kinh (World Bank 2009). However, this is because data are disaggregated by group classification rather than by language(s) spoken (World Bank 2009; see also La 1993 on rural/urban differences in Vietnamese competence among Tay). The successful performance of these groups in Vietnamese-medium education is used by many to argue against mother tongue-based education. They have not recognised the serious weakness in their reasoning, that is, that competence in the language of instruction is a key factor in educational success.

4.2.2 Origins of Mother Tongue-based Education in the Region

In Southeast Asia, the idea of education based on learners' first languages has historically come from two sources: religion and communism. Beginning with religious sources, both Buddhism and Christianity have made use of local languages. Buddhist temples in a number of linguistic minority areas have taught boys and men literacy in their first languages in addition to Pali.[5] One example of this practice is among Khmer speakers in Vietnam, and another example involves several ethnolinguistic minority groups in Myanmar and Thailand (Kosonen 2005, 2009; Owen 2008). As in some African contexts (Spolsky 2004), Christianity in Southeast Asia has promoted the use of NDLs in education, particularly in literacy. Many of the writing systems for minority languages developed by Christian missionaries in the 19th and 20th centuries are still in use in non-formal education throughout the region (Kosonen 2008; Smalley 1994). Likewise, the current official *quoc ngu* orthography for writing Vietnamese was developed by Portuguese and French missionaries in the 17th century (Lo Bianco 2002).

In addition to religion, the influence of Marxist-Leninist ideology in Vietnam and Laos brought about strong top-down support for the use of local languages, particularly in Vietnam (Vu 2008; Kosonen 2009; World Bank 2009). However, what seems to be policy support on paper has mainly remained rhetoric and has not yet been implemented to its full potential.

Current thinking about people's home languages has been positively influenced by applied academic study and by development agencies supporting educational development. In Thailand, academic institutions such as the Research Institute for Languages and Cultures of Asia of Mahidol University and the Linguistics Department and the Linguistics Institute at Payap University have played a major role in minority language development during the past few decades. As a result, few languages in Thailand remain unwritten. These institutions have also begun to apply their linguistic research to multilingual education. In Vietnam, government agencies such as the National Institute of Linguistics in Hanoi as well as the Vietnamese National Front for Liberation have developed writing systems for previously unwritten languages. The National Institute of Linguistics has also been involved in developing learning and teaching materials in NDLs. In Cambodia and Thailand, non-governmental agencies (NGOs) have played a key role in language development (Kosonen and Young 2009).

4.2.3 *Some Challenges of Writing Non-dominant Languages*

Mainland Southeast Asia is a diverse region in terms of orthographies and scripts. The four national languages of the countries discussed here use four different scripts. We will first define key orthographic concepts, and note that there is a great deal of confusion over these concepts in the region. First, we consider a script to include 'the graphic form of the units of a writing system (e.g. the Roman vs. the Cyrillic alphabet)' (Crystal 1999: 299). A modified Roman script with additional diacritics marking tone is used for Vietnamese. The Khmer, Lao and Thai languages have their own scripts, all of which are based on southern Indian scripts that came to Southeast Asia with Buddhism, and all of which have been adapted to create orthographies for minority languages. A writing system is 'a system of visual marks on a surface' to record a spoken language (ibid.: 368), and this is the basic requirement for a language to be used in mother tongue-based literacy. An orthography is 'a standardized system for writing a particular language. The notion includes a prescribed system of spelling and punctuation' (ibid.: 244), implying that efforts have been made by stakeholders to agree on a set of rules that all will follow. Finally, an alphabet is a set of symbols, usually letters, which represent the sounds of the language; this is the most common approach to developing writing systems for previously unwritten languages, an approach which lends itself to teaching literacy through phonics approaches.

Decision-making on orthographies for NDLs has varied by country. Cambodia, for example, has a system of government approval for any proposed orthographies; there have been discussions but limited capacity to implement such a system in Laos; and Thailand has a somewhat laissez-faire approach where any orthography can be developed and used, though some basic guidelines exist. Finally, Vietnam's top-down ethnic classification (as mentioned above) has led to centralised choice of the most prestigious 'dialect' as the basis for language development in general, and orthography development is denied for those language communities not officially recognised by the government. Observers have noted that this approval process is so bureaucratic that it practically blocks all efforts of orthography development (SEAMEO 2009).

There are a number of issues related to writing NDLs in the region. First, the existence of ancient scripts for some languages (such as Cham, Kammuang, Mon, Sgaw Karen and Shan) raises differences of opinion. Some members of these speech communities want to continue using the original scripts, while others favour orthographies based on the scripts of the respective national languages. Governments would naturally prefer the latter, presumably for assimilationist reasons, along with the widespread belief that literacy transfer from L1 to L2 is facilitated by use of the same script. There is occasionally opposition from non-dominant groups who feel their own scripts best represent them linguistically or in other ways. Likewise, some speakers of national languages such as Khmer, Lao or Thai oppose the writing of NDLs in 'their' scripts, which must 'break spelling rules' to reflect different sound systems and tones. Western research demonstrates that effective transfer happens across writing systems (Bialystock 2001; Kenner 2004) and suggests that use of the same script is not likely to resolve learning challenges where the two languages are highly divergent in terms of phonemes, tones and so on. However, we must acknowledge that where technical and financial resources are lacking, imperfect solutions may pave the way for non-dominant languages to be used in education.

Another issue is that many orthographies for NDLs were developed in the 19th and 20th centuries by Western missionaries who lacked proper linguistic training (Smalley 1994). These less-than-ideal writing systems are still in use, and people have developed strong attachments to them, making it difficult to propose revisions. Competition is also generated where orthographies were developed in parallel by different actors, and/or where there are different varieties of the same language (ibid.). Another type of competition arises with languages that are spoken in more than one country, especially where governments are promoting use of the same scripts used for their respective national languages. In the worst cases, the choice of a script that differs from that of the national language can be seen by a government as a secessionist political act.

Government promotion of national scripts may be implicit or explicit in the process of developing NDLs. In Cambodia, for example, all new orthographies developed over the past decade have adapted the Khmer script (UNESCO 2007b: 56–59, 2008b: 44–47), ostensibly for the presumed benefits of transferring to Khmer literacy. It is not clear whether other options were considered (such as the Roman script used to write some of these same languages across the border in Vietnam) or whether local language communities could voice their preferences. In Thailand all new orthographies are supposed to be adaptations of the Thai script, but no approval system exists. For example, recent efforts to develop an orthography for Patani Malay, one of the largest NDLs of Thailand, have been challenged by differences of opinion regarding three different scripts: Arabic, Roman and Thai (Paramal 2008; Premsrirat 2008, 2009).

These experiences would suggest that while the politics of decision-making cannot be avoided, orthographical development processes would be well served to take linguistic and educational perspectives into greater consideration (UNESCO 2008b: 187–189 provides some useful suggestions). From a rights-based perspective it seems clear that decisions about any specific language should involve stakeholders from the speech community.

4.2.4 Current Thinking about Languages in Education

The idea of using minority languages for formal instruction is relatively new in the region. Most L1 use has been in the non-formal sector, at the early childhood or adult literacy levels, implemented by NGOs and civil society organisations. However, the past two decades have seen a growing interest in the region;

apart from Laos and a few other countries; in using learners' first languages for learning, both for rights-based reasons and to improve educational access and quality, especially for girls, in light of Education for All and the UN Millennium Development Goals (see, e.g., Benson 2004, 2005; Kosonen and Young 2009; UNESCO 2008b). In many cases, international agencies have been at the forefront of promoting mother tongue-based education, and governments have been somewhat receptive; however, decision-makers' levels of awareness, along with public attitudes, lag behind.

While recognising that certain ethnic minority groups are not benefiting from schooling in national languages, ministries of education tend to focus on national languages rather than considering greater use of the L1. Typical approaches include teaching the national language to minority learners beginning as early as possible, preferably at the preschool level, and 'strengthening' national language skills with minimal use of the L1. The concept of bilingual or multilingual education is often misunderstood; for example, 'bilingual education' often makes people think of programmes teaching the national language and English. Even the weakest models with minimal use of the mother tongue (such as oral L1 use by unqualified 'teaching assistants') have been considered bilingual education. Fortunately, despite these challenges, we can report that pilot bilingual projects using NDLs for instruction have been initiated in three of our four case countries, excepting only Laos.

4.3 Points from the Ethiopia Report: Comparison and Contrast with the Asian cases

There are three points raised in the research done on Ethiopian language-in-education policies and practices that are interesting to compare and contrast with the four case countries from the Southeast Asia region. The first point is how national policy affects practice; the second is how policies and practices can have unintended effects; and the third is how centralisation versus decentralisation can affect policy implementation. All three points from the Ethiopia report (see also Benson et al., this volume) provide lessons in themselves, but when analysed from a Southeast Asian perspective offer additional insights.

4.3.1 Theoretically Sound Language-in-Education Policy

The Ethiopian national language-in-education policy calls for L1-based teaching and learning for the entire eight years of primary schooling, while the national language (L2) and the international language (L3) are taught as subjects. To a great extent this policy represents a theoretically sound approach to language and learning because it builds on the learner's strongest language for initial literacy, development of reading and writing skills, and academic content instruction. The teaching of two additional languages as subjects is also theoretically sound, though

Heugh *et al.* (2007) point out that in practice teachers are not prepared to use second or foreign language methodology, nor do they generally have the language competence they need to teach effectively, at least not in the L3 (English). Further, the switch to English as a medium of instruction at the secondary level is not adequately supported because current conditions do not generate sufficient English language competence on the part of students or teachers. Despite these limitations, the primary education policy represents theoretically sound decision-making, and demonstrates that Ethiopia has made a serious commitment that few other multilingual countries have to building a strong foundation in each learner's best language. What remains is for the Ethiopian government to back its policy with appropriate resource allocation, and for development agencies and donors to support national languages (including NDLs) in addition to international ones.

The effectiveness of the Ethiopian policy is supported by higher results from the grade 8 national examinations in the regions that have implemented the full eight years of L1-medium schooling. While it is unlikely that language of instruction is the only factor in play, the cases of the three fully compliant regions (along with others that have followed national policy to a great degree) give us a rare view of what can be done educationally when the school invests in long-term development of the learners' first language.

The Ethiopian language-in-education policy at primary level provides a strong example for Asian countries, most of which lack coherent language-in-education policies of any kind. Further, those countries with good written policies have, up to now, failed to implement them. In this section we look at language-in-education policies by country, beginning with the weakest on a continuum ranging from no policy or practice to more encouraging combinations of policy-related communications and practice.

No explicit policy or practice: Laos has no explicit policies relating to the use of NDLs. The Constitution stipulates the use of the Lao language and script for official purposes, which has been interpreted as allowing *only* the national language in education (Kosonen 2007, 2009; Leclerc 2010a). Until recently, this interpretation has blocked efforts by various agencies to introduce NDLs into education, and made the debate very sensitive politically. The situation has improved in recent years, at least on paper, as the current National Socio-Economic Development Plan (NSEDP 2006) promotes the use, learning and teaching of the roughly 20 NDLs for which there are existing orthographies. The plan also promotes the further development and maintenance of NDLs in the context of targeting the poorest areas of the country. The country's Education for All (EFA) plan actually recommends the use of minority learners' mother tongues to improve educational quality (Lao PDR 2005), as do regional SEAMEO initiatives (2009) in which Lao officials have participated. As yet there are no NDLs in education, though small-scale pilot projects in pre-primary and primary education are being considered in collaboration with international agencies. Whereas support for NDLs over the years has come more often from Lao People's Revolutionary Party leaders rather than Ministry of Education officials, the latter have indicated at recent regional conferences that attitudes toward NDLs are becoming increasingly positive.

It would thus be timely for Laos to consider lessons from Ethiopia, especially since the contexts are quite similar in terms of linguistic diversity. Laos might adopt 'enabling' language policies for non-dominant groups which would give them the right to use their languages in society as well as at home. This could be supported by adoption of an explicit language-in-education policy to spell out the parameters for NDL use, using the excellent model for primary education provided by Ethiopia.

Enabling policy, little implementation: In Vietnam, the use of ethnic minority languages in society and in education is supported by policy documents including all four Constitutions as well as various education laws, decrees, decisions and circulars, yet few mention the language of instruction (Bui and Bui 2009; Kosonen 2009; Vu 2008). Thus Vietnamese remains the main language of instruction at all levels of education, even in predominantly non-Vietnamese-speaking areas, though NDLs are taught as school subjects in some of these areas. Contradictory decisions have been issued at different times by different sources, creating a great deal of confusion regarding actual policy (Kosonen 2004, 2009). The terminology has also been confusing, leading to quite different conceptions of bilingual education and the study of NDLs from those found in neighbouring countries. According to Vu (2008) there were attempts to use NDLs alongside Vietnamese in the 1960s and 70s, but shortages of NDL-proficient teachers blocked effective implementation, and current lack of awareness implies that little useful experience in bilingual education was gained at that time.

Despite the apparent gaps between policy and practice, recent initiatives in formal education have been enabled by policies supporting NDLs. One large-scale, internationally funded government programme focusing on ethnic minority schooling makes use of non-professional teaching assistants who speak local languages; another small-scale pilot preschool programme supported by Save the Children recruits children's mothers to work as teaching assistants to promote oral communication in the L1. There are also some preschool programmes that start with learners' home languages (Hoang 2009). These programmes represent small steps toward improving education for NDL speakers because they facilitate oral communication, but they are a far cry from developing L1 literacy as a basis for learning additional languages and academic content. L1 literacy is, however, the aim of a recent pilot programme developed by the ethnic minority research department of the Ministry of Education and Training, supported by UNICEF with Benson's technical assistance. This programme has adopted a fully bilingual approach based on mother tongue development from preschool through the end of primary in schools in three provinces, representing three NDLs – Hmong, J'rai and Khmer (Bui and Bui 2009; SEAMEO 2009; Vu 2008).

If any of these recent educational initiatives lead to change, the gaps between policy and practice in Vietnam may be narrowed. While Ethiopian education policy already provides theoretical support for bilingual literacy such as Vietnam is now piloting, Ethiopia might also learn from Vietnam in its efforts to implement such a strong L1 approach throughout the country.

Some policy support, some action: In both Cambodia and Thailand, activities using NDLs have preceded policy-making by government authorities. These countries have allowed latitude for non-dominant groups and their partners, i.e. advocacy groups, academics and NGOs, to experiment with the use of NDLs in society and in education, at least to some extent. Over the past few years, both countries have undergone processes of review of previously unwritten policies regarding language-related matters, though no theoretically sound approaches such as Ethiopia's has been proposed by either Ministry of Education. There is reason for optimism in Thailand, however, as two pilot projects have intensified debate at the Ministry of Education as well as in the media (Aluyufri 2008; Kosonen 2008; SEAMEO 2009; Tienmee 2009). Particularly significant is an action research project supported by Mahidol University in southern Thailand using Patani Malay, a widely spoken NDL, for long-term literacy development and learning (*Bangkok Post* 2010a, 2010b; Premsrirat 2008, 2009). A policy conference organised in Bangkok in July 2008 (NLP 2008) appears to have paved the way for approval of Thailand's first written language and language-in-education policy, which was signed by the prime minister in 2010. It is not yet clear how the new policy will be operationalised, but at least it provides – for the first time – official support for NDLs in education in Thailand.

In Cambodia, L1-based educational projects of various scales have been operating for a decade, and now progress is being made in formal education. The most influential programmes of bilingual education in formal and non-formal education, supported by CARE International and International Cooperation for Cambodia (ICC) in the Ratanakiri province, have served as a model for further initiatives by the Ministry of Education, Youth and Sports (MoEYS) (CARE International Cambodia 2004; Kosonen 2007; Middelborg 2005; Noorlander and Ven 2008; Siren 2009; Sun 2009; Thomas 2002; UNESCO 2007b). As a result, MoEYS has adopted a system to approve newly developed NDL orthographies and learning materials, and as of 2010 has a plan to implement primary bilingual education in five provinces (see below for elaboration).

Even if the contexts of language development, materials and teacher training in multilingual Southeast Asia do not currently support strong first language-based schooling, a language-in-education policy like Ethiopia's provides an example to work toward. This would mean that these highly centralised education ministries would need to loosen their grip somewhat, at least in ethnic minority areas. Both Thailand and Vietnam would be well served to take Ethiopia's example, since recent efforts demonstrate their willingness to invest in greater L1 development than most other initiatives in the region.

4.3.2 Negative Effects of Prioritising the Dominant Language

A problematic issue raised in the Ethiopian context is how further schooling in the dominant language can hurt L1-based programmes and indeed overall learning by sending the wrong signals about which language really counts. Whether intentional or unintentional, the following Ethiopian Ministry of Education activities send the message that *only* English is important:

- the teaching of English L3 as a subject beginning at grade 1, instead of teaching the widely spoken national language, Amharic (which begins later and has not been given enough attention);
- the costly and time-consuming work of the English Language Improvement Project to raise the English language proficiency of all primary teachers (albeit insufficiently, through minimal contact hours and a 'distance education' component);
- the use of (South African) English-medium educational television programming at the secondary level, also at great expense;
- the exclusive use of English as the language of testing for secondary and tertiary education, including teachers' college entrance examinations.

(Heugh et al. 2007; Benson et al., in this volume)

It also appears that the difficulties experienced by Ethiopian learners of the international language – whether caused by teaching approaches, teachers' own limited competence or overall limited meaningful exposure to the language, or a combination of these – have convinced parents and policymakers that even more time needs to be allotted to foreign language study at the primary level. The Ethiopian case demonstrates that over-emphasis of a dominant language, in this case an international one, impacts negatively on earlier levels of education even where there is policy support for L1 development.

The Ethiopian study (ibid.) indicates that at least two language learning 'myths' are in operation in Ethiopia: 'the more dominant language, the better' and 'the earlier, the better'. Unfortunately these myths are also alive and well in the Southeast Asia region, despite evidence that ethnolinguistic minority learners are severely disadvantaged by submersion in the dominant language. In the case of Vietnam, for example, the persistent low achievement and high dropout and failure rates associated with ethnic minority learners (Kosonen 2006; World Bank 2009) tend to generate calls for even more Vietnamese language in the schooling system, and at earlier stages. As Kosonen found in 2004, 'Most officials interviewed for this study see the teaching of Vietnamese to ethnic minority children as early as possible as the best way to alleviate the situation' (p. 5). Similarly, at a national teleconference on ethnic minority education in 2008, the Minister of Education said that the education level of ethnic students was 'obviously' not in line with that of students in the rest of the country, and that the way to improve their level was through 'good and effective preparation in the Vietnamese language' (Teleconference 18 April 2008, unofficial translation).

Vietnamese beliefs and attitudes are, unfortunately, not unique in the Southeast Asia region. When faced with better quality data on education, now disaggregated by ethnicity or region, education officials must acknowledge that speakers of NDLs do not generally perform as well as speakers of dominant languages (Kosonen and Young 2009; Lao PDR 2004). Yet the solutions they propose, like Vietnam's, buy into myths about language, focusing on more, better, earlier use of dominant languages instead of bilingual approaches. In our experience, apart from some academics, representatives of international organisations and 'enlightened' civil servants, many stakeholders including parents in Cambodia, Thailand and Laos believe in the same myths. To illustrate the issues we will continue with the example of Vietnam.

In Vietnam, priorities of the MOET Department of Ethnic Minority Education are the extension of Vietnamese-medium preschool programmes into ethnic minority areas, investment in boarding schools for younger ethnic minority learners, the improvement and 'strengthening' of Vietnamese language learning at all levels, and the creation of a sixth primary year so that Vietnamese can be 'mastered' (EMED 2007). It may be noted that boarding and 'semi-boarding' (weekday) schools were expanded for ethnic minority learners according to an official 1996 decision by the prime minister as a strategy to provide equal educational opportunities for ethnic minority people, especially in mountainous areas (Kosonen 2004; Trần Kiều 2002; World Bank 2009). They have normally been directed toward older students and are associated with improved school success, mostly because children (especially girls) are released from family and farm labour and given conditions such as electric lights for evening study (Ministry of Education and Training 2008); however, it was reported at the above-mentioned teleconference in April 2008 that boarding schools are now being put into operation for all ages. Despite the government message that boarding schools are run under local leadership, the entire effort is reminiscent of historical treatment of Native Americans, Aboriginal Australians or the Sámi in Northern Europe, whose children were taken out of their social and cultural environments so that they could be more easily assimilated both culturally and linguistically (e.g. Dunbar and Skutnabb-Kangas 2008).

None of these activities prioritising the learning (and 'mastery') of Vietnamese attend to people's own languages and their potential for promoting learning. Reviewing the Ethnic Minority Education division's priorities, the only reference to ethnic minority languages is their study as subjects in upper primary and possibly secondary school (EMED 2007). Further, in contrast to the many remarks at the 2008 teleconference about improving ethnic minority learners' Vietnamese language proficiency, there was only one brief mention of the teaching of ethnic minority languages when the speakers called for a symposium to 'study and clarify the scientific issues' (Teleconference 18 April 2008, unofficial translation). The public dialogue has tended to neglect existing activities promoting learning through the learners' first languages, including the study of ethnic minority languages as subjects, the use of teaching assistants from the communities, or the UNICEF-supported bilingual pilot project. It remains unclear if the focus on Vietnamese is based on conscious efforts to undermine non-dominant languages or simply a lack of understanding of how the mother tongue contributes to language (and all other) learning.

One lesson that can be taken from the Ethiopian case is that language-in-education policy and practice should cover the entire educational system coherently, and that the aims of schooling should be balanced against the existing language competence of students and teachers as well as what is humanly possible based on principles of language learning. Examination of the Ethiopian policy could be a useful first step for educational stakeholders in Cambodia, Thailand and Vietnam to better understand how L1 development contributes to the learning of content and additional languages. If and when Laos also starts working on L1-based education, this balance between aims and possibilities will also be worth serious consideration.

4.3.3 Policy Implementation and Decentralisation

Each region of Ethiopia can make decisions about how the languages of the region will be used in primary education, with reference to an enabling and theoretically sound national language-in-education policy. As already noted, three regions have fully applied the national policy, while others are in various stages of compliance. This implies that each region can make decisions based on a realistic understanding of the languages spoken in each district, town and school and develop support mechanisms for curriculum, materials and teacher training. In this section we will explore three aspects of decentralisation as they apply to Southeast Asia: first, how decentralisation may facilitate the practice of first language-based bilingual or multilingual education; second, how decentralisation may work against good practice if dominant regional languages are given priority over learners' mother tongues; and third, how linguistic heterogeneity may or may not be dealt with effectively.

Decentralised decision-making that facilitates policy implementation: Decentralisation appears to have resulted in appropriate language use in schooling in many regions of Ethiopia, or at least those with one or two main languages. Each regional education bureau seems best suited to knowing which languages and language-related resources are needed, and some decision-making can be devolved to district and local levels as needed. Heugh *et al.* (2007) provided an example of local empowerment when they described a school-based decision that one teacher would specialise in the international language, allowing the others to teach in the mother tongue. For the still highly centralised Southeast Asian countries, this is a particularly important lesson learned, and one which could positively impact on current policies and practices, including ongoing pilot programmes. In fact, decentralisation of educational administration is currently being debated throughout the region, but progress is particularly slow in Laos and Vietnam.

Effective decentralisation implies that a number of conditions be met, and these conditions may or may not be present in Ethiopia or in the four Southeast Asian countries discussed here. One condition is a certain level of capacity for decision-making on the part of education staff; another is a budget so that decisions can be carried out. An additional condition is some level of understanding of participatory democracy so that communities are involved in the decision-making processes that affect them.

As we have noted, local decision-making in the Southeast Asian country cases is quite constrained at this point, especially in Vietnam and Laos. However, the concept of 'local curriculum' may provide some latitude for local participation and empowerment in all four cases, particularly because the local curriculum component includes local language study. The local curriculum component is widely used in low-income countries, including to some extent the four countries discussed here, in an effort to make centralised national curriculum more relevant to all learners. It is usually open to local interpretation and may include local skills, traditional and cultural practices, visits by community experts, and so on. In our experience, because little direction is provided from the central level, schools are often at a loss as to what to teach in this component, so local language study can become a concrete solution to the problem. In Vietnam, the study of NDLs is allowed to take up as much as 20% of the primary education curriculum, even if only a handful of NDLs are currently available. Laos has a similar 20% allowance for local curriculum that could be used for L1 teaching if resources were made available. In Cambodia, government primary schools have a 2-hour slot per week for 'local life skills', and curriculum of this component is developed at the local level (Jan Noorlander, personal communication 25 September 2008). Finally, as of 2001, Thailand allows schools to tailor up to 30% of the learning time to local needs, and in some minority areas this slot is used for teaching local languages, including Bisu, Chong, Mon, Lahu Shi and Patani Malay (Kosonen 2007). Regarding local curriculum, what might be needed are linguistic resources, including language learning materials and teachers with the appropriate L1 literacy.

Decentralisation as a danger to mother tongue-based education: While most Ethiopian regions indicate they are working in a few languages, Benson *et al.* (this volume) report that even the regions most consistent with national policy are not working with *all* learners' first languages. The three regions that have been most compliant with the eight-year mother tongue primary schooling policy are relatively homogeneous, that is, they represent large groups that speak the regional or 'nationality' language: Afan Oromo in Oromiya region, Somali in Somali region and Tigrinya in Tigray region. It is clearly more challenging to implement eight years of L1-based schooling in regions characterised by greater linguistic diversity. Yet even the so-called homogeneous regions should be encouraged to meet the needs of speakers of less widely spoken minority languages. The case of India should send up a warning flag for Ethiopia: decentralised language policy may not meet everyone's needs if it allows only the 'larger' regional languages to dominate – this is only a regional reproduction of the official language decision at national level, rather than truly serving the educational needs of all learners (Jhingran 2008).

Decentralisation might also be problematic if local stakeholders are not well informed as to the pedagogical and linguistic reasoning behind L1-based schooling. In Ethiopia, Heugh *et al.* (2007) found that parental pressure had forced provincial education authorities – often against their better judgement – to bring English-medium instruction into upper primary in their provinces, despite the fact that national policy supported L1 instruction through the end of grade 8. The researchers attribute this pressure to belief in myths about languages and learning as well as to the negative impact of prioritising English beginning in grade 9. As mentioned above, when it comes to dominant languages, myths like 'the earlier, the better' are alive and well throughout Southeast Asia, so some direction from educational decision makers could be useful.

If decentralisation can create obstacles to first language-based schooling, can a more centralised approach be recommendable? We have already noted that the Southeast Asian cases tend to operate in highly centralised ways, even if there is some latitude for L1 teaching within the local curriculum component. The Ethiopian case could conceivably be seen as effective decision-making at the central level, due to adoption of a sound language-in-education policy for primary schooling and promotion of its implementation in the country's administrative regions. The Ethiopian study shows that that national policy implementation could be strengthened if more financial and technical support from the centre were earmarked for the development of materials and curriculum in 'nationality languages' (L1s) and/or if implementation of the national policy were promoted in some way by the Ministry of Education, possibly by providing incentives to the administrative regions. This might work in centralised cases such as Vietnam and Laos, if their governments are willing to take a stand on L1-based learning and promote it countrywide. The Vietnamese Ministry of Education and Training currently requires all educational pilot projects to submit their curricula for review and approval, which demonstrates the degree of control maintained by the centre at this time; this could be positive if the L1-based bilingual pilot demonstrates results that the government is interested in expanding beyond the three languages and three provinces of the pilot.

Thailand may be more comparable to Ethiopia in that the central government has more of a guiding and less of a controlling role in education. Because the new language policy has yet to be interpreted in education, language-of-instruction issues have not yet been concretised. As mentioned above, at least two L1-based multilingual projects have contributed to policy development, run not by the Ministry of Education but by a university and a local NGO in collaboration with local education authorities (*Bangkok Post* 2010a, 2010b; Premsrirat 2008, 2009; SEAMEO 2009; Tienmee 2009). However, there are centralised leanings even in Thailand; for example, an apparently effective primary non-formal MLE pilot in Pwo Karen (Kosonen and Young 2009; UNESCO 2007b; UNESCO 2008b) was abruptly closed down by high-level provincial education authorities in 2007 for undisclosed reasons. As in the case of Vietnam, it is difficult to know whether the educational focus on the dominant language to the detriment of non-dominant languages is due to conscious effort or to lack of understanding of learning processes, or even due to alternative educational goals that do not correspond to international development initiatives.

Dealing effectively with linguistic heterogeneity at the regional, district and local levels: As noted above, decentralised decision-making in Ethiopia has permitted many regions to adopt appropriate languages in education, but the regions with most diversity are having greater difficulty adopting and implementing policies that resemble the national policy. Decentralisation implies budget decisions as well, and regions serving more ethnolinguistic groups logically require greater investment of human and financial resources for linguistic development, curriculum and materials development and teacher training. The concept of decentralising services and decision-making is relatively new in Southeast Asia; however, there have been useful lessons learned regarding diversity in Cambodia and Thailand, particularly in the non-formal education sector, which could offer new insights for Ethiopia. Before discussing these cases, we will refer to a special case in the Pacific region: that of Papua New Guinea, a small country with approximately 850 languages.

The case of Papua New Guinea (PNG) is important in at least two ways: (1) the extent to which NDLs are used in education, and (2) the positive impact of language use in non-formal education (NFE) on formal education. No other country uses NDLs as widely as does PNG, where around 400 languages are currently used as media of instruction, and where the goal is to include all 850 (Ikupu 2008). While the system is not without problems, many of the technical and practical challenges in terms of language development and multilingual education have been sorted out, and the quality of teaching and learning is reportedly much improved since the days of English-medium schooling (Ikupu 2008; Kaplan and Baldauf 2003; Klaus 2003; Litteral 2005; Siegel 1997). The PNG case shows that linguistic diversity is not an obstacle to first language-based MLE if the political will exists. The PNG experience is particularly instructive because of the multiplicity of languages that are being used. However, the challenge remains to extend L1-based education beyond preschools and the early primary grades.

NDLs entered the PNG education system through a nationwide non-formal education (NFE) movement in the 1980s, requiring a massive endeavour to develop previously unwritten languages. This was done in a highly decentralised manner, with NGOs and local communities playing essential roles. NFE programmes in pre-primary and adult literacy thus introduced hundreds of local languages for instruction in their respective communities. Based on positive experiences in NFE, and extending basic education beyond L1-based preschools, a reform of the formal education system was undertaken in the 1990s, replacing English with the mother tongue as medium of instruction in the first three grades. L1-based preschools and primary schools are run by local communities, who make decisions about the language of instruction, form committees to oversee the community schools, choose teachers and otherwise contribute to the operation of the schools (ibid.).

Beginning with NFE is an effective strategy which could be recommended for Ethiopian languages that have not yet been brought into formal schooling. At a 2003 meeting in Laos to explore educational language policy and practice, Benson called NFE a 'foot-in-the-door strategy' because it is not as threatening to education officials as formal education, and because it provides opportunities to develop writing systems and materials in local languages that can be further developed for use in formal settings (Benson 2003). Indeed, interest and experience in L1-based learning has been generated in both Thailand and Cambodia by starting with adult literacy and/or alternative out-of-school youth programmes in learners' first languages.

In Cambodia, NFE has had a positive effect on national education policy as well as on formal education (Kosonen 2009; Thomas 2008). Until recently the language of instruction at all levels of education was Khmer, the national language. In the late 1990s five minority languages were introduced as languages of instruction in the Eastern highlands in pilot projects run by international NGOs in close collaboration with provincial education authorities and local ethnic minority communities. These projects in the NFE sector gave birth to formal education experimentation using the newly created orthographies (CARE International Cambodia 2004; Middelborg 2005), and a system for orthography and materials approval was developed within MoEYS.

The positive results of L1-based schooling in Cambodia have influenced policy as stated in the Education Law of 2007, which gives local authorities the right to choose the language(s) of instruction in areas where Khmer Lue languages, i.e. NDLs related to Khmer as well as Jarai, an unrelated NDL, are spoken, representing a giant step towards acknowledging the importance of NDLs to education in Cambodia (Noorlander and Ven 2008; Thomas 2008; UNESCO 2008b). Unfortunately, the law fails to mention the three largest NDLs – Cham, Chinese and Vietnamese – which are commonly considered immigrant languages that do not deserve the same treatment as Khmer-related NDLs. Earlier drafts of the law gave some ethnic minority groups the right to mother tongue instruction in early primary school, but the final version is weaker. Fortunately, additional NDLs are now being developed, and the CARE community schools model (Noorlander and Ven 2008; Siren 2009; Sun 2009) has provided the basis for a set of official guidelines recently adopted by the MoEYS. These guidelines delineate how bilingual primary education will be expanded in the formal system of five highland provinces beginning in 2011 (MoEYS 2010).

One important reason for the great strides made in Cambodia is the major role played by minority communities themselves. This role has been carried out mainly through the formation of Language Committees (for NFE projects) and Community School Boards (for formal programmes). These groups consist of community members who have worked in language development, curriculum development, the production of learning materials in NDLs, and the identification of local teachers with appropriate linguistic and cultural knowledge (Siren 2009; Sun 2009; Thomas 2002). The CARE-supported Highland Children's Education Project (HCEP) is a particularly good example of what can be done when the community 'owns' the project through School Board activities, including community governance of project schools, employment (at reasonable salary levels) of local teachers who are native speakers of the learners' languages, and community participation in developing mother tongue-based curriculum (Care International Cambodia 2004; Noorlander and Ven 2008). Many of these options could be explored in the more diverse regions of Ethiopia, in an attempt to put language development and school decision-making into the hands of those whose children will benefit.

4.4 Discussion and Conclusions

In many ways, the Ethiopian national language-in-education policy is unprecedented among multilingual low-income countries, including its adherence to language and learning principles, its far-reaching implications for all mother tongues, and its effective implementation on a regional level. Ethiopian policy and practice are advanced relative to the stage of development of multilingual education in Mainland Southeast Asia, as our case countries have illustrated. At the same time, this discussion has raised a number of issues that suggest that there are things these two different parts of the world have in common, as well as things they – and we – can learn from each other.

To begin with, it seems there is a focus common to all four of the Southeast Asian cases and Ethiopia on improving dominant language competence among speakers of non-dominant languages. This is understandable given the power and importance of dominant languages for further education, employment and so on. However, a single-minded focus on the L2 (and L3 in the Ethiopian case) causes stakeholders to forget the usefulness of the L1 for learning all curricular content as well as additional languages, never mind seeing multilingualism and multiliteracy as appropriate educational goals in themselves.

In the case of the Mainland Southeast Asian countries, the focus on dominant language 'strengthening' has thus far prevented mother tongue-based multilingual education from existing as anything but NFE programmes and pilot projects in the formal systems of education. It is difficult to know if this is due to lack of information about languages and learning, concerns about national unity, ethnocentrism of dominant groups, concerns about financing, discrimination against non-dominant languages and their speakers, or a combination of these. In the cases of Laos and Vietnam there are written policies favouring language rights for all. The case of Ethiopia would suggest that understanding can be gained as multilingual education is implemented and people see the results, particularly if testing is done in both/all languages. However, Ethiopia is also focused on improving learners' competence in a more distant dominant language, English, and the choice of English as medium of instruction for secondary schooling has had a decidedly negative effect on the use of learners' mother tongues at lower levels. All indications are that despite Ethiopia's policy promoting a solid L1-based education, decision makers are confused about how the L1 supports learning in general – as well as how it supports learning an L2 and even an L3. Further, even if such understandings can be reached, practical challenges must be overcome with regard to teachers' language competence and use of relevant language teaching methods.

However, the Ethiopian case may serve as a model for the Southeast Asian countries in a few respects. First, it demonstrates that a theoretically sound approach to mother tongue-based multilingual education, at least at the primary level, is possible in a multilingual country and can lead to educational success for speakers of non-dominant languages. Next, it shows how decentralisation can lead to effective decision-making regarding implementation of mother tongue-based education, with the caveats that technical and financial supports may still be needed from the centre, and that heterogeneous regions should not limit learners to schooling in a single regional language. It also seems that in the Ethiopian context there has been respect for people's choices about their own languages and traditional scripts, though we do not know enough about community involvement in linguistic decision-making to say that this has happened in all cases. Finally, the Ethiopian policy of teaching through a foreign language at the secondary level, despite its negative effects on the system, demonstrates the difficulties of promoting official language learning along with academic content learning. We hope that the Southeast Asian countries can find lessons learned in all of these aspects of the Ethiopian experience, and that Ethiopian decision makers can continue searching for ways to make the education system more effective.

At the same time, the Southeast Asian case countries have offered us some unique perspectives that can contribute to discussions in both Ethiopia and other contexts. One is how Soviet influence regarding languages and ethnicity has played out in present-day countries such as Vietnam and Laos, where identifying and unpackaging language competence(s) can be challenging due to sometimes arbitrary top-down ethnic classification, but where at the same time there are written rights-based policies in place that may enable mother tongue-based schooling to be implemented. Ethiopia was also exposed to Soviet influence during the long-running Marxist DERG regime in the 1970s and 80s (Leclerc 2010b), which could at least partially explain its language-in-education policy favouring non-dominant languages. Even with this shared influence on attitudes toward NDLs, Ethiopia has gone further than Vietnam, and even than China, in implementing its written policy. This comparison demonstrates that an understanding of the history and politics of each context can provide insights into attitudes towards languages and education.

The Southeast Asian cases might offer Ethiopia some lessons on the use of different scripts as the basis for orthographies for previously unwritten languages that are to be introduced in the education system. A quick count of the 34 languages mentioned in Heugh *et al.* (2007, Appendix E) found that they were almost equally divided between two main scripts, Sabean/Ethiopic (used for two dominant languages, Amharic and Tigrinya) and Roman (used for Afan Oromo, another widely spoken Ethiopian language), but that many languages are shifting to Roman. We do not have enough information to compare the linguistic, political or religious factors involved, but we do know that Southeast Asian languages use a variety of scripts. Our cases have demonstrated the many practical considerations involved in developing orthographies, which would suggest that any remaining unwritten Ethiopian languages might consider using neighbouring languages as the basis of their own orthographies, and that the local language communities be involved in decision-making (e.g. UNESCO 2008b: 187–189). In addition, the Southeast Asian cases demonstrate that orthography development can and should take place even for less widely spoken NDLs, so for Ethiopia to implement its language-in-education policy consistently, it cannot focus only on its largest languages.

A final lesson from the Southeast Asian country cases is how initial introduction of non-dominant languages in non-formal education facilitates bringing mother tongue-based programmes into the formal sector. Early childhood education and adult literacy have both played important roles throughout Asia and the Pacific region in initiating processes of language development, creating bodies of literature written in non-dominant languages, and alerting people to the potential these languages offer in promoting learning. Some Southeast Asian preschool programmes targeting ethnic minority children have surprisingly high enrolment rates. In Thailand, for example, more than 75% of children 3 to 5 years old are enrolled in early childhood education programmes (UNESCO 2008a). As this is a net rate, it stands out as a remarkable achievement, even globally. Nevertheless, many children who speak NDLs do not have access to early childhood education programmes, even in Thailand. Clearly the potential of NFE programmes for serving as platforms for introducing mother tongue-based education has not been fully exploited even in Southeast Asia, and this point could be made with the heterogeneous Ethiopian regions that have not yet found ways to bring learners' mother tongues into formal schooling.

In conclusion, this discussion of language-in-education policy and practice in Ethiopia and in Mainland Southeast Asia has brought about useful comparisons and contrasts, highlighting lessons learned and offering new insights into how L1-based programmes can be fostered. This demonstrates how much can be learned when multilingual countries share their experiences, and it suggests that there is a need for greater 'South–South' cooperation and collaboration in non-dominant language issues. We are reminded that insights into local problems and challenges can be found in far-away Southern contexts in addition to the obvious neighbouring countries or high-income Northern countries. We hope that this chapter, and the whole book for that matter, represent important steps towards this kind of collaboration among academics and practitioners alike.

Notes

1   The authors are grateful to David Bradley, Carl Grove, Jan Noorlander, Dennis Malone, Susan Malone, Richard Noonan, Vu Thi Thanh Huong and our editors for their invaluable comments and insights.
2   This reference to 'others' is problematic in the Southeast Asian context, where governments have classified people according only to officially recognised ethnic groups.
3   Similar classification has been practised in regions without direct Soviet influence, but in this region the phenomenon is found in China, Laos and Vietnam, where Soviet models were emulated.
4   Although North Korea also follows a variation of Marxist-Leninist ideology, planning for NDLs has not been an issue due to its relatively homogeneous population.
5   Pali is an ancient Indo-Aryan language in which the earliest Buddhist scriptures are written; it is also the liturgical language of Theravada Buddhism, the majority religion in Cambodia, Laos and Thailand.

References

Aikman, Sheila and Pridmore, Pat (2001). Multigrade schooling in 'remote' areas of Vietnam. *International Journal of Educational Development* 21: 6, 521–536.

Aluyufri, Sabe Abdullah (2008). *The role of Patani Malay in Thailand's Southern Border Provinces.* Paper presented at the International Conference on National Language Policy: Language Diversity for National Unity. Bangkok, 4–5 July 2008.

Bangkok Post (2010a). *Bilingual education pays off for border students,* 11 July 2010.

Bangkok Post (2010b). *Teaching in the mother tongue,* 3 October 2010.

Barnes, Dayle (1974). Language planning in mainland China: standardization. In J. A. Fishman (ed.), *Advances in Language Planning.* The Hague: Mouton, 457–477.

Benson, Carol (2003). *Mother tongue-based bilingual education: What, why and how?* Paper commissioned by Sida for Symposium on Language of Instruction, UNICEF. Vientiane, Laos, October 2003.

Benson, Carol (2004). *The importance of mother tongue-based schooling for educational quality.*

Background paper for EFA Global Monitoring Report 2005. In UNESCO, *Education for All: The Quality Imperative*. Paris: UNESCO. (www.efareport.unesco.org)

Benson, Carol (2005). *Girls, educational equity and mother tongue-based teaching*. Policy document, 14 pp. Bangkok: UNESCO Bangkok. (http://unesdoc.unesco.org/images/0014/001420/142079e.pdf)

Bialystock, Ellen (2001). *Bilingualism in Development: Language, Literacy and Cognition*. Cambridge: Cambridge University Press.

Bradley, David (2005). Introduction: Language policy and language endangerment in China. *International Journal of the Sociology of Language* 173, 1–23.

Bradley, David (2008). *Language policy for transnational minorities of Thailand*. Plenary presentation at International Conference on National Language Policy: Language Diversity for National Unity. Bangkok, 4–5 July 2008.

Bradley, David and Bradley, Maya (2002). Language policy and language maintenance: Yi in China. In Bradley, David and Bradley, Maya (eds), *Language Endangerment and Language Maintenance*. London: Routledge Curzon, 77–97.

Bui, Thi Ngoc Diep and Bui, Van Thanh (2009). Language-in-education policies in Vietnam. In Kosonen, Kimmo and Young, Catherine (eds), *Mother Tongue as Bridge Language of Instruction: Policies and Experiences in Southeast Asia*. Bangkok: Southeast Asian Ministers of Education Organization (SEAMEO), 109–116.

CARE International Cambodia (2004). Cambodia: Highland Children's Education Project (HCEP), Ratanakiri Province. In King, Linda and Schielmann, Sabine (eds), *The Challenge of Indigenous Education: Practice and Perspectives*. Paris: UNESCO, 113–122.

Chazée, Laurent (1999). *The Peoples of Laos: Rural and Ethnic Diversities*. Bangkok: White Lotus.

Crystal, David (1999). *The Penguin Dictionary of Language*. 2nd edition. London: Penguin.

Dunbar, Robert and Skutnabb-Kangas, Tove (2008). *Forms of education of Indigenous children as crimes against humanity?* Expert paper written for the United Nations Permanent Forum on Indigenous Issues (PFII). New York: PFII. [On the PFII site: 'Presented by Lars-Anders Baer, in collaboration with Robert Dunbar, Tove Skutnabb-Kangas and Ole Henrik Magga'] (http://www.linguistic-rights.org/tove-skutnabb-kangas/Forms_of_education_of_indigenous_children_as_crimes_against_humanity.pdf)

EMED (2007). *Functions and responsibilities of the Ethnic Minority Education Department* (pursuant to Decision No. 4499/QD-BGD DT dated 23 August 2007 of Education and Training Minister). Official English translation presented at the Consultative Workshop on Ethnic Minority Education in Hanoi on 1 December 2007.

Heugh, Kathleen, Benson, Carol, Bogale, Berhanu and Gebre Yohannes, Mekonnen Alemu (2007). *Final Report: Study on Medium of Instruction in Primary Schools in Ethiopia*. Research report commissioned by the Ministry of Education, Addis Ababa, September to December 2006.

Hoang Thi Thu Huong (2009). A mother tongue-based preschool programme for ethnic minority children in Gia Lai, Vietnam. In Kosonen, Kimmo and Young, Catherine (eds), *Mother Tongue as Bridge Language of Instruction: Policies and Experiences in Southeast Asia*. Bangkok: Southeast Asian Ministers of Education Organization (SEAMEO), 180–187.

Ikupu, Andrew (2008). *Papua New Guinea: One model of mother tongue and MLE policy in education*. Plenary presentation at the Second International Conference on Language Development, Language Revitalization and Multilingual Education in Ethnolinguistic Communities. Bangkok, 1–3 July 2008. (http://www.seameo.org/_ld2008/document.html)

Jhingran, Dhir (2008). *India: Language situation and language-in-education policies.* Plenary presentation at the Second International Conference on Language Development, Language Revitalization and Multilingual Education in Ethnolinguistic Communities. Bangkok, 1–3 July 2008. (http://www.seameo.org/_ld2008/document.html)

Kaplan, Robert B. and Baldauf, Richard B. (2003). *Language and Language-in-Education Planning in the Pacific Basin.* Dordrecht: Kluwer.

Kenner, Charmian (2004). *Becoming Literate: Young Children Learning Different Writing Systems.* Stoke-on-Trent: Trentham Books.

Kingsada, Thongphet (2003). Languages and ethnic classification in the Lao PDR. *Waalasaan Phasaa Lae Xiwit/Language and Life Journal* 1/2003, 24–39.

Klaus, David (2003). The use of indigenous languages in early basic education in Papua New Guinea: A model for elsewhere? *Language and Education* 17: 2, 105–111.

Kosonen, Kimmo (September 2004). *Language in Education Policy and Practice in Vietnam.* Commissioned study. Hanoi: UNICEF.

Kosonen, Kimmo (2005). Education in local languages: Policy and practice in South-East Asia. In *First Language First: Community-based Literacy Programmes for Minority Language Context in Asia, 96–134.* (http://unesdoc.unesco.org/images/0014/001402/140280e. pdf)

Kosonen, Kimmo (2006). Multigrade teaching among ethnic minority children: the language issue. In Cornish, Linley (ed.), *Reaching EFA through Multi-grade Teaching: Issues, Contexts and Practices.* Armidale, NSW Australia: Kardoorair Press, 239–258.

Kosonen, Kimmo (2007). Vernaculars in literacy and basic education in Cambodia, Laos and Thailand. In Liddicoat, Anthony J. (ed.), *Issues in Language Planning and Literacy.* Clevedon, UK: Multilingual Matters, 122–142.

Kosonen, Kimmo (2008). Literacy in local languages in Thailand: Language maintenance in a globalised world. *International Journal of Bilingual Education and Bilingualism* 11: 2, 170–188.

Kosonen, Kimmo (2009). Language-in-education policies in Southeast Asia: an overview. In Kosonen, Kimmo and Young, Catherine (eds), *Mother Tongue as Bridge Language of Instruction: Policies and Experiences in Southeast Asia.* Bangkok: Southeast Asian Ministers of Education Organization (SEAMEO), 22–43.

Kosonen, Kimmo and Young, Catherine (eds) (2009). *Mother Tongue as Bridge Language of Instruction: Policies and Experiences in Southeast Asia.* Bangkok: Southeast Asian Ministers of Education Organization (SEAMEO). (http://www.seameo.org/images/stories/Projects/2009_MotherTongueBridgeLang/MT_compendium_Final_Book-08-05-09.pdf)

Kosonen, Kimmo, Young, Catherine and Malone, Susan (2007). *Promoting Literacy in Multilingual Settings.* Bangkok: UNESCO. (http://unesdoc.unesco.org/images/0015/001507/150704e.pdf)

La Cong, Y. (1993). Tieng Viet trong doi song cac dan toc thieu so [Vietnamese in the life of ethnic minority people]. *Nhung van de chinh sach ngon ngu o Viet Nam [Language Policy Issues in Vietnam],* NXB KHXH, Hanoi.

Lao PDR (2004). *Lao National Literacy Survey 2001: Final Report.* Ministry of Education. Department of Non-formal Education. Bangkok: UNESCO, Asia-Pacific Regional Bureau for Education. (http://www.unescobkk.org/ips/ebooks/documents/LaoNatL-iteracy2001/loasLiteracy.pdf)

Lao PDR (2005). *Education for All (EFA) National Plan of Action 2003–2015.* Ministry of Education. Bangkok: UNESCO Bangkok.

Lao PDR (2007). *Population Census 2005.* Vientiane: National Statistics Centre. (http://www.nsc.gov.la/PopulationCensus2005.htm)

Leclerc, Jacques (2010a). Laos. In *L'Aménagement Linguistique dans le Monde [Language Planning Around the World].* Quebec: TLFQ, Université Laval. (http://www.tlfq.ulaval.ca/axl/asie/Laos.htm)

Leclerc, Jacques (2010b). Éthiopie. In *L'Aménagement Linguistique dans le Monde [Language Planning Around the World].* Quebec: TLFQ, Université Laval. (http://www.tlfq.ulaval.ca/axl/afrique/ethiopie.htm)

Lewis, M. Paul (ed.) (2009). *Ethnologue: Languages of the World,* 16th edition. Dallas, TX: SIL International. (http://www.ethnologue.com/)

Litteral, Robert (2005). Vernacular education in Papua New Guinea. Commissioned background paper for EFA Global Monitoring Report 2005. EFA Global Monitoring Report 2005. In UNESCO, *Education for All: The Quality Imperative.* Paris: UNESCO. (www.efareport.unesco.org)

Lo Bianco, Joe (2002). Vietnam: Quoc Ngu, colonialism and language policy. In Gottlieb, Nanette and Chen, Ping (eds), *Language Planning and Language Policy: East Asian Perspectives.* Richmond: Curzon, 159–206.

Middelborg, Jørn (2005). *Highland Children's Education Project: A Pilot Project on Bilingual Education in Cambodia.* Bangkok: UNESCO.

Ministry of Education and Training (2008). *The Transition of Ethnic Minority Girls from Primary to Secondary Education.* Hanoi: MOET/UNICEF/UNESCO/UNGEI.

Ministry of Education, Youth and Sport (26 August 2010). Guidelines on the implementation of bilingual education programs for indigenous children in highland provinces (No. 2972). Phnom Penh: MoEYS.

NLP (2008). *International Conference on National Language Policy: Language Diversity for National Unity.* Organised in Bangkok on 4–5 July 2008 and sponsored by the Royal Institute of Thailand, Ministry of Education, Australian Education International, SEAMEO, UNICEF, UNESCO, SIL International, UNICEF and Thai Airways.

Noorlander, Jan and Ven, Churk (2008). *Cambodia's Highland Community Education Program.* Paper presented at the Second International Conference on Language Development, Language Revitalization and Multilingual Education in Ethnolinguistic Communities. Bangkok, 1–3 July 2008. (http://www.seameo.org/_ld2008/document.html)

NSEDP (2006). *National Socio-Economic Development Plan (2006–2010).* Vientiane, Committee for Planning and Investment, Lao People's Democratic Republic, October 2006.

Owen, Robert Wyn (2008). *Language use, literacy and phonological variation in Khuen.* Unpublished MA Thesis in Linguistics. Chiang Mai: Payap University.

Paramal, Waemaji (2008). *Success and challenges in developing a writing system for Patani Malay.* Paper presented at the International Conference on National Language Policy: Language Diversity for National Unity. Bangkok, 4–5 July 2008.

Pholsena, Vatthana (2006). *Post-war Laos: The Politics of Culture, History and Identity.* Singapore: Institute of Southeast Asian Studies.

Premsrirat, Suwilai (2008). Language for national reconciliation: Southern Thailand. *EENET – Enabling Education. Special Edition: Language.* Issue 12, August 2008, 16–17. (http://www.eenet.org.uk)

Premsrirat, Suwilai (2009). *Bilingual education for national reconciliation in Southern Thailand: A role for Patani Malay and Thai.* Paper presented at SEAMEO's regional meeting on the dissemination of project results and identification of good functioning models, 'Project on Mother Tongue as Bridge Language of Instruction in Southeast Asian Countries: Policy, Strategies and Advocacy'. Bangkok, 24–26 February 2009.

Schliesinger, Joachim (2003). *Ethnic Groups of Laos*. Vols 1–4. Bangkok: White Lotus.

SEAMEO (2009). *Project on Mother Tongue as Bridge Language of Instruction in Southeast Asian Countries: Policy, Strategies and Advocacy*. Proceedings of the regional meeting on the dissemination of project results and identification of good functioning models. Bangkok, 24–26 February 2009. Bangkok: Southeast Asian Ministers of Education Organization (SEAMEO).

Siegel, Jeff (1997). Formal vs. non-formal vernacular education: The education reform in Papua New Guinea. *Journal of Multilingual and Multicultural Development* 18: 3, 206–222.

Siren, Un (2009). The mother tongue as a bridge language of instruction in Cambodia. In Kosonen, Kimmo and Young, Catherine (eds), *Mother Tongue as Bridge Language of Instruction: Policies and Experiences in Southeast Asia*. Bangkok: Southeast Asian Ministers of Education Organization (SEAMEO), 148–152.

Skutnabb-Kangas, Tove (2000). *Linguistic Genocide in Education – or Worldwide Diversity and Human Rights?* Mahwah, NJ: Lawrence Erlbaum Associates.

Smalley, William A. (1994). *Linguistic Diversity and National Unity: Language Ecology in Thailand*. Chicago, IL: University of Chicago Press.

Spolsky, Bernard (2004). *Language Policy*. Cambridge: Cambridge University Press.

Stalin, Joseph (1950). Marxism and Problems of Linguistics. Published in the June 20, July 4, and August 2, 1950 issues of Pravda. In J. V. Stalin: *Marxism and Problems of Linguistics*, Foreign Languages Publishing House, Moscow. (http://www.marxists.org/reference/archive/stalin/works/1950/jun/20.htm)

Stites, Regie (1999). Writing cultural boundaries: National minority language policy, literacy planning, and bilingual education. In Postiglione, Gerard A. (ed.), *China's National Minority Education*. New York: Falmer, 95–130.

Sun, Neou (2009). Education policies for ethnic minorities in Cambodia. In Kosonen, Kimmo and Young, Catherine (eds.), *Mother Tongue as Bridge Language of Instruction: Policies and Experiences in Southeast Asia*. Bangkok: Southeast Asian Ministers of Education Organization (SEAMEO), 62–68.

Thomas, Anne (2002). Bilingual community-based education in the Cambodian highlands: A successful approach for enabling access to education by indigenous peoples. *Journal of Southeast Asian Education* 3 (1), 26–58.

Thomas, Anne (2008). *Community ownership strengthens multilingual nonformal education in the Cambodian Highlands*. Paper presented at the Second International Conference on Language Development, Language Revitalization and Multilingual Education in Ethnolinguistic Communities. Bangkok, 1–3 July 2008. (http://www.seameo.org/_ld2008/document.html)

Tienmee, Wanna (2009). *The Mon-Thai bilingual project, Wat Wang Wiwekaram School, Kanchanaburi province*. Paper presented at SEAMEO's Regional Meeting on the Dissemination of Project Results and Identification of Good Functioning Models, 'Project on Mother Tongue as Bridge Language of Instruction in Southeast Asian Countries: Policy, Strategies and Advocacy'. Bangkok, 24–26 February 2009.

Trần Kiều (2002). *Education in Vietnam: Current State and Issues*. Hanoi: Thế Giới Publishers.

UNESCO (2003). *Education in a Multilingual World*. UNESCO Education Position Paper. Paris: UNESCO. (http://unesdoc.unesco.org/images/0012/001297/129728e.pdf)

UNESCO (2005). *First Language First: Community-based Literacy Programmes for Minority Language Context in Asia*. Bangkok: UNESCO. (http://unesdoc.unesco.org/images/0014/001402/140280e.pdf)

UNESCO (2007a). *Advocacy Kit for Promoting Multilingual Education: Including the Excluded*. Bangkok: UNESCO Asia and Pacific Regional Bureau for Education, 5 booklets. (http://unesdoc.unesco.org/images/0015/001521/152198e.pdf)

UNESCO (2007b). *Mother Tongue-based Literacy Programmes: Case Studies of Good Practice in Asia*. Bangkok: UNESCO Asia and Pacific Regional Bureau for Education. (http://unesdoc.unesco.org/images/0015/001517/151793e.pdf)

UNESCO (2008a). *Education for All Global Monitoring Report 2008: Education For All By 2015: Will We Make It?* Paris: UNESCO. (http://unesdoc.unesco.org/images/0015/001548/154820e.pdf)

UNESCO (2008b). *Improving the Quality of Mother Tongue-based Literacy and Learning. Case Studies from Asia, Africa and South America*. Bangkok: UNESCO Asia and Pacific Regional Bureau for Education. (http://unesdoc.unesco.org/images/0017/001777/177738e.pdf)

Vu, Thi Thanh Huong (2008). *Ethnic minority languages in Vietnam: Policy and implementation issues*. Paper presented at the Second International Conference on Language Development, Language Revitalization and Multilingual Education in Ethnolinguistic Communities. Bangkok, 1–3 July 2008. (http://www.seameo.org/_ld2008/document.html)

World Bank (2009). *Country Social Analysis: Ethnicity and Development in Vietnam*. Washington, DC: The International Bank for Reconstruction and Development/The World Bank

5

MLE AND THE DOUBLE DIVIDE IN MULTILINGUAL SOCIETIES

Comparing Policy and Practice in India and Ethiopia

Ajit Mohanty

5.1 Introduction

Questions of maintenance of diversity – biological as well as cultural – are often met with gross ideological rhetoric in the modern world. In most cases, the state commitments are seldom translated into reality; the gaps between ideology, policies, plans and ground level implementation are quite appalling. Skutnabb-Kangas (2000) shows how the state policies and actual practices in respect of languages lead to loss of linguistic diversity by denial of linguistic human rights in education and various forms of neglect of minority mother tongues. The world's linguistic diversity is threatened as never before; 90% of the existing languages are predicted to disappear by the end of the current century. While maintenance of linguistic diversity depends on a host of complex factors, use of languages in education is seen as a powerful force in survival and development of languages (Fishman 1991; Skutnabb-Kangas 2000). Thus, language policies and practices in education throughout the world need to be examined and assessed both for their immediate consequences for quality of education and their long-term impact on maintenance or loss of linguistic diversity. The Ethiopian study of language-in-education issues (Heugh *et al.* 2007) is a positive example of such an exercise with significant implications and lessons far beyond the immediate context of Ethiopian education. This chapter seeks to examine aspects of the Indian language policy and practice in education in light of this insightful study of the role of languages in education in Ethiopia. In this comparative reflection, we focus on two broad themes: the language-in-education policy and the challenges for multilingual education (MLE). It is shown that multilingualism in India as well as other South Asian countries is characterised by a hierarchical relationship among languages with some languages giving their speakers greater power and access to resources compared with other languages. At a macro level, this hierarchical multilingualism is broadly structured as a double divide – one between English, the elite language of power, and the major regional languages; and, the other, between the regional languages and the dominated languages of the Indigenous and tribal[1] minorities. In the absence of a clear language policy in education, the complex processes of negotiating the linguistic double divide are reflected in the positioning of English, Hindi, regional majority languages and other Indigenous/ minority languages in education and educational practices in respect of these languages in the multilingual hierarchy. The marginalisation and educational neglect of Indigenous, tribal and minority (ITM) languages lead to educational failure, capability deprivation and poverty of the minority linguistic groups, particularly the tribal mother tongue speakers (Mohanty 2008a). Some recent attempts to deal with language disadvantage of tribal children in India, through experimental programmes of multilingual education, are briefly analysed in view of the Ethiopian findings.

5.2 The Double Divide and Language Policy in Education

Multilingual societies are generally characterised by hierarchical power relationships among languages and their speakers. Some languages empower their speakers giving them privileged access to resources whereas others contribute to marginalisation and disadvantage for the community of their users. Large-scale social neglect and discrimination have led to impoverishment of languages and loss of linguistic diversity all over the world. Chances of survival and development of many languages are severely restricted due to their exclusion from significant domains of power, official recognition, legal and statutory use, trade, commerce and education. Such neglect and prolonged deprivation strip languages of their instrumental vitality and contribute to their cumulative weakness which is often used to justify further neglect that continues to make them weaker in a vicious circle of language disadvantage (Mohanty *et al.* 2009: 278–291). With English as the dominant language in post-colonial India, as in South Asia and other parts of the world, the linguistic hierarchy has created major power gaps in the society which can be seen as a double divide (Mohanty 2010) between English and major languages and between major languages and the ITM languages.

In Pakistan, of the three official languages – English, Urdu and Sindhi – English is the language of power and Urdu is promoted as the language of nationalism and identity whereas nearly 72 other languages are struggling for a place in the hierarchy (Rahman 1998). Thus, there is a clear divide between English and Urdu (as well as other major languages including Sindhi and Punjabi), on one hand, and another divide between the major languages and minor ones, on the other. Nepal has over 100 languages out of which Nepali is promoted as the major national language (Nurmela, Awasthi and Skutnabb-Kangas in this volume). Nevertheless, English is the language of the elite, popular aspirations and power. This has created a three-tiered hierarchy with English at the top, Nepali in the middle and other languages at the bottom. Bengali nationalism and rejection of Urdu dominance were major forces leading to the creation of Bangladesh as a separate nation with Bengali as the only official language. However, English is clearly the elite language with greater power compared to Bengali. There are over 39 other languages in Bangladesh, which remain neglected and marginalised (Mohanty 2007). In Bhutan, the major state language is Dzongkha, with English occupying a major and preferred place in the language-in-education policy of the country. In the current debate over the National Educational Framework of Bhutan, the primacy of English remains unquestioned and the dominant place of Dzongkha is assured, whereas the role of nearly 29 other languages in education remains uncertain (Royal Education Council, Bhutan and iDiscovery Education 2009).

The linguistic double divide in South Asian countries shows two typically common characteristics: (a) English is the major language of power, and (b) one or few national level languages have a dominant status, symbolically supported as the language(s) of national identity. Thus, English is the most sought after language in South Asia but, oddly enough, it is never viewed as a language of national identity (Dasgupta 1993). In fact, in these South Asian countries, English has established itself as the most powerful language, often benefiting from competing linguistic identities and assertions. The conflicts between Hindi and Tamil (as well as other Indian languages) in India, between Sinhala and Tamil in Sri Lanka, between Urdu, Punjabi, Sindhi and major languages of other communities in Pakistan, and between Urdu and Bengali in Bangladesh have helped English to the position of power.

While English has dominated the major languages of national and regional communication in South Asia, the influence of these languages themselves has remained limited to their dominance over ITM languages. They have failed to counter the growing dominance of English partly because of conflicting interests and identities. As a result, there is a divide between English and major/dominant national languages, which Ramanathan (2005a) calls the English–Vernacular divide. The other linguistic divide is between the dominant national languages and the ITM languages and it is characterised as the Vernacular–Other divide (Mohanty 2010). Mohanty (2010) has analysed the nature and implications of the double divide in Indian society.

Like India (and the other South Asian countries), Ethiopia can also be seen as having a double divide situation with a chasm between English, which is evidently the most sought after language, and Amharic and another between Amharic and the other mother tongues. In both countries, the dilemma of choice of language-in-education centres on the need to balance between English and the languages of national and regional identities. In both India and Ethiopia, there is a popular demand for English. The number of English-medium private schools in India is rapidly increasing; nearly 25% of the schools in India are private English-medium schools. Government-run schools teach English only as a language subject unlike Ethiopia where English is also used as a medium of instruction (MoI) with popular demand to bring English MoI to earlier grades. The popular demand in both the countries for English is related to its instrumental value in the globalising world and to what Heugh *et al.* (2007) call the 'washback' effect of promoting English in education. Higher and technical education in India (as also in Ethiopia) is almost exclusively in English as the MoI and this strengthens the popular view that competence in English is essential for educational success.

The dominant role of English and popular aspirations to acquire the language cannot be ignored and, at the same time, language policy and practice in education must accommodate the nationalistic and regional identities emotionally associated with mother tongues. In India, the regional languages as well as Hindi serve the need to assert nationalism for the majority and they take over the role of mother tongues in the conflict between Indigenous and exogenous languages. Hence, as is evident from the various modifications to the Three Language Formula[2] (TLF) of the Government of India (see Mohanty 2008b, for discussion), the rhetoric of mother tongue in the policy debate is hijacked by the dominant regional languages and, in the process, the claims of the ITM languages are easily neglected without much concern. As Panda (2009: 121) notes, official languages of the states in India are treated as 'default mother tongue of all children' and ITM languages are often stigmatised as dialects.

Lack of clarity in the distinction between regional language and mother tongue, as in the TLF, reinforces the Vernacular–Other language divide. It formalises the imposition of the regional or state languages, including Hindi and other major languages (such as Oriya, Telugu, Tamil, etc.) as the teaching language or MoI on minority and tribal language children, whose MT is not the regional language. The subsequent modifications of the TLF sought to address this anomaly, by suggesting the use of tribal languages as languages of early schooling for tribal children. However, this provision in the TLF as well as other policy documents 'mostly remained untranslated into practice' (Mohanty 2006: 247) and ITM languages have remained neglected and marginalised, caught in the underside of the Vernacular–Other language divide.

Thus, in both India and Ethiopia, the gaps between language policy and practice in education arise out of the compulsion to assert national and Indigenous identities without sacrificing the aspirations for better English. The Ethiopian study belies this compulsion to prioritise competence in English as a major indicator of quality education. It is true that the broader objectives of education and classroom achievement are also taken as indicators of quality education but the acquired competence in English remains the major benchmark.

This compulsion also guides how the linguistic double divide in India is negotiated; achievement in English in school, even in regional language-medium government schools, is a major factor guiding policy. Recent policy decisions in most of the states in India show the national obsession to strengthen the presence of English in school practices. Some states, such as Andhra Pradesh, have decided to start English-medium sections in the government-run schools. The National Knowledge Commission of India (2009) has recommended that teaching of English needs to move down to the first year of schooling in all government schools in order to 'democratise' English. English is now taught in grade 1 in the government schools, at least as a second language, in a majority of the states in India. As in Ethiopia, practices in Indian states tend to bring English to earlier grades and, in some cases such as the *Kendriya Vidyalaya* (Central School) system, English is used to teach 'prestigious subjects' like mathematics and science whereas Hindi or other languages are used to teach the 'less prestigious' subjects like history and social sciences. Hindi used to be the second language subject in most non-Hindi states in India. Now it has been replaced by English and it is relegated to the position of a third language subject in most states. The National Curricular Framework (NCERT 2005) recommends teaching through mother tongue but does not see any problem with early teaching of English. This is where the language policy and practice in education needs to be informed by the findings of the Ethiopian study to realise that quality teaching of English is not achieved at the cost of mother tongues; rather, strengthening of mother tongues must be viewed as a necessary condition for quality teaching of English.

The Vernacular–Other language divide impacts on Indian education by disadvantaging ITM language communities, pushing them into submersion education in the dominant languages and progressively invisibilising these languages in schools. School programmes deny children's rights to use their mother tongues and have a clear subtractive effect on them. At the national level, while all of the 22 languages listed in the Constitution of India as official languages are used as languages of teaching or MoI and as school subjects, the use of other languages in schools has declined over the years (Mohanty 2008b). In 1970, the number of languages taught as subjects in schools was 81 and, by 1998, it had declined to 41. In the primary grades (grades 1 to 5), the actual number of languages used as MoI declined from 43 in 1990 to 33 in 1998. Thus, only 11 of the languages not listed as official languages of India are used as MoI in primary grades. Mother tongues get only rhetorical support in policy documents in India, including the Constitution of India (http://www.india.gov.in/govt/constitutions_of_india. php; see Mohanty (2006, 2008b) for discussion). The Constitution of India (Article 350A) calls for 'adequate facilities for instruction in the mother tongue at primary stage of education to children belonging to minority groups'. However, the Indian federal policy in respect of languages in education was never categorically stated and, as indicated earlier, the TLF remained just an unsure formula falling well short of a clear policy document. In fact, the TLF, initially intended to deal with the divergent language-in-education practices in different regions in India by suggesting a uniform pattern of three languages in school education, opened up many more issues than it solved. The built-in ambiguities in respect of mother tongues and regional languages and lack of a clear stand in respect of Hindi and English contributed to the chaos in the applications of the formula across the states in India. Further, education is a concurrent topic in India, which means that the central and the state governments have joint jurisdiction over education. This has led to divergent state practices (and varying interpretations of federal recommendations such as the TLF), as in the case of Ethiopia. The recent Right of Children to Free and Compulsory Education Act 2009 (http://edu-cation.nic.in/Elementary/free%20and%20compulsory.pdf) passed by the Indian Parliament provides for education for 6 to 14 year olds as a right but it fails to guarantee education in mother tongues; Article 29 (2) (f) of the Act (Chapter V) says, 'medium of instruction shall, *as far as practicable*, be in child's mother tongue' (emphasis added).[3] This has led to a lot of protests from language rights activists in India. For example, Panda (2009: 122) states that 'the right to education needs to be linked to the right to receive education in one's preferred language'.

The increasing dominance of English in education in India and Ethiopia (and many other countries in the world) raises some issues in respect of language policy and practice in education, which continue to be in flux, seeking to accommodate to divergent linguistic interests. The trilingual or multilingual policy in Ethiopia regulates the use of the mother tongue as medium of instruction, particularly at the primary level, learning of the national language Amharic as a subject, and transition to English as an international language at grade 9 (and also 7 and 5, in reality). However, the actual practices in the states in respect of the point of intro-duction of English in the school programme are quite divergent. Further, it seems the distinction between teaching of a language as a school subject and using it as the medium of teaching is clearly maintained in the Ethiopian policy. The Indian policy formulations, such as the TLF, lack clarity in this respect. The Ethiopian policy is trilingual based on the mother tongue, Amharic and English except for Amharic mother tongue students for whom it is bilingual. The Three Language Formula in India, besides failing to differentiate between language as a school subject and as a medium of teaching, also resulted in anomalies in respect of the number of languages for students in school education. By suggesting teaching in tribal languages, the TLF virtually becomes a four-language formula for tribal children – tribal mother tongue, major state language, English and Hindi. For the Hindi mother tongue students, learning of another Indian language was suggested but never implemented, reducing the TLF to a bilingual formula for these chil-dren. Turning back to the question of English in education, it remains a foreign language both in India and in Ethiopia; it is neither a mother tongue (except for a small community of Anglo-Indian speakers in India) nor a widely used sec-ond language for most people. In terms of language education policy, schools in Ethiopia are required to switch to English medium by grade 9, although in prac-tice this occurs earlier in some regions. In India, the issue of English as an Indian language or a foreign language continues to be debated (Dasgupta 1993) mostly from urban upper- and middle-class perspectives. In reality, however, English has a very limited presence in rural and tribal areas, and culturally it is an alien language for most people in India. This makes the pedagogy of English a formidable challenge to which Indian responses are grossly inadequate.

Our analysis of classroom practices in teaching English in different parts of India (Mohanty, Panda and Pal 2010) shows that English-medium schools for the upper and lower social class children espouse very different strategies to negotiate the English–Vernacular divide. Ramanathan (2005a, b) also observed that schools in India socialise students to divergent models of English literacy. Our study (Mohanty *et al.* 2010) shows that pupils from the lower social strata are actually taught English in Hindi (or in other mother tongues).[4] Further, the schools make various adjustments in choice of textbooks and evaluation procedures to accommodate to the basic reality that there is no home support for English for the children from the lower social strata. The situation in government schools in the tribal areas is even more difficult as teachers have a very low level of competence in English. For tribal mother tongue pupils, who may have some exposure to the regional major language (e.g. Oriya) but almost no exposure to English, it is twice removed from their reality. Mohanty *et al.* (2010) show that classroom teaching of English remains marginal in the tribal areas of Orissa, although English is prescribed in the curriculum for all schools in state. This is a strategy seeking to negotiate the formidable double divide – the English–Vernacular (Oriya) and Vernacular (Oriya)–Tribal language divides. Thus, it is necessary to rethink English teaching practices in India, perhaps taking some cues from the Ethiopian practices and their evaluation. The analysis of the Ethiopian situation (Benson *et al.*, this volume) does show how best this can be done through late-exit multilingual education. Problems and prospects of multilingual education in India will be discussed next in light of the Ethiopian findings.

5.3 Multilingual Education in India

The language policy and practice in education in India have not responded to its multilingual context (Mohanty 2008b). Promotion of high levels of academic achievement is a major objective of education and, as Heugh *et al.* (2007) suggest, language policy and practice in education must support this objective while, at the same time, seeking to develop high levels of academic literacy and communicative skills in languages, which pupils in a multilingual society need. As in the Ethiopian context, education of students in India must necessarily foster proficiency in languages of functional significance – MT, languages for regional- and national-level communication and an international language for wider communication. This involves development of competence in two to three languages for the dominant language communities, and at least four languages for tribal mother tongue children. School educational practices in India do involve multiple languages but they can be characterised only as nominal forms of multilingual education (Mohanty 2006, 2008b). Multilingual education (MLE) involves two or more languages of teaching or MoI in subjects other than the languages themselves (Skutnabb-Kangas and McCarty 2008) and it seeks to develop high levels of multilingualism and multiliteracy (Mohanty, Panda, Phillipson and Skutnabb-Kangas 2009). International research evidence and the Ethiopian study show that effective MLE starts with development of MT proficiency, through teaching in the MT as the medium of instruction for at least six to eight years of initial schooling, and gradually develops proficiency and literacy skills in other languages used systematically as languages of teaching at some point in school education (Skutnabb-Kangas and Mohanty 2009).

In the absence of any clear policy of mother tongue and multilingual education in India, tribal mother tongue children are forced into submersion education in the major regional/official language of the state, which has a subtractive effect on their mother tongues (Mohanty 2006). As pointed out, neglect of tribal languages in education, the mismatch between home language and school language and the language barrier in schools perpetuate inequalities leading to capability deprivation and poverty (Mohanty 2008a). The language disadvantage of tribal children, facing the formidable double divide in dominant language schools, is a major factor in their school failure. This problem in tribal education in India led to various short-term attempts at mother tongue-based education including some transitional programmes to facilitate smooth transition from mother tongue to school language (Mohanty 1989, 2006). Recently, some states with large tribal populations have launched mother tongue-based MLE for tribal children. Similar programmes of MT-based MLE were launched in Andhra Pradesh in the year 2004 in eight tribal languages and, two years later, in Orissa in ten tribal languages (see Mohanty, Mishra, Reddy and Ramesh 2009, for details). The mother tongues of the tribal children, written in the script[5] of the major state language, are used in these MLE programmes as languages of teaching and literacy instruction for three to five years of primary education. The state majority language (L2) – Telugu in Andhra Pradesh and Oriya in Orissa – is introduced as a language subject for development of oral communication skills in the second year and for reading and writing skills from the third year onwards. These programmes envisage use of L2 as a language of teaching (along with L1) from the fourth year of primary schools, with L1 (MT) continuing as a language subject. The teachers in the MLE programme are from the tribal language community and speak the tribal mother tongue (L1) and the state majority language (L2). The MLE programmes follow the common school curriculum of the state but make efforts to integrate the Indigenous cultural knowledge systems in developing the textbooks and curricular materials. An intervention programme in Orissa, called *MLE Plus* (MLE+), uses cultural pedagogy emphasising culture- and community-based approaches to MLE to foster collaborative classroom learning and cultural identity (Panda and Mohanty 2009). The MLE+ programme is implemented as special intervention in eight of the Government MLE schools in Saora and Kui tribal languages.

The MLE and MLE+ programmes in India have been evaluated, and they show positive effects on children's classroom achievement, school attendance and participation, parental and community attitudes and involvement (see Mohanty *et al.* 2009; Panda and Mohanty 2009). Panda and Mohanty (2010) evaluated the classroom achievement of children in a cross-sequential study in which the students joining grade 1 in the years 2007, 2008 and 2009 in MLE and MLE+ programmes and their non-MT counterparts were tested at the end of each grade over a three-year period (2007–2009) from grades 1 to 3. Thus, achievement measures for grade 1 children were taken for three batches of students in 2007, 2008 and 2009. Similarly, two batches of grade 2 students were tested in the years 2008 and 2009 and one batch of students of grade 3 was tested in 2009. Classroom achievement measures were taken for Mathematics, Language (MT for the MLE and MLE+ and Oriya for the non-MT programmes) and Environmental Studies. Table 5.1 gives the percentage of scores of the children in different programmes in the three school subjects and overall performance combining all the subjects.

As the evaluation shows, children in non-MT-medium schools with the subtractive form of dominant language-medium programmes had the poorest performance compared to the MLE and MLE+ programmes. MLE+ children had better performance compared to the MLE programmes. The differences across the different types of programmes were significant. It is also noteworthy that when teaching was in a non-MT language children's performance deteriorated over the grades. This suggests that there is a negative impact of the forced submersion in a dominant language on classroom learning. Quite clearly, mother tongue-based education makes a positive difference in classroom performance of children.

A National Multilingual Education Resource Consortium (NMRC) has also been set up in India (see NMRC website www.nmrc-jnu.org for details) to facilitate and augment MLE activities and to take up formative evaluation of the programmes. The reports of NMRC on the MLE programmes in Andhra Pradesh and Orissa (Manoharan and Nag 2009; Nag and Manoharan 2009) point to some problems in transition from L1 (mother tongue) to L2 (state language) and in the introduction of English and Hindi in the existing programmes. The NMRC reports on the MLE programmes in Orissa and Andhra Pradesh raise some questions about the early-exit nature of MLE in India. It may be noted that the children in the MLE schools are scheduled to join the regular majority language (Telugu/Oriya) medium school programmes in the states from the sixth year of schooling onwards. Thus, the initial experimental programmes of MLE in India can be seen as early-exit programmes in which MT is used as a language of teaching for three to four years and as a language subject up to the fifth year of primary level education. It is evident from the various evaluations of these programmes that they provide better quality education for tribal children, compared to the common programmes of submersion education. However, the Ethiopian findings suggest that early transition from MT to L2 and English may be somewhat

TABLE 5.1 Classroom achievement of children in different types of school programmes; Grade 1 (2007–2009), Grade 2 (2008–2009) and Grade 3 (2009)

School	Non-MT schools			MLE schools			MLE+ schools		
Subject	Gr. 1 N=190	Gr. 2 N=111	Gr. 3 N=72	Gr. 1 N=171	Gr. 2 N=112	Gr. 3 N=63	Gr. 1 N=382	Gr. 2 N=253	Gr. 3 N=112
Language	40.93	31.96	29.62	42.21	40.58	40.51	47.31	48.02	53.18
Maths	40.22	30.81	27.57	47.35	40.47	44.33	51.68	50.67	54.04
Env. sci.	27.05	27.45	22.89	31.13	26.91	35.40	31.82	29.57	36.35
Overall	36.07	30.07	26.69	40.23	35.99	40.08	43.60	42.75	47.86

Key: Gr. = Grade; MT = Mother Tongue; MLE = Mother tongue-based Multilingual Education; Env. sci. = Environmental sciences better than the forced submersion in a second language, but late-exit programmes of MLE, which use MT as a language of teaching for six to eight years, are more effective than the early-exit programmes. Thus, the Ethiopian report has far-reaching implications for MLE programmes in India and it calls for reappraisal of their transition plans. It also shows that the burden of the linguistic double divide remains a potential problem for MLE programmes in India, which are under pressure to accommodate the major state language, English and Hindi within the primary level programme of education. Negotiating the Vernacular–Other language (MT) divide and English–Vernacular divide is a formidable challenge for MLE in India. Nevertheless, the Ethiopian findings show that it can be done effectively. The MLE programmes in India are experimental programmes implemented in about 500 schools in Andhra Pradesh and Orissa. While both states have plans to extend the programme to several new schools and to other tribal languages in their attempts at better education for tribal children, there seems to be no change in the state policy in this respect nor in the long-term plans, which are conspicuous by their absence. Despite regional variations and diverse practices, Ethiopia's language-in-education policy can be expected to provide a good model and the study by Heugh *et al.* (2007) has recommendations for a road map for effective MLE programmes under very difficult and challenging conditions. The Ethiopian findings carry some hope for a better future of the MLE programmes in India and elsewhere in the world.

Notes

1 Indigenous or Aboriginal communities in India are officially called 'tribes' (ādivāsi) and are listed as 'scheduled tribes' which are identified on the basis of 'distinct culture and language', 'geographical isolation', 'primitive traits', 'economic backwardness', and 'limited contact with the out groups' and also, sometimes, on political considerations. The Anthropological Survey of India, in its People of India project, has identified 635 tribal communities of which 573 are so far officially notified as Scheduled Tribes. Here the term 'tribe' (rather than 'Indigenous peoples') is used specifically in the Indian context in its formal/official and neutral sense.

2 In 1957, the government of India proclaimed the Three Language Formula (TLF) as a framework for languages in education. Initially it recommended use of three languages in school-level education: (1) Regional language or mother tongue as the language of teaching, (2) Hindi or an Indian language (for Hindi mother tongue children), and (3) English as a third language. Subsequently, the TLF was severally modified by the government of India and variously interpreted by the state governments.

3 See Dr. Giridhar Rao's blog 'MTM education in RtE Bill' at http://bolii.blogspot.com/2009/01/mtm-education-in-rte-bill.html; see also 'Education Bill – three critiques by Anil Sadgopal' at http://bolii.blogspot.com/2009/01/education-bill-three-critiques-by-anil.html.

4 It should be noted that use of students' L1 to promote L2 proficiency can be an effective strategy and it facilitates cross-linguistic transfer in respect of conceptual, pragmatic, metacognitive and metalinguistic understanding (Cummins 2007). Systematic and skilful application of bilingual or multilingual instructional strategies for teaching of L2 is supported by research evidence. However, in schools in India, teaching

English in Hindi or students' L1 is neither systematic nor purposeful; it is, rather, used to compensate for lack of support for the English language in that particular milieu and also for the poor proficiency among the teachers and students in the language.
5 Tribal languages in India do not have any exclusive writing system; they are usually written in the script of either the dominant regional language or another major language. However, in recent years, some tribal languages, such as Santali, have developed their own writing systems.

References

Cummins, Jim (2007). Rethinking monolingual instructional strategies in multilingual classrooms. *The Canadian Journal of Applied Linguistics*, 10(2), 221–240.

Dasgupta, Probal (1993). *The otherness of English: India's auntie tongue syndrome.* Delhi: Oxford University Press.

Fishman, Joshua A. (1991). *Reversing language shift: Theoretical and empirical foundations of assistance to threatened languages.* Clevedon: Multilingual Matters.

Heugh, Kathleen, Benson, Carol, Bogale, Berhanu and Gebre Yohannes, Mekonnen Alemu (2007). *Final report: Study on medium of instruction in primary schools in Ethiopia.* Ethiopia: Ministry of Education.

Manoharan, Pramila and Nag, Shivani (2009). *Andhra Pradesh MLE: Status Report.* New Delhi: NMRC. (www.nmrc-jnu.org).

Mohanty, Ajit K. (1989). Psychological consequences of mother tongue maintenance and the language of literacy for linguistic minorities in India. *Psychology and Developing Societies*, 2(1), 31–51.

Mohanty, Ajit K. (2006). Multilingualism of the unequals and predicaments of education in India: Mother tongue or Other tongue? In García, Ofelia, Skutnabb-Kangas, Tove and Torres-Guzmán, María E. (eds), *Imagining multilingual schools: Language in education and glocalization.* Clevedon: Multilingual Matters, 262–283.

Mohanty, Ajit K. (2007). Introduction. In Skutnabb-Kangas, Tove (ed.), *Bilingualism or not: The education of minorities.* New Delhi: Orient Longman, xvii–xxvi.

Mohanty, Ajit K. (2008a). Perpetuating inequality: Language disadvantage and capability deprivation of tribal mother tongue speakers in India'. In Harbert, Wayne, McConnell-Ginet, Sally, Miller, Amanda and Whitman, John (eds), *Language and poverty.* Clevedon: Multilingual Matters, 102–124.

Mohanty, Ajit K. (2008b). Multilingual Education in India. In Cummins, Jim and Hornberger, Nancy (eds),Vol. 5, *Bilingual education. Encyclopaedia of language and education* (2nd edition). New York: Springer, 165–174.

Mohanty, Ajit K. (2010). Languages, inequality and marginalization: Implications of the double divide in Indian multilingualism. *International Journal of the Sociology of Language*, 205, 131–154.

Mohanty, Ajit K., Mishra, Mahendra Kumar, Reddy, N. Upender and Ramesh, Gumidyala (2009). Overcoming the language barrier for tribal children: MLE in Andhra Pradesh and Orissa, India. In Mohanty, Ajit K., Panda, Minati, Phillipson, Robert and Skutnabb-Kangas, Tove (eds), *Multilingual education for social justice: Globalising the local.* New Delhi: Orient Blackswan, 278–291.

Mohanty, Ajit K., Panda, Minati and Pal, Rashim (2010). Language policy in education and classroom practices in India: Is the teacher a cog in the policy wheel? In Menken, Kate and García, Ofelia (eds), *Negotiating language policies in schools: Educators as policy makers.* London: Routledge, 211–231.

Mohanty, Ajit K., Panda, Minati, Phillipson, Robert and Skutnabb-Kangas, Tove (eds) (2009). *Multilingual education for social justice: Globalising the local*. New Delhi: Orient Blackswan.

Nag, Shivani and Manoharan, Pramila (2009). *Orissa MLE: Status Report*. New Delhi: NMRC (also in www.nmrc-jnu.org).

National Knowledge Commission. (2009). *National Knowledge Commission Report to the Nation 2006–2009*. New Delhi: Government of India.

NCERT (2005). *National curriculum framework 2005*. New Delhi: National Council of Educational Research and Training.

Nurmela, Iina, Awasthi, Lava Deo and Skutnabb-Kangas, Tove (this volume). Enhancing quality education for all in Nepal through indigenized MLE: the challenge to teach in over a hundred languages.

Panda, Minati (2009). Discriminating against mother tongue. *Combat Law*, May–August, 120–122.

Panda, Minati and Mohanty, Ajit (2009). Language matters, so does culture: beyond the rhetoric of culture in multilingual education. In Mohanty, Ajit K., Panda, Minati, Phillipson, Robert and Skutnabb-Kangas, Tove (eds), *Multilingual education for social justice: Globalising the local*. New Delhi: Orient Blackswan, 295–312.

Panda, Minati and Mohanty, Ajit (2010). Classroom achievement of tribal children in dominant Oriya medium and mother tongue based MLE and MLE+ programmes in Orissa: a cross-sequential study. Unpublished ZHCES-BvLF Interim Project Report, Jawaharlal Nehru University, New Delhi.

Rahman, Tariq (1998). *Language and politics in Pakistan*. Karachi: Oxford University Press.

Ramanathan, Vaidehi (2005a). Ambiguities about English: Ideologies and critical practice in vernacular-medium college classrooms in Gujarat, India. *Journal of Language, Identity and Education*, 4(1), 45–65.

Ramanathan, Vaidehi (2005b). *The English–Vernacular divide: Postcolonial language politics and practice*. Clevedon: Multilingual Matters.

Royal Education Council, Bhutan and iDiscovery Education (2009). *Draft National Educational Framework of Bhutan*. New Delhi: iDiscovery.

Skutnabb-Kangas, Tove (2000). *Linguistic genocide in education – or worldwide diversity and human rights?* Mahwah, NJ: Lawrence Erlbaum.

Skutnabb-Kangas, Tove and McCarty, Teresa L. (2008). Key concepts in bilingual education: Ideological, historical, epistemological, and empirical foundations. In Cummins, Jim and Hornberger, Nancy (eds), Vol. 5, *Bilingual Education, Encyclopaedia of Language and Education* (2nd edition). New York: Springer, 3–17.

Skutnabb-Kangas, Tove and Mohanty, Ajit K. (2009). *Policy and Strategy for MLE in Nepal. Report by Tove Skutnabb-Kangas and Ajit Mohanty. Consultancy visit 4–14 March 2009*. Sanothimi, Bhaktapur, Nepal: Multilingual Education Program for All Non-Nepali Speaking Students of Primary Schools of Nepal. Ministry of Education, Department of Education, Inclusive Section. (http://www.tove-skutnabb-kangas.org/en/articles_for_downloading.html).

6

ENHANCING QUALITY EDUCATION FOR ALL IN NEPAL THROUGH INDIGENISED MLE

The Challenge to Teach in Over a Hundred Languages

Iina Nurmela, Lava Deo Awasthi and Tove Skutnabb-Kangas[1]

6.1 Introduction: The Sociocultural, Linguistic and Political Background

All educational language planning needs to be based on an analysis of the historically grounded political, sociocultural and linguistic situation in the country. Therefore we start with a short background presentation. Nepal's population was reported to be 28,584,975 in the census figures released in July 2011 (http: www.census.gov.np/). The population has increased by over five million since the census of 2001. In 1971 it was 11,555,983. About 40% of the Nepalese are under the age of 15. The people of Nepal represent different languages, cultures, social, 'caste' and ethnic backgrounds, also due to geographical variations in the country (eight of the world's highest mountains are in Nepal, in the Himalayas). The census of 2001 noted 102 'social groups' and '59 officially recognized caste and ethnic groups' (Yadava and Turin 2006: 7, quoting the census).

The 2001 census recorded 92 languages, while the *Ethnologue*, 16th edition, claims 124 living languages and Yonjan-Tamang (2006) claims over 143 languages. The Indo-Aryan language group is the largest in terms of the number of speakers (some 80% of all speakers) while the Tibeto-Burman branch has the largest number of languages (57). The rest are Austro-Asiatic and Dravidian, with one linguistic isolate, Kusunda (Yadava and Turin 2006: 7). Nineteen languages are estimated as being on the verge of extinction (Yadava and Grove 2008). Fewer than 20 languages have more than 100,000 speakers. The literacy rate in the 2001 census was 54%: 65% for males, 42% for females. With 2005–2007 data, the literacy rate for adults (15 years and older) was 56.5% (70.3 for males, 43.6 for females; for youth between 15 and 24 it was 79.3% (85.3 for males, 73.0

for females) (*Global Education Digest 2009*, Table 15, p. 192). Nepali is the main language of teaching. Teaching Indigenous, tribal and minority (ITM) children through the medium of a language that they do not understand obviously contributes to the low literacy rates (see *National Assessment*, 2008).

> The national literacy rate in Ecuador, for example, was 91% in 2001 but that of indigenous groups was 72%; in Viet Nam the rates in 2000 were 87% nationally, 17% for ethnic minorities and merely 5% for some indigenous groups. Nepal's Dalit population has a significantly lower adult literacy rate than the rest of the population.
>
> *(EFA Global Monitoring Report 2009: 96)*[2]

Nepal suffered from ten years of insurgency. It ended in 2006 when a Comprehensive Peace Accord was signed between the government and CPN-Maoists. This included a commitment to crafting a new constitution. In November 2007 the Parliament passed an Interim Constitution. Elections took place in April 2008. Of the CA members, 33.16% are women (http://www.can.gov.np/); 36.3% represent Indigenous peoples (Ram Bahadur Magar Thapa, one of the Indigenous MPs, personal information to TSK, 6 October 2009). The oaths at the solemn opening of the Constituent Assembly were taken in 29 languages, of which 21 were Indigenous (ibid.). The political situation in the country is still (July 2011) extremely vulnerable and power struggles are visible. The daily life is difficult and constant power cuts, shortage of food and fuel, difficult transport, a malfunctioning infrastructure, strikes, kidnappings, etc. make any planning haphazard. Both domestic and external interests clash.

Still, there is a lot of optimism, and educational language planning is going forward. In this chapter we present in some detail Nepal's planning and implementation processes, starting from Nepal's international commitments and proceeding to national commitments and developments, with all the various challenges. We are especially interested in the role of the various mother tongues in education. A recent Multilingual Education Programme (2006–2009) is presented and lessons from it are drawn and discussed. At the end, some similarities and differences in relation to the Ethiopian case are discussed.

6.2 Educational Language Planning: Nepal's International Commitments

Nepal's Education for All *EFA National Plan of Action* (2001) adopted the six goals to be achieved by 2015, articulated in the Dakar Framework for Action (http://www.unesco.org/education/efa/ed_for_all/dakfram_eng.shtml). About 50.1% of Nepal's school-age population speaks a language other than Nepali as a mother tongue. Given the ethnic, social and linguistic diversity of Nepal, an additional 7th goal of EFA was identified (*EFA National Plan of Action (2001/15)*, to ensure the right of Indigenous peoples and linguistic minorities to quality basic and primary education through their mother tongues. Nepal's EFA goals thus respect linguistic and ethnic diversity.

In addition to many of the more general UN human rights instruments, Nepal's government has voted for or ratified the two major UN instruments regarding the rights of Indigenous peoples. International Labour Organization (*ILO*) *Convention No. 169 on Indigenous and Tribal Peoples in Independent Countries* (see http://www.ilo.org/ilolex/cgi-lex/convde.pl?C169) was ratified by Nepal in September 2007, and it entered into force one year later. The Convention, as a treaty, creates binding legal obligations for those States which ratify it. Thus far, only 22 states have done so, Nepal being the first state in Asia.[3] There is also a lively debate, with sometimes harsh criticism of the government, in relation to ILO 169.[4] Nepal also voted in favour of the adoption of the United Nations' General Assembly *Declaration on the Rights of Indigenous Peoples* (UNDRIP) of 13 September 2007 (http://www.un.org/esa/socdev/unpfii/en/drip.html). The UNDRIP does not, strictly speaking, create binding legal obligations, but the moral obligations are still major.

Both give ITM children a right to mother tongue-medium education, especially when interpreted together with other instruments, and comments to these. The most important instrument here is the UN *Convention on the Rights of the Child* (CRC[5]), and several opinions expressed by treaty bodies.[6] Two will be mentioned; these can then be compared with the implementation plans of the Government.

The *Committee on the Rights of the Child* held at their 34th Session in 2003 a Day of General Discussion on the Rights of Indigenous Children. They recommend 'that States parties ensure access for indigenous children to appropriate and high quality education' (E/C.19/2004/5/Add.11, Annex, p. 10). Interpreting this access, they recommend that:

> States parties, with the active participation of indigenous communities and children [. . .]
>
> b) implement indigenous children's right to be taught to read and write in their own indigenous language or in the language most commonly used by the group to which they belong, as well as the national language(s) of the country in which they live;[7]
>
> c) undertake measures to effectively address the comparatively higher drop-out rates[8] among indigenous youth and ensure that indigenous children are adequately prepared for higher education, vocational training and their further economic, social and cultural aspirations;
>
> d) take effective measures to increase the number of teachers from indigenous communities or who speak indigenous languages, provide them with appropriate training, and ensure that they are not discriminated against in relation to other teachers;

e) allocate sufficient financial, material and human resources to implement these programmes and policies effectively.

An extremely important recent *General Comment* was made with regard to Indigenous children and their rights under the CRC by the treaty body established under the CRC, the Committee on the Rights of the Child.[9] The Committee noted that the CRC was the first UN core human rights treaty to include specific references to Indigenous children in a number of provisions. The Committee also noted that the specific references to Indigenous children in the CRC 'are indicative of the recognition that they require special measures in order to fully enjoy their rights' (para. 5). See also the General Comment on 'The right to education', Art. 13 in the UN International Covenant on Economic, Social and Cultural Rights, ICESCR.[10] Several new recommendations have appeared in 2009 or are being developed by two new UN bodies on Indigenous and minority rights.

6.3 Educational Language Planning: Development of the Government's National Commitments

6.3.1 Development of Primary Education: Change from Nepali as the Only Language of Instruction to Mother Tongue-medium in Early Grades

Multilingualism appears to have developed in Nepal as a necessity for people's survival in difficult terrains and isolated areas in the mountains, hills, plains and the valleys where daily communication in one language was impossible. Multilingualism has thus evolved as an indigenous construct and has been in practice for generations to maintain social relations and facilitate commercial transactions (see Awasthi 2004). The existence of immense diversity of languages and cultures in Nepal proves that multilingualism thrived in the past, prior to the spread of the monolingual ideologies, promoted by the Nepali state under the influence of the British Empire in India. The systematic destruction of local languages through glorification of one dominant language can be attributed to the work of the Macaulay Minutes of 1835 in India at the regional level. In Nepal, this led to the Wood Commission Report of 1956. Both had the same mission to accomplish: the spread of English in India and the spread of Nepali in Nepal (see Phillipson 1992, 2009; Prasad 2001; Awasthi 2004). Just as English proved to be a means of Anglicising India and creating linguistic power hierarchies, so did Nepali for the spread of mainstream language and culture across Nepal. The power of Nepali contributed significantly to invisibilising the language resources of the Indigenous/tribal peoples and minority groups (ITMs), and made them inconvertible to other resources, including political power (see Skutnabb-Kangas 2000, Chapter 6, Globalisation, Power and Control). The insurgency ending in 2006 can also be interpreted claiming that the linguistic power hierarchies resulting from the monolingual orientations might have contributed to the loss of cultural cohesion and have increased social and economic cleavages, leading to majority/minority splits, social tensions and class conflicts in the country (see Raj 2004).

Until the adoption of the Interim Constitution in 2007, the Nepali language was the single language of government affairs, business and education. The medium of instruction (MOI) in primary education for the general population (since 1951) was mostly Nepali, but from fairly early on also English in private schools in the capital. There is no teaching of Nepali as a (second language) subject. One of the major causes of children's 'dropout', class repetition and failure is attributed to the use of Nepali (or English), instead of children's mother tongues in early grades. According to a study by EDSC (1997: 95) on the National Achievement Level of Grade 3 Students 'the parents of the top 10 schools' students were from the Nepali mother tongue group whereas the parents of the bottom 10 schools' students came from non-Nepali speaking group'. As the statistics show, sooner or later ITM children get frustrated and stop coming to school, i.e. the structure of the education with a non-comprehensible MOI pushes them out.

> The National Language Policy Recommendation Commission in Nepal pointed to this problem as early as 1994 (Yadava and Grove 2008: 24). The children enrolled at primary level tend to 'drop out' from the schools. In some cases, the students leave the school and enrol again. For these students it takes nine to twelve years to complete the primary education. This is an indication of a great educational loss. 'The majority of the school dropouts are found in grade (1–2)', Yadava and Grove state (p. 24).
>
> *(Skutnabb-Kangas and Mohanty 2009: 20)*

Awasthi stated (2004: 286) in his study *Exploring Monolingual School Practices in Multilingual Nepal*:

> The existing medium of instruction (MOI) practices do not allow NNS [= non-Nepali-speaking] children to receive education through their mother tongues (see chapters 5, 8, 9 and 10). Teaching in schools operates in Nepali despite the fact that a majority of school children in non-Nepali speaking areas speak other language(s) than Nepali. [. . .] My evidence suggests that the Nepali-only practice in classrooms has devastating effects on NNS children's school performance and on their self-esteems.

But the harm done to Indigenous children goes further than push-out, repetition and failure rates The lack of appreciation of Indigenous culture and language by the dominant society has led to feelings of inferiority, humiliation and self-hate when speaking one's native language (Hough *et al.* 2009: 147).[11] The 'harm' is detailed in Skutnabb-Kangas and Dunbar (2010).

Nepal's new governments seem to have shown awareness of the need and interest in improving the mother tongue (MT)-based MLE. Government's changed policy intentions on MLE were already visible in 2006 but the implementation arrangements were not given due consideration in the *Interim Constitution* (2007). However, the political changes reiterated the need for providing mother tongue-medium (MTM) education for children in the early grades. Both the *Interim Constitution 2007* (http://www.nic.gov.np/download/interim-constitution.pdf) and the *National Curriculum Framework* (NCF 2007) ensure the *right of every child to have their education through the medium of their mother tongue during the first grades of their school years*. Further, the *Three Year Interim Plan (2007–10)* reiterates the government's commitment to ensuring children's education through their mother tongues in primary schools.

Lately, education authorities, urged by the Indigenous organisations have realised that serious efforts are needed to really implement Nepal's general mother tongue-based MLE policies, sometimes said to be the best in the whole of South Asia. The current government programme states: 'All Nepalese will get an opportunity to complete their basic education in their mother tongues' (*EFA National Plan of Action (2001–15)*). The necessary policies for implementing mother tongue-based MLE[12] thus exist but the socio-cultural and political conditions have slowed down the process. In the current context of Nepal, the MLE policies are vital, and appear to be one effective means towards healing the wounds caused by the conflict; they can provide a basis for harmonising relations. Thus, MLE is believed to ultimately help sustain peace and regain prosperity in Nepal (see Awasthi 2004; Dahal 2005).

6.3.2 Today's Situation: Good Policy – How About Implementation?

Statistics disaggregated by the language of the child in relation to enrolment, literacy and push-out rates are inadequate; most statistics are about all children, regardless of language background. The statistics of the *Joint Evaluation of Nepal's Education for All 2004–2009 Sector Program* (2008) show that net enrolment among *all* primary school age children in Nepal has increased from 84.2% in 2004 to 91.9% in 2008. *EFA's Global Monitoring Report 2009* (p. 59) praises Nepal (in Text Box 2.7, with the title 'Nepal – also on fast-forward towards UPE' (UPE = Universal Primary Education):[13]

> In recent years Nepal has registered rapid progress towards UPE. The NER [Net Enrolment Rate] for 2004 stood at 79% – up from 65% in just five years. Numbers of children out of school have fallen from 1 million to 700,000. And survival to grade 5 has increased from 58% to 79%. The fact that this progress was sustained during a civil conflict that ended only in 2006 points to a remarkable achievement. Nepal's experience demonstrates

that even the most deeply-rooted problems and inequalities are susceptible to public policies (see also EFA Global Monitoring Reports 2009 and 2010 for particularly important reforms).

Despite the government efforts, a *Joint Evaluation of Nepal's Education for All 2004–2009 Sector Program* (2008), however, gives a fairly challenging picture of the reality in schools. Multilingual classes pose a challenge to most teachers. Sometimes preschool classes are used to teach ITM children basic skills in Nepali language to facilitate learning in primary grades but often there are no efforts to support their learning: the low performance by non-Nepali speaking students is viewed as a matter of fact.

This 2008 EFA evaluation also discusses the wrong perceptions of consequences of learning through the medium of the mother tongue. These misconceptions are widely held views in Nepal (see also section 6.7 below):

'Some perceived that learning mother tongues would hold their children back from learning Nepali and thus disadvantage them further. By extension of the same argument, quite a few people consulted wanted schools to [use English as MOI] from Grade 1 on the assumption that this would mean that children would learn English faster, regardless of practical consideration such as availability of English speaking teachers.' (ibid.: 20) 'These perceptions' – the evaluation argues – 'suggest a need for more awareness-raising at all levels as to how language and literacy learning takes place. Reassurance that mother tongue learning need not hinder, but can support, success in a second and third language is much needed. The evaluation invites the development of a more nuanced policy, which details a range of approaches that might be appropriate in the many different language contexts that exist across Nepal'. (ibid.: 43–44)[14]

This is being said in Nepal, but it is important to ask who – education authorities, parents, or others – feel this way. Who are questioning MTM education and advocating English? Do they represent ITMs – or dominant language speakers (including those elites who have had their education through the medium of English)? These views come often from dominant-language speakers and education authorities who *claim* to be quoting Nepali-speaking and ITM parents. In the field, the Programme staff (see below) mostly heard people demanding MT-based MLE, despite sometimes being worried about whether the children would learn Nepali or English sufficiently this way. A two-page leaflet (see below) tries to address some of these worries. Indigenous organisations also are *demanding* MTM education.

Under the *Education for All programme (2004–09)*, jointly funded by the Government of Nepal and development partners, the Ministry of Education introduced in 2006 a *Multilingual Education programme* (see below; see also Nepal Ministry of

Education and Sports 2006; World Bank 2007). The on-going interventions are extremely crucial for the Ministry as a model-building exercise to consolidate the MLE initiatives and to expand the programme through the School Sector Reform Plan launched from 2009.

6.4 The Multilingual Education Programme 2006–2009

6.4.1 The MLE Programme Goals

One central element of EFA was the *Multilingual Education Programme aiming at all non-Nepali Speaking Students in Primary Schools of Nepal* (hereafter 'The MLE programme') for which the government utilised technical assistance provided by Finland. It was to achieve five interconnected objectives:

1   creating a conducive policy environment for MLE;
2   developing an institutional structure that will facilitate a bottom-up implementation of sustainable MLE and coordinate MLE activities;
3   strengthening the capacity at central, district and community levels to implement MLE;
4   creating and establishing models of learning environments that facilitate the non-Nepali speaking students' learning and prepare them to continue their education after the primary level;
5   establishing models of creating support networks of schools implementing MLE.

The MLE programme included a small-scale intervention to build models of MLE in primary schools. Seven schools in six districts (out of 75 districts and 32,000 schools in the whole country) began work with MLE in 2007. In an effort to suggest a model for nation-wide implementation, the pilot experience was cascaded by the pilot school communities themselves into two more schools in each district in 2009. The number of schools currently implementing MTM-based education is very small. However, it has opened ways for the expansion and consolidation of MLE interventions, building on the lessons learnt and gains made so far.

6.4.2 Work in Communities and Schools

The choice of pilot districts, schools and languages was prepared meticulously to ensure a just representation of the four language families, of the three regions of Nepal: the mountains, hills and the lowlands of Terai/Madhesh, and of different stages of language endangerment – both very endangered languages and also languages spoken by large numbers of people were selected. For the purposes of creating models for the diverse MLE settings in the country, the pilots included both monolingual and multilingual student populations. The final decision of schools was taken by the district-level Indigenous peoples' organisations and the District Education Offices. The pilot languages included Rasuwa Tamang, Palpa Magar, Athapaharia Rai, Rana (Tharu), Uranw, Tharu/Maithili, Santhali and Rajbangsi in the districts of Rasuwa, Palpa, Dhankuta, Kanchanpur, Sunsari and Jhapa.

There was a lack of teaching and learning materials in languages other than Nepali. Grade 1 subject matter textbooks had been translated into seven other languages, and grade 2 textbooks into three languages, but these were never printed, due to heavy criticism from ITMs. They were opposed to the contents which did not reflect their own cultures and traditions. During the MLE programme, ITM groups expressed their wish to write their own textbooks and reference materials. As soon as the decision on the pilot schools was taken in June 2007, and the schools and communities showed readiness and commitment to enter into this process, the MLE Team in cooperation with relevant stakeholders initiated the process of preparing culturally relevant mother tongue-medium supplementary reference material in the pilot communities.

Indigenous knowledge (IK) holders of the communities were invited to the schools to tell children culturally relevant stories in their mother tongues. Children listened to these elders, wrote down the stories and drew pictures. The stories were typed up in the mother tongues, translated into Nepali and English, and printed, each in three languages, in Kathmandu. These eight booklets are an example of teaching materials with appropriate cultural contents. The teachers in the pilot schools use the readers widely as materials for mother tongue lessons, and the children enjoy reading them. To ensure the continued motivation and commitment of the pilot schools to the work of the MLE programme, posters based on the stories were designed and distributed to the schools shortly after the field visits. Producing the posters was also to assure the ITM communities that whatever is 'collected' from them will also be 'returned to them'. Every child also got an A4-sized set of the posters, and it was easy to see the excitement and delight of the children when they looked at them, showed the materials to their parents and grandparents, and discussed with them.

In the future, to avoid problems of distribution of books from the centre – which can sometimes take up to months – the texts could be typed, illustrated and printed in each district. This is also done in Ethiopia, and it enables Ethiopian children to have books that they can take home, as opposed to the glossy English-medium books printed by multinational publishers in South Africa where these books are so expensive that schools cannot afford to have them for each child, and the children are not allowed to take them home (Heugh 2009).

During the last year of the programme implementation, children in the pilot schools received teaching with the eight ITM languages as MOIs, in first, second and third grades. The first grade textbooks in all school subjects in the eight languages were printed in September 2009 and the second and third grade textbooks in all school subjects were developed and printed later in 2009.

They were written locally by school staff and community members. The School Management Committees validated the language and content of the textbooks before printing.

6.4.3 Identifying Core Issues for Implementation and Forward Planning

Experiences from the pilot districts and from the central level partner agencies, institutions and organisations were collected in two different attempts to identify the core issues in the implementation of MLE. In 2008, a group of central level officials and academics wrote a Concept paper for MLE (Bajracharya *et al.* 2008).[15] In 2009, a Research and Expert (R&E) Team wrote a review of MLE based on information from a wide variety of individuals and groups active in MLE implementation (Acharya 2009).

The findings of the two undertakings concurred on most points and outlined the following issues that need to be addressed in planning the MLE implementation (these can be compared with issues in other countries; the challenges are very similar):

- *Implementation guidelines*: The implementation guidelines relating to mother tongue as a medium of instruction need to be developed and disseminated. Clear guidelines to facilitate the implementation of MLE need to be reinforced based on the outcomes of the MLE programme.
- *Financial resources*: It has been shown by international experience that MLE does not increase the overall costs in the education sector.[16] However, at the early phase of implementation, the government may need to make larger investments in materials production and teacher preparation and training. Class size is also an important general financial issue in quality education.
- *Materials development*: Mechanisms to develop materials locally in different mother tongues must be developed. The supply of MT/MLE books everywhere needs to be ensured.
- *Human resources*: Urgent attention needs to be given to the redeployment and appointment of mother tongue-speaking teachers. In-service and pre-service teacher training programmes must be developed for mother tongues as both subjects and MOIs.
- *Teacher training* must also respond to the needs of teachers working *in non-conventional settings* (multi-grades etc.) and of those who teach *Nepali as a second language* and *English as a foreign language*.
- *Advocacy, sensitisation and orientation*: Advocacy information through various media on the value and outcomes of MLE should be offered to guardians, teachers, school principals, education officers and other concerned parties at all levels. Meeting the expectations and priorities of communities should be a priority.

- *Ensuring MLE in all language scenarios*: MTs and MLE should be promoted and strengthened from monolingual to multilingual school settings and in all languages, whether they have a script or a written system or are based on an oral tradition.
- *Coordinating MLE activities*: MLE implementation should be harmonised among the line agencies and between the central and district level education authorities. MLE should also be included in both early childhood education and non-formal education programmes.
- *Creation of resources*: To collect local knowledge, stories, practices and technologies and human resources for teachers and students in one permanent venue, Language and Indigenous Resource Centres should be founded within the existing Resource Centres.[17]

The two reviews diverged slightly on the issue of the extent to which mother tongues would be offered as the MOI. The R&E review recommends the mother tongues as the MOI for grades 1–3, after which some subjects would be taught in the second language. From grade 6 onwards the medium of instruction would be the second language only (Nepali or a regional language). The Concept paper (Bajracharya *et al.* 2008: 5–6) envisions the use of MTs as MOI for 'at least through primary level [5 years] but preferably for the first 6–8 years'. It also anticipates an expansion of MLE in secondary and tertiary education by introducing MT as a subject in the long run; in the short term, provisions for this would be created (ibid.: 7).

A major policy-related conclusion of the R&E review was that several international MLE-related human rights provisions that Nepal has agreed to comply with have, in fact, been recognised. The efforts, however, are sporadic and in some instances inconsistent with each other. The need is therefore to consolidate them all. The Concept paper is somewhat more sceptical. The July 2009 *Report on the situation of indigenous peoples in Nepal* by the United Nations Special Rapporteur on the situation of human rights and fundamental freedoms of indigenous peoples, James Anaya (Anaya 2009), commends Nepal on its ratification of the ILO 169 and many of the government's initiatives, but Anaya also presents many points of criticism, some also on education.[18] His recommendations include the following:

> In order to meet the Millennium Development Goals, Nepal has proclaimed free education at the primary level (grades I to V). Efforts to fulfill this objective are in place, but investment levels need to be sufficient to reach the most marginalized communities, including investment in scholarships, training of teachers speaking indigenous languages, and textbooks in indigenous languages.
>
> *(Anaya 2009: para 44)*

The *MLE Implementation Guidelines* working group (see below) reviewed all these recommendations when formulating the steps to initiate the MLE on a broader basis. Functional linkages between the different line agencies (especially curriculum development, teaching materials development and teacher education) are crucial and need MLE harmonisation. Teaching Nepali as a second language to non-Nepali-speaking children still needs to be established as part of the standard curriculum. The textbooks for Nepali as a second language are also urgently needed.

6.5 Working to Ensure Continuation After the MLE Programme

There were many activities in the MLE Programme to ensure the continuation of the work after the programme came to an end (December 2009). Experiences were widely shared in national seminars and workshops as well as recorded in a documentary video produced in 2009. A large number of programme reports and many other publications were prepared, ranging from leaflets for parents, teachers and politicians, through materials for schools, teachers and educational authorities, to research-oriented publications. These can and will be used for years to come.

The MLE work plan with the NCED included international consultancies, combined with developing and printing of training manuals and self-learning materials, to support the development of MLE expertise in teacher training. Both active materials writers from the different language groups in Nepal, and the mother tongue teachers from the MLE Pilot schools participated. The resulting *MLE Teacher Training Manuals* were piloted first in three districts (Ilam, Jhapa, Sunsari) and four languages groups (Bantawa Rai, Limbu, Uranw and Rajbangsi) in June–July 2009. A second MLE teacher training focused on seven of the languages that CDC had developed MT-as-a-subject textbooks in (Limbu, Bantawa Rai, Maithili, Bhojpuri, Awadhi and Tharu). The participants learned different pedagogical methods on how to teach teachers to teach through the medium of the MTs in linguistically both homogeneous and heterogeneous (multilingual) classes (see Taylor, this volume).[19]

A seminar on Nepali as a second language, both the theoretical background and practical issues, was held in August 2009; the concept of Nepali as a second language is new. There is an urgent need to clarify the concept, to create Nepali L2 guidelines and to start preparations to teach Nepali as a subject to children with non-Nepali mother tongues. The presentations and discussions in the seminar have been printed as a booklet and distributed to educationists, linguists, education authorities, local governments, NGOs and education development partners.

A two-page popular introduction to MLE for parents, education authorities, media and politicians, 'Why mother-tongue-based multilingual education?' was prepared in March 2009, with the purpose of developing more MLE awareness

(Skutnabb-Kangas 2009a). It gives short research-based answers to the following questions, heard many times:

1   Why should children be taught mainly through the medium of their mother tongue (MT) in school for the first 6–8 years? They know their MT already?
2   Parents want children to learn Nepali and English. If children are taught mainly through their MT the first many years, how do they learn Nepali and English?
3   Isn't it enough if children have the first 3 years in the MT and then the teaching can be in Nepali?
4   Parents want English-medium schools. What are the likely results?

The leaflet concludes with the statement: 'Mother-tongue based MLE for the first 6–8 years, with good teaching of Nepali as a second language and English as a foreign language, and possibly other languages too, with locally based materials which respect local Indigenous knowledge, seems to be a good research-based recommendation for Nepal.' The leaflet has been translated into Nepali and distributed widely.

The experiences and results of all these activities have been used in the process of developing *MLE Implementation Guidelines* in March 2009. The programme implementation through the piloting experiences increased tremendously the pedagogical awareness of the importance of learning through the mother tongues among education authorities and community members. A group of officials from different education line agencies developed the draft MLE Implementation Guidelines; these were discussed in several seminars and with the participants of the NCED *Training of Trainers* workshops.

In August 2009, the Guidelines were reviewed by the highest education authorities of Nepal. The education officials emphasised that MT-based MLE will need to be developed according to demand, and that the local communities need to have the key role in initiating MLE at community/school level. The draft Guidelines suggest that school communities themselves will be able to initiate the discussion on the possibility to start the MLE in any school in Nepal. It was proposed at the seminar that Village Development Committees and municipalities could act as the bodies to approve the demands from the communities. The schools could then develop plans and move forward with the support of the District Education Officers. One way could be to develop an MLE strategy at the central level, to include MLE in the national curriculum frameworks, and support communities in capacity building programmes for developing MLE. As a conclusion of the Ministry seminar, an MLE Technical Team was established, comprising different line agencies of the Ministry of Education.

The approach in the MLE Implementation Guidelines is to guarantee the MT-based MLE to both continue in pilot areas, and to expand the activities beyond the model building schools. When schools in different parts of Nepal will get more experience in MTM education, it will be possible to move forward with a nationwide *National Strategy for Mother-Tongue-Based Multilingual Education*. The Continuous Assessment System (CAS) should be an integral part of MLE implementation. The *School Sector Reform Programme* has introduced the CAS in basic education, opening ways for MLE-based education through internal tests and portfolio assessments. It is vital that testing should take place in the language of instruction.

6.6 Challenges in MLE and Reflections on the MLE Programme

A few of the many challenges in implementing MLE will be described, together with some reflections on central concepts and issues.

6.6.1 Linguistically Diverse Villages

Nepal has pockets that are culturally and linguistically very diverse. These are located mainly in the south of the country, in the lowlands of Terai (Awasthi 2004). Two of the piloting districts located in Terai, Jhapa and Sunsari are very multilingual. The pilot school students speak three different languages: Nepali, Uranw and Tharu/Maithili in Sunsari and Nepali, Santhali and Bengali in Jhapa. The students in Kanchanpur, the third Terai piloting district, are all speakers of Rana (Tharu).

The schools adopted slightly different solutions when they started implementing mother tongues as MOIs in grades 1–3. In one locality, they created an Uranw class for grades 2–3 and a bilingual Tharu/Maithili and Nepali class for grades 2–3. They also created a trilingual class for all students in grade 1 where the teacher was supposed to teach in the three languages simultaneously. The observed learning opportunities for each language group in the trilingual grade 1 class were not promising. Taylor (this volume) describes and analyses this situation.

In Jhapa, the school began implementing mother tongues as MOIs in grades 1–2 only. They created one bilingual class for Nepali- and Rajbangsi-speaking students (grades 1–2) and one class for Santhali students (grades 1–2). In the bilingual class the teacher started by using the two languages simultaneously but after some discussion on some other possibilities with the programme staff, officers from the central education agencies, school staff and community representatives, he decided to try an adaptation of the method of alternative half-days. He would teach half of the day in Nepali and the second half in Rajbangsi.

In Kanchanpur the student population was monolingual but some of the teachers did not speak Rana Tharu. The school redeployed the MT-speaking teachers for grades 1–3 to enable the implementation of Rana Tharu as the MOI. The Nepali-speaking teachers were assigned to higher grades were the MOI was still Nepali. In addition, the teachers stayed after school every Friday to develop materials in the MT for the purposes of textbook production.

Since these multilingual classrooms are common already all over the world and will continue to become still more common with rapidly progressing urbanisation, experimenting with several models and proper evaluation of long-term results is essential. Placing the right teachers in the right places and matching their linguistic competencies with those of the students is essential, as is in-service training of teachers.

6.6.2 The Indigenous Approach

Multilingual education in Nepal is hoped to ensure quality education for all in the long run, but the primary beneficiaries should be those who have previously faced disadvantage linguistically, culturally and pedagogically. The ITM child in any one of the country's villages aspiring to learn does not represent the dominant language or the dominant culture. Who, then, is able to make the decisions and plans that guarantee her equitable opportunities?

The approach in the development and implementation of the MLE programme has been one that begins in the villages and with the languages, traditions, aspirations and skills of the ITM peoples, with the belief that they know best what they need, and possess most of the skills necessary to achieve their goals (see Hough *et al.* (2009) and Yonjan-Tamang *et al.* (2009) for more information about privileging Indigenous knowledges). Throughout the programme, people from pilot schools and villages have been brought together with the district education offices and officers from central level education agencies to discuss issues in MLE. The pilot experiences in local level materials development and the implementation of mother tongues as the media of instruction in grades 1–3 have been central in visualising a nationwide way forward in MLE, ultimately leading to MLE in grades 1 to 8 in basic education.

Foreign experts offering technical assistance are able to share knowledge on MLE from linguistically similar countries, combining theory and practice. But as they lack knowledge of the languages and cultures of the ITM peoples in Nepal, and as models and practices are rarely directly transferrable from one setting to another, the role of local people is crucial in accepting and negotiating the knowledge into practice. It is a general practice that local and central government officials participate in the decision-making and implementation activities. However, the gaps still exist between the importation of ideas and ideologies and the knowledge of systems that operate locally (see Hancock 1991: 119). Dominant language-speaking local or central level officials are most often ill-informed or have 'conventional-wisdom-based' or imported ideologies. Although most Nepalese officials do not seem to resist the MTM education in the country, they often lack the Indigenous knowledge. This calls for a need to empower the IK holders. This means that in order to create and implement MLE – teaching methodologies, content, emphasis on oral and/or written traditions – that is relevant to the ITM peoples, the mother tongue teachers, IK holders and other community members must be strongly involved.

In the case of Nepal, many of the ITM languages are spoken by a very small number of people but even some of the bigger ITM languages have low retention rates. For example, only 48% of Magar children and 69% of Uranw children learn the language as their native tongue (Yonjan-Tamang 2006). The IK holders and community elders can be the key people to help implement MLE programmes, especially within these ITM groups. An example comes from Aotearoa where the approach has been implemented in cultural and linguistic revitalisation movements. The Māori educator Linda Tuhiwai Smith (1999: 111) states that women and elders 'were often those who had retained "traditional" practices, had been taught by elders, were fluent in the language and had specialized knowledges pertaining to the land, the spiritual belief systems and the customary lore of the community'.

An Indigenous approach also necessitates the use of the local languages and the use of interpreters in all situations. This has unfortunately not been successful during all programme activities. Most of the seminars and workshops were in English or English and Nepali, and even when there was interpretation sometimes, this was not done nearly to the extent that it should have been done. This shows that mother tongues need to be used more across the programme, if we are serious about multilingual education and respect for all languages. We must have the time (and resources) to interpret and to give everyone their voice in whichever language they want. This attitude of thinking that it is impossible or even unnecessary to use Indigenous languages (or not even having thought about the issue) is visible in the whole of the development sector internationally,[20] and also in Nepal where English is used as lingua franca even though it is not an official language of the country. The Nepali language seems to have taken the same route that English has followed over time.

6.6.3 Oracy and Literacy

Textbooks for mother tongues as subjects have been written for some of the ITM languages. Most of the ITM languages in Nepal are oral in their traditions. However, there is no regard for the oral traditions of ITMs in Nepal today. We need to see how orate and literate people are defined and what the implications of these definitions are for orate ITMs in Nepal and elsewhere. We have looked at the definitions in the online Thesaurus of Word (see Skutnabb-Kangas 2009b):

LITERATE, adjective

1. many of the workers were not literate ABLE TO READ/WRITE, educated, schooled. ANTONYM illiterate.

2. her literate friends EDUCATED, well-educated, well-read, widely read, scholarly, learned, knowledgeable, lettered, cultured, cultivated, sophisticated, well-informed. ANTONYM ignorant.
3. he was computer literate KNOWLEDGEABLE, well-versed, savvy, smart, conversant, competent; ANTONYM ignorant.

(Thesaurus, Word, online)

These definitions give the impression that a literate person is in many ways positive. If you are orate ('not literate'; ORATE as an adjective does not exist in the Thesaurus), you are NOT educated or knowledgeable or cultured or sophisticated or well-informed or smart or competent. You are the opposite of all these positive characteristics. 'Illiterates' are IGNORANT. We can ask, where fairness is. Everybody should be defined either positively, in terms of what they are and know: 'literate' versus 'orate', or BOTH should be defined negatively, in terms of what they are NOT and do NOT know: 'inorate' versus 'illiterate'. It is unfair to define one group positively in terms of what they are/know ('literate') but define the other group negatively, in terms of what they are NOT/do NOT know ('illiterate'). This hierarchises people. More accurate definitions might be:

ORACY: High levels of spoken language proficiency; to be a competent speaker or storyteller. An *orate* is an individual who communicates through listening and speaking but not reading and writing; orates often have superb memory strategies in comparison with persons considered literate because orates carry their entire 'library' in their heads. *Orature* is oral literature.

(Skutnabb-Kangas and McCarty 2008: 11)

One might ask why we need to define these concepts.

The concepts we use are almost never neutral. In contested arenas such as bilingual education, words and concepts frame and construct the phenomena under discussion, making some persons and groups visible, others invisible; some the unmarked norm, others marked and negative. Choice of language can minoritise or distort some individuals, groups, phenomena, and relations while majoritising and glorifying others. Concepts also can be defined in ways that either hide or expose, and rationalize or question power relations.

(Skutnabb-Kangas and McCarty 2008: 3)

It is clear that the concept 'literate' participates in making ITMs and their cultures 'invisible', 'marked' and 'negative'; it 'minoritises' them, and hides and rationalises power relations instead of exposing and questioning them. The existence of paradigms in literacy research also makes this clear:

Literacy can be defined as the ability to read and write. Yet this definition masks two different paradigms informing literacy research and practice. *Autonomous* views characterise literacy as abstract, neutral, and independent from the social context and language users (Ong, 1982). *Ideological* views characterize literacy as socially and historically situated, fluid, multiple, and power-linked. Educationally, an *autonomous* view emphasizes discrete language skills, often taught through direct instruction and scripted phonics programs. An *ideological* view binds reading and writing to oracy, emphasizing the development of different literacies (and multiliteracies) for different purposes through meaningful social interaction and critical examination of authentic texts.

(Skutnabb-Kangas and McCarty 2008: 3–4)

As stated above, most of the ITM languages in Nepal are oral in their traditions and these may include 'praise-songs, word games, proverbs, riddles, tongue twisters . . . arithmetic puzzles, dilemma tales, fables, myths and legends' (Reagan 1996: 26, 21) which are also common in African languages. They all have an educational side; for example, dilemma tales aim to stimulate discussion on a specific problem, and proverbs develop the child's reasoning power and skill required for decision-making and settling disputes. Similarly, a tale is

not just history but an educational story. The stories are manifestations of the memory, the origin and history of the group, the deeds of their great men and women, their victories and defeats in war, their experiences which led to individual and group successes and those which led to individual and group failure.

(N. Uka quoted in Reagan 1996: 27)

For example, the Rai have a fascinating tradition of composing songs on the spot; they have even sung songs about MLE during seminars. These all should be a part of the mother tongue curriculum; they should come first before the introduction of written language and literature. The introduction of written language and a literary tradition will change the culture (e.g. Reagan 1996; Mühlhäusler 2003).

All this is something the ITM people/s should be aware of and discuss when they start developing scripts and building a literary repertoire. There is so far very little discussion about the values and benefits of oral cultures and traditions in Nepal. It seems in Nepal too that it is assumed that a written language is more developed and therefore all ITM groups will want to move away from oral traditions. Today literacy is glorified and made into a norm that cannot be questioned, while oracy in adults is stigmatised and made into something to be ashamed of. Everybody HAS to be literate. People who are orate are made to feel that it is their own fault; they 'ARE' stupid and ignorant, and their oral culture is not worth maintaining. Perhaps it is inevitable (and beneficial?) in the long run that *some* oral traditions disappear, or at least change as all cultures do, but children who currently grow up in oral environments should not be subjected to education that is comprised mostly of reading and writing. As a way of learning, this is culturally irrelevant. In fact, both oracy and literacy have drawbacks and benefits, and these have to be clarified. It may be possible to combine the benefits of both in well-conducted MLE so that those who want it, can maintain the benefits of oral traditions at the same time as they become literate at a high level in both or all languages.

6.7 Some Comparisons with the Ethiopian Case

There are many similarities between Ethiopian and Nepalese MLE situations. Both countries are rich in many kinds of diversity, and multilingualism has been a common practice for generations. Nepal has very recently developed an official language policy similar to the Ethiopian Education and Training Policy of 1994 to ensure the use of ITM languages in the early years of primary education. Combining Early Childhood Development Programmes entirely based on the mother tongues, and then implementing the first five years of school proper as a condensed MLE programme guarantees the use of these mother tongues as MOI for eight years (as in some regions in Ethiopia). Even when all of it is not in school proper, it nevertheless recognises the value of the students' mother tongues and their potential as academic languages. It also ensures the development of curriculum, textbooks and other reference materials (materials have today been developed in over 20 mother tongues). Ethiopia has been able to include 23 languages in MTM education since 1994. It should be possible for Nepal, with similar socio-economic conditions, to achieve at least the same number very soon. As opposed to Ethiopia which again may be going back to English-medium, by 2015 Nepal aims to provide basic education to all non-Nepali speaking children in their mother tongues. This is an extremely ambitious aim.

The context of the development of MLE is similar in relation to many aspects: teachers in Nepal have a similar (low) level of training; the attitudes of parents are complex and multiple. Similar myths about language learning, and the role of Nepali and English exist among the different stakeholders; many people in both Nepal and Ethiopia also seem to believe that local languages cannot be used to teach academic content. There is very little knowledge about second language learning in Nepal at local, regional and central levels; this is also the case in Ethiopia. However, the benefits of MLE were immediately observed in ITM classrooms in both countries: classroom interaction between students and teachers increased visibly when the teachers began teaching in the students' mother tongue.

There are also differences, and reflecting on some of them can be useful in Nepal. In Ethiopia, teacher training has been offered in the different ITM languages. This has ensured that teachers are competent in their own mother tongue, and that the ITM languages have a developed pedagogical vocabulary. This seems to lead to a prolonged use of ITMs in education, which in turn benefits student learning. In Nepal, teacher training exists in Nepalese only, with the exception of curriculum and in-service training manuals to teach the mother tongue as a subject for some ITM languages, and arrangements are being made to enable the study of various mother tongues at university level. L2 strategies are also introduced in teacher training programmes. The Ethiopian results can encourage the relevant Nepalese central agencies to further develop teacher training in ITM languages.

The development of MLE in Nepal has also different challenges from those in Ethiopia. First of all, the Nepalese regions are generally much more heterogeneous than in Ethiopia. The best Ethiopian match would be SNNPR with 21 languages in primary education. Many of the villages and schools in Nepal are multilingual and require different models and solutions from those that can be designed in schools with an initially monolingual student population. Secondly, the dominant language in Nepal and therefore in the Nepalese education system is Nepali which is for many of the ITM speakers also their second language. It is the language of administration and media, and has enjoyed a very high status in the country. As the districts are generally linguistically heterogeneous, students hear Nepali in their everyday life. This is different in Ethiopia where the position of Amharic is not as strong in all parts of the country as that of Nepali in Nepal. Even if English is also prevalent in Nepal, it is probably not yet a similar threat as in Ethiopia; it is still unusual that English would be learned subtractively, at the cost of Nepali or even ITM languages. In Ethiopia, the main threat to the maintenance and use of ITM languages is English, a foreign language in the country. Thus, while English is also deemed important in Nepal, due to tourism and the great number of Nepalese workers abroad, it does not (yet) represent a similar threat to ITMs in Nepal; instead, it is the Nepali language that may be learned subtractively.

At the moment most of the ITM languages in Nepal are in the earlier phases of standardisation and development; many (up to 70 languages) are solely oral. There may be a need to develop scripts, grammars and some literature for as many as over a hundred languages. Alternatively, or in addition, oral education could be further developed by the speakers of ITM languages with strong oral traditions. This has been different in Ethiopia where a written form for several languages was developed hundreds of years ago.

The fact that Ethiopian educational administrators have, during the last few years, gone back to more and earlier English-medium education, at the cost of MLE, despite the incredibly positive research results from eight years of mother tongue-based MLE can function as a warning to Nepal. Information about positive research results is necessary but not sufficient for rational decision-making. Power politics need to be integrated into educational planning.

6.8 Concluding Remarks on Ways Forward

Nepal's experience with MLE has proved to be a clear departure from rote memorisation, towards a meaningful engagement with learning. The focus in MLE was thus shifted from 'teaching' to 'learning', with a view to fostering children's understanding and creativity. The model-building initiatives in MLE schools demonstrated that the classroom becomes joyful, provided that schools give space to children's languages, cultures and knowledges (see also Panda and Mohanty 2009 on some suggestions for how it can be done). These were some of the observations that the Head teachers of the pilot schools made during the programme evaluation session held in Kathmandu in September 2009.

Despite these encouraging stakeholders' observations, the old usual misconceptions (see interviews in Awasthi 2004) are also visible at both policy and practice levels. These were what the two-page leaflet (see section 6.5) tried to articulate and dispel.[21] The main sources of these fallacies (see Skutnabb-Kangas, in press) seem to be the anglophile elites who seem to be the role models, but who unfortunately appear to be ill-informed about the benefits of MLE for facilitating children's learning. Nonetheless, these elites have succeeded in influencing parents and education officials due to their social and economic capital. Owing to this influence, ordinary parents are bound to follow their paths. As a result, English has been chosen as a medium of instruction at the early stages of children's education by many parents (see *Joint Evaluation of Nepal's Education for All 2004–2009 Sector Programme Evaluation Report 1/2009*). A question that Indigenous organisations are addressing in many countries, together with informed parents, teachers and education authorities and supported by researchers and international organisations is how these misconceptions and fallacies should be handled. Most ITM parents and community organisations are positive towards MLE, but many middle-class people are causing confusion. Politicians, educational decision makers, including staff at various administrative levels, and teachers certainly need more information. This will hopefully lead to some reorientation – which is vital for the success of MLE – but information alone bears little weight in power struggles. In general, though, there is today strong political support for MLE, but more technical and pedagogical backing competence is still limited. Since MLE can be implemented more effectively in collaboration with non-government organisations and local bodies, including Village Development Committees and municipalities, awareness-raising and information about MLE at all levels is urgently needed. Cultural differences in how to tackle the various challenges, and what role outsiders (development partners, international organisations, etc.) might play also need consideration.[22]

Information about results of well-conducted MLE is still sparse in Nepal because the concept of MLE is relatively recent. (However, the Newar communities in Kathmandu have had one mainly Newar-medium school, Jagat Sundar Bhownekuthi school, since the early 1990, with 322 students in the year

2009–2010, and have had very good results.[23]) Interestingly, the student performance in the MLE programme schools described in this article shows some signs of improvement and the available records indicate positive effects on children's participation, retention and learning. Although a full picture will be available only when an assessment has been conducted after the completion of a first three-year cycle, Nepal's MLE interventions seem to lay a foundation for generating evidence to demystify the existing misconceptions.

The MLE programme has a strong focus on the use of local knowledge and methodologies, with a view to indigenising school pedagogy through adopting a bottom-up planning process. Nepal needs to make Regional Education Directorates and District Education Offices more responsive to MLE needs of children at local levels. Nepal also needs to make local government more accountable for MLE promotion in schools.

The MLE interventions also emphasise the need for reorienting teachers for change in their attitudes and behaviours. Recognising the centrality of teachers in Nepal's school system, efforts have been made to help them prepare their instructional plans together with (other) knowledge holders (see Taylor, this volume, for the concept of Funds of Knowledge), for developing appropriate materials at the local level, and encourage them to facilitate children's learning, also by employing a continuous formative assessment process. Training of teachers, materials writers, education administrators, and decision-makers both through practice and on specialised university courses is essential.[24]

The MLE programme in Nepal has also attempted to make parents and education staff aware of the fact that early exit from mother tongue-medium education does not work. The current MLE initiatives will be continued throughout the basic education, up to grade 8, giving enough ground for gaining competence in mother tongues and providing a broad base for transition to the second language. Throughout the MLE implementation, evidence will be collected and documented, to demonstrate how MLE contributes to developing children's full potential and how it can produce better results, with enhanced performance.

Notes

1 We would like to thank the school staff, parents and other community members in the six pilot districts; the MLE project team: David Hough, Päivi Ahonen, Amrit Yonjan-Tamang, Dheeraj Gurung, J. B. Tamang and Ratna Lama; the Inclusive Education Section, and the Concept paper team. Päivi Ahonen was initially intended to be one of the authors of this chapter and collected some of the background data that we have used, but had to withdraw because of other urgent commitments. Our heartfelt thanks to Päivi for her contribution!

2 The Dalits are the so-called untouchables – see, e.g. http://www.dalitnetwork. org/go?/dfn/who_are_the_dalit/C64

3 As of 22 September 2010, they include nine South American states (Argentina, Bolivia, Brazil, Chile, Colombia, Ecuador, Paraguay, Peru and Venezuela), five Central American states (Costa Rica, Guatemala, Honduras, Mexico and Nicaragua), four

European states (Denmark, Netherlands, Norway and Spain), as well as Central African Republic, Dominica, Fiji and Nepal. See: http://www.ilo.org/ilolex/cgi-lex/ratifce.pl?C169.

4 All national-level Indigenous organisations use their energies for informing their members of how ILO 169 can be used. Om Gurung (2009), on the other hand, presents fairly harsh criticism of the ratification. He lists challenges that constrain an effective implementation of the Convention, also claiming that the ratification was done for political reasons, to pacify Indigenous organisations, and that the government is deliberately misinterpreting the Convention, especially in relation to land rights and the right to self-determination, stirring up 'ethnic' conflict instead of developing federalism and a deeper democracy.

5 See http://www2.ohchr.org/english/law/crc.htm; Nepal has ratified the CRC.

6 See Skutnabb-Kangas and Dunbar (2010) for a thorough discussion of ITM children's right to education and violations of that right.

7 This recommendation comes from ILO 169, Art. 28, para. 1 which, however, has the addition 'wherever practicable'.

8 We prefer the term 'push-out', rather than the usual 'drop-out'. In most cases, children do not 'drop out' voluntarily; it is the organisation of the education (in classes where the children do not understand the teaching languages) that pushes them out. The term 'drop-out' reflects deficiency-based theories, which blame the Indigenous students, their characteristics, their parents and their culture for lack of school achievement. Hereafter, we use 'push-out', except in quotations.

9 General Comment No. 11 (2009), 'Indigenous children and their rights under the Convention', Committee on the Rights of the Child, Fiftieth session, 12–30 January, 2009: Document CRC/C/GC/11 (http://www.crin.org/docs/GC.11_indigenous_New.pdf).

10 08/12/99. E/C.12/1999/10, General Comments, by the UN Committee on Economic, Social and Cultural Rights, (http://www.unhchr.ch/tbs/doc.nsf/%28symbol%29/E.C.12.1999.10.En?OpenDocument).

11 Similar harm was described in detail in Mauritius, at an International Hearing on the Harm done in Schools by the Suppression of the Mother Tongue, 20–24 October 2009. See the Report, Findings and Recommendations, at http://www.lalitmauritius.org, 27 Oct 2009, Documents.

12 From now on, 'MLE' is taken to mean mother tongue-based multilingual education.

13 The other country receiving applause is Ethiopia, in Box 2.6: 'Ethiopia – moving into the UPE fast lane', p. 58.

14 These are not new issues in Nepal. Alan Davies (2009) describes in an article, aptly called 'Professional Advice vs Political Imperatives', a 1982/83 Survey of English Language Teaching, set up by the Ministry of Education in Nepal, with three Nepalese and three outsider experts. On the basis of research-based knowledge on language learning and interviews and tests in Nepal (students and teachers were given an English language test) they wanted to recommend that English language teaching as a subject be started only in Grade 8. Availability and language competence of teachers were crucial for the recommendation. A necessary compromise was reached in negotiations with politicians and educational authorities: grade 4. The same misconceptions that are still flourishing were evident. At the same time, the reality and importance of the political imperatives has to be acknowledged. Davies does not mention Indigenous and minority children at all; once again, they are invisibilised.

15 The Concept paper (Bajracharya et al. 2008) was developed as one result of a 3-day intensive course (taught by Tove Skutnabb-Kangas), with representatives of Nepalese education authorities and language specialists. It deals with issues about what MLE is, why it is required in Nepal, various possible models of MLE and how to implement them, Nepal's MLE-related international law and human rights obligations, current

policy, practices and efforts related to MLE in Nepal, and possible (short-, middle- and long-term) future directions for MLE in Nepal.

16 See, e.g., Nikièma and Taryam Ilboudo 2009, this volume. See also articles by François Grin at http://www.unige.ch/eti/ecole/organisation/departements/dfr/dfr-corps-enseignant/pages-personnelles/francois-grin.html#cv.

17 This was discussed in the first stages of the programme during a visit by an MLE coordinator, Dr Mahendra Kumar Mishra, from Orissa, India, where such community centres are in operation. There is also a National MLE Resource Consortium at the Jawaharlal Nehru University, New Delhi (http://www.nmrc-jnu.org/); one of the two directors, Professor Ajit Mohanty, has also consulted with the MLE Programme.

18 Adequate opportunities for education are lacking for indigenous communities (para. 26); 'Land-loss and forced displacement over time has resulted in the dissolution of communities, the break-up of families, and the attendant lack of registration of many members of Adivasi Janajati [indigenous] communities, making access to simple services such as health and education a challenge, if not an impossibility' (para. 41); 'Although the Ministry of Education is now promoting the objective of multilingual education through various plans, many community members interviewed by the Special Rapporteur expressed concern that education in their mother tongues was not available for their children' (para. 44).

19 Professor Taylor was the international consultant in both these 2-week training courses (see Taylor 2010).

20 See, e.g. Widin 2010 for a critical description.

21 The Indian National Multilingual Education Resource Consortium (http://www. nmrc-jnu.org/) has produced a similar leaflet in Oriya, Telugu, Hindi and English (see Mohanty, Panda and Skutnabb-Kangas 2009); it has been translated into several tribal languages. These fallacies seem to be similar in many if not most countries.

22 See the long quote about outsiders from Nurmela in Heugh and Skutnabb-Kangas (2010: 324).

23 The first batch of students, seven girls and six boys, graduated in 2009, all with very high marks (Nirmal Man Tuladhar, emails to TSK August–October 2009; thanks!).

24 Tribhuvan University in Kathmandu (Department of Linguistics, Professor Yogendra Yadava) has already initiated this in 2009 with an MA-course in MLE.

References

Acharya, Sushan (2009). *Report on MLE Policy and Strategy*. Bhaktapur, Nepal: MLE Programme, Inclusive Education Section, Department of Education.

Anaya, James (2009). *Promotion and protection of all human rights, civil, political, economic, social and cultural rights, including the right to development. Report by the Special Rapporteur on the situation of human rights and fundamental freedoms of indigenous people, James Anaya. Addendum: Report on the situation of indigenous peoples in Nepal*. Human Rights Council, Twelfth session, Agenda item 3. United Nations, General Assembly, A/HRC/12/34/ Add.3. 20 July 2009.

Awasthi, Lava Deo (2004). *Exploring Monolingual School Practices in Multilingual Nepal*. Ph.D. thesis. Copenhagen: Danmarks Pædagogiske Universitet/Danish University of Education.

Bajracharya, Pradeep, Bhattarai, Prem, Bhattarai, Toya, Dahal, Madhav, Gautam, Geha Nath, Pant, Hari Ram, *et al.* (2008). *Multilingual Education and Nepal. A Concept Paper*. Bhaktapur, Nepal: MLE Programme, Inclusive Education Section, Department of Education (also as an Appendix in Skutnabb-Kangas and Mohanty 2009).

Dahal, Dev Raj (2005). *Nepal: Supporting Peace Processes Through a Systemic Approach. Study prepared for the Berghof Foundation for Peace Support.* (http://www.nepaldemocracy. org/).

Davies, Alan (2009). Professional Advice vs Political Imperatives. In Alderson, Charles J. (ed.), *The Politics of Language Education. Individuals and Institutions.* Bristol: Multilingual Matters, 45–63.

EDSC (1997). *National Achievement Level of Grade 3 Students.* Educational and Developmental Service Centre. Kathmandu.

Education for All Programme (2004–09). Keshar Mahal: Ministry of Education.

EFA Global Monitoring Report 2009. Overcoming Inequality: Why Governance Matters. Paris: UNESCO and Oxford: Oxford University Press.

EFA National Plan of Action (2001–15). Kathmandu: Ministry of Education and Sports.

Global Education Digest 2009. Comparing Education Statistics Across the World. Montreal: UNESCO Institute of Statistics.

Gurung, Om (2009). Major Challenges for Implementing ILO Convention 169 in Nepal. Paper presented in a three-day seminar 'Should States Ratify Human Rights Conventions?' Organised by the Center of Advanced Studies, Oslo, Norway, August 18–20, 2009. (http://www.jus.uio.no/english/research/areas/intrel/projects/should-states-ratify-project/gurung-final-major-challenges-of-ilo-implemen.pdf).

Hancock, Graham (1991). *The Lords of Poverty.* London: Mandarin.

Heugh, Kathleen (2009). Into the cauldron: An interplay of indigenous and globalised knowledge with strong and weak notions of literacy and language education in Ethiopia and South Africa. *Language Matters, Studies in the Languages of Africa,* 40: 2, 166–189.

Heugh, Kathleen and Skutnabb-Kangas, Tove (2010). Multilingual Education Works When 'Peripheries' Take the Centre Stage. In Heugh, Kathleen and Skutnabb-Kangas, Tove (eds), *Multilingual Education Works: From the Periphery to the Centre.* New Delhi: Orient BlackSwan, 316–342.

Hough, David, Thapa Magar, Ram Bahadur and Yonjan-Tamang, Amrit (2009). Privileging Indigenous Knowledges: Empowering MLE in Nepal. In Mohanty, Ajit, Panda, Minati, Phillipson, Robert and Skutnabb-Kangas, Tove (eds), *Multilingual Education for Social Justice: Globalising the Local.* New Delhi: Orient BlackSwan, 146–161. The same article is in Skutnabb-Kangas *et al.* (eds) (2009).

Interim Constitution of Nepal (2007). Kathmandu: Nepal Law Book Society.

Joint Evaluation of Nepal's Education for All 2004–2009 Sector Programme (2008). Evaluation Department, Norad.

Mohanty, Ajit, Panda, Minati and Skutnabb-Kangas, Tove (2009). *Why Mother-tongue-based MLE?* New Delhi: National Multilingual Education Resource Consortium. Jawaharlar Nehru University. (http://www.nmrc-jnu.org/nmrc_publications.html). [Also in Adivasi Oriya, Banjara, Hindi, Gondi, Kolami, Konda, Koya, Kui, Kuvi, Oriya, Saora, Savara and Telugu].

Mühlhäusler, Peter (2003). *Language of Environment – Environment of Language. A Course in Ecolinguistics.* London: Battlebridge.

National Assessment of Grade 5 Students (2008). Assessment commissioned by Department of Education, conducted by Full Bright Consultancy and Chirag. Kathmandu: Department of Education.

National Curriculum Framework for School Education in Nepal (NCF) (2007). Sanothimi, Bhaktapur: Government of Nepal, Ministry of Education and Sports, Curriculum Development Centre.

Nepal Ministry of Education and Sports (2006). *Flash I Report 2064 (2007–08)*. Sanothimi, Bhaktapur, Nepal: Ministry of Education and Sports, Department of Education.

Panda, Minati and Mohanty, Ajit (2009). Language Matters, so Does Culture: Beyond the Rhetoric of Culture in Multilingual Education. In Mohanty *et al.* (eds), 295–312. The same article is in Skutnabb-Kangas *et al.* (eds) (2009).

Phillipson, Robert (1992). *Linguistic Imperialism*. Oxford: Oxford University Press.

Phillipson, Robert (2009). *Linguistic Imperialism Continued*. Delhi: Orient BlackSwan [also New York: Routledge].

Prasad, Chandrabhan (2001). *The Impure Milk of Lord Macaulay?* (http://www.ambedkar. org/chandrabhan/Theimpure.htm).

Raj, Prakash A. (2004). *Maoists in the Land of Buddha: An Analytical Study of the Maoist Insurgency in Nepal*. New Delhi: Nirala Publications.

Reagan, Timothy (1996). *Non-Western Educational Traditions: Alternative Approaches to Educational Thought and Practice*. Mahwah, NJ: Lawrence Erlbaum.

Skutnabb-Kangas, Tove (2000). *Linguistic Genocide in Education – Or Worldwide Diversity and Human Rights?* Mahwah, NJ: Lawrence Erlbaum. [South Asian updated edition in 2008, Delhi: Orient BlackSwan].

Skutnabb-Kangas, Tove (2009a). Why mother-tongue-based multilingual education? Kathmandu: Multilingual Education Program for All Non-Nepali Speaking Students of Primary Schools of Nepal. Ministry of Education, Department of Education, Inclusive Section (http://www.tove-skutnabb-kangas.org/en/articles_for_downloading.html, in Nepali or English).

Skutnabb-Kangas, Tove (2009b). Literacy and Oracy in Mother-Tongue Based Multi-Lingual Education. Public Lecture, Mahatma Gandhi Institute, Mauritius, 24 October 2009. ((http://www.tove-skutnabb-kangas.org/en/PowerPoint_presentations.html).

Skutnabb-Kangas, Tove (in press). Mother tongue medium education. In *The Encyclopedia of Applied Linguistics*, General Editor Carol A. Chapelle; Volume *Bilingual Education*, Area Editors Jasone Cenoz and Durk Gorter; Oxford: Wiley-Blackwell.

Skutnabb-Kangas, Tove and Dunbar, Robert (2010). *Indigenous Children's Education as Linguistic Genocide and a Crime Against Humanity? A Global View*. Gáldu, Resource Centre for the Rights of Indigenous Peoples, www.galdu.org. Read it at http://www.e-pages. dk/grusweb/55/.

Skutnabb-Kangas, Tove and McCarty, Teresa (2008). Clarification, ideological/epistemological underpinnings and implications of some concepts in bilingual education. In Volume 5, Cummins, Jim and Hornberger, Nancy H. (eds), *Bilingual Education. Encyclopedia of Language and Education*, 2nd edition. New York: Springer, 3–17.

Skutnabb-Kangas, Tove and Mohanty, Ajit (2009). *Policy and Strategy for MLE in Nepal. Report by Tove Skutnabb-Kangas and Ajit Mohanty. Consultancy visit 4–14 March 2009.* Kathmandu: Multilingual Education Program for All Non-Nepali Speaking Students of Primary Schools of Nepal. Ministry of Education, Department of Education, Inclusive Section. (http://www.tove-skutnabb-kangas.org/en/articles_for_downloading.html).

Skutnabb-Kangas, Tove, Phillipson, Robert, Mohanty, Ajit and Panda, Minati (eds) (2009). *Social Justice through Multilingual Education*. Bristol, Buffalo and Toronto: Multilingual Matters.

Skutnabb-Kangas, Tove, Phillipson, Robert, Panda, Minati and Mohanty, Ajit (2009). MLE Concepts, Goals, Needs and Expense: English for All or Achieving Justice? In Mohanty *et al.* (eds), 313–334. The same article is in Skutnabb-Kangas *et al.* (eds) (2009).

Taylor, Shelley K. (2010). MLE Policy and Practice in Nepal: Identifying the Glitches and Making it Work. In Heugh, Kathleen and Skutnabb-Kangas, Tove (eds), *Multilingual Education Works. From the Periphery to the Centre.* Hyderabad: Orient BlackSwan, 204–223.

Three Year Interim Plan (2007–10) (2007). National Planning Commission. Kathmandu.

Tuhiwai Smith, Linda (1999). *Decolonizing Methodologies: Research and Indigenous Peoples.* Dunedin: University of Otago Press.

Widin, Jaqueline (2010). *Illegitimate Practices. Global English Language Education.* Bristol, Buffalo and Toronto: Multilingual Matters.

World Bank (2007). *Project Paper on a Proposed Additional Financing (Grant) in the Amount of SDR 38.7 Million (US$60,0 Million Equivalent) to Nepal for the Education For All Project.* Bangkok: World Bank, Human Development Unit, South Asia Regional Office. (41346-NP.)

Yadava, Yogendra P. and Grove, Carl (eds) (2008) [1994]. *The Report of National Languages Policy Recommendation Commission.* Kathmandu: Central Department of Linguistics, Tribhuvan University, Kirtipur, Kathmandu, Nepal.

Yadava, Yogendra Prasad and Turin, Mark (2006). Indigenous Languages of Nepal: A Critical Analysis of the Linguistic Situation and Contemporary Issues. In Yadava, Yogendra P. and Bajracharya, Pradeep L. (eds) *The Indigenous Languages of Nepal (ILN). Situation, Policy Planning and Coordination.* Lalitpur: National Foundation for Development of Indigenous Nationalities (NFDIN), 6–46.

Yonjan-Tamang, Amrit (2006). *Languages of Nepal: Present Situation and Language Planning in Nepal* (in Nepali). Kathmandu: Indigenous Linguistic Society of Nepal (Adivasi Bhasabigyan Samaj).

Yonjan-Tamang, Amrit, Hough, David and Nurmela, Iina (2009). The Nepal Multilingual Education Program: Year One of Planning and Implementation. In Mohanty *et al.* (eds), 241–249. [also in Skutnabb-Kangas *et al.* (eds) 2009].

7

MLE FROM ETHIOPIA TO NEPAL

Refining a Success Story

Shelley K. Taylor

7.1 Introduction

The results of Heugh, Benson, Bogale and Gebre Yohannes' (2007) seminal work on MLE in Ethiopia show that mother tongue-based multilingual language education (MLE) can be successfully introduced and implemented in less wealthy countries with high levels of ethno-linguistic diversity if only the political will is there. This chapter[1] deals with an MLE programme implemented in Nepal 2007–2009. Like the Ethiopian MLE programme, Nepal is not wealthy, yet Nepalis are ambitiously implementing a visionary project. They intend to extend MLE from 15 to 100 languages over the next several years (Nurmela, Awasthi and Skutnabb-Kangas, this volume). With challenging new programmes come implementation difficulties and glitches to work out. Two such glitches are reviewed in this chapter, not to take away from this laudable effort, but to maximise its success.

Oral reports of educators whom I met while delivering two workshops for MLE teachers and materials developers, and documentary evidence reviewed since, indicated that a key aspect of MLE was being misconstrued; namely, the number of linguistic groups that could be combined in any particular classroom. Educators remarked that MLE was the perfect way to handle the linguistic diversity typical of many Nepali classrooms. This comment suggested that MLE was being interpreted as a panacea for high levels of societal multilingualism and the educational challenges that it poses.[2] The present chapter recognises that many educational models designed in and for Western contexts must be reconceptualised to account for the social, linguistic and economic realities of countries such as Nepal. Therefore, it adopts a multilayered approach in its review of key tenets of MLE and analysis of how misinterpreting these tenets can undermine the theoretical underpinnings of the programme. It also takes a multilayered, context-sensitive approach to viewing implementation glitches and examining how materials development fits into the overall picture. To begin, the bases of MLE are reviewed.

7.2 Key Concepts of MLE and Key MLE Practices Internationally

7.2.1 Key Concepts of MLE

Over a decade ago, Tove Skutnabb-Kangas edited a book entitled *Multilingualism for all* (Skutnabb-Kangas 1995b). In her introductory chapter, she outlined what 'multilingual language education' (MLE) was all about and how it could look when implemented in schools (Skutnabb-Kangas 1995a). She drew from Hugo Baetens Beardsmore's (1995) work in the European School system, which entailed European Union members' children being schooled in their mother tongue (L1) (L1-based instruction) throughout the primary years, regardless of their country of residence. These children would then go on to learn another language (L2) (they could choose between English, French and German) as a subject in primary school, followed by learning a third language (L3) as a subject. For their L3, the children could choose to study any other official EU language, provided that the school offered it. Once the children had enough exposure to their L2 and L3 as subjects, they were gradually introduced to using their L2 (or in non-obligatory subjects even L3) as the medium of instruction. In secondary school, students would take about half of the curriculum in their L2. At the time, Skutnabb-Kangas (1995a) remarked that while multilingualism has long been valued in elite circles, it has generally not been broadly accepted, especially for children from stigmatised linguistic and cultural backgrounds, like immigrant children. In Western countries, not much has changed since she made that observation.

Skutnabb-Kangas (1995b) invited contributors to *Multilingualism for all* to 'imagine' whether Baetens Beardsmore's (1995) MLE model of schooling would work in different national contexts and how it could be applied. While all of the contributors endorsed MLE in principle, most predicted implementation difficulties in their national contexts. The exception was E. Annamalai's (1995) paper describing the Indian context where trilingualism was already part of the school system. The major drawback that he noted was that, although children experienced trilingual schooling, including in their state language, many were not receiving L1-based instruction. In a talk given by Anvita Abbi (2008) in Delhi, she questioned the usefulness of the three-language formula in India (Hindi, the state language, and English) for the same reason as Annamalai (1995) a decade earlier. She noted that the three-language formula did not provide for L1-based instruction. Instead, Abbi (2008) recommended a four-language formula, beginning with children's L1 as the medium of instruction in the primary years.

While three- or four-language versions of MLE are not even issues in many wealthy countries such as Canada (Taylor 2009a), they are currently being implemented in India and Nepal (Jhingran 2009; Mohanty, Mishra, Reddy and Ramesh 2009; Nurmela, Awasthi and Skutnabb-Kangas, this volume; Yonjan-Tamang, Hough and Nurmela 2009). The last two articles describe a Nepali MLE project. These papers, combined with Benson, Heugh, Bogale and Gebre Yohannes (this volume) and Heugh, Benson, Bogale and Gebre Yohannes' (2007 and this volume) seminal work on MLE in Ethiopia, are clear examples of how MLE can be successfully introduced and implemented in schools with high levels of ethnolinguistic diversity in less wealthy countries if the political will is there.

As García, Skutnabb-Kangas and Torres-Guzman note in their book *Imagining multilingual schools*, the key criterion for multilingual language education is the number of languages of instruction: 'Multilingual education is education where more than two languages are used as languages of instruction in subjects other than the languages themselves' (García *et al.* 2006: 13). They caution that it is not enough for a school to be 'linguistically diverse' (i.e. to have students that speak many different L1s) (ibid.). Student multilingualism does not constitute MLE in and of itself.

In order for schools that offer more than two languages of instruction to function well, Skutnabb-Kangas suggests the following principles for multilingualism through education:

1   Support (i.e. use as the main language of education for the first eight years) the language that is least likely to develop to a high formal level.
2   Group children with the same L1 together initially – mixed groups are not positive initially, especially for cognitively demanding, decontextualised subjects (i.e. subjects that are highly print-based or where measures are not taken to make oral instruction comprehensible to L2/L3-speakers).
3   Ensure that all children become high-level bilinguals, not only minority-language children.
4   Equalise the status of all children's L1s and their knowledge of the language of instruction (i.e. either all children know the language of instruction or no children know the language of instruction, or efforts are made so that they alternate between knowing and not knowing it).[3]
5   Ensure that teachers are bi- or multilingual – though a high level of competence in a minority language is more important for a teacher than a high level of competence in a majority language (e.g. Nepali).
6   Ensure that foreign languages be taught with the child's L1 as the starting point by teachers who know the child's L1.[4]
7   Ensure that children study both their L1 (i.e. a minority or Indigenous language) and L2 (e.g. Nepali in Nepal) as compulsory subjects all the way through to school completion.
8   Use both languages as medium of education in some phase of the children's

education, but the progression between languages, and how much each is used when, varies for minority versus majority children.

(Skutnabb-Kangas 1995a, adapted from pp. 12–14)

These principles must be interpreted flexibly in light of the linguistic heterogeneity and complexity of different settings around the world in which MLE is being implemented. As Benson (2009) notes, MLE in settings such as Nepal must be context-sensitive; still certain principles must be maintained (e.g. delivering a substantial chunk of daily instruction through the medium of children's L1) for a programme to qualify as MLE.

In contrast to the time when Skutnabb-Kangas (1995b) initially inquired into how applicable the European Schools MLE model could be in other contexts and how multilingualism develops and plays out, a multitude of researchers are now working in this area. This increased research and professional interest in MLE has revealed a need to rethink or develop new theories to capture and account for the dynamics of child multilingual development and the intricacies of multilingual societies such as Nepal. As Skutnabb-Kangas, Phillipson, Panda and Mohanty (2009) explain:

> Theoretical concepts and categories are temporally embedded to begin with; they continue to evolve through the flow of knowledge, practices, and analytical processes. Those in the field of MLE are no exceptions. The models and concepts in the field of bilingualism/multilingualism and [Bilingual Education]/MLE (such as 'balanced'/additive/subtractive bilingualism) which proved to be extremely powerful explanatory tools are now becoming inadequate for dealing with linguistic heterogeneity and complexity around the globe. Even the common categorical labels such as monolingualism, bilingualism, multilingualism are being increasingly problematised.
>
> *(ibid.: 315)*

Jessner's (2006) dynamic model of multilingualism offers a theoretical refinement for understanding the development of multilingualism. Her model suggests that multilinguals are qualitatively different from monolinguals or bilinguals as all of their linguistic systems interact in novel ways. According to Jessner (2006), multilinguals have different sorts of metalinguistic awareness and therefore process cognitive information differently from bi- or monolinguals (see also Mohanty 1995). Jessner (2006) posits that the languages that multilinguals share at the linguistic level enhance their knowledge of all of the languages in their linguistic repertoire. Furthermore, she suggests that different multilingual individuals reap the metalinguistic advantages of their multilingualism differently, suggesting that we are on the very eve of research into understanding the dynamic processes involved in multilingualism.

Despite the magnitude of challenges that Skutnabb-Kangas *et al.* (2009) and Jessner's (2006) work identify as coming into play and demanding consideration in any attempt to introduce MLE into settings with the extent of linguistic diversity that Nepal has, one concept that has been the mainstay of bilingual education still holds: Cummins' (1981) work on the level of proficiency in an L2 that children need to succeed academically when receiving L2-based instruction; specifically, cognitive-academic language proficiency (CALP).

7.2.2 BICS, CALP and the Need for L1-based Instruction

The thread that keeps running through Skutnabb-Kangas' (1995a) principles of multilingual development through education is that continued L1-support is necessary for minority-language children to meet academic success. This thread is understandable in light of Cummins' (1981) distinction between basic interpersonal communication skills (BICS) and CALP, and the time required to develop CALP. Whereas children may sound proficient in an L2 within two years of starting to learn the language, they do not develop sufficient CALP (i.e. depth of vocabulary; deep understanding of linguistic and culturally based properties of an L2) until they have learned it for four, six, eight or ten years, depending on their situations. As Cummins (2009) notes, research continues to support the validity of this concept developed in the context of bilingual development and bilingual education and, given my experiences in Nepal, it continues to hold true for multilingual development through MLE.[5]

Heugh *et al.*'s (2007) work in Ethiopia provides empirical support for Cummins' (1981, 2009) claim and Skutnabb-Kangas *et al.*'s (2009) call for continued L1-support. In their study, Heugh *et al.* (2007) found that students who received eight years of L1-based instruction outperformed students who transitioned to L2-based instruction after four or six years (see also Benson *et al.* and Heugh *et al.* in this volume). Notably, the Ethiopian study not only replicates the findings of earlier studies conducted in Western settings (e.g. Collier and Thomas 1989, 1999) that supported Cummins' (1981, 2009) psycholinguistic rationale for CALP, but it does so in Africa. The fact that the construct holds in a setting renowned for its linguistic heterogeneity supports its robustness – and the psycholinguistic premise of L1-based MLE. Still, there is another strong argument in favour of MLE in Nepal and around the world.

7.2.3 Linguistic Human Rights

Skutnabb-Kangas (1998: 23) identifies the following as necessary conditions of linguistic human rights (LHRs) at the individual level. An individual must be able to: (a) fully learn, use in most official situations (including schools) and identify with her L1(s) and have that identification accepted and respected by others; (b) learn (one of) the official language(s) of the country of residence and thus become bilingual (or trilingual, as the case may be); (c) not have a change of L1 imposed, which encompasses supposedly 'voluntary' language shift if the individual does not know about the possible long-term consequences of such a shift (i.e. an uninformed shift would be viewed as imposed rather than fully voluntary), and (d) profit from the state education system, no matter what her L1. Skutnabb-Kangas (1998, 2000) argues that, presently, many minority individuals cannot fully learn their L1 (e.g. develop both oracy and literacy) or use their L1 in official settings such as schools. They cannot become balanced bilinguals with the help of the school (those who do so often succeed despite the school). Many cannot derive maximum benefit from state education. And many cannot control whether their L1 will remain a fully known language that they can transfer to their children if they so wish – they are forced to shift languages. In short, they do not have linguistic human rights. Their lack of LHRs not only limits their educational prospects, but it also limits their economic prospects, denies their legal rights and constitutes an illegal abuse of human rights (Skutnabb-Kangas and Dunbar 2010).

7.2.4 From Right . . . to Practice: The Case of Nepal

When the Maoist government came into power in Nepal in 2007, it introduced an Interim Constitution guaranteeing Indigenous and minority children the right to L1-based instruction (Nurmela *et al.* this volume). Offering L1-based instruction in Indigenous languages was a major change from the prior system whereby Nepali was the mandatory medium of instruction for all children, despite their varied L1s. The Nepali-medium mandate had come (directly or indirectly) from the Nepali monarchy, an authoritarian regime that held power for more than 240 years, and was part of the greater hegemonic, nationalist ideology that promoted 'one religion', 'one culture' and 'one language' in the name of 'national unity' (Awasthi 2004; Yadava 2007). Though Nepal was a multilingual country, a single language (Nepali) was granted primacy with all the power, recognition and prestige that ensued while the remaining languages were minoritised, impoverished and marginalised (Skutnabb-Kangas and McCarty 2008; Yadava 2007). State-imposed dominance of one language, Nepali, impeded linguistic 'minority' children's rights to L1-based education (i.e. their LHRs), whether their L1 was an Indigenous (tribal) or a minority language. Therefore, it was remarkable when, following the change in government in Nepal, the governments of Nepal and Finland introduced an MLE project in Nepal.

The purpose of the Nepali MLE project was to develop the capacity of Indigenous/minority communities to create L1-based programmes in the primary years in local schools and to institute culturally relevant pedagogy (i.e. teaching that was culturally familiar and relevant to the local children). In Hough, Thapa Magar and Yonjan-Tamang's (2009) terms, the goal was to institute critical indigenous pedagogy. An additional goal of the project was to develop linguistically/culturally responsive teaching materials. The project also aimed to develop the capacity of the Nepali Ministry of Education and Sports and the National Centre for Educational Development (NCED) to prepare trainers of trainers; namely, the teachers who would teach subsequent groups of teachers in future pilot districts and schools how to implement MLE programming. Under the auspices of the project, the NCED prepared teacher training manuals in nine languages first, and completed manuals in 15 languages by summer 2009.

I conducted two workshops for materials writers and teacher trainers, both of which focused on theoretical and practical aspects of MLE laid out in the locally developed 'MLE framework' (Taylor 2010). One aspect of the way the programme was implemented in some parts of Nepal undermined the theoretical underpinnings of MLE and created roadblocks to achieving programmatic goals. I outline this issue first, and then describe a more practical issue that arose with regard to materials development and preparing materials developers and teacher trainers to introduce culturally/linguistic responsive pedagogy to subsequent groups of MLE teachers in indigenous and minority settings.

7.3 Glimpses of Glitches

7.3.1 'Monolingual' Versus 'Multilingual' Multilingual Language Education?

The main issue that arose in the first workshop involved homogeneous versus het-erogeneous linguistic groupings of children in MLE classrooms. It also involved the advisability of grouping two, three or more linguistic groups together in any given classroom. To explain, given the high level of societal multilingualism in Nepal, it stood to reason that some workshop participants had been teaching in schools with children from more than one linguistic group in the same classroom. This was less noticeable prior to implementation of the MLE programme as, under the old system, all children whose L1 was not Nepali were 'submersed' in Nepali as the medium of instruction. Under the MLE system, the issue of individual L1s came to the forefront of language teaching provisions. The pro-gramme began with teachers in seven pilot schools working with nine languages, which meant that most schools had homogeneous groupings from the inception stage onwards although some had heterogeneous groupings. It was understand-ably easier for schools to accommodate same-language groupings in communities with relatively homogeneous Indigenous language groups than in communities with more heterogeneous Indigenous language groups.

Nurmela et al. (this volume) note that schools adopted slightly different solu-tions to the issue of multiple L1s. Some initial misunderstandings of what was required for optimal L1 learning were resolved, as Nurmela et al. (this volume) describe with regard to the classroom in Jhapa District. To explain, while in many cases homogeneous classrooms were formed (i.e. with children from one Indigenous language background), other classrooms grouped children from two language backgrounds together. In one school, children from three Indigenous language groups and Nepali-speaking children were grouped together (see Nurmela *et al.* this volume). The latter model, in particular, differed substantially from the European School model, which was designed on the assumption that all children in a classroom would share the same L1. Contradictory though it may seem, the European School model of MLE as reflected in linguistically homogeneous groupings of children became referred to as 'monolingual' classrooms (i.e. monolingual *multilingual language education*) in the Nepali MLE context. Classrooms comprised of children from more than one language group became referred to as 'multilingual' classrooms (i.e. multilingual *multilingual language education*). To simplify the discussion, I will refer to the first option as 'single-L1' and the second as 'multi-L1' MLE groupings.

Models also differed in terms of whether several teachers taught their own specialty courses in one classroom ('subject teaching') or one classroom teacher stayed in the classroom for the whole day and taught all the subjects ('grade teaching'), either in a single-grade or mixed-grade classroom. Table 7.1 (below) summarises the different linguistic and grade groupings adopted in pilot school classrooms in terms of different 'models'.

The six models presented in Table 7.1 differed in terms of the number of L1s and grades found in a classroom (i.e. single-L1 or multi-L1s; single-grade or mixed-grades). There were four single-L1 models and two multi-L1 models. The *single-L1* version featured L1-medium instruction during maths, social studies, art, science, health and physical education lessons. The children also learned English and Nepali as subjects beginning in grade 1. The *multi-L1* version featured a bi-/tri-/multilingual teacher delivering L1 instruction to children from two, three or four different L1 groups, depending on how the programme was designed locally.

In one school, 75% of the children were Indigenous peoples and spoke four different L1s between them (Nurmela, personal correspondence, 28 January 2009). Three of the languages shared features and older children from those three language backgrounds might gradually come to understand the two that were not their L1s to some extent, but the fourth language would likely remain unintelligible to them without extended socialisation with speakers of that language (Baquedano-López and Kattan 2007).

Over the course of my stays in Nepal to conduct trainer of trainers and materials development workshops in 2009, I had the opportunity to view film footage of the grade 1 classroom that included children from four language groups in a multi-L1 classroom. I also had the opportunity to engage in conversation with participants from the school in which that multi-L1 classroom was housed. They informed me that their typical way of teaching that grade was to repeat the same lesson in four different languages, subject after subject, since they were multilingual in all four of the children's L1s. For example, a social studies teacher would start by delivering a lesson in Language A, then deliver the same lesson

TABLE 7.1 Different classroom organisations in the MLE pilot schools (adapted from Nurmela, forthcoming)

MODEL	Main features of classrooms	Languages used	Status of the school
Model I	Single-L1, Single-grade, Subject teaching	Rana (Tharu) in grades 1, 2 and 3 in Kanchanpur	Enough classrooms All teachers speak the students' L1 – enough L1 teachers
Model II	Single-L1, Single-grade, Grade teaching	Athapaharia (Rai) in grades 1, 2 and 3 in Dhankuta	Enough classrooms Some teachers cannot speak the students' L1 – L1 teachers for first 3 grades only
Model III	Single-L1, Multi-grade, Grade teaching	Santhal in a combined Grade 1/2 classroom in Jhapa	Lack of classrooms for MLE purposes Most teachers cannot speak the students' L1 – lack of L1 teachers (only 1)
Model IV	Single-L1, Multi-grade, Subject teaching	Uraw in a combined Grade 2/3 classroom in Sunsari	Lack of classrooms for MLE purposes All teachers are multilingual in the students' L1s
Model V	Multi-L1, Single-grade, Subject teaching	Tharu, Maithili, Uraw and Nepali in Grade 1 classroom in Sunsari (simultaneous use of all four languages by one teacher)	Lack of classrooms for MLE purposes All teachers are multilingual in the students' L1s – enough L1 teachers
Model VI	Multi-L1, Multi-grade, Grade teaching	Tharu/Maithili and Nepali in a combined Grade 2/3 classroom in Sunsari (simultaneous use of both languages) Rajbangsi and Nepali in a combined Grade 1/2 classroom in Jhapa (half-day instruction in Rajbansi and half-day instruction in Nepali)	Lack of classrooms in both schools for MLE purposes Not enough teachers speak the students' L1s (Jhapa)

Notes:
Subject teaching: the general practice in Nepal is that, even in primary schools, teachers teach their own subject rather than all subjects in one classroom.
Grade teaching: refers to the situation whereby one teacher teaches all the subjects in one classroom (it can also be a multi-grade classroom)

in Language B, then in Language C and, finally, in Language D. Then the next subject teacher (e.g. mathematics) would come into the room and follow the same procedure.

Technically, the children were all receiving L1-based instruction in all four languages and their teachers were delivering L1-based instruction to all four linguistic groups in the classroom; however, the children were only in grade 1 and the three languages that were not their L1 were not yet comprehensible to them, meaning they only understood the language of instruction for 25% of the school day. How did grade 1 students just learning how to 'do school' react? The film footage showed unruly student behaviour when instruction was in the languages they did not understand.

Compared to the former system of Nepali submersion, the teachers also reported advantages to the approach: (a) the children understood the topics of instruction (even if presented in a speeded-up format to accommodate multiple presentations in multiple languages), and (b) the children, their parents and community members were very aware of their LHRs and were happy that the children now had the right to receive even a modicum of L1-based instruction. That is, the programme carried great symbolic weight no matter how it was implemented or what percentage of the day children actually heard their L1. For them, the programme meant honouring their linguistic/cultural heritage and their LHRs. Evidence of this satisfaction was the fact that the normal attrition rate for children had dropped: Whereas the norm is for 50% of Indigenous children to drop out of school in grade 1, these children kept coming back to school day after day (Nurmela, personal communication, 28 January 2009; Nurmela et al. this volume).

It is telling that a multi-L1 MLE programme that created a daunting teaching environment should be so appreciated, and this example speaks to how bad the situation was before the MLE programme was implemented. To contextualise how this could be so, it is useful to include one workshop participant's explanation of why retention rates were so low before implementing the MLE programme. The participant in question related an incident in which one child was hit by another child on his first day of grade 1. When the injured party tried to tell his teacher about it in the only language the child knew upon entering school – his non-Nepali L1 – his teacher slapped him for not speaking Nepali (a language as yet unknown to the child). As a result of that injustice, the first day of grade 1 ended up being the child's first and last day of school, since he never returned.

Though the limited amount of L1-based instruction that the children received was an improvement, the situation was far from ideal from an MLE perspective, as is discussed later; however, it is useful to stress the positive side of what Nepal is attempting to do, despite limited resources. When I inquired into why the classroom (which numbered approximately 100 grade 1 children in January 2009) was not split along linguistic lines since such a large class size is clearly not ideal for a grade 1 classroom, the teachers participating in the workshop said space and monetary considerations at the community level impeded their dividing the group up into two classrooms. Neither was it possible to invite volunteers into the classroom to divide the children up linguistically and aid the teacher; people need to be paid for any work they do, and the school could not afford to pay 'volunteers'. Heugh's (2009) words about the significance of implementing MLE in Ethiopia: MLE 'can and does happen in one of the poorest countries in Africa' cannot be emphasized enough (p. 112). Skutnabb-Kangas and Heugh (2010) offer countless Tables where Ethiopia and Nepal figure prominently in major indicators of national poverty – child malnutrition, infant mortality rates, low life expectancies, similar human development index, etc. Benson *et al.* (this volume) also provide clear examples of Ethiopia's poverty level and, nonetheless, they also draw on hard data and rich contextual evidence that supports the viability of successfully introducing MLE system-wide in a poor country. Taken together, the Ethiopian and Nepali examples show that where there is a will, there is a way.

7.3.2 Introducing Culturally/Linguistically Sensitive Pedagogy in Teacher Training Workshops

A key issue in MLE is how to incorporate teachers' and learners' experiences, knowledge and skills into the programme and how to develop learning materials and teacher training that is locally specific and relevant. I based my training workshops on Moll and González' (1997) 'funds of knowledge' (FoKn) approach to teaching as it best captured the intents of the Nepali and Finnish programme developers (bottom-up processes, participatory pedagogy, capacity building, critical indigenous pedagogy, etc.). The term refers to the knowledge base and strategies that children learn at home and in their local community. Moll and González (1997) stress that minority-language children and children from other marginalised backgrounds do not arrive in school with no language and no prior knowledge, contrary to the stereotypes and misconceptions that some teachers may hold of children from backgrounds different from their own. Teachers need to learn about the 'cultural practices or bodies of knowledge and information that households use to survive, get ahead or to thrive' (Moll 1992: 21). To do so, teachers must become students of their students, draw on their students' background knowledge and build their conceptual schemata, an approach that has long been recognised as a highly effective way to teach children (Barnes 1992; Cummins 2009; Wells and Ball 2008).

To gain this understanding, teachers must move beyond marginalising stereotypes, monolingual ideologies, and deficit constructions of minority-language children, their parents, their communities and their knowledge base. When teachers develop classroom cultures that value children's FoKn, the classroom becomes 'a comfortable place where the parents, teachers, community and students become active members in a successful educational process' (Moll and Gonzales 2004: 156). The silencing process that can result in individuals becoming 'tongue-tied' or afraid or incapable of speaking in their L1 has all too frequently been part of classroom cultures (Taylor 2009b). Similarly, teacher knowledge must be recognised to avoid teachers becoming silenced as well.

Moll and González' (1997) observation of teachers not sharing their students' FoKn did not pertain to the teachers at the pilot schools as they were typically from the children's home communities and spoke the same languages as the children; however, their observation did pertain to the materials developers (even though they too spoke the same languages as the children). The materials developers were so cognisant of the tenets of critical indigenous pedagogy (e.g. the need to seek out traditional knowledge holders' wisdom and incorporate indigenous knowledge into materials) that they experienced writer's block. To 'unblock' them, I designed workshop activities in which we discussed how their local knowledge was valid too, and how they could also seek out children and community members' knowledge about locally relevant topics and strategies; they did not have to limit themselves to seeking out elders in their communities. I explicitly introduced the notion of FoKn to the materials writers (and teacher-participants) as they were under the impression that 'local knowledge' was not within their grasp. They expressed great trepidation about knowing where to start in terms of preparing local materials. I explained that, from a FoKn perspective, local-specific information on topics ranging from agriculture (local flowers, plants, trees and seeds), water distribution and management, animal care and veterinary medicine, home farm economy or home business economy, mechanics, carpentry, masonry, electrical appliances, indigenous/minority remedies, herbal cures and midwifery, biology and mathematics all qualified as 'local knowledge'. When the materials writers heard about such familiar topics and realised that they had knowledge that constituted local knowledge, which they could write about, and when teachers realised that they could elicit their students' FoKn, they felt empowered. This process in no way interfered with their desire to consult traditional knowledge holders; however, it did succeed in getting participants out of the mental 'straitjacket' of feeling that elders were the only community members with any valuable knowledge. The participants came to understand that families and local communities know best what constitutes local knowledge in their contexts.

I also introduced 'semantic webs' as a useful teaching technique to draw out the children's FoKn. All in all, these sessions heightened the participants' understanding of their ability to make manuals and self-learning materials 'local specific', based on their own experiences, and in line with the United Nations Declaration on the Rights of Indigenous Peoples (United Nations 2007) and previous work done on the MLE project in Nepal by Hough *et al.* (2009) and Yonjan-Tamang *et al.* (2009).

One specific activity involved showing teacher-participants that their students could write classroom books *à la Freinet*. Célestin Freinet was a teacher who introduced the 'learning printing technique' to children in his classroom in France in 1924. They used a printing press to reproduce texts that they wrote themselves.

The pupils wrote compositions about their personal experiences, then presented them to the class and finally printed them themselves. The texts were compiled into class journals and school newspapers (Clandfield and Sivell 1990; History of Freinet pedagogy, n.d.). The Freinet approach was pertinent because, when I conducted my second workshop eight months after the first, the teachers reported difficulties as there were not enough materials in the children's L1s to sustain L1-based instruction. Though the MLE project team had developed a certain amount of exemplary and durable L1 materials, they were costly and time-consuming to produce. I suggested adopting a language experience approach whereby the children would draw pictures to illustrate stories and adults would transcribe key sentences. The materials could then be compiled to make classroom books on given topics.

The participants brainstormed activities that grade 1 children enjoyed doing in their free time after school. As Nepal has jungles with tigers and elephants in the southern Terai region, and the snowy Himalayas to the north, many different activities were mentioned. These included hopping on and off water buffalo in rivers, catching birds, killing birds with slingshots, finding birds' eggs in nests, etc. I asked the workshop participants to write a short text that represented children's age-appropriate interests using child-appropriate language in their L1. They then developed texts and pictures illustrating those themes and religious festivals (e.g. Naag Panchami). By interweaving a FoKn approach throughout this and related materials development projects, the participants grew to trust their instincts about local knowledge. This was a major achievement as it meant that the participants (both professional materials developers and classroom teachers) felt more confident about developing local materials.

One difficulty that remained unresolved by the end of the second workshop involved encouraging participants to adopt a 'small c' approach to local culture. That is, they primarily equated local culture with religious/cultural celebrations (a 'big C' approach to culture) rather than recognising how all aspects of daily life also counted as local 'culture' (e.g. animal care, midwifery). Potentially, a problem could arise with equating 'Celebrations' with local culture: the children might find always 'translating' Nepali national curriculum into a monothematic approach to local culture repetitive. Therefore, I tried to encourage the participants to envision local culture in a broader manner.

Over the course of the two 14-day-long workshops, the participants made a great deal of progress in understanding the socio-political and psycholinguistic foundations of MLE, programme models and variables, and linguistically/culturally sensitive pedagogy. This understanding was needed to be able to deliver MLE pedagogy in multilingual school settings. Furthermore, after years of external silencing, they stopped imposing internal silencing on their L1s and started to embrace L1 materials development techniques.

7.4 Discussion and Conclusion

In the case of the multi-L1 grade 1 classroom described above, Skutnabb-Kangas' (1995a) principle of grouping only children with the same L1 together initially (alternating instruction in the two languages on different days, or some similar arrangement) was either misunderstood or overlooked because of local constraints. The form of instruction delivered in that setting (teaching Lesson X in Language A, then in Languages B, C and D) is best described as 'consecutive interpretation': not MLE. In fact, what the teachers described related more closely to the model of multilingual classrooms (not MLE) described by Cummins (2007) in the Canadian context. In that context, provisions are sometimes made for children to produce work in their L1, but L1-based instruction is never provided since the sole medium of instruction is the dominant language (English). While the multi-L1 arrangement was rooted in a sincere wish to provide linguistically/culturally responsive pedagogy to large numbers of linguistically diverse students, it could be viewed as 'MLE as panacea' or 'easy solution' and did not result in optimal learning situations.

The classroom that mixed four L1s was an unfortunate mix of a partial understanding of the theoretical bases of MLE and a lack of resources. The participants reported that there was neither extra space within the school nor extra money in the community to build another classroom. This lack of economic resources blocked the teachers from dividing the classroom to create a better learning environment for the 100+ grade 1 children and a better teaching environment for themselves. It should be noted that they were doing miracles given the highly demanding nature of their teaching situation. Had the teachers had a better understanding of key tenets of MLE, they might have said it was impossible to implement the programme under those conditions. Given their understanding of L1-based instruction at the time, community demand for their LHRs, community support for the programme, economic constraints and the high level of linguistic heterogeneity in the community, the model of MLE implemented in that grade 1 classroom was not ideal, but it met the community members' needs at that time and place.

While the readers can appreciate and understand the MLE programme's genesis in that classroom, the fact remains that L1-based instruction for only 25% of the instructional time is insufficient for a programme to qualify as 'MLE'. The multi-L1 setting constituted a unique and interesting pedagogical innovation, but did not constitute MLE per se as it would not have developed the children's CALP. Rather, it would have been preferable to group the children by linguistic groups in multi-grade classrooms. In that case, even if not all of the instruction was geared to their grade level, they would have understood the medium of instruction and incidentally developed their L1 oracy and literacy skills throughout the entire school day, providing them with a rich L1 base on which to build CALP.

MLE teachers are not able to implement 'best practices' such as peer/group work and collaborative learning in multi-L1 classrooms with over 100 children. Neither are they able to draw on parent-volunteers to create smaller, linguistically homogeneous groupings to help implement those kinds of practices, given the socio-economic realities of Nepal. Many layers of constraints must be considered to understand the sorts of roadblocks that teachers may face when trying to implement 'best practices' in MLE.

The other glitch in the programme (e.g. materials production) was addressed when the teachers and material writers gained access to the MLE workshops that I offered. They gained better understanding of what 'local' knowledge entailed and, especially by the end of my second workshop, expressed feelings of greater confidence in their own local knowledge and ability to develop 'local' L1 materials. Furthermore, in summer 2009 the NCED developed teacher training materials to be disseminated during training of trainer sessions. Therefore, it is reasonable to expect that the material glitches that arose were 'growing pains' that can be remedied.

While there were glitches in the system, glitches commonly occur when implementing new programmes. It is not surprising that they occurred in the course of introducing L1-based instruction that, in time, will be offered in over 100 languages on a limited budget. What was remarkable about the Nepali MLE programme was the enormous amount of good will, hard work and appreciation of all parties concerned: the children, parents, teachers, educators from the school level up to the Ministry of Education and NCED, and even up to the politicians in the Constituent Assembly.

A major goal of the MLE programme was to cut the attrition rate, which workshop participants informed me generally reached as high as 50% in grade 1 (see also Skutnabb-Kangas and Heugh, this volume). Given the previously described incident of a child being physically punished for not speaking his L2 on the first day of school – the first time he was exposed to it – it is not surprising that the grade 1 children in the multi-L1 classroom enjoyed their school experience despite being in an over-crowded classroom and learning in a very complicated linguistic situation. Their home language, culture and background knowledge were valorised in the programme, and they kept coming back to school day after day.

Should the MLE programme planners have delayed its implementation until all teachers had received MLE training, all materials writers were comfortable with how to develop L1-based curricular materials and there were enough L1-based materials for all children in all subjects? Or is it better that the programme was piloted and experience was gained of what glitches required fixing? In answer to those questions, we return to the case of the grade 1 classroom and its retention rate. The fact that the children 'talked with their feet' answers the questions: yes, it was better to start right away. As a result, children stayed in class right up to the last day of the grade 1 school year rather than 'closing the book' on their school career at the end of their first day. Glitches can be fixed, but opportunities lost often do not arise again. The fact that the children thrived despite a situation that was extremely challenging for them and their teachers confirms the findings of the authors of an extensive Report on Mother Tongue and Bilingual Education in sub-Saharan Africa for the Association for the Development of Education in Africa-UNESCO Institute of Education that, 'Language is not everything in education, but without language, everything is nothing in education' (Alidou *et al.* 2006: 6). MLE programmes are good for children.

In conclusion, while there are still some glitches in the system, the remarkable way in which the Nepalis have implemented MLE so far suggests that they will continue to experiment with how far the MLE model will stretch to deal adequately with the complexities of their linguistic heterogeneity and socio-economic realities. In so doing, they will find a way to create a uniquely Nepali version of MLE. The will is certainly there on the part of official and civil society, and this is key to longer-term success.

Notes

1   I would like to thank Tove Skutnabb-Kangas for her insightful feedback on an earlier draft of this paper, and Kathleen Heugh for her support throughout the writing process. Additional thanks go to Iina Nurmela for showing me her pilot school video and allowing me to adapt her Table (Nurmela forthcoming), as well as to Roz Stooke and Dawn Fyn.
2   See Nurmela *et al.* (this volume) for further discussion of this topic.
3   For instance, if two language groups are in the same classroom, a bilingual teacher could use one language as the medium of instruction in the morning and the other in the afternoon, or use the two languages on alternate days. In so doing, children's L1s would be used for 50% of the time, and they would only be exposed to an L2 for 50% of the time. Neither group would be exposed to L2-based instruction longer than the other group: an equitable solution.
4   This does not mean that the L1 should remain the medium of instruction throughout a child's entire instruction in a foreign language and should not be construed as espousing the grammar-translation method; what is meant is that when a child is first introduced to a foreign language such as English, it should be introduced in the child's L1 not (in the case of Nepal) through their L2, Nepali.
5   The author acknowledges the debates and controversies about BICS and CALP, yet argues nevertheless that in contexts such as Nepal, the distinction, however approximate, is an important tool in the provision of effective education for marginalised children.

References

Abbi, Anvita (2008). *Multilingual education in phases: Questioning the three language formula.* Paper presented at the 2008 Multilingualism and Intercultural Dialogue in Globalization Conference (11–12 December). Delhi, India.
Alidou, Hassana, Boly, Aliou, Brock-Utne, Birgit, Diallo, Yaya Satina, Heugh, Kathleen and Wolff, H. Ekkehard (2006). *Optimizing learning and education in Africa – the language factor: A stock-taking research on mother tongue and bilingual education*

in sub-Saharan Africa. Paris: ADEA-UIE. (http://www.adeanet.org/adeaPortal/adea/biennial-2006/doc/document/B3_1_MTBLE_en.pdf).

Annamalai, E. (1995). Multilingualism for all – an Indian perspective. In Skutnabb-Kangas, Tove (ed.), *Multilingualism for all.* Lisse, the Netherlands: Swets and Zeitlinger, 215–220.

Awasthi, Lava Deo (2004). *Exploring monolingual school practices in multilingual Nepal.* Ph.D. thesis. Copenhagen: Danmarks Pædagogiske Universitet [Danish University of Education].

Baetens Beardsmore, Hugo (1995). The European School experience in multilingual education. In Skutnabb-Kangas, Tove (ed.), *Multilingualism for all.* Lisse, the Netherlands: Swets and Zeitlinger, 21–68.

Baquedano-López, Patricia and Kattan, Shlomy (2007). Growing up in a multilingual community: Insights from language socialisation. In Auer, Peter and Wei, Li (eds), *Handbook of multilingualism and multilingual communication.* Berlin: Mouton de Gruyter, 69–99.

Barnes, Douglas (1992). The teacher's control of knowledge. *From communication to curriculum* (2nd edn). Portsmouth, NH: Boynton Cook Publishers Heinemann, 108–138.

Benson, Carol (2009). Designing effective schooling in multilingual contexts: The strengths and limitations of bilingual 'models'. In Mohanty *et al.* (eds), 60–78.

Clandfield, David and Sivell, John (1990). *Cooperative learning and social change: Selected writings of Célestin Freinet.* Toronto: Our schools/Our Selves Education Foundation.

Collier, Virginia P. and Thomas, Wayne (1989). How long? A synthesis of research on academic achievement in a second language. *TESOL Quarterly* 23, 509–531.

Collier, Virginia P. and Thomas, Wayne (1999). Making US schools effective for English language learners, Part 2. *TESOL Matters* 9:5, 1, 6.

Cummins, Jim (1981). The role of primary language development in promoting educational success for language minority students. In California State Department of Education (ed.), *Schooling and language minority students: A theoretical framework.* Los Angeles: Evaluation, Dissemination and Assessment Center, California State University, 3–49.

Cummins, Jim (2007). Rethinking monolingual instructional strategies in multilingual classrooms. In Lyster, Roy and Lapkin, Sharon (eds), Theme Issue: Multilingualism in Canadian Schools. *Canadian Journal of Applied Linguistics* 10:2, 221–240.

Cummins, Jim (2009). Fundamental psychological and sociological principles underlying educational success for linguistic minority students. In Mohanty *et al.* (eds), 21–35.

García, Ofelia, Skutnabb-Kangas, Tove and Torres-Guzman, María E. (2006). Weaving spaces and (de)constructing ways for multilingual schools: The actual and the imagined. In García, Ofelia, Skutnabb-Kangas, Tove and Torres-Guzmán, María E. (eds), *Imagining multilingual schools: Languages in education and glocalization.* Clevedon, England: Multilingual Matters, 3–47.

Heugh, Kathleen (2009). Literacy and bi/multilingual education in Africa: recovering collective memory and expertise. In Mohanty *et al.* (eds), 95–113.

Heugh, Kathleen, Benson, Carol, Bogale, Berhanu and Gebre Yohannes, Mekonnen Alemu (2007). *Final Report: Study on Medium of Instruction in Primary Schools in Ethiopia.* Research report commissioned by the Ministry of Education, Addis Ababa, September to December 2006. (http://www.hsrc.ac.za/research/output/outputDocuments/4379_Heugh_Studyonmediumofinstruction.pdf).

History of Freinet pedagogy (n.d.). History of Freinet pedagogy. (http://freinet.org/icem/history.htm).

Hough, David A., Thapa Magar, Ram B. and Yonjan-Tamang, Amrit (2009). Privileging indigenous knowledges: Empowering MLE in Nepal. In Mohanty *et al.* (eds), 146–161.

Jessner, Ulrike (2006). *Linguistic awareness in multilinguals: English as a third language.* Edinburgh: Edinburgh University Press.

Jhingran, Dhir (2009). Hundreds of home languages in the country and many in most classrooms – coping with diversity in primary education in India. In Mohanty *et al.* (eds), 250–267.

Mohanty, Ajit K. (1995). *Bilingualism in a multilingual society. Psycho-social and pedagogical implications.* Mysore: Central Institute of Indian Languages.

Mohanty, Ajit, Mishra, Mahendra Kumar, Reddy, N. Upender and Ramesh, Gumidyal (2009). Overcoming the language barrier for tribal children: MLE in Andhra Pradesh and Orissa, India. In Mohanty *et al.* (eds), 278–291.

Mohanty, Ajit, Panda, Minati, Phillipson, Robert and Skutnabb-Kangas, Tove (eds) (2009). *Multilingual education for social justice: Globalising the local.* New Delhi: Orient BlackSwan.

Moll, Luis C. (1992). Bilingual classroom studies and community analysis: Some recent trends. *Educational Researcher* 21:2, 20–24.

Moll, Luis C. and González, Norma (1997). Teachers as social scientists: Learning about culture from household research. In Hall, Peter M. (ed.), *Race, ethnicity and multiculturalism: Policy and practice.* Missouri Symposium on Research and Educational Policy, Vol. 1. New York: Garland Publishing, 89–114.

Moll, Luis C. and González, Norma (2004). Beginning where the children are. In Santa Ana, Otto (ed.), *Tongue-tied: the lives of multilingual children in public education.* Lanham, MD: Towman and Littlefield Publishers, 152–156.

Nurmela, Iina (forthcoming). Omakielinen opetus monikielisissä kouluissa Nepalissa [Mother tongue medium teaching in multilingual schools in Nepal].

Skutnabb-Kangas, Tove (1995a). Introduction. In Skutnabb-Kangas, Tove (ed.), *Multilingualism for all.* Lisse, the Netherlands: Swets and Zeitlinger, 7–20.

Skutnabb-Kangas, Tove (ed.) (1995b). *Multilingualism for all.* Lisse, the Netherlands: Swets and Zeitlinger.

Skutnabb-Kangas, Tove (1998). Human rights and language wrongs: A future for diversity. In Benson, Phil, Grundy, Peter and Skutnabb-Kangas, Tove (eds), *Language rights.* Special Issue, *Language Sciences* 20:1, 5–27.

Skutnabb-Kangas, Tove (2000). *Linguistic genocide in education: Or worldwide diversity and human rights?* Mahwah, NJ: Lawrence Erlbaum.

Skutnabb-Kangas, Tove and Dunbar, Robert (2010). *Indigenous children's education as linguistic genocide and a crime against humanity? A global view.* Gáldu, Norway: Resource Centre for the Rights of Indigenous Peoples.

Skutnabb-Kangas, Tove and Heugh, Kathleen (eds) (2010). *Multilingual education works: From the periphery to the centre.* New Delhi: Orient BlackSwan.

Skutnabb-Kangas, Tove and McCarty, Teresa (2008). Clarification, ideological/epistemological underpinnings and implications of some concepts in bilingual education. In Volume 5, *Bilingual Education*, Cummins, Jim and Hornberger, Nancy H. (eds), *Encyclopedia of Language and Education*, 2nd edition. New York: Springer, 3–17.

Skutnabb-Kangas, Tove, Phillipson, Robert, Panda, Minati and Mohanty, Ajit (2009). MLE concepts, goals, needs and expense: English for all or achieving justice? In Mohanty *et al.* (eds), 313–334.

Taylor, Shelley K. (2009a). The caste system approach to multilingual education in Canada: Linguistic and cultural minority children in French immersion. In Mohanty *et al.*, 162–180.

Taylor, Shelley K. (2009b). Tongue-tied no more? Beyond linguistic colonialization of multilingual children in the public school system. *Race, Ethnicity and Education* 12:3, 417–426.

Taylor, Shelley K. (2010). Beyond bilingual education: Multilingual language education in Nepal. *Colombian Journal of Bilingual Education/GiST Education and Learning Research Journal*, 4, 138–154.

United Nations (2007). United Nations Declaration on the Rights of Indigenous Peoples. (http://www.un.org/esa/socdev/unpfii/en/drip.html).

Wells, Gordon and Ball, Tamara (2008). Exploratory talk and dialogic inquiry. In Mercer, Neil and Hodgkinson, Steve (eds), *Exploring talk in school*. Thousand Oaks, CA: Sage, 167–184.

Yadava, Yogendra P. (2007). *Linguistic Diversity in Nepal Perspectives on Language Policy*. Paper presented at the Seminar on Constitutionalism and Diversity (22–24 August). Kathmandu, Nepal. (http://74.125.77.132/search?q=cache:6KgHrJ1aIRMJ: www.seameo.org/_ld2008/doucments/Presentation_document/Yadava_Linguistic_ Diversity_Nepal.pdf+Uranw+Ethnologue&cd=1&hl=en&ct=clnk&gl=dk&lr=lang_ da|lang_en|lang_fi&client=firefox-a).

Yonjan-Tamang, Amrit, Hough, David and Nurmela, Iina (2009). 'All Nepalese children have the right to education in their mother tongue' – but how? The Nepal MLE program. In Mohanty *et al.* (eds), 241–249.

8

SETTING A TRADITION OF MOTHER TONGUE-MEDIUM EDUCATION IN 'FRANCOPHONE' AFRICA

The Case of Burkina Faso

Norbert Nikièma and Paul Taryam Ilboudo

The commitment of the international community in the 1990s to promote quality 'education for all' has engendered a new trend in 'francophone' Africa towards the experimentation of mother tongue first education in primary school (Halaoui 2005; Nikièma, forthcoming) in an environment where mother tongues (MTs) were forbidden from use in the school area. We focus here on the case of Burkina Faso where such experimentation gained momentum in the mid-1990s after a first short-lived attempt between 1979 and 1984. This chapter highlights the successes and the challenges to be met by the major experiment known as the MEBA-OSEO (Ministry of Basic Education and Literacy-Oeuvre Suisse d'entraide ouvrière/Swiss Labour Assistance) formula, drawing parallels where applicable, with the Ethiopian case described in Chapter 1 above.

8.1 Sociolinguistic Situation and Context of Language Education Policy in Burkina Faso

Burkina Faso (Upper-Volta, until 1984) is a landlocked West African country sharing borders with Ivory Coast, Ghana, Togo, Benin, Niger and Mali. It is a multi-ethnic and multilingual country where 59 local languages (referred to as 'national languages' in the constitution) are spoken by a population of nearly 15 million. There are no statistics on the multilingual competence of speakers. On the basis of answers to the question, 'Which language do you speak at home?' in the 1985 population census, 15 languages stood out as the most widely spoken. Forty-six languages are each spoken by fewer than 100,000 speakers; 12 languages have between 100,000 and 800,000 speakers and only one (Mòoré, sometimes also known as Mossi) is spoken by several million (50.4% of the population). The 15 most frequently spoken languages are also dominant in their particular territories and are spread over fairly large areas within provinces and/or regions. The greatest linguistic heterogeneity is encountered in the south-western part of the country, with some 40 languages or so spoken within a relatively small area (Kedrebeogo 1997). Jula (or Dioula) serves as a lingua franca in this area and is accepted and readily learned by speakers from various ethnic groups when the need arises.[1] The proportion of respondents who declared they spoke French at home was 0.3%. The overall proportion of speakers of French is estimated at 11–17%.

Burkina Faso is divided into 13 regions headed by governors, and regions are subdivided into provinces (45 altogether) headed by high commissioners. Decentralization and local community participation and empowerment, however, are recent concepts and new areas of national endeavour. The type of autonomy in administration and education evident in Ethiopia is not paralleled in Burkina Faso.

8.1.1 Post Independence Language Policy in Education

As elsewhere in 'francophone' Africa, Upper-Volta inherited, and Burkina Faso still implements, a 'one nation, one language' policy, in which French is the only official language and the only language of the legal, justice and public administration systems. The 'French only' policy continued in education during the first decade after independence (1960), in formal education (primary and secondary schools). It continued also in non-formal education (NFE) in the *École d'Éducation Rurale* (rural education school) system open to young adults, and in literacy programmes offered in evening schools (*Cours d'adultes*). Local languages were not mentioned in the constitution and their use was forbidden in school, where French was made obligatory (Decree 289bis of 3 August 1965).

In the 1970s, an evaluation of the NFE programme was conducted in the *École Rurale* system. The NFE experiment was found unsuccessful given the high drop-out and failure rates, and the inability of graduates to communicate through the local languages, the knowledge and new agricultural techniques they had acquired in French. The early 1970s also marked the beginning of the implementation of a literacy programme in the framework of a 'joint Upper-Volta–UNESCO project for equal access of girls and women to education'. Adult literacy was offered for the first time in five local languages. Before then, only private bodies, namely, Catholic and Protestant Missions and a few private associations, were involved in literacy provision in these languages.

The implementation of the literacy component of the Upper-Volta–UNESCO project was preceded by important policy decisions, namely, the establishment of a National Language Academy, *Commission Nationale des Langues Voltaïques*, in 1969, and of language committees in the early 1970s and later. By 1976, ten national language committees had been created. Providing the local languages with adequate, standardised writing systems and orthographies were major tasks of the language committees. They proposed a national alphabetic script (adapted from Latin) for the national languages. This script was made official in 1979 and each national language had to select the symbols needed in its specific orthography from the national list.

In 1974, the government created an *Office National pour l'Éducation Permanente et l'Alphabétisation Fonctionnelle et Sélective* (National Office for Permanent Education and Functional and Selective Literacy, ONEPAFS). From then on, adult literacy was conducted only in local languages as explicitly decreed in 1978.

As a result of the language education policy between the early 1960s and the early 1980s, a situation of diglossia developed where high-status functions and levels of prestige were associated with French and French language education, while low-status functions and prestige were associated with MTs and mother tongue-medium education (MTE). Adult literacy in the MT/L1 was looked down upon by the elite and those who attended formal school. Such a situation reinforces a loss of confidence in, and weakens the loyalty to, L1.

8.1.2 Challenges of Formal Education and the Motivation for Bilingual Education

A diagnostic study of formal education focusing on primary education was conducted in the mid-1970s. The main challenges of the system were described to be, *inter alia*, low internal and external efficiency of the system,[2] marked by the following:

- low rates of promotion;
- high repeat and drop-out rates;
- only 22 out of 100 pupils who started primary school completed it in 6 years (the normal duration of primary);
- only 17 of 100 passed the end of primary school certificate;
- 34% of boys and 42% of girls fell back into illiteracy; and
- only 17 of 1,000 pupils enrolled in the first grade would receive the baccalaureate (end of high school diploma) 13 years later.

Although over half of the time in school was devoted to learning French, only 20–25% of the pupils could read or write adequately by the end of primary.

The study also highlighted:

- the very high cost of an education with such low achievement;
- the alienating nature of the education offered; and
- the inadequate, selective and discriminatory, nature of education.

The system was clearly in need of the profound reform which began in 1979. It was then decided to experiment with three major national languages (Fulfulde,

Jula and Mòoré) as media of instruction (MoI) throughout primary, along with French, first as a subject and later as an MoI. The experimental schools were selected in the rural areas where those languages are spoken. However, there were heated debates (see Nikièma 2000) over the soundness of the initiative. Some stakeholders, most notably the primary school teachers' trade union, supported it even though they criticised some aspects of implementation (cf. SNEAHV 1980). Others, the elite in general and city dwellers, strongly criticised it. Bilingual education, with the use of MTs in primary school, was objected to on several grounds (see below) and which mirror some sentiments in Ethiopia (Chapter 1).

- There was strong scepticism about the possibility of teaching mathematics and the sciences in local languages.
- Many equated MTM education with low-quality education and were also convinced that the use of the MTs of the children would hinder their mastery of French. This in turn would have detrimental effects on learning, since French is the sole MoI in formal education.
- Starting in the mother tongues was viewed as a waste of time since secondary and higher education are in French.
- Bilingual education might be unfair, since it could not possibly be offered in all 59 languages.
- It would be too costly and unaffordable, no matter how many languages were used.

The reform along with the experiment on MTE was interrupted in 1984 when the first experimental school children were in grade 5, that is, one year before the completion of a normal cycle, and therefore their achievement in the primary school-leaving certificate could not be assessed. Nevertheless, a nation-wide symposium convened on education policy in 1994 concluded that it was necessary to take up the MTE programme once again. The government itself took no steps to do this; instead, it encouraged private initiatives to explore alternative education programmes. Four NGOs and associations cooperating with the Ministry of Basic Education and Literacy (MEBA) undertook to experiment with MTE again in formal education, using various models/formulas as summarised in Table 8.1.

The 1996 Law of Orientation of Education (LOE) was a decisive measure which made basic education compulsory for children aged 6–16, thus extending it from primary to the first four grades of high school. The law also gave to national languages the new status of languages of education in the following terms (article 4): 'the languages of education are French and the national languages'. There was, however, no implementation decree and thus, no real plan to develop multilingual education. A new LOE of July 2007 renewed the same status for national languages and added the precision that they could be used both in teaching and in evaluation.

TABLE 8.1 Bilingual models/formulas used from the mid-1990s onwards

Supporting NGO/Association; Programme start	Type and duration of schooling	Bilingual model/formula
Public school	Classical school; 6 years	Monolingual French-medium throughout.
OSEO★ (1994)	Bilingual schools; 5 years	8 mother tongues used throughout the system but with a gradual decrease in duration in favour of French.
UNICEF (1995)	Satellite schools; 3 years	8 mother tongues used for the first two years, then exclusive use of French as a medium the remainder of the school cycle; schooling is pursued in a nearby classical school in French.
Tin tua (1995)	Banmanuara; 5 years	One mother tongue (Gulmancema) used for the first two years, then exclusive use of French as a medium the remainder of the school cycle.
Save the Children USA (1995)	Community schools; 4 years	One mother tongue (Mòoré) used for the first two years, then exclusive use of French as a medium the remainder of the school cycle.

★ OSEO: Oeuvre Suisse d'entraide ouvrière (Swiss Labour Assistance)

8.2 The Multilingual Education Model and its Implementation

The multilingual education model supported by OSEO (Swiss Labour Assistance) began as a bilingual programme for primary school. It offers MT education in eight national languages, for a period of five years. MTM education is offered within an early-exit bilingual programme involving a transition to French as a medium of instruction in the third and fourth years of primary. However, the teaching and learning of the MT as a subject has recently been extended beyond primary school for four years into junior high school. For those children who are able to access the newly established preschools (since 2003 and very few at present), the teaching of and through the MT can start at this level and therefore run from preschool through primary and into junior high school. It is this model, now known as the *Continuum d'Éducation de Base Multilingue* (CEBAM) – multilingual basic education continuum – which is the main focus of this chapter.

8.2.1 The Initial Phase of Bilingual Primary Schools, Écoles Bilingues

In its initial, experimental phase (1994–1998), the now multilingual programme began as a 4-year, Mòoré-French bilingual programme devised for 55 children who were nine years old and over, and who, according to official regulations, were thus 'too old' to access formal school. The programme was to provide an opportunity for these students to catch up with their peers. Through this programme they would be prepared for the primary school exit examinations which are normally offered after six years of schooling. It was believed that this experiment would support the claim that developing basic skills and academic competence while using the mother tongue or a familiar language will facilitate the acquisition tasks and lead to better learning in the foreign/second language (FL/L2). The curriculum for the first few years of public school was adapted or translated into Mòoré (including history, geography, science and mathematics). By the beginning of the third year, the pupils were supposed, through a specially designed method for learning French, to be able to use the same textbooks as school children in the fifth year of the classical school system. In the fourth year, the pupils were to be prepared to sit for the end of primary school examination (entirely in French).

The general aims of the bilingual programme were:

- to raise the internal efficiency of primary education;
- to improve the external efficiency and the relevance of education;
- to promote the local culture;
- to promote gender equity; and
- to encourage a better participation of the communities in the affairs of the schools.

For example, parents were asked to take turns in class to teach stories and other folklore and oral traditions to their children in the local languages (songs, music, how to play musical instruments, dance, etc.).

The results of the experiment were quite encouraging: the experimental school pupils scored a 52.83% success rate at the certificate in 1998 after four years of schooling (compared with a departmental 42% success rate). The children who passed the end of primary school certificate examination were allowed to pursue their studies in secondary school, and those who scored high enough (and were under 15 years of age) were given scholarships. A comparative study of the cost of primary education in one of the experimental schools and in a classical school in the same department (Korgho 2001: 17) revealed that schooling cost CFA 77,447 (about US\$ 172) for a bilingual child and CFA 104,962 (about US\$ 233) for a classical pupil. The chances of earning the school-leaving certificate at the end of the cycle was 72% for a bilingual child and 14% for a child in the classical system.[3] In other words, none of the objections to MTE alluded to above, including the fear of additional cost, was substantiated in the experiment.

8.2.2 The Extension of Bilingual Primary Schools

These results aroused the interest of all stakeholders in education. After the initial phase, a 5-year programme was devised for school-age (6- to 8-year-old) children. The proportions of time for each language per grade are as follows:

> *First year:* Mother tongue/National Language 90%; French 10%
> *Second year:* Mother tongue/National Language 80%; French 20%
> *Third year:* Mother tongue/National Language 50%; French 50%[4]
> *Fourth year:* Mother tongue/National Language 20%; French 80%
> *Fifth year:* Mother tongue/National Language 10%; French 90%.[5]

The government allowed the extension of the MEBA-OSEO bilingual education formula to public schools with the financial and technical support of OSEO. Various measures were also taken in favour of the innovation, as follows.

- OSEO supported in-service teacher training programmes as well as technical support (preliminary sociolinguistic studies, adaptation and reproduction of sufficient textbooks in various languages, etc.); MEBA recently introduced bilingual education modules in the training programmes of primary school teachers and inspectors.
- The Ministry of Education (MoE) authorised parents to ask for the transformation of classical 6-year schools to 5-year bilingual schools; so, unlike the 1979–84 reform, these changes were never imposed.
- The choice of the local language and of the dialect for textbooks is left to parents. No restriction is imposed on which or how many languages can be used. Seven other national languages thus entered the programme which is currently using eight national languages throughout primary school along with French.
- Some private schools also chose to use the bilingual programme. In 2003, the Catholic Mission decided progressively to switch to the bilingual formula in all its primary schools.[6]

8.2.3 The Multilingual Basic Education Continuum (CEBAM)

By 2003, the initially remedial programme had turned into a complete and fully articulated multilingual programme encompassing both formal and non-formal education, extending from preschool to junior high. On the basis of the 1996 LOE, formal basic education is conceived of as a continuum with three inter-connected and interdependent components: preschool centres, bilingual primary schools, and junior high schools.

8.2.3.1 Preschool Centres

Bilingual education is offered in *Espaces d'Éveil Éducatif* (spaces for educational awakening) or 3E centres for 3- to 6-year-old children. The first 3E centres were opened in 2003 in selected villages that already hosted a bilingual school. There are three grades in a 3E centre. Cognitive development activities include draw-ing, graphism, mathematical awakening activities and the learning of oral French. All subjects are taught using MTM education (in the same national languages used in bilingual primary schools). The programme had 41 3E centres in 2009/2010 with about 3,000 children (slightly more than 50% are girls).

8.2.3.2 Bilingual Primary Schools

Their number grew to 78 public and 37 private schools by the 2007–2008 school year, with a total of 14,000+ pupils. The schools are in rural, semi-urban and urban areas, including Ouagadougou, the capital city, and Bobo-Dioulasso, the second largest city. As evident in Table 8.2, from June 1998 to June 2008 over 5,000 pupils received their primary school-leaving certificate in the 4–5-year programme.

TABLE 8.2 Success rates of bilingual schools at the school-leaving certificate (CEP)

Year	Bilingual schools				Classical schools	
	Number of schools	Number of national languages	Number of candidates	Number of laureates	% success rate after 4–5 years (if no repeats)	% success rate at national level after 6 years (if no repeats)
1998	2	1	53	28	52.83	48.60
2002	4	2	92	77	83.69	62.90
2003	3	1	88	56	63.64	70.01
2004	10	4	259	245	94.59	73.73
2005	21	6	508	463	91.14	69.01
2006	40	7	960	741	77.19	69.91
2007	47	7	1,182	836	70.73	66.83
2008	75	7	1,852	1,142	61.66	58.34
2009	94	8	2,825	1,984	72.23	73.68
2010	91	8	2,834	1,711	60.37	
Total number of candidates/ laureates			10,706	7,283		
Average % success rate 2002–2010					68.03	

From 2007–2008 onwards, a trilingual model has been undergoing experimentation in five so-called 'Franco-Arabic schools' and *madressas* around Ouagadougou and Ouahigouya, a secondary town in the north, which offer schooling in French and Arabic.

8.2.3.3 Special Junior High Schools or CMS

The sharp decrease in the time devoted to MT courses from the third year of primary schooling onwards was blatantly at odds with the proclaimed option of the MEBA-OSEO model to aim at additive bilingualism. The programme took advantage of provisions of the 1996 LOE according to which formal basic education extends across the first four years (or 'first cycle') of high school (henceforth 'junior high school'). The government authorised the opening of new junior high schools known as *'collèges multilingues spécifiques'* or CMS ('specific multilingual high schools') for 13–18-year-old adolescents who had completed primary education in a bilingual school. Two such colleges were created, first in 2003 in Loumbila in the vicinity of the first two experimental bilingual schools, and then in 2005 in Dafinso (Bobo-Dioulasso) in the Jula-speaking area. The multilingual programme in the two *collèges* includes the strengthening of the MTs used as MoI in primary school and the learning of one of the three major national languages (Jula, Fulfulde or Mòoré) as an L2 for national integration and the promotion of a national language environment in secondary school. Two and four hours per week are devoted to L1 and L2 (national language) courses, respectively.

By adding L1 and national L2 language courses for four years in junior secondary school (excluding preschool which is optional and not yet accessible to many), there is now the potential for a 9-year period in which the MT is included in the formal system from primary through junior high in the MEBA-OSEO multilingual education model.[7] In addition, multilingual education is promoted through the introduction of a third, national language, in junior high school. The CMS programme also includes pre-professional training as well as the usual programme of classical junior high schools.

Table 8.3 provides information on aspects of the internal efficiency of the two CMS of Loumbila (opened in 2003) and Dafinso (opened in 2005).

The performances of CMS pupils, with an enriched programme, can be compared with those of other purely classical *collèges* known as CEG or *Lycée*, as shown in Table 8.4.

The internal efficiency of CMS schools is comparable to, and often better than, that of neighbouring *collèges* and *lycées*. There have been no tracer studies to follow the achievement of bilingual children elsewhere other than in a CMS, except in the case of Tanyoko, a private school in the Loumbila department. Some of the challenges in promoting national languages in secondary school are touched on below.

TABLE 8.3 Internal efficiency of the two CMS (2003–2006)

School term				
CMS Loumbila	Variable	6th grade	5th grade	4th grade
2003/4	Class size	54		
	Promotion	70.35%		
	Repeat	27.78%		
	Drop-out	01.8%		
2004/5	Class size	66	38	
	Promotion	78.79%	52.63%	
	Repeat	18.18%	39.47%	
	Drop-out	03.03%	07.90%	
2005/6	Class size	128	60	20
	Promotion	55.56%	68.33%	70.00%
	Repeat	37.30%	20.00%	30.00%
	Drop-out	07.14%	11.67%	00.00%
CMS Dafinso	Variable	6th grade	5th grade	4th grade
2004/5	Class size	59		
	Promotion	64.41%		
	Repeat	35.59%		
	Drop-out	00.00%		
2005/6	Class size	88	43	
	Promotion	81.40%	65.12%	
	Repeat	16.28%	34.88%	
	Drop-out	02.32%	00.00%	

Adapted from Ilboudo (2009: 116)

TABLE 8.4 Average internal efficiency (in percentages) of classical high schools in the same province as CMS Loumbila (School year 2005/6)

Institution	Promotion	Repeat	Drop-out
Lycée Privé J.Edouard	50.31	30.82	18.87
CEG de Zitenga	49.65	18.29	25.36
Lycée Communal de Ziniaré	33.31		
CEG de Dapelgo	24.52	27.15	44.38
Lycée Provincial de Bassy	56.60	29.85	13.54
Lycée El Micayah	42.42	41.28	14.30
CEG de Donsin	62.76	24.47	12.77
CMS de Loumbila	62.31	33.17	4.52

Source: MESSRS/DEP 2005 quoted by Ilboudo (2009: 117)

8.2.4 Innovative Features of the Multilingual Programme

Innovative features of multilingual programme described here *inter alia* include the following.

- There has been effective introduction of multilingual MTM education (MTE) in a formal education context where MTs had been denied a role for decades. Eight national languages are currently used in the programme and other languages are being considered. MTE is also now introduced in 'Franco-Arabic' schools in a trilingual (MT-French-Arabic) formula.
- There has been provision of MTE within an educational continuum from preschool through primary and into junior high, with a potential of at least nine years of multilingual education.
- There is an opportunity for out-of-school children between the ages of 9 and 11 to catch up with their peers because of the shortening of the schooling period in bilingual programmes. The programme is a 4-year schooling formula known as AFI-D (*Alphabétisation-Formation Intensive pour le Développement* ('intensive literacy and training programme for development', cf. Ilboudou and Nikièma 2010). Students may pursue their studies in secondary school if they do obtain the primary school-leaving certificate and choose to do so.
- A synergy has been established between the two educational subsystems that had earlier coexisted in parallel. Those who begin in non-formal education have new opportunities to access formal education.
- The effective pursuit of quality education and of the goals of UNESCO's Education for All (EFA) is possible through a programme that offers educational services to all ages and grades (children, adolescents and adults) and it reduces exclusion.
- National integration is supported along with a multilingual culture in basic education which can extend through junior high school.

8.3 Lessons Learned, Issues, Challenges and Prospects

8.3.1 Lessons Learned

Several lessons can be learned from the multilingual school experiment.

- African mother tongues can be efficient tools of learning at school. No one thought those experimental school children who 'wasted so much time' learning in their MTs would perform so well and have such high success rates at national exams (see Table 8.2).
- National languages can facilitate teaching and accelerate learning, including the learning of a second/official/international language. It is surprising that those children are able to pass the primary school-leaving certificate after only five (or four) years of schooling although all the examinations are in French exclusively. The argument that the earlier you start in French (or English in Ethiopia, Chapter 1) the better can, therefore, be challenged.

- Governments, decision-makers and even the elite can accept and support mother tongue education even in francophone countries when there is good evidence of their efficacy in schools.
- The bilingual school encourages and even enhances parental participation. Not only do literate parents follow their children's work at home; literate and orate parents take turns to teach the cultural and production part of the curriculum.
- MLE is implementable, sustainable, affordable and arguably not more costly than monolingual education in a foreign language. The reduction of repeat and drop-out rates in this programme, combined with the improvement of school completion rates has a positive effect on the cost-effectiveness of the programme, as shown by Korgho (2001) and Remain-Kinda (2003).[8]

8.3.2 Issues and Challenges

There are, however, several issues and challenges of varying degrees of importance that must be dealt with, relating to such areas as (among others) the model, the criteria of evaluation of the multilingual programme, the general perception of bilingualism and the fate of local languages, teacher training, and the expansion of the programme.

8.3.2.1 The Number of MTs to be Introduced in Formal Education

The multilingual strategy using several other languages in addition to the three national languages introduced during the 1979–1984 reform seems to be well accepted and even welcomed. But the question arises now as to the feasibility and soundness of pursuing both vertical extension of MTM education through the grades to junior secondary, and horizontal extension to more schools and in more languages at the same time. Our feeling is that given the prevailing negative attitudes towards multilingualism (e.g. the belief that linguistic diversity poses a threat to national unity) it would not be strategic or realistic at this point to advocate the use in formal education of more than the 15 most commonly spoken languages identified in Kano (1994). Their successful integration appears as a condition for the integration and the acceptance at a later stage of demographically smaller languages. In our context, government has not developed a clear policy and integrated the consequences and costs of MTM education into a rigorous plan of action. The Nepalese example (Nurmela et al., this volume) and the Papua New Guinean case where over 400 local languages have been brought into the formal education system (Malone and Paraide, forthcoming) are spectacular examples of very bold commitments to MTM education despite their linguistically complex and diverse environments. Such examples need to be known and inspire decision-makers in this part of the world.

8.3.2.2 Additive Bilingualism

The option to work towards additive bilingualism, which requires keeping the MTs throughout the educational system and using them as languages of instruction in basic education for no less than 50% of the time (Heugh 2006), is among the biggest of challenges once the introduction of local languages in education is accepted. This is because the real goals of MTM education are not yet fully understood and/or appreciated in our context. The sceptics and those who oppose MTE argue that the apparently good results of bilingual children are to be explained by such factors as the small class sizes, the good conditions of studies in experimental schools and other Hawthorne effects, rather than the use of MTs or a familiar language. Yet, none of the well-resourced schools in Ouagadougou has ever attempted or envisioned a shorter 5- or 4-year schooling cycle of the type that has been successful in the experimental bilingual programmes, or any other strategy for reducing linguistic exclusion.

The Conference of Ministers in charge of education in 'Francophone Africa' (CONFEMEN) now recognises that 'taking the local languages into account in the curricula is beneficial to national languages and to French' (AIF 2003: 1). But it is not the impact of MTE on cognitive development, the effectiveness of learning and the overall quality of education that is appreciated. Apparently, in their understanding, 'being beneficial to French' is a *conditio sine qua non* for the introduction and maintenance of the local languages in formal education. The Ministers go so far as to declare that:

> Africa needs . . . a strong and powerful French language, because the state of health of educational systems depends on that language. Thus the quality of education in all the States that have chosen this language as the 'partner' of their development, hinges on a good mastery of French, the language of access to information and to knowledge.
>
> *(Ibid.)*

There is no provision in this excerpt for the conception of local languages as languages of access to information and knowledge, and the Ministers did not suspect that there is no scientific, research-based evidence to support their claim.

8.3.2.3 The Hard Pressure of French

Teachers in the multilingual programme also often believe, just like in the Ethiopian context discussed in Chapter 1, and contrary to research findings, that the sooner students begin to learn French and the more time that is devoted to it, the better. This situation, and the fact that local languages and the subjects taught in them are not assessed in the primary school-leaving certificate, which is conducted exclusively in French, exert pressure on teachers in the multilingual programme to switch to French MoI sooner than advocated in the curriculum and in teachers' guides (Alidou *et al.* 2008: 83ff.). The precision in the 2007 LOE that the national languages can be used both in teaching *and in assessment* paves the way to a satisfactory solution to the problems raised.

8.3.2.4 Implementing a Strong MTM Education Programme

In such a context, it is doubtful that research findings which show that eight years of MT/familiar language instruction is the minimum time required in African countries to ensure long-term positive effects; or six years 'if there is a switch to a language which functions as L2 across many domains of society and it is sufficiently well resourced and class sizes do not exceed 30 learners per teacher' (Heugh *et al.* 2007: 103–104, 127 and Chapter 1, this volume), will be received with enthusiasm. In many 'francophone' countries, where even the success-ful implementation of a transitional, early-exit bilingual model is an important achievement, there is a need to imagine strategies to first ensure the acceptance of MTs at school and then progressively work towards the maintenance of MTs throughout the educational system.

Nevertheless, the findings in the study of the Ethiopian case are very relevant and can be supported even in our small and young experience with MTE. As illustrated in 8.1 above, Burkina Faso has experimented with several schooling formulas or models of bilingual education. The differences between the models lie in the time devoted to L1-medium and to French-medium instruction. The two 'competing' 5-year programmes leading to the primary school-leaving certificate are the MEBA-OSEO and the *Banma nuara* 1 (CBN1) school formulas. In CBN1 schools, MTE lasts two years and is used essentially to ensure initial literacy. In the MEBA-OSEO formula, MTE lasts three years (after which L1 becomes a subject) but it extends beyond initial literacy to cover such subjects as history, geography, L1 and L2 grammars, mathematics and natural sciences. The two pro-grammes fare rather well in terms of student performances when compared to traditional schools, but there are appreciable differences also when compared with each other. The findings in the study of the Ethiopian case shown in Chapters 1 and 10, this volume, suggest the prediction that *of two bilingual models, the perform-ances are better in the one that retains L1 longer and/or uses it as a medium in a greater number of academic subjects.* If, for the sake of comparison, we take success rates at the school-leaving certificate (CEP) as one key indicator of good performance, the prediction is borne out. According to Association *Tin Tua* (ATT) (2005, 2006, 2008) the CBN1 Gulmancema-French programme presented 819 candidates for CEP examinations in the eight years between 2000 and 2008 (except 2003 when there were no candidates). There was a success rate of 57.63% (472 laureates) during this time. The MEBA-OSEO multilingual programme (eight national lan-guages and French) presented 7,819 candidates for the same official examinations between 2002[9] and 2009, and the average success rate is 70.90% (5,544 laureates).

We believe the better performances in the MEBA–OSEO formula are due to the longer time devoted to, and the greater number of subjects taught in, MTM.

The multilingual programme in Burkina Faso has reached the point where it is now possible to work towards an increase in the time devoted to MTM, now that local languages are accepted even in junior high school, and to target the full 10-year compulsory basic education cycle (rather than just the six years of primary).

8.3.2.5 The Need for Tracer Studies

We also need a study to demonstrate the positive effect, overall, of MTE on learning in general and on the performance of students in secondary school. The two CMS are not able to cater for the needs of all the children who have gone through bilingual education. Yet there are no tracer studies to show how the thousands of pupils who do not attend a CMS perform in the traditional *collèges* where they pursue their studies.

8.3.2.6 The Training of Trainers

The duration and content of teacher training is another challenge. Not only is the current in-service training formula quite costly, the duration of the training is much too short (three weeks). The training mostly focuses on the mastery of the orthography of the national LOI (two weeks), the mastery of specific methodologies and of the new terminologies created to teach the various disciplines (one week). This is clearly insufficient both in duration and in content. Only recently has training in MTE been included in the initial training of school teachers in their *Écoles Nationales des Enseignants du Primaire* (national primary school teacher training schools) and in the initial training programmes for inspectors. The curricula of such training are still rather experimental. In-service training will also have to be continued for some time.

8.3.2.7 Scaling up the Multilingual Programme and the Education Continuum

Another challenge is the extension and the scaling up of the multilingual programme and the education continuum (cf. section 8.2.3). For the first time in history, the Minister of Basic Education has been asked by a member of parliament to explain why the MEBA–OSEO bilingual programme is still not offered on a large scale. MEBA has indeed not been able to satisfy the close to 300 demands by parents in 2004 and 2005 for new bilingual schools or the transformation of classical schools to bilingual schools (Alidou *et al.* 2008). This may dampen parents' enthusiasm and create doubts about government's intention to promote MTM education. It appears that the best strategy for the extension of the bilingual programme is for MEBA first to answer the numerous demands by parents and then progressively also to offer multilingual MTE.

The challenges to be addressed in extending multilingual education to secondary school are equally numerous. Teacher training at this level does not take MTE into consideration. Although there are only two CMS, there has been a shortage of instructors to cover the contents of L1 teaching. There are materials for L2 courses, but there are still no textbooks or guides for the L1 courses, and teachers feel unprepared to teach those contents in the national languages as required. There is still a lot to be done to prepare the national languages to serve as media of instruction beyond the level of basic literacy. There is also no incentive to invest efforts in painstakingly developing courses in those national language disciplines that are not evaluated at the official Brevet d'Etudes du Premier Cycle (BEPC) examination.

8.3.3 Prospects

The issues and challenges are still numerous but the programme has managed to set a framework for an extended use of local languages throughout primary education and beyond. There seems to be good will on the part of the government to meet the challenges and to promote MTE. OSEO handed over the full responsibility of the programme to MEBA in December 2007 when it was believed that the implementability of a multilingual education policy and the adequacy of the model had been demonstrated and that political will was now required to make of MTM education a system-wide option. MEBA asked for an evaluation of the programme, which was conducted by ADEA in 2008 (cf. Alidou *et al.* 2008), as well as a strategic plan to extend the provision of MTE within its 10-year education development plan. As an application of the new 2007 LOE, a 2008 decree recognised bilingual education as an option in primary education and MEBA is expected to initiate a decree indicating which subjects will be written in the national languages in official examinations.

Notes

1 Jula is also a lingua franca in neighbouring Ivory Coast and its Bambara variety is the dominant language of Mali.
2 Internal efficiency is measured by indicators such as success rates, grade-to-grade promotion rates, cycle completion rates, low drop-out rates, etc.; while external efficiency is measured by indicators such as the number of pupils who pursue their studies or who find jobs after their studies.
3 Remain-Kinda (2003) later showed financial advantages of extending this bilingual education formula within the framework of the 10-year development plan of education in Burkina Faso.
4 Transition to French-medium during grades 3 and 4 is regarded as an early-exit bilingual model in African countries. It is significant that efforts are being made to extend the teaching of the MT, as a subject and for further literacy development, to

the end of grade 5; and also to extend MTE into recently introduced preschools and also into junior high school.

5   The concept of 'junior primary' is unknown in the system; the 5th year is part of primary. In the classical, 6-year system, the first two grades form what is known as '*Cours Préparatoire*' (CP); the next two grades as '*Cours Élémentaire*' (CE) and the last two grades as '*Cours Moyen*' (CM). Primary school lasts six years (shortened to five in the bilingual system).

6   The Catholic Church handed over its schools to the government in 1969, at a time when there were too few public schools. Now that there are enough public schools, it has decided to recover them progressively from the government.

7   *Preschool* (which is only well-developed in cities) has three one-year grades (petite section, moyenne section, grande section). The '*continuum d'éducation multilingue*' attempts to integrate preschool in the system, but this has not yet been accomplished.

8   The findings in Halaoui *et al.* (2006) concur with evidence in Toe-Sidibé (2002) about the internal efficiency of bilingual schools: 'the data place bilingual schools at the top when compared with traditional schools. The claim that bilingual schools have lower rates of casualties is confirmed' (Halaoui *et al.* 2006: 33ff.).

9   2002 is the year when the first school-age pupils to do their schooling in the 5-year bilingual formula sat for the primary leaving certificate. The cohorts of the preceding years were 9–14-year-old children who had a 4-year bilingual schooling cycle.

References

AIF [Agence Intergouvernementale de la Francophonie] (2003). *Mémorandum issu de la réunion des Ministres en charge de l'éducation des pays de l'Afrique subsaharienne francophone* [Memorandum of the meeting of Education Ministers in Francophone sub-Saharan African countries]. Multigraphié.

Alidou, Hassana, Batiana, André, Damiba, Aimé, Kaboré-Paré, Afsata and Rémain-Kinda, Emma (2008). *Le continuum d'éducation de base multilingue au Burkina Faso: une réponse aux exigences de l'éducation de qualité*. Evaluation du programme de consolidation de l'éducation bilingue et Plan d'Action stratégique opérationnel 2008–2010. Rapport d'étude. [The multilingual basic education continuum in Burkina Faso: a response to the quality imperative in education. Evaluation report]. Ouagadougou: MEBA.

ATT (Association *Tin Tua*) (2005). Bilan des résultats au CEP des centres banma nuara (CBN) de l'association tin tua. [Results of the Banma nuara schools of the Tin tua association at the school leaving certificate]. Fada N-Gourma, ms.

ATT (Association *Tin Tua*) (2006). Brève présentation de l'association tin tua. Objectifs et activités en éducation de base. [Brief presentation of the Tin Tua Association. Objectives and activities in basic education]. Septembre 2006. Fada: Association *Tin Tua*. 24 pp.

ATT (Association *Tin Tua*) (2008). Résultats des écoles primaires bilingues de *Tin Tua* au CEP (EPBTT), session de juin 2008. Campagne 2007–2008. [Results of bilingual Tin Tua primary schools at the primary school-leaving certificate, June 2008, 2007–2008 campaign]. Fada: Association *Tin Tua*.

Halaoui, Nazam (2005). *Langues et systèmes éducatifs dans les états francophones d'Afrique subsaharienne. Un état des lieux. [Languages in the Education Systems of Francophone Sub-Saharan African States. Taking stock of the situation]*. Paris: Editions Autrement Frontières.

Halaoui Nazam, Nabolle, Martin, Nikièma, Norbert, Sanwidi, Ignace, Souili, P. François and Tapsoba, Judith (2006). *Evaluation du programme Education Bilingue au Burkina Faso.*

Rapport définitif. [Evaluation of the Bilingual Education Programme in Burkina Faso. Final study report]. Ouagadougou: MEBA-OSEO.

Heugh, Kathleen (2006). Theory and practice – Language Education Models in Africa: research, design, decision-making and outcomes. In Alidou *et al.*, 55–84.

Heugh, Kathleen, Benson, Carol, Bogale, Berhanu, and Gebre Yohannes, Mekonnen Alemu (2007). *Final report: Study on medium of instruction in primary schools in Ethiopia.* (http://www.hsrc.ac.za/research/output/outputDocuments/4379_Heugh_Studyonm ediumofinstruction.pdf).

Ilboudo, Paul Taryam (2009). *L'éducation bilingue au Burkina Faso. Une formule alternative pour une éducation de base de qualité* [Bilingual education in Burkina Faso: an alternative education formula for quality basic education in Burkina Faso]. Tunis: ADEA.

Ilboudo, Paul Taryam and Norbert Nikièma (2010). Implementing a multilingual model of education in Burkina Faso: successes, issues and challenges. In Heugh, Kathleen and Skutnabb-Kangas, Tove (eds), *Multilingual Education Works: From the Periphery to the Centre.* Delhi: Orient BlackSwan, 239–261.

Kano, Hamissou (1994). Les langues nationales parlées dans les ménages au Burkina. Une analyse des données observées au recensement de la population de décembre 1985. [The national languages spoken in Burkina Faso. An analysis of the data from the population census of December 1985]. In DGINA (ed.), *Les langues nationales dans les systèmes éducatifs du Burkina Faso: état des lieux et perspectives.* Actes du colloque organisé du 2 au 5 mars 1993 à Ouagadougou. Ouagadougou: DGINA, 25–34.

Kedrebeogo, Gérard (1997). Linguistic diversity and language policy: the challenge of multilingualism in Burkina Faso. *Hemispheres, Journal of the Polish Academy of Sciences* 12, 5–27.

Korgho, Albert (2001). *Etude comparative des coûts de formation entre les écoles classique et bilingue de Nomgana dans le département de Loumbila.* [A comparative study of the cost of training in a classical school and in a bilingual school in Nomgana in the department of Loumbila]. Ouagadougou: OSEO.

Malone, Susan and Paraide, Patricia (forthcoming). Mother tongue first bilingual education in Papua New Guinea. *International Review of Education*, special issue.

Nikièma, Norbert (2000). Bibliographie annotée de propos et prises de positions de nationaux sur les langues nationales dans l'éducation au Burkina Faso. [Annotated bibliography of opinions and viewpoints of nationals on the use of national languages in education in Burkina Faso]. In Nikièma, Norbert and Salo, Samuel (eds), *Mélanges en l'honneur du professeur Coulibaly Bakary. Cahiers du CERLESHS*, 2e Numéro spécial 2000, 107–122.

Nikièma, Norbert (forthcoming). A L1 first, multilingual model to meet the quality imperative in formal basic education in three 'francophone' West African countries. *International Review of Education*, special issue.

Remain-Kinda, Emma (2003). *L'impact d'une généralisation de l'éducation bilingue sur le Plan Décennal de Développement de l'Education de Base: cas des écoles bilingues* [The consequences of a generalisation of bilingual education for the Ten Year Development Plan of Basic Education: the case of bilingual schools]. Mémoire de fin de formation à la fonction d'inspecteur de l'enseignement du premier degré (IEPD), ENSK. Koudougou: ENSK.

SNEAHV (1980). Le SNEAHV face à l'introduction des langues nationales dans l'enseignement [The teachers' trade union's standpoint with respect to the introduction of national languages in teaching]. In *Travaux du XXVIe Congrès tenu à Bobo-Dioulasso du*

30 au 4 août 1980. La Voix des Enseignants Voltaïque, Organe du Syndicat National des Enseignants Africains de Haute-Volta (SNEAHV), 61–66.

Toe-Sidibé, Suzanne (2002). L'impact de l'éducation bilingue sur l'efficacité interne de l'école au Burkina Faso: cas des provinces d'Oubritenga et du Sanmatenga [The impact of bilingual education on the internal efficiency of school in Burkina Faso: the case of the provinces of Oubritenga and Sanmatenga]. Mémoire de fin de formation des inspecteurs de l'enseignement du 1er Degré. Koudougou: ENSK.

9

'THERE IS NO SUCH THING AS "KEEPING OUT OF POLITICS"'

Arabisation and Amazigh/Berber Mother Tongue Education in Morocco

Ahmed Kabel

9.1 Introduction

Language and language-in-education are pressing issues in the postcolonial world. Not only do they have direct bearing on ethical questions of justice, equality, pluralism and citizenship in an increasingly fragmented and polarised world system, they are equally enmeshed in both banal and aggressive forms of nationalism and 'modern' technologies of governmentality. Although problems of language and education are hardly independent of other material and objective realities and structures of domination and inequality, they usually form effective channels of political mobilisation and rationalisation either by states or elites and are, as a consequence, subscribed to larger political and strategic agendas, thus forming the locus of political struggle and contestation. A nuanced understanding of language and language-in-education, therefore, needs to take stock of the broader political and ideological context in which they are embedded. In this chapter, I draw attention to the politics of language and language-in-education in Morocco, more specifically medium of instruction and mother tongue teaching as a subject. I start by giving a sketch of the Moroccan sociolinguistic situation and language-in-education policy in independent Morocco. I then move on to discuss the political nature of Arabisation both as official state policy and as an elite political project and how the latter, among other factors, has dramatically impacted on the implementation of the policy in education. The second part of the chapter is concerned with the deeply ideological character of the Amazigh/Berber language[1] and education policy project. The ideological underpinnings of Amazigh/Berber planning, namely the choice of script and corpus, and the obstacles of enacting the policy are discussed in light of the political agendas of both the state and Amazigh and non-Amazigh elites. The chapter will conclude with a brief account of the relevance of the Ethiopia study to language-in-education policy in Morocco. But before dealing with these questions in detail, a description of the sociolinguistic situation in Morocco is in order.

9.2 The Current Sociolinguistic Situation

Given its strategic location at the crossroads of Europe, North Africa and the rest of the continent, Morocco has long been the subject of multiple influences. This long history is reflected among other things in its linguistic makeup. There are two autochthonous macro language varieties used in the country: Arabic and Amazigh. The first includes at least three main varieties, namely Moroccan Arabic (itself composed of several regional/social dialects), Standard Arabic and Classical Arabic. Berber, on the other hand, is composed of three regional dialects, Tashelhit in the south-west, Tarifit in the north and Tamazight in the middle. For endogenous languages, the legacy of colonial and postcolonial domination,[2] French is the dominant foreign language. Spanish, which is spoken in the north but is not of wide currency, will not be considered here. English which has already started making important inroads into the educational system and the economy will not be considered either.

9.2.1 Classical Arabic

Classical Arabic is the idiom of the Qur'an and Prophet Mohammed's sayings, a corpus of foundational Islamic texts that have been preserved for over 14 centuries. Classical Arabic is also the language of Qur'anic exegesis and theological writing, classical grammar, philosophy and religious rituals and practice as well as ancient and classical poetry and literary art forms. Contrary to what some researchers claim (Ennaji 1991), Classical Arabic is not a language of the past, a euphemism for a dead language. It is equally a language of the present. A great deal of theological writing is still conducted in this idiom as are a great number of texts by religious scholars. However, Classical Arabic remains marginal to the daily language practices of both formally educated and uneducated Moroccans. For the latter, the language is virtually incomprehensible. For the former, who received secular education in postcolonial Morocco, proper understanding is hardly achieved without the assistance of a good dictionary.

9.2.2 Modern Standard Arabic

Modern Standard Arabic is a 'modernised' version of Classical Arabic which emerged as a result of the pressure for postcolonial nation building, 'development' and 'modernisation' and it came about exclusively through the technologies of language planning and policy. Modern Standard Arabic is the language of television, newspapers, modern literature, political discourse, and (at least officially) administration and education. The requirements of 'modernisation' initiated major 'simplifications' of Classical Arabic, which concerned all levels of language form (phonology, morphology, grammar) and content (lexicon) (Ennaji 2005; Mitchell 1986). The new lexicon consists of new word coinages and borrowings from mainly French and English to serve emerging communication and expressive needs. As opposed to Classical Arabic, Modern Standard Arabic has simple sentence structure and word order. Phonologically, the impact of dialectal Arabic is very much in evidence. Innovations in several domains, the spread of mass media, mass education and literacy as well as the increasing and widespread proliferation of government bureaucracy have all substantially impacted on the spread, importance and prestige of this variety. Compared to its classical parent variety, it is far less difficult to the average formally uneducated Moroccan.

Although Classical and Modern Standard Arabic carry a certain degree of prestige in their respective domains, they are not the mother tongue of Arabic-speaking Moroccans; the latter's first language is Moroccan Arabic (also known as Dialectal or Demotic Arabic). These linguistic distinctions are not merely of theoretical interest; they have significant import in educational policy and practice, as we shall see below.

9.2.3 Moroccan Arabic

Moroccan Arabic is the mother tongue of all Arabs in Morocco and the second language of Amazigh speakers. Moroccan Arabic is used in the most mundane and intimate spheres of social and private life. It is also used as lingua franca between speakers of Amazigh and Moroccan Arabic. In comparison to the two other varieties, Moroccan Arabic has far simpler lexis, phonology, morphology, syntax and pragmatics (Ennaji 2005). However, using Moroccan Arabic as a macro variety is a misleading simplification, to say the least. There exist tremendous levels of regional variation within Moroccan Arabic which undermines the hypothesis that Moroccan Arabic is monolithic (see Table 9.1). One can even venture to state that some varieties might verge on mutual unintelligibility. On the other hand, in addition to regional variation, there is also variation related to class and level of formal education (usually inter-related) with 'demotic' Moroccan Arabic and 'Educated' Moroccan Arabic (Youssi 1995; Mitchell 1986; see Table 9.1). The latter variety is generally spoken by formally educated Moroccans in certain formal or semi-formal domains of language use such as on television, radio and education. Recently, newspapers and magazines, for both ideological and commercial motives, have started using this 'brand' as their main language of publication. Politicians also use 'Educated' Moroccan Arabic to rally supporters and promote their political agenda.

TABLE 9.1 Varieties of Arabic and Amazigh

Macro varieties	Examples	
	Arabic	Amazigh
Regional varieties	Tetounai, Fassi, Bidaoui	Tashelhit, Tarifit, Tamazight
Dialect vs Standard	Dialectal, Demotic or Moroccan Arabic Educated Moroccan Arabic Modern Standard Arabic Classical Arabic	Tashelhit, Tarifit, Tamazight vs Standard Berber
Urban/Rural	Aaroubi Arabic, Mdini Arabic	Mountain Berber/City Berber

9.2.4 Amazigh

Berber, also known as Amazigh, is an Afro-Asiatic language whose speakers are scattered throughout North Africa in Egypt, Libya, Tunisia, Algeria, Mauritania and Morocco. Tuareg, a group of nomads with a distinctive dialect and who have created the Tifinagh script now used in Morocco, inhabit vast areas in Northern Niger, Mali and Burkina Faso.

In Morocco, although no official census data is available, estimates vary widely as to the representation of Berbers. Generally, estimates range from 40% (Crawford 2001) to 60% (Sadiqi 2003), thus reflecting not only difficulties in getting census data but, more importantly, lack of consensus over who is or who is not an Amazigh and a 'Bérbérophone' for that matter. There are three varieties of Berber spoken by three segments of the Amazigh population inhabiting three dis-contiguous geographic areas: Tarifit in the north, Tamazight in the Middle Atlas and Tashelhit in the south-west of Morocco. The three varieties have existed in Morocco for at least 5,000 years (Boukous 1995a: 18; 1995b). Largely owing to historical and geographic factors, the three varieties have evolved into virtually mutually unintelligible linguistic systems (although there seems to be a continuum along geographically contiguous areas from the south-west to the north and north-east). Nevertheless, although the three varieties possess different lexicons and phonological systems, they share a fundamentally similar syntactic structure. Not unlike Moroccan Arabic, there is wide variation within each of the three varieties, with estimates postulating the existence of hundreds of different dialects (Boukous 1979) (see Table 9.1). Berber, like 'demotic' Moroccan Arabic, is used in everyday contexts of language use and also utilised for communal interaction and as a vehicle for transmitting Amazigh cultural heritage and traditions. Berber has largely borrowed from Latin, Moroccan Arabic and French. However, the overwhelming majority of loan words come from Moroccan Arabic (Ennaji 1991, 1997). These borrowings are the outcome of the extension of the use of Amazigh to domains previously dominated by Moroccan Arabic or are generally a result of the long history of language contact. Although these borrowings maintain their roots, they mostly acquire Berber morphological and phonological form. On the other hand, Amazigh has also important influences on Moroccan Arabic, which encompass lexicon, grammar and phonology and phonetics (Chtatou 1997). This largely explains the difficulties that speakers of Moroccan Arabic and Middle Easterners encounter when communicating with each other. Moroccans are said to speak 'Berberised Arabic'. Amazigh has recently been used on television, radio, and in newspapers and education. More of this below.

9.2.5 French

French carries a (heavy) legacy of colonialism. For the great majority of formally educated Moroccans, French is a second or a third language. However, its being a second language does not make its status *secondary*. As perhaps with other European symbolic goods, it enjoys tremendous prestige and is vied for in circles of power and influence. The language is generally spoken by an urban, middle and upper class and intellectual elite and exerts an aura of open-mindedness and 'modernity' and, in this sense, is an essential gate-keeping mechanism for social mobility and to the centres of power. The special position that French enjoys is a result of colonial policy, postcolonial dependency and elite politics. Despite the declared policy of Arabisation, French remains the dominant language of business, administration and higher education, domains where high level and 'sociolinguistically proper' functioning depends to a large extent on the mastery of this language (Sadiqi 2003).

9.3 Language-in-education Policy in Independent Morocco

Since independence in 1956, Morocco has effected numerous reforms in its constitution. Along with the foundational creeds of the nation, there has always been one constant, however: every constitution stipulates that Arabic is the official language of Morocco. In this capacity, Arabic is proffered the *de jure* status of the language of the government, administration, economy and education. The process of implementation was characterised more by rupture than by continuity. Between 1957 and 1964, progressive Arabisation of the elementary education was implemented despite a (brief temporary) retreat from this policy during 1958. Arabisation of administration was launched in 1960. Four years later, the government issued a statement stipulating the obligatory Arabisation of the judiciary. Arabisation of secondary education was effected according to subject matter starting with the social sciences and then scientific and technical subjects. In 1983, the secondary cycle was completely Arabised. For higher education, Arabisation concerned mostly the social sciences and humanities. The sciences were still predominantly taught in French. In 1990, the first 'Arabised' baccalaureate holders were to join universities.

9.4 The Current Charter for Educational Reform

After all the protracted, unsystematic and inefficient implementation of Arabisation and several other initiatives, in 2000, a Charter for Educational Reform was produced that had as an objective the complete overhaul of the educational system. The Charter was an extremely ambitious project which ran the whole gamut of educational philosophy, policy, curriculum and pedagogy. The document was designed to provide orientations and guidelines for implementation for a ten-year period between 2000 and 2009. Only those elements of immediate interest to language policy will be dealt with here. The Charter states that 'within education, the Kingdom of Morocco adopts clear, coherent and constant language policy' (Charte Nationale d'Education et de Formation 1999: 30). The document outlines three main relevant policy orientations: the reinforcement of Arabic language teaching, diversification of the languages of science and technology and, for the first time, an 'opening up' to Amazigh/Berber.

Interestingly, the current Charter for Educational Reform does not explicitly address, at least in name, the question of Arabisation although the ideological and legitimatory premises underlying the policy remain in full force. The Charter made it clear that Arabic is (still) the national and official language and gave recommendations for its modernisation in terms of language planning, the encouragement of production and translation in Arabic and the formation of Arabic language experts and teacher trainers. Equally importantly, the Charter recommended that an academy be established and take in charge projects of language planning, implementation and evaluation.

The second major element in the policy is the diversification of the language of instruction of science and technology. The Charter states that 'optional' branches of science and technology will be opened at tertiary level institutions where Arabic will be the medium of instruction. At the same time, other 'highly' specialised research and training units will be set up in the foreign language that offers the best scientific 'performances' and the easiest means of communication. The latter statement leaves the door open for speculation, whether that 'superior' language is French or English. In addition, the languages of instruction at the secondary and tertiary levels will be streamlined so that students will pursue their higher education in the language they employed in their high school. This of course is a recipe for confusion.

Perhaps the most innovative element in the policy is the explicit reference to Berber. For the first time in the history of educational reforms in Morocco, the latter was given explicit and clear recognition. The Charter points out that regional educational bodies have the capacity to choose the use of Berber or any other local dialect to facilitate the learning of the 'official language', meaning Arabic. It is important to say here that Berber and local dialects can be used to facilitate the learning of Arabic, as medium of instruction to teach the medium of instruction! In addition, the Charter stipulates that research bodies for the 'linguistic and cultural development' of Berber will be created as well as teacher training and curriculum development programmes. This section of the Charter predates and constitutes the foundation for subsequent decisions regarding the establishment of IRCAM (Institut Royal de la Culture Amazighe) and the inclusion of Berber mother tongue instruction as a subject in 2003.

9.5 The Politics of Arabisation

From its inception, Arabisation policies have been a fundamentally political affair and their implementation a matter of political expediency. After independence in 1956, the hegemony of the French language was uncontested. It continued its monopoly over major sectors of the bureaucracy, economy and education. But not for so long, at least at the level of discourse. The nationalists soon launched a policy of Arabisation. *Technically*, Arabisation is understood as the replacement of French as the official language of education and administration with Arabic (Grandguillaume 1998: 18). However, it would be naive to believe that Arabisation is merely a matter of *technically* and *nominally* substituting one language for another. Arabisation cannot be understood without taking stock of the political, sociological and cultural politics which gave it rise. Foremost, Arabisation was employed as the paramount tool for harnessing legitimacy by the nationalists and the monarchy after independence (Grandguillaume 1983). Decolonisation from France also necessitated a kind of (official) cultural detachment from the coloniser and thus a return to an (imagined) past unsullied by French interference. Arabisation in this sense was the vehicle, to use Ngũgĩ (1986), for 'decolonising the mind'.

On the other hand, Arabisation was employed as a tool for manufacturing a sense of national identity predicated on a 'common' Arab and Islamic heritage, to the exclusion of Amazighs and their cultural heritage. In this sense, Arabisation promoted a sense of unity and was aimed at creating, to employ Anderson's (1991) overused book-title phrase, an 'imagined community' without which the political authority of the nascent state would be unfounded. Political authority through Arabisation similarly had to be legitimated with reference to appurtenance to the larger Arab and Islamic *Umma* (nation). In this case, Arabisation meant not only national but also 'inter-national' unity. Soon after independence, certain segments of Moroccan society found themselves gradually dispossessed of their power by a French-educated elite. The traditionalists, as they were called, had their eyes on the benefits that would accrue from the adoption of Arabic as the language of education and bureaucracy (Boukous 1999: 77). These traditionalists needed to make sure that Arabisation became official policy so that their interests would not be compromised but, at the same time, they would have to enhance the linguistic capital of their children by securing for them a bilingual (French-Arabic) education (Grandguillaume 1983).

Nevertheless, whatever the differences between the traditionalists and the modernists, both tendencies converged on the devaluation and delegitimisation of the mother tongues of Moroccans, namely, Moroccan Arabic and Amazigh. In the words of the late Mohamed Abid Al-Jabiri, a distinguished Moroccan intellectual and Arabist of Berber origin, total Arabisation 'must aim at eliminating French as the language of civilisation, high culture and daily practice and *must especially eliminate the local dialects, Berber or Arabic*' (1973: 146, emphasis added). For the traditionalists, the dialects are parasitic outgrowths, and are therefore a hindrance that has to be eliminated as a condition for purifying tradition. For the modernists, dialects are antiquarian legacies of a backward past and an impediment to progress and modernisation which have to be fulfilled through the homogenisation of the linguistic landscape that modernity implies, precisely like what their Jacobin white overlords in Paris had in mind. Finally, it is undoubtedly clear that Arabisation was targeted for the masses, regardless of their ethnic appurtenance, who, in order to be disciplined and ruled, have to be denied precisely the means of power and control, prominent among which was the French language. The paradox reached its tragicomic climax with 'top education Ministry personnel sending their children to French-language schools while they engineer Arabisation policies for the nation at large' (Sirles 1999: 125–126). No wonder. Their ilk in top government circles was fervently professing the same faith. Even the most ardent champions of 'Arabisation for the whole of Moroccan people' (read, the masses), including the chief of the nationalist movement, had thrown the lot of their children in with the several establishments of the '*Mission laïque française*' (Dalle 2001: 54).[3]

9.6 Implementing Arabisation

In addition to the ambivalent and contradictory aspects of the policy, there were similarly serious problems with the implementation of Arabisation. 'One of the setbacks Arabisation has suffered', writes Hammoud, 'is a remarkable lack of consistency and continuity in its execution. It has been at the mercy of changing ministers and coalitions until pronouncements were made about it by the king' (1982: 229, cited in Redouane 1998: 200). Similarly 'the inadequacy in planning by the Ministry of Education, as well as lack of coordination among the offices and public administrations have been the biggest problems for efficient language planning in education' (ibid.). Related to this is the heavy centralisation of all planning and execution activities and lack of accountability and independent expertise.

Although there is consensus among educators that the use of Arabic as a medium of instruction helps students to assimilate course content and leads to higher levels of achievement (Mouhssine 1995: 58), the policy, however, suffers from serious shortcomings. While achievement might be enhanced at the elementary and secondary schools, university success largely depends on the mastery of French. Most scientific and technical subjects at tertiary institutions are taught in French. Textbooks and course materials are also in French. The instructors and professors are trained in France or had their training through the medium of French. The dominance of French as the language of science and education and as a perceived crucial factor for socio-economic progress compromises effective implementation of Arabisation. Hammoud, for instance, asserts that 'the convenient long-term reliance on French as an advanced language of wider communication and a medium facilitating access to the modern world of science and technology has made Arabisation harder and harder to achieve' (1982: 228, cited in Redouane 1998: 199). Additionally, 'French must be kept in order to remain in contact with Europe and the rest of the world', and therefore a complete implementation of Arabisation, officials believed, 'will lead to linguistic isolation, which will have negative ramifications for the socio-economic development of the country' (Ennaji 1988: 10). In such geopolitical context it is only patently normal that French would continue as the de facto official language of bureaucracy, economy and higher education. Indeed, French continued to enjoy its status as the 'unofficial official language' and is closely 'associated with public administration, with technical and scientific matters . . . and modernity' (Elbiad 1991: 34). This produced the adverse effect, namely the devaluation of the Arabic language and the elevation of the status of French.

The success of the use of Arabic as medium of instruction was additionally compromised by purely linguistic determinants, namely the phenomenon of diglossia. The diglossic, triglossic (Youssi 1995: 29–31) or quadriglossic (Ennaji 2005: 49) realities have had a direct impact on the nature of language use inside classrooms. Prior to the current Charter, in theory, instruction in Moroccan schools had to be carried out through the medium of the standard. In this respect, pedagogical intervention in Standard Arabic had to be dissociated from Moroccan Arabic and Amazigh/Berber, the mother tongues of the students. In fact, the teaching of Standard Arabic was meant to 'correct' and 'remedy' the deficiencies inherent in the dialects and the habits of mind they were thought to inculcate. Medium of instruction in this respect was more about remedial work than about actual teaching. Even with the recommendations of the new Charter, spoken dialects are not used in their own right, but only as tools for enhancing the acquisition of Standard Arabic. On the other hand, in practice, it is difficult to state that Standard Arabic was systematically used as the medium of instruction. Given the rife contradictions in the policy, it was a mixture of Moroccan Arabic, Standard Arabic and French that was used in the classroom. Instruction was mainly conducted in the medium of 'Educated Moroccan Arabic'. This resulted in a deep ambivalence towards and devaluation of spoken dialects, including Moroccan Arabic and Amazigh (Mouhssine 1995: 53). This clearly has implications for perceptions of the use of dialects as medium of instruction.

Related to this issue is the part played by language attitudes as a crucial factor in the implementation of Arabisation. Different segments of Moroccan society hold different and ambivalent perceptions towards Arabisation. Bentahila (1983: 123–124), for instance, identified at least four contrasting trends. The traditionalists hold dearly to the policy and consider the language a guarantor of cultural identity and heritage and a criterial component of Moroccanness. The nationalists consider Arabisation as a way to strengthen political ties with other Arab nations and work towards establishing Arab unity. The modernists and bureaucrats are sceptical about (if not hostile to the idea of) the usefulness of Arabisation and are primordially concerned with establishing an efficient educational system capable of preparing graduates to deal with the challenges of the 'modern' world. These 'Françisants', (Ennaji 2005: 188), hold powerful positions in higher education and the economy and are major decision-makers in most administrative sectors. For these groups, Arabic is not a lucrative commodity at the linguistic market-place and may consequently compromise the whole project of modernisation and development.

On the other hand, there are claims advanced regarding the political and even security costs of Arabisation. Some writers have expressed apprehension concerning the radicalising effects of Arabisation. Their eyes were certainly on 'neighbouring countries (Algeria)' where, according to one author, rapid Arabi-sation has led to the festering of 'fundamentalism, xenophobia, chauvinism and obscurantism' (Berdouzi 2000: 21). Ennaji and Sadiqi follow suit by affirming that 'Arabisation policy has indirectly contributed to the development of Mus-lim fundamentalism and has paved the way for the growth of Islamist demands' (2008: 50). 'Muslim fundamentalist leaders', the authors drudge on, 'are reluctant to speak French and make use of Standard/Classical Arabic to rally the masses in their struggle for power' (Ennaji and Sadiqi 2008: 50). Putting aside the rather loose use of the word 'fundamentalism', these fantastic statements fall like a house of cards when put to the factual test. Just one example will suffice. Nadia Yassine, the daughter of Abdessalam Yassine, the founder of the officially banned 'funda-mentalist' association '*Al Adl Wa Al Ihssan* (Justice and Charity)' and second in line of command in the association, has the following biographical information on her personal website: 'She went to French-cultural-mission schools for her primary and secondary education, respectively at Paul Cezanne primary School in Rabat, Descartes's High School in Rabat and Victor Hugo High School in Marrakech' (http://www.nadiayassine.net). But Nadia is not any kind of French mission pupil. 'From the latter she earned her high school diploma with distinc-tion in the year of 1977.' Nadia Yassine, whose association (and father) is labelled as fundamentalist by Ennaji (referred to above), did not have to bear the brunt of Arabised education, and therefore morph into a fundamentalist. Neither is she reluctant to speak French; according to the same website, 'she gave interviews to multiple radio and television stations from around the world: ARTE, France 3, France 5, BBC, Radio Orient, Oumma TV, Radio Canada' and even her first book 'Toutes voiles dehors' was written in French and was published in 2003 by 'Altereditions' in France and by 'Le Fennec', a French publisher in Morocco. This, to conclude, does not look like a biography of someone who 'is reluctant to speak French', if the latter is at all a defining feature of 'fundamentalists'.

9.7 Amazigh Language-in-Education

May 1994 was a milestone in the history of Berber culture, language and education in Morocco. At May Day parade, seven teachers were arrested and interrogated by the police for carrying banners written in *Tifinagh*, the then unofficial writing system for Amazigh and the symbol of the Berber cultural movement. The incident drew international media and human rights coverage, and the Amazigh 'problem' soon occupied political centre stage. Three months later, King Hassan II, in his address on August 20, declared for the first time that Berber dialects are 'one of the components of the authenticity of our history'. Following the lead of his father, King Mohammed VI declared in October 2001 that Amazigh/Berber is 'a principal element of national culture' and ordered the establishment of IRCAM which would be the sole official body to be in charge of the development and promotion of Amazigh/Berber language, culture and education. Three years later, the first Amazigh-as-a-subject classes were held in primary schools across the Berber-speaking regions. The initial plan devised by both the Ministry of Education and IRCAM stipulated the gradual inclusion of Berber at the elementary levels from first to sixth grade. This is clearly a tremendous achievement and certainly calls for celebration. However, the process of planning and implementation has been a rather bumpy road.

9.8 Planning Berber

9.8.1 Choice of Script

The choice of an orthographic system is far from being a matter of technical validity or even educational viability. Since Amazigh/Berber was mainly a spoken language, the first challenge for IRCAM was to adopt a writing system. There were three options available for language planners: the adoption of Arabic, Latin or Tifinagh script. After heated debates and lengthy deliberations, agreement was impossible to reach among the clashing camps. The decision was delegated (or rather relegated) to IRCAM Administrative Council which opted for the use of Tifinagh (see Table 9.2). Contrary to what can be expected, the debate about the choice of script did not revolve around the educational, pedagogical or technical viability of each of the available options. The locus of the whole tedious deliberations was about politics and ideology (Errihani 2006). The arguments, counter-arguments and accusations focused on the symbolic and political implications of each potential choice. Those who were in favour of the Latin script were intent on severing any ties with the Arabic language and culture, setting the Berber project on a totally different course and joining the ranks of the international Amazigh movement exemplified in the radical Algerian Kabyle activists. For their opponents, the advocacy of a Latin script is a ploy that smacks of neo-colonialist and separatist overtones and is indeed a rejuvenation of the Berber Decree promoted by the French during the Protectorate to separate Amazighs from Arabs.

TABLE 9.2 Tifinagh script

ⴰ	ⴱ	ⴳ	ⴳⵯ	ⴷ	ⴹ	ⴻ	ⴼ	ⴽ	ⴽⵯ	ⵀ
ya	yab	yag	yagʷ	yad	yaḍ	yey	yaf	yak	yakʷ	yah
a	b	g	gʷ	d	ḍ	e	f	k	kʷ	h
[a]	[b/β]	[g/ɟ]	[gʷ]	[d/ð]	[d̴]	[e]	[f]	[k/ç]	[kʷ]	[h]
ⵃ	ⵄ	ⵅ	ⵇ	ⵉ	ⵊ	ⵍ	ⵎ	ⵏ	ⵓ	ⵔ
yaḥ	yaɛ	yax	yaq	yi	yaj	yal	yam	yan	yu	yar
ḥ		x	q	i	j	l	m	n	u	r
[ħ]	[ʕ]	[x]	[q]	[i]	[ʒ]	[l]	[m]	[n]	[u]	[r]
ⵕ	ⵖ	ⵙ	ⵚ	ⵛ	ⵜ	ⵟ	ⵡ	ⵢ	ⵣ	ⵥ
yaṛ	yagh	yas	yaṣ	yac	yat	yaṭ	yaw	yay	yaz	yaẓ
ṛ	gh	s	ṣ	c	t	ṭ	w	y	z	ẓ
[r̴]	[ɣ]	[s]	[s]	[ʃ]	[t/θ]	[t̴]	[w]	[j]	[z]	[z̴]

The Latin script was anything but palatable to the Islamists who perceived in it an attempt to alienate the Berbers from their Islamic heritage. On the other hand, the advocates of Arabic script were accused of being campaigners of Arabisation and plunging headlong into the bosom of Arab nationalism and the state.

The choice of Tifinagh as the official script on the part of the Administrative Council was informed by subtle political calculations. From a political standpoint, the most damaging choice for the state (and IRCAM by extension) was the Latin script. In the minds of Arabophones and Islamists, resonances of the Berber Decree, neo-colonialism and treason would be inevitable and the state would be compelled to intervene to appease the tension and thus compromise the whole initiative. On the other hand, the association of the Latin script with the Kabyle activists could also be a major factor in the further politicisation of the 'Amazigh problem' and its 'extra-territorialisation' beyond the borders of Morocco, which might propel it out of control. The porous character of the nation state in post-modern times makes any 'trans-national' choice a threat to its 'sovereignty'. These forms of 'transpolitics' highlight the 'translocal dimensions of all local cultural processes' and the fact that questions of identity '*transcend* the formal political institutions of state bureaucracies' (Silverstein 2004: 8). For the state, Tifinagh would be a harmless choice. At least, the Berber problem was once and for all irrevocably contained within the confines of national territory and should be a far better choice than Latin, and politically as viable as the choice of Arabic.

9.8.2 Corpus Planning

The first major task facing IRCAM after the choice of the Tifinagh script was the standardisation of the spoken dialects. The difficulty of planning a unified

Amazigh/Berber corpus resided in the existence of three mutually unintelligible varieties, which gave rise to the question of which variety to choose. But given the deeply political and ideological implications of opting for and reaching consensus on one of the varieties, the decision was to create one single macro variety. This macro variety will be allotted the status of a standard language. The actual process of standardisation, on the other hand, reveals a subtle ideological project espoused by the Amazigh/Berberist planners, namely 'de-dialectalisation' and 'purification'.

9.8.3 The Politics of Linguistic Engineering

The resolution to invent a macro variety was informed by political motivations in a similar fashion to the selection of script. The existence of a macro variety that would be imposed on the speakers of the three dialects is an expedient scenario for the state. The uniformisation of the Amazigh dialects implies a potential homogenisation of the three Berber communities with the aim of diffusing any potential attempt to mount claims for autonomy in any of the three Berber regions. More specifically, given the persistent and increasingly vocal demands of the Rif activists for autonomy or even independence, homogenisation can be a powerful instrument for neutralising these demands and diffusing separatist schemes.[4] Conversely, officialisation of each variety would entail the consolidation of regional identities and fuelling of calls for autonomy or political rights. Linguistic homogenisation and standardisation of the Amazigh curriculum extend and consolidate state penetration in those regions. As was stated above, the standardisation of Berber conceals an ideological programme promoted by Berberist planners. Before tackling these schemes, we will briefly refer to the technical aspects of Amazigh standardisation.

The strategies for corpus planning are explicitly spelled out by the current (i.e. in September 2010) Rector of IRCAM, Ahmed Boukous. For him, the main goal is the standardisation of Berber as a 'common national language'. The reasons of this formulation will be outlined below. For the moment, let us linger for a while on the technicalities of standardisation. For Boukous, the normalisation project should be carried out according to two principal and successive phases. The first stage concerns the standardisation of each of the three different dialects. The rationale behind this exercise was to ensure the conditions for 'linguistic and cultural security' on the one hand, and to form the basis for the 'unification' of the three dialects in the form of 'Standard Amazigh/Berber', on the other. The second phase consists of the elaboration of the standard language where the central task should be to 'manage divergences'. The management of variation consists of either integrating competing forms as, like in music, similar variations on a theme and let 'the linguistic market' decide on their fate or else drastically incorporate some variants into the system and exclude others (Boukous 2004: 18). The rationale for these technologies was to engineer a standardised version of the language and at the same time to preserve its diversity and richness. This is definitely a tall order and a contradictory process. Moving away from 'sociolinguistic-speak', the unstated motive behind standardisation is 'de-dialectalisation'.

First, any kind of standardisation enterprise cannot be achieved without reducing variability.[5] In this very respect, standardisation is not so much the accommodation of variation as the imposition of 'invariability'. The treatment of the variants as 'functionally redundant' or 'superfluous', as in the case of Berber here, rests on the assumption that variation is chaotic and inordinately unsystematic, and standardisation will therefore bring the vernacular into 'disciplined linguistic order'. But variation is not random and does serve important sociolinguistic functions; as Cooper pointed out, 'when variants . . . serve as markers of our identity, we may be loath to abandon them, namely in the name of a soulless efficiency' (1989: 132). The standardisation and normalisation of a language have implications for a certain degree of objectification and fixity that run against the openness and vitality of the spoken forms of the language. Therefore, despite solemn disclaimers, at the heart of normalisation is a process of minimising the dialectal traits of the varieties; in short, standardisation stands for 'de-dialectalisation'.

As a discourse, standardisation sets limits on what can and cannot be included and, in the process, produces new orders of linguistic reality, culminating in the generation of a stratification of the 'standard' and 'non-standard' varieties of the language. Standardisation inevitably leads to the devaluation of dialects. And given the generative nature of discourse, the same logic will mechanically transfer to the users of those varieties. Thus the linguistic variety which people use will equate with social class stratification. The first important sequel of linguistic standardisation is the production of an immediate socio-economic rift between those who have written literacy/ies and those who possess mainly oral literacy/ies. The significance of formal literacy and the material and symbolic profits that accrue from it also form a source of prestige for the emerging class of formally literate Berbers and, by implication, exacerbate the predicament of the already disadvantaged Amazigh orates.

The claim that standardising the three varieties will ensure 'linguistic and cultural security' is far from an accurate appraisal, as shall be presently argued. The creation of a macro variety, which in essence is an artificial language, may undermine the linguistic security of the native speakers of the varieties, especially if one considers the hierarchisation of standard and non-standard linguistic forms. The learning of the standard may well approximate the learning of a second language, alienating young learners from their dialect. On the other hand, as the standard and the dialect will have different functional distributions, diglossia is most likely to be the order of the day. The dialect or local variety will continue to be used in the most intimate and mundane domains of daily discourse while the standard will occupy other 'higher' spheres of language use such as education. An immediate consequence would threaten to disrupt the continuity between home and school, which is fundamental to educational and linguistic security. The discontinuity between home and school, too, has direct bearing on gender equity and inequalities among the young and the elderly. It affects the human dynamics between those who stay at home (mainly women), the elderly and their children, with the result that the linguistic security of those who will not be able to learn the standard language (women, the elderly) will be even more compromised. As for cultural security, the development of a potentially artificial language and its inclusion in education poses questions regarding the appropriacy of using it as a vehicle for cultural transmission and revival.

If de-dialectalisation is a process targeting issues of variation within Amazigh/Berber, purification is the parallel mechanism employed for handling 'interlingual' variability. Although this is not an explicitly stated aim of the planners, there are indications in which these concerns have been central to the rationalities of the planning process. Language planners have prioritised a 'cleansing' of Berber by focusing on the lexicon as the central locus of contamination. In the first booklet of Amazigh vocabulary, the criteria for vocabulary development and elaboration were laid out explicitly and unequivocally. When several varieties of a similar concept are present, a hierarchy of selection criteria is developed and strictly observed (Ameur et al. 2006: 7–8). The first criterion in the hierarchy is 'authenticity'. The second criterion relates to the geographic diffusion of the item while the third concerns the creation of neologisms if an item does not meet the above mentioned criteria. Among the three, authenticity reigns supreme. In the words of the planners, '*un mot Amazigh, pris dans son sens premier ou avec une extension semantique, a le primat sur les autres*' (Ameur et al. 2006: 8).[6] Although authenticity is never defined in such corpus planning documents, it would not be difficult to infer what it means from practice. Authenticity encompasses the essential *formal* elements, such as etymology, morphology and phonotactics which confer upon an item the status of an Amazigh/Berber word. The other more substantive side of authenticity, namely *sociolinguistic* authenticity (how speakers relate to the word and how the word serves functional uses), was largely ignored. The emphasis on authenticity as a primary selection criterion rationalised the exclusion of other 'less authentic' (both French and Arabic) words. Therefore, even though a word is of wider currency, it is considered less worthy of inclusion in the standard corpus merely because of its suspect (formal) authenticity. Neologisms were treated in like fashion. In the absence of authentic concepts, neologisms have to be coined even in the existence of words of wider use. Given that coinage relies exclusively on purely formal and linguistic considerations, formal authenticity again remains primary. While such persistent attempts to purge Amazigh/Berber of lexical 'impurities and contamination' generated perfectly *formally* 'acceptable' coinages, it conversely produced '*sociolinguistic monsters*' in the process.

The primary goal of standardisation in this case has been the 'authentication' of the language through de-dialectalisation and purification. While this has to a large extent succeeded, one needs to take stock of the sociolinguistic and educational consequences.

The perceived 'authenticity' of the standard is diminished because of a large number of sociolinguistic factors. Indeed, sociolinguistic considerations would lead to the rejection of the standard as an artificial entity. Amazigh language planners had plenty of lessons to learn from the fate of Arabic, especially with regard to the perceived differences between prescription and usage. This is in relation to reverse logic, 'since the rules of Arabic grammar are based on prescriptive rules instead of actual usage, they will remain hopeless and unattainable goals for the vast majority of Arab learners' (Ibrahim 1989: 42, cited in Dorian 1994: 480), and practices of this kind 'may threaten the very success of the effort to promote the standard language' (Dorian 1994: 479–480). Paradoxically, such practices may only promote the success of the political and ideological agenda of powerful elite circles with the result of alienating the language from the masses. Alienation entails, as was pointed out above, the diglossic competition between the vernacular and standard, a potentially serious by-product of these planning processes. Educationally, purification leads to 'de-bilingualisation'. By imposing strictly hygienic principles on the language (Cameron 1995), a decoupling between Berber and Moroccan Arabic is created. It is just unrealistic, to say the least, to obliterate, with a stroke of a lexical 'corpus', hundreds of years of language contact and cross-influence between Arabic and Berber and subject the Berber language to a severe reality of impoverishment and linguistic isolation. This will ultimately lock innocent speakers into a perennial reality of linguistic chauvinism and separatism, not quite different from their nationalist counterparts. The implications this has for pedagogy concern the perceived mutual exclusiveness of Berber vis-à-vis other languages and therefore the insignificance of attempting to make and forge connections between them. In addition to concerns over *linguistic* authenticity in standardisation, there is equally a fixation on authenticity in the Berber cultural curriculum, which reveals once more a subtle form of cultural politics.

9.9 Implementing Amazigh: Problems and Obstacles

One of the serious obstacles to the effective implementation of Berber as a subject is centralisation and monopoly of all implementation capacity and decision-making in the hands of the Ministry of Education. The mission of IRCAM is limited to conducting linguistic and pedagogical research and putting forward curricula and recommendations that will then need to receive the final blessing of the Ministry. The latter then proceeds to put into practice those recommendations in and on its own terms. However, as Errihani points out, 'while IRCAM fulfils its role by researching, proposing, and recommending, the same cannot be said of the Ministry of Education, which has been accused of hardly acting on IRCAM's recommendations' and 'protracted inaction and inability to seriously implement IRCAM's recommendations' (2006: 146). The IRCAM therefore is no more than a consultative body and has only suggestive power. Its recommendations as a consequence remain no more than a public relations façade and a means to 'officialise' the Berber education project. These observations cast doubt over the seriousness of the official establishment to adopt and implement a clear language policy. Clearly, one of the obstacles to the success of Berber education is the ambiguous status of Berber. Although there is a clear official 'opening up' to Berber, the language has not yet been granted the status of a national language. This ambivalence underplays positive reception among different parties and mini-mises the chances of the success of the project.

In addition to inefficiencies in planning and policy, Amazigh education is encountering serious challenges in its practical implementation. As was the case with Arabisation, there is the proverbial dissonance between policy and exe-cution. The implementation of Berber has been beset by similar inadequacies of planning, inefficiency, inconsistencies in practice, lack of accountability and vision, dearth of resources and the lack of ideological commitment on the part of policy makers. The following passage from a former IRCAM official summarises it all and it is useful to quote him at length.

> The news about Tamazight language teaching are [sic] quite grim and the prospects look bleak. As of now, there is hardly any teaching in third year, even though the book for this year had been printed. Berber was supposed to be introduced at the Junior High School level, but it has not been. At the university level, departments of Berber or at least teaching and research units, were supposed to be created. Nothing of that has been done. The Ministry, the Academies and the Universities are dragging their feet.
>
> (Jilali Saib, cited in Buckner 2006: 426)

The first damaging weakness was lack of teacher training for Berber teach-ers. Prior to the implementation of Berber education, no extensive, specialised teacher education programme was devised. There was no specialised corps of Berber teachers; all of them were teachers of either Arabic or French. These pro-spective teachers were given only two weeks of training in the form of workshops in 2003. But even this meagre pedagogical training diet pales in comparison with only three days in 2004. Matters were made worse by the fact that the teachers are required to use a new language with a completely new script. There are teachers who are assigned to teach children a language they do not themselves speak or in which they have shaky competence at best. Even for those who already speak one of the varieties, the standard language presents many a difficulty. To give an example, 'one Berber teacher explained that while he is a native speaker, he himself often struggles with the vocabulary because the dialect he and his students speak has been influenced heavily by Arabic and French over the years' (Buckner 2006: 428). Teacher trainers and supervisors did not fare any better.

Not only was pre-service training not provided, the instructors did not receive in-service training either, leaving them to their own devices as to what and how to teach and assess, thus paving the ground for inadequacies in pedagogical practice. In the absence of sound training and practice being under enormous pressure, teachers usually fall back on discredited teaching methods and classroom techniques. 'When visiting almost any classroom where Berber is being taught' writes Errihani, 'one is faced with archaic methods of drilling students and a heavy reliance on translation between Moroccan Arabic and Berber' (2006: 150). Teachers are not of course to blame; they do their utmost in the most unfavourable teaching conditions, class sizes are usually large and there is often more than one grade level in the same class. On top of lack of teaching resources, instructors have found themselves with three additional hours of Berber a week. This has raised questions not only about scheduling, teaching load and the capacity to deal with lesson planning, homework and evaluation. It has also raised concerns about the feasibility of teaching three languages when the time available barely allows them to teach two, resulting in fears about the inability to teach any of the languages effectively. As would be expected, this state of affairs has led to a great deal of resentment amongst Berber instructors. This was aggravated by the lack of incentives either in terms of recognition or financial compensation, which has pushed some teachers to stop teaching Berber and stick to the teaching of either Arabic or French.

9.10 Attitudes

Attitudes towards Berber and its inclusion in education are equally instrumental in shaping the outcomes of Berber education. The centrality of attitudes to language policy and language-in-education policy is expressed in the following passage by Lewis:

> No policy will succeed which does not do one of three things: conform to expressed attitudes of those involved; persuade those who express negative attitudes about the rightness of the policy or seek to remove the causes of disagreement. . . . Knowledge about attitudes is fundamental to the formulation of a policy as well as to success in its implementation.
>
> *(1981: 262)*

Berber has been the subject of negative attitudes even among some Amazigh-speaking elements who perceive in it a source of stigma and backwardness. Political reasons are also involved in this regard. In the words of a student, 'Although I am a Berber, I am against teaching Berber in schools because this will have disastrous political consequences'. Another student puts it less radically by saying that 'there is no harm in teaching Amazigh/Berber, but the harm may come from extremists or some Amazigh/Berber fanatics' (Ennaji 2005: 179). Negative attitudes are similarly held by elites. Some political leaders do not have a clear stance on the issue of Berber while others, especially those subscribing to an Arab nationalist or Islamist agenda, may even hold very negative and rejectionist attitudes towards it; the intellectual vanguard are no exception.

Regarding attitudes towards Berber education, Errihani (2008) recently conducted a small-scale study to tap into the perceptions of students concerning this issue. The results that transpired from the questionnaire revealed that, regardless of their ethnic affiliation (Arab or Berber), the overwhelming majority of students were against the mandatory nature of Berber education and believed that the learning of Amazigh should be optional. In addition, many of those surveyed are sceptical about the usefulness of Berber. Indeed, none of the participants stated that Berber is useful. Errihani attempted an explanation by affirming that Amazigh language and culture 'have been viewed in negative light for so long that they might have become convinced of the validity of such judgement' (2008: 422), which is perhaps a direct result of the historical fact 'Berber has been marginalised for several centuries' and that 'this is the first time in Moroccan contemporary history that Berber may be introduced in the official educational system' (Ennaji 2005: 179). Another reason behind this stance 'may be the practical and pragmatic way of thinking' that has led the participants 'to finally realise that the linguistic market of Morocco has long been saturated by much more instrumental languages' (Errihani 2008: 423). Berber, in this respect, is not a much coveted commodity on the market. Not only did the respondents believe that the language is not prestigious, they more importantly stated that the language represents backwardness and is associated with an archaic, traditional way of life. These findings corroborate those of an earlier study which concluded that 'attitudes towards Berber and Arabic–Berber bilingualism were almost entirely negative, reflecting the fact that . . . there is little respect for Berber, which many, if not most, students may regard as worthless dialects' (Marley 2004: 38), a fact which 'represents a major obstacle to the implementation of the language policy of maintaining and promoting Amazigh by teaching to all Moroccans' (Errihani 2008: 426).

In light of the Ethiopia study and previous research evidence, the effectiveness of the use of mother tongues as media of instruction hardly warrants further elaboration. The benefits for the Moroccan context should be evident, although the politics of that is a formidable force to be reckoned with. In comparative perspective, Arabic, like Amharic, is the dominant language of wider communication and is a second language for speakers of other languages. Similar difficulties arise when Arabic is used as medium of instruction for Amazigh speakers and when Berber is taught only as a subject. A way forward, informed by the Ethiopia study, is to employ Amazigh/Berber as medium of instruction in the Berber-speaking regions and teach Arabic as a subject to Amazigh speakers during the early years of schooling. French can be happily delayed. This suggestion dovetails with an important recommendation the study makes regarding the decentralisation of decision-making. The Berber language education project is heavily centralised and bureaucratised with the Ministry of Education monopolising decision-making, which has had adverse effects on both policy and practice, thus bearing testimony to the fact that 'countries with top-down decision-making tend to implement a single educational model with little regard for diversity in terms of language attitudes and use, exposure to national and/or official languages, goals of schooling and so on' (Benson, Heugh, Bogale and Gebre Yohannes, this volume). A decentralised system wherein the different Amazigh-speaking regions elaborate policies and make locally educationally sound decisions is likely to be a more viable alternative to the current regime. 'The decentralized education system in Ethiopia', Benson *et al.* (this volume) write, 'appears to favour development of locally appropriate policies and practices that serve the languages and cultures of each region'. Matters pertaining to teacher training, professional development, materials design and assessment will also have to be addressed at the regional level. The Ethiopia study also underscores the crucial significance of language attitudes in the implementation and potential success of multilingual education. The discussion of how language attitudes shape perceptions of the effectiveness and desirability of Arabic and Amazigh language instruction resonates strikingly with the issues raised by Benson *et al.* (this volume) notably that the use of 'less developed' languages will have negative effects on the cognitive development of students, will lower their achievement and will compromise their chances of future success. Hopefully, implementing multilingual education within an educationally progressive framework will alter these perceptions and ultimately increase the value capital of mother tongues. Here lies the immense transformative potential of the Ethiopia project.

In his famous essay 'Politics and the English Language', George Orwell argued that 'in our age there is no such thing as "keeping out of politics."' 'All issues', he continued, 'are political issues, and politics itself is a mass of lies, evasions, folly, hatred and schizophrenia'. Although one may not share the particularly bleak and totalising portrayal of politics that Orwell drew, it seems fair to state that indeed in matters linguistic and educational there is no such thing as 'keeping out of politics', and that language and language-in-education policy is beset by 'a mass of lies, evasions, and schizophrenia', a touch of Machiavellian logic and, to borrow Nietzsche, 'the will to power'. Hence the title of this chapter.

Notes

1   Since both Berber and Amazigh are heavily ideologically loaded terms, I will use both terms interchangeably.
2   Morocco was under French Protectorate from 1912 to 1956. Spanish colonisation of parts of Morocco ended in 1975, although the northern enclaves of Ceuta and Millelia still remain under Spanish colonial rule to this very day.
3   Mission laïque française is an official French association whose goal is to spread French language and culture abroad through schooling. Its main focus is on secular education. (http://www.mlfmonde.org).
4   The Rif is a predominantly mountainous region located in the northern part of Morocco. This region was colonised by Spain and witnessed some of the most heroic episodes of local resistance against colonisation. The resistance movement was led by

Muhammed ben Abdel-kerim Al Khattabi who in 1926 declared the Rif region as an independent republic 'with a government and a flag'. He was later defeated by a coalition of French and Spanish forces. His was only an ephemeral dream as his declared republic survived no more than three years. But the dream remains a milestone in the history of the Rif and forms the historical reference for independence tendencies in the region.

5   There have been other discussions about 'harmonisation' of different African languages (Prah 1998) or of different varieties (Alexander 1989), which appear to accommodate inclusive practices of standardisation. However, the situation in Morocco is exceptionally fraught with political sensitivity and the context is different from the ones which Prah and Alexander consider.

6   An Amazigh lexical item, taken in its primary meaning or semantic extension, has the absolute priority over other items.

References

Alexander, Neville (1989). *Language Policy and National Unity in South Africa/Azania*. Cape Town: Buchu Books.

Al-Jabiri, Mohamed A. (1973). *Adwaa ala Moshkil Ataalim fi al Maghreb*. Beirut: Arab Unity Center.

Ameur, Meftaha, Bouhjar, Aicha, Elmedlaoui, Mohamed and Iazzi, El Mehdi (2006). *Vocabulaire de la Langue Amazighe (Français-Amazighe)*. Rabat: El Maarif Al-Jadida.

Anderson, Benedict (1991). *Imagined Communities: Reflections on the Origin and Spread of Nationalism*. New York: Verso.

Bentahila, Abdelali (1983). *Language Attitudes among Arabic-French Bilinguals in Morocco*. Clevedon: Multilingual Matters.

Berdouzi, Mohamed (2000). *Rénover l'Enseignement: de la Charte aux Actes*. Rabat: Renouveau.

Boukous, Ahmed (1979). La Situation Linguistique au Maroc: Compétition Symbolique et Acculturation. *Revue Littéraire Mensuelle*, 602–603, 5–21.

Boukous, Ahmed (1995a). La Langue Berbère: Maintien et Changement. *International Journal of the Sociology of Language*, 112, 9–28.

Boukous, Ahmed (1995b). *Société, Langues et Cultures au Maroc: Enjeux Symboliques*. Rabat: Publications de la Faculté des Lettres et Sciences Humaines.

Boukous, Ahmed (1999). *Dominance et Différence: Essai sur les Enjeux Symboliques au Maroc*. Casablanca: Éditions Le Fennec.

Boukous, Ahmed (2004). La Standardisation de l'Amazighe: Quelques Premises. In Ameur, Meftaha and Abdellah Boumalk (eds), *La Standardisation de l'Amazighe*. Rabat: Publications de l'Institut Royal de la Culture Amazighe, 11–22.

Buckner, Elizabeth (2006). Language Drama in Morocco: Another Perspective on the Problems and Prospects of Teaching Berber. *Journal of North African Studies*, 11: 4, 421–433.

Charte Nationale d'Education et de Formation (1999). Ministère de l'Education Nationale, de l'Enseignement Supérieur, de la Formation des Cadres et de la Recherche Scientifique. (http://www.men.gov.ma/viescolaire/Documents/Charte_Fr.pdf).

Chtatou, Mohamed (1997). The Influence of the Berber Language on Moroccan Arabic. *International Journal of the Sociology of Language*, 123, 101–118.

Cameron, Deborah (1995). *Verbal Hygiene*. London: Routledge.

Cooper, Robert L. (1989). *Language Planning and Social Change*. New York: Cambridge University Press.

Crawford, David (2001). How Berber Matters in the Middle of Nowhere. *The Middle East Report*, 219, 20–25.

Dalle, Ignacio (2001). *Maroc 1961–1999: Espérances Brisées*. Paris: Maisonneuve et Larose.

Dorian, Nancy C. (1994). Purism vs. Compromise in Language Revitalization and Language Revival. *Language in Society*, 23: 4, 479–494.

Elbiad, Mohamed (1991). The Role of Some Population Sectors in the Progress of Arabization in Morocco. *International Journal of the Sociology of Language*, 87, 27–44.

Ennaji, Moha (1988). Language Planning in Morocco and Changes in Arabic. *International Journal of the Sociology of Language*, 74, 9–39.

Ennaji, Moha (1991). Aspects of Multilingualism in the Maghreb. *International Journal of the Sociology of Language*, 87, 7–25.

Ennaji, Moha (1997). The Sociology of Berber: Change and Continuity. *International Journal of the Sociology of Language*, 123, 23–40.

Ennaji, Moha (2005). *Multilingualism, Cultural Identity and Education in Morocco*. New York: Springer.

Ennaji, Moha and Sadiqi, Fatima (2008). Morocco: Language, Nationalism and Gender. In Simpson, Andrew (ed.), *Language and National Identity in Africa*. Oxford: Oxford University Press, 44–60.

Errihani, Mohamed (2006). Language Policy in Morocco: Problems and Prospects of Teaching Berber in Morocco. *Journal of North African Studies*, 11: 2, 143–154.

Errihani, Mohamed (2008). Language Attitudes and Language Use in Morocco: Effects of Attitudes on 'Berber' Language Policy. *Journal of North African Studies*, 13: 4, 411–428.

Grandguillaume, Gilbert (1983). *Arabisation et Politique Linguistique au Maghreb*. Paris: Maisonneuvean and Larose.

Grandguillaume, Gilbert (1998). Arabisation et Légitimité Politique en Algérie. In Chaker, Salem (ed.), *Langues et Pouvoir de l'Afrique du Nord à l'Extrême-Orient*. Aix-en-Provence: Edisud, 17–23.Hammoud, Mohamed Salah-Dine (1982). *Arabicization in Morocco: A Case Study in Language Planning and Language Policy Attitudes*. Ph.D. dissertation, University of Texas, Austin.

Ibrahim, Muhammad H. (1989). Communicating in Arabic: Problems and Prospects. In Coulmas, Florian (ed.), *Language Adaptation*. Cambridge: Cambridge University Press, 39–59.

Lewis, Glyn E. (1981). *Bilingualism and Bilingual Education*. Oxford: Pergamon Press.

Marley, Dawn (2004). Language Attitudes in Morocco Following Recent Changes in Language Policy. *Language Policy*, 3, 25–46.

Mitchell, Terry F. (1986). What is Educated Spoken Arabic? *International Journal of the Sociology of Language*, 61, 7–32.

Mouhssine, Ouafae (1995). Ambivalence du Discours sur l'Arabisation. *International Journal of the Sociology of Language*, 112, 45–61.

Ngũgĩ wa Thiong'o (1986). *Decolonising the Mind: The Politics of Language in African Literature*. Portsmouth, NH: Heinemann.

Prah, Kwesi Kwaa (ed.) (1998). *Between Distinction and Extinction. The Harmonisation and Standardisation of African Languages*. Cape Town: The Centre for Advanced Studies of African Society.

Redouane, Rabia (1998). Arabisation in the Moroccan Educational System: Problems and Prospects. *Language, Culture and Curriculum*, 11: 2, 195–203.

Sadiqi, Fatima (2003). *Women, Gender and Language in Morocco.* Leiden and Boston: Brill.

Silverstein, Paul (2004). *Algeria in France: Transpolitics, Race, and Nation.* Bloomington and Indianapolis: Indiana University Press.

Sirles, Craig A. (1999). Politics and Arabization: The Evolution of Postindependence North Africa. *International Journal of the Sociology of Language,* 137, 115–129.

Yassine, Nadia. About Nadia Yassine. (http://www.nadiayassine.net/en/service/whoisshe.html).

Youssi, Abderrahim (1995). The Moroccan Triglossia: Facts and Implications. *International Journal of the Sociology of Language,* 112, 29–43.

10

IMPLICATIONS FOR MULTILINGUAL EDUCATION

Student Achievement in Different Models of Education in Ethiopia

Kathleen Heugh, Carol Benson, Mekonnen Alemu Gebre Yohannes and Berhanu Bogale

10.1 Introduction

In this chapter we focus on the relationship between type of bi/trilingual MTM education model and student achievement in Ethiopia by examining three sets of system-wide assessment data of grade 8 students over a period of eight years (2000–2008). In our *Final Report: Study on Medium of Instruction in Primary Schools in Ethiopia* (Heugh, Benson, Bogale and Gebre Yohannes 2007, and in Chapter 1, this volume) we have drawn attention to what appear to be correlations: on an inclined scale, between highest number of years of MTM education (hereafter MTM) and highest level of achievement; and on a declining scale, between lowest number of years of MTM and lowest achievement. We have also noted the potential risks of reverse planning, which involves a decreasing emphasis on the current/official language policy implementation and a return to an earlier policy or towards one which neutralises the current official policy. The most recent set of system-wide student assessment data became available in 2009 and we have been able to reconsider our earlier analysis of the data from the 2000 and 2004 assessments in order to identify and track trends which coincide with changing language policy emphases. We have thus triangulated our field data from late 2006 with this longitudinal analysis of student assessment results, along with qualitative data provided by informants in Ethiopia during 2009–2010. We believe that the data from Ethiopia offer the international community some of the most relevant system-wide information available to demonstrate the positive relationship between mother tongue-based bi/trilingual teaching and learning and improved student achievement. Our data also demonstrate a clear correlation between a precipitous switch to English-medium education and a decline in student achievement.[1]

The implementation of a strong mother tongue-based bilingual education policy for Amharic speakers and trilingual policy for most Ethiopian pupils, despite myriad challenges in this low-income country (e.g. Wagaw 1999; Smith 2008; Terefe 2010), appears to have been exceptionally successful over the 10–12-year period from 1994 to the commissioning of our study by the Ministry of Education in 2006. We now believe that the timing of our data collection coincided with a turning point in what had until that time been a successful trajectory of policy implementation. Increasing pressure towards earlier use of English medium posed a risk to the successful continuation of MTM. However, it is significant that within a decade, MTM education was being offered in 23 Ethiopian languages with language development in at least 36 languages, partially enabled by language planning activities decentralised to the level of each regional administration (cf. Chapter 1). Wagaw (1999) had warned that this could result in uneven development and further marginalisation of ethnolinguistic communities. This was especially in relation to more linguistically heterogeneous regions, like SNNPR (Southern Nations, Nationalities and Peoples Region) and Benishangul Gumuz, in contrast with more homogeneous Amhara and Oromiya regions, and this has indeed been the case. Yet, there have been remarkable successes, and progress in some languages has encouraged development in others. In SNNPR this has resulted in the development of 12 languages for use as medium of instruction (MoI) to grade 4, eight of which were used as MoI to grade 6 until a regional policy change in 2004, and all 12 continuing as a subject through the end of primary at grade 8. In fact, since our data collection, language teams have continued to develop an additional nine languages in this region for subject teaching, though not yet as languages of teaching and learning across the curriculum. Interestingly, in SNNPR it has been possible to decentralise language development a step beyond the regions to the Zonal Education Bureaus, and there are even cases of further decentralisation to the woreda (local government) level. To date, we estimate that language development activities thus far make it possible for at least 84% of children in Ethiopia to receive MTM even if this potential has not always been realised. Addis Ababa is a striking example of lost potential, where Amharic is used as MoI whether it is the L1 or L2, and whether or not students could be served with MT materials and programmes developed in other regions.

As noted in Chapter 1, while the intent was to implement eight years of MTM in each region, the semi-autonomous nature of regional decision-making with relation to the federal government policy has allowed for variation. Thus, in terms of bilingual and multilingual education theories and models, the case of Ethiopia offers a microcosm of different degrees of mother tongue development and second/foreign language introduction prior to a switch in medium to English. The purpose of this chapter is thus to show the relationship between the different iterations of bi/multilingual education and the results of three national assessments in 2000, 2004 and 2008. While the Ministry of Education (MoE) commissions assessments at both grade 4 and grade 8, we have focused on the latter because international research has shown that grade 4 is too early to demonstrate the long-term efficacy of a language education policy (e.g. Thomas and Collier 2002). Earlier studies on language education in African settings have shown that student achievement after six to eight years of a literacy/language programme are likely to demonstrate useful data, which point towards secondary enrolment, retention and successful completion of secondary schooling (Heugh 2006a). This analysis of the Ethiopian system provides further insights into the connection between greater mother tongue development and improved school performance, with implications for policy not only for Ethiopia but for other linguistically diverse countries worldwide.

10.1.2 Salient Differences between Regions and Approaches to Mother Tongue Use

Ethiopia thus offers researchers something of an authentic 'laboratory' in which it is possible to compare student achievement in regionally different 'models' of education. As shown in 1.3 (Benson *et al.*, this volume), regional practices range from eight full years of mother tongue-medium instruction (MTM/MTE) to six, four or none at all. English (foreign language) medium is introduced at grades 9, 7 or 5 depending on the other languages used. Amharic (L2) medium is used as a back-up option in some more heterogeneous regions that do not, at this stage, have the available resources to offer instruction through all learners' home languages.

Admittedly, the Ethiopian regions cannot offer laboratory-like conditions that are decontextualised from socio-economic, sociolinguistic, geographic and climatic differences. These differences need to be taken into consideration when analysing the educational achievement data. For example, Somali and Afar regions are extremely remote and sparsely populated, with many people living in nomadic communities where students rarely have access to more than two or three years of non-formal primary education. Both of these regions border countries with which Ethiopia is in military conflict or under threat of it. Despite the relative linguistic homogeneity of Afar, there are pastoralists who speak Afan Oromo, and administrators in the towns use Amharic. In Somali, travel outside of the capital, Jijiga, is dangerous and beset with brigands, some of whom have crossed the border from Somalia. Because abductions are common, families fear for their daughters who are about to reach puberty, as they may be abducted between home and school. Another risk to schooling not directly related to military or other conflict is early marriage, which contributes to significant gender disparity and very low throughput of girls to the end of primary school in these regions (see also *Introduction*, Skutnabb-Kangas and Heugh, in this volume). Gambella region, which borders the Sudan, is characterised by internal civil strife and tropical disease and, similar to Afar and Somali regions, could not be expected to compare favourably with less disadvantaged regions in terms of educational attainment and throughput.

Conditions for relatively more favourable educational outcomes are present in Amhara, Oromiya, Harari and SNNPR regions. Harari, for example, has better socio-economic conditions, and its capital, Harar, is a thriving business centre surrounded by lush agricultural lands. SNNPR, while susceptible to floods along the Rift Valley, has several rivers which provide good irrigation for agricultural pursuits, resulting in significantly lower incidence of hunger there than in Somali and Afar. On the surface then, we could expect relatively more favourable educational outcomes in Harari and SNNPR, though SNNPR is highly diverse.

The city-state of Dire Dawa has been severely affected by several years of devastating floods, which have destroyed large portions of the city and resulted in the closure of schools for extended periods. High achievement could thus not be expected there, but we might expect that schools in Addis Ababa, the capital city of the country, would be better resourced. We might also expect that exposure to English as a foreign language (FL) would be greater in Addis, and that student achievement would be among the highest in the country.

These contextual factors are important to keep in mind when examining the assessment data. If current theories of bi- and multilingual education (e.g. García and Baker 2007; Thomas and Collier 2002; Heugh 2006a; Benson 2009; Cummins 2009; Mohanty *et al.* 2009; Skutnabb-Kangas, in press) hold true in Ethiopia, students with eight years of MTM should do better than those with six, who should do better than those with four – all things being equal. However, given that conditions are not the same across Ethiopia, we would expect that students in the more remote, resource-poor and linguistically heterogeneous regions would have lower levels of achievement than those with more favourable conditions. In the next section, we discuss the different levels of MTM with regard to results from the three sets of system-wide assessment data for grade 8 students.

10.2 Analysis of the System-wide Assessment data 2000–2008 by MTM Level

10.2.1 System-wide Assessment in Ethiopia

At the time of our 2006 study, we recognised the value of system-wide assessment in offering a snapshot of the relationship between MoI and achievement. Gebre Yohannes (2005) had already drawn attention to the higher achievement in 2000 among students with eight years of MTM who were assessed in their mother tongue (MT), as opposed to students with fewer years of MTM, particularly those assessed in English. This effect was also apparent in the 2004 assessment data. Table 10.1 shows the mean achievement scores of all students assessed in their MT, alongside all of those assessed in English, in the three grade 8 assessments to date. It should be noted that the average scores are generally low across the curriculum, which can be attributed to poverty, poor educational resources and overly content-heavy or inappropriate curriculum (cf. Bamgbose 2000; Obanya 2002;

TABLE 10.1 Weighted mean achievement scores by mother tongue vs. English medium of instruction for three national assessments of grade 8 students

Year of assessment	MoI & assessment	English	Maths	Biology	Chem.	Physics	Average %
2000	MTs (MTM 8)	37.41	42.73	57.85	45.41	–	45.85
	Eng.	39.07	36.20	42.40	38.00	–	38.92
2004	MTs (MTM 8)	40.65	42.60	47.30	43.19	39.62	42.67
	Eng.	41.43	39.43	35.93	37.28	31.53	37.12
2008	MTs (MTM 8)	38.30	34.30	44.00	37.30	34.60	37.70
	Eng.	38.70	34.00	34.90	33.20	30.70	34.30

Source: adapted from MoE/NOE 2001, MoE/NOE 2004, GEQAEA 2008

Ouane 2003; Alidou *et al.* 2006). Such low results might in other circumstances call into question the validity of the assessment tools, but these scores are within the range of other system-wide studies in Africa, even those found in wealthier countries like South Africa (e.g. as reported in Heugh 2006a), as well as in multi-country studies (e.g. Mothibeli 2005). Thus we are satisfied that the scores are representative of the realities in Ethiopian education, and they serve our purpose to determine whether or not there is evidence that different medium of instruction choices result in higher or lower achievement among grade 8 students.

Table 10.1 demonstrates that such evidence has indeed been found. Across all three systemic assessments, students with eight years of MTM assessed in their MT outperform students who switch to English medium earlier. The only exception is with regard to English as a subject, where overall, students who switch to English medium earlier than grade 9 actually outperform the MTM students (see our region-specific discussion below), which may be explained by differences in the amount of exposure to the foreign language. It is noteworthy that overall achievement appears to have declined significantly according to the 2008 assessment. However, biology, chemistry and physics results are consistently higher for MT than for English groups through grade 8 across all assessment periods. The gap in mathematics achievement is wider between the MT and English groups in the first two assessments, narrowing considerably in the most recent assessment. The gap in achievement in English between the two sets of students also narrowed significantly by 2008. On the surface it appears that students learning mathematics through English have caught up with those learning mathematics through the MT. Paradoxically, MT learners have caught up with English-medium learners in the English language.

Particularly in mathematics, there is a significant and worrying decline in overall achievement. The average achievement in English language has also declined across both groups, as have each of the science subjects. This overall decline has occurred during the same period during which there has been a shift towards

English medium in upper primary education in many regions. As a result, fewer students than before have been receiving MTM education to the end of grade 8. As noted in Chapter 1, Amhara region changed in 2006 from eight years of MTM (MTM 8) to a mixture of English and MT in grades 7–8 (i.e. English medium for mathematics and science). SNNPR changed from six to four years of MTM, and teacher education across the entire education system, even for those who will teach in local language, is moving towards English medium in the name of teacher 'professionalisation'.

The 'washback effect' of English through secondary and higher education seems to have gained momentum since 2004, increasing since our collection of field data, while student achievement has declined over the same period, and may be continuing in the same trajectory unless the issues are addressed. The English Language Improvement Programme (ELIP), beginning in 2005, syphoned off 42% of the entire teacher education budget of Ethiopia in an attempt to improve all teachers' English proficiency, diverting attention and vital resources away from implementing the national policy of delivering quality teaching and learning through learners' mother tongues. Further, ELIP and other pro-English initiatives have been interpreted by teachers and teacher educators as enhancing their career opportunities beyond the classroom rather than as facilitating improvement of student learning outcomes.

For a clearer picture of what happens to students required to switch to English as MoI at different stages of their schooling and/or being assessed through English before grade 8, we have disaggregated the data on student achievement from Table 10.1. The following tables 10.2, 10.3 and 10.4 illustrate the relationship between mother tongue-medium education MTM/MTE and achievement in those regions which have used eight, six and four years of MTM education, as well as zero (but six years of Amharic as a second language/L2), respectively, in each of the three assessments, beginning with the year 2000 in Table 10.2.

It should be noted that the Somali region did not participate in the 2000 assessment, nor was physical science assessed. Even so, it is possible to see the consistency in achievement, where students with eight years of MTM scored significantly higher than those with fewer years of MTM in all of the subjects except English. There are relatively clear differences in achievement in mathematics and sciences amongst those students with eight years of MTM (Tigray, Oromiya and Amhara) and those with six (Addis Ababa, Dire Dawa and SNNPR) or four (Gambella), which would suggest that MTM helps students to understand curricular content.

Interestingly, English achievement is highest in Harari region (where English is used for some subjects, maths and science, in grade 7–8) and Addis Ababa (where English is used for all grade 7–8 subjects). Why might this be? Prior research in African countries has shown that in areas where MTM is better resourced, six years of MT allow students to succeed in all subjects including the additional language, and that in areas where MTM is less well resourced, eight years of MT may be required (e.g. Heugh 2003, 2006a, b). In fact, Harari region has six years

TABLE 10.2 Year 2000 grade 8 achievement scores by region and years of MTM

Region	MOI	English %	Maths %	Biology %	Chem. %	Average %
Tigray	MTM 8	39	45	56	47	46.75
Oromiya	MTM 8	39	40	56	45	45
Somali	MTM 8	—	—	—	—	—
Amhara	MTM 8	34	44	61	45	46
Harari	MTM 6+8 (Eng MoI maths & sci. from gr. 7)	45	40	48	43	44
Addis Ababa	MTM 6 (L2 Amharic estim. 50%)	46	39	44	40	42.25
Dire Dawa	MTM 6 (L2 Amharic estim. 50%)	39	37	41	39	39
SNNPR	MTM 6 (L2 Amharic estim. 50%)	37	36	43	36	38
Gambella	MTM 4	36	27	37	33	33.25
Benishangul Gumuz	MTM 0 (L2 Amharic 6 yrs)	40	36	43	41	40
Afar	MTM 0 (L2 Amharic 6 yrs)	34	36	39	36	36.25

Source: data from MoE/NOE 2001, tables 4.4, 4.21, 4.38 and 4.55; table modified from Heugh *et al.* 2007: 79.

of full MTM plus some in grades 7–8, while being somewhat better resourced than elsewhere. Similarly, pupils in Addis Ababa are relatively privileged, and more exposed both to Amharic and to English. These factors rather than medium of instruction may explain the higher English assessment results in these two areas, yet despite their advantages, average overall student achievement is still lower than in regions with eight years of MTM.[2]

What is clear from the 2000 assessment data is that a shift to English medium before six years of MTM does not result in improved English language achievement.

Thus far the research on multilingual education has not, at least not in African contexts, pinpointed the optimal minimum number of years for MTM education prior to a shift in medium of instruction (see also discussion of second language acquisition in the introductory chapter of this volume). We know it appears to be somewhere between six and eight years in situations where English is the de facto *second language* of the country (i.e. where there is a long history of administration, legal systems and infrastructure in English, even if it does not function as such in everyday life of most people. Clearly a longer period of MTM would be called for where the L2 is not as well established in the country.

Prior to examining the Ethiopian case, we have not had an opportunity to examine comparative school achievement data in a system attempting to use an entirely *foreign language* as MoI, which is the case of English here. The Harari data may therefore be particularly relevant, since there are assessment data for students with both six and eight years of MTM (i.e. some subjects in MTM for six years and other subjects for eight years). However, there are extenuating circumstances in Harari in that an over-supply of primary teachers in the region had allowed the REB to allocate specialist English teachers to lower primary classrooms. Our team recommended this practice to other regions because of its potential to use teachers more proficient in English for language teaching, however, lack of human resources prevented most from doing so.

As a final note on the 2000 data, student achievement averaged at least 40% in six regions. It is widely accepted that any individual student should achieve an average of at least 50% by the end of primary (grade 8 in Ethiopia) to have a chance of succeeding at secondary school. Regions with overall averages of less than 40% would have had very few students with high enough averages to proceed through secondary school (see below for further discussion of language proficiency and achievement).

As shown in Table 10.3, the 2004 assessment differed from 2000 with its inclusion of physical science as an additional subject, and its omission of Gambella region. This prevents us from seeing how students with four years of MTM fared in comparison to those with more or fewer years. Nevertheless, the 2004 results show that students with eight years of MTM have higher scores across the curriculum, especially in mathematics and science, than those with six years of MTM or those with Amharic L2 medium.

MTM 8: As they did four years earlier, the regions with eight years of MTM have similarly high overall levels of achievement, except for Somali region, which seems out of kilter. Somali's results may be explained by the difficult conditions mentioned above; in addition to being resource-poor, it is geographically marginalised, sparsely populated and shares 60% of its border with Somalia, a country with which Ethiopia is in frequent military conflict. Despite Somali region's disappointing results in comparison with the other regions with eight years of MTM, Somali students do not do less well than the regions with six years of MTM, and they outperform both SNNPR and better resourced Addis Ababa. In comparison with the latter two regions, Somali does better than would be expected given its challenging circumstances.

MTM 6 + 8: Harari region, with its six years of MTM plus some use of the MT in grades 7–8, achieves the next-best levels of overall achievement, and the

TABLE 10.3 Year 2004 grade 8 achievement scores by region and years of MTM

Region	MOI	English %	Maths %	Biology %	Chem. %	Physics %	Average %
Tigray	MTM 8	39.1	44.4	49.1	43.0	39.5	43.0
Oromiya	MTM 8	41.6	42.8	48.3	43.6	39.3	43.2
Somali	MTM 8	42.4	42.6	36.3	37.8	34.5	38.6
Amhara	MTM 8	39.1	41.4	48.3	44.6	41.8	43.0
Harari	MTM 6+8 (Eng MOI maths & sci. from gr. 7)	46.8	43.4	39.4	42.5	35.1	41.5
Addis Ababa	MTM 6 (L2 Amharic estim. 50%)	42.3	40.5	33.7	35.9	31.1	36.7
Dire Dawa	MTM 6 (L2 Amharic estim. 50%)	42.4	41.0	37.7	38.2	33.5	38.6
SNNPR	MTM 6 (L2 Amharic estim. 50%)	41.0	39.7	36.8	37.5	31.3	37.4
Gambella	MTM 4	—	—	—	—	—	—
Benishangul Gumuz	MTM 0 (L2 Amharic 6 yrs)	37.0	33.3	31.2	34.5	28.4	33.7
Afar	MTM 0 (L2 Amharic 6 yrs)	39.6	36.6	32.0	33.8	30.7	34.6

Source: data from MoE/NOE 2004, tables 10, 18, 26, 34, 42 and 50; table modified from Heugh *et al.* 2007: 79.

highest English language results. The latter could be due to using English language teachers, as mentioned above. It is also possible that Harari's 'model' of six years of MTM for some subjects and eight for others facilitates cognitive and linguistic development in a way others do not, but we do not have the sociolinguistic or classroom data needed to support this claim. It may be noted that although Harari student performance is comparable to regions with eight years of MTM in mathematics and chemistry, they fare less well in physics and biology.

MTM 6: After Harari, achievement in regions with six years of MTM is slightly lower. Students are competitive in English and mathematics but do less well than the MTM 8 students in the science subjects. The apparent advantages of Addis Ababa and Dire Dawa urban centres do not appear to compensate for their use of six, rather than eight, years of MTM. There is no significant difference in English results between regions with eight years of MTM and those with six. SNNPR shows an improvement over its 2000 English scores, which raises its overall achievement to a level comparable to the two city-states, despite the fact that SNNPR is largely rural, geographically distant from urban centres, and linguistically heterogeneous. The case of SNNPR shows that dealing with multiple languages does not have a negative effect on overall achievement; rather the reverse holds true. (In fact, Addis Ababa, despite its obvious advantages as the capital city, uses only Amharic and English in school, invests little effort in MT or local language education and achieves the lowest student average scores of the three six-year MTM education programmes.)

MTM 0: Finally, as we might expect, the two regions with no MTM but six years of L2 Amharic medium, perform less well than the others. Whereas Benishangul Gumuz appeared to be doing comparatively better than expected in 2000, this has not been sustained in 2004 and we regard the 2000 data as anomalous.

In the 2004 assessment data, the number of regions averaging 40% or above overall falls to four (from six in 2000), of which all use six to eight years of MTM. Addis Ababa and Benishangul Gumuz, using only Amharic and English as MoI, show significant declines in achievement since 2000, which may be explained by the fact that Amharic is the L2 of approximately 50% and 90%, respectively, of students and both use only two languages, Amharic and English. In sum, in regions where students' achievement average 40% or above, the students are expected to learn three languages (MT, Amharic L2 and English) in primary school.

The 2008 data[3] indicate a marked decline in results from both earlier assessments. Tigray is the only region that comes close to maintaining its earlier student achievement levels, and it is the only region where average overall achievement is above 40%. As suggested earlier (also Chapter 1), this decline occurs during the same period as a shift in focus away from MTM and towards English in upper primary schooling. Amhara region, for example, shifted from MTM 8 to a mixed MTM 6+8, introducing English MoI for mathematics and sciences from grade 7 onwards; and in SNNPR, MTM 6 was reduced to MTM 4.

In general the 2008 assessment data confirm for the third time that students with eight years of MTM outperform most of the others, with some regional variation probably due to non-linguistic factors (e.g. in Somali region). The next-best results come from regions with six years-plus of MTM, i.e. those who still use the MT for some subjects (but not mathematics and science) in grades 7 and 8. Amhara region, which has shifted to this six-plus model, has slightly improved English scores but significant declines in mathematics and the sciences, suggesting that the switch to English MoI has not provided improved understanding of these subjects. Harari region, which has had this model even longer, has also experienced a decline since 2004. While it is possible that the 2008 assessment instruments were unusually difficult or less reliable, we find this is unlikely, as they were thoroughly piloted and trialled in 2006 and this was the third systemic assessment conducted in Ethiopia. Increasing expertise and improved conditions for reliable assessments would be likely to render more rather than less reliable data. The coincidence of this overall decline with the shift to earlier introduction of English

TABLE 10.4 Year 2008 grade 8 achievement scores by region and years of MTM

Region	MOI	English %	Maths %	Biology %	Chem. %	Physics %	Average %
Tigray	MTM 8	38.30	40.40	48.00	44.60	39.40	42.18
Oromiya	MTM 8	36.90	32.30	45.50	35.90	34.40	38.62
Somali	MTM 8	39.90	30.40	38.40	31.60	29.90	34.04
Amhara Earlier partial use of English MoI from 2006	MTM 6+8 (Eng. MoI maths & sci. from gr. 7)	40.50	37.20	35.90	36.80	33.40	36.76
Harari	MTM 6+8 (Eng. MoI maths & sci. from gr. 7)	40.00	34.90	35.30	36.20	31.50	35.58
Addis Ababa	MTM 6 (L2 Amharic estim. 50%)	39.60	33.40	34.20	31.90	30.50	33.92
Dire Dawa	MTM 6 (L2 Amharic estim. 50%)	36.40	35.70	33.70	31.60	29.40	33.36
SNNPR Earlier use of English MoI, since 2004	MTM 4 (L2 Amharic estim. 50%)	40.00	34.70	36.60	34.90	31.60	35.56
Gambella	MTM 4	37.00	26.00	34.70	29.00	27.50	30.84
Benishangul Gumuz	MTM 0 (L2 Amharic 6 yrs)	35.80	30.60	32.90	31.20	29.40	31.98
Afar	MTM 0 (L2 Amharic 6 yrs)	38.40	37.90	34.80	31.90	30.50	34.6

Source: data from GEQAEA 2008, tables 17, 18, 20, 21, 22, 23 and 24

MoI is thus significant in our analysis (Chapter 1; Gebre Yohannes 2009; Heugh 2009, and discussion below).

The two six-year MTM city-states, Dire Dawa and Addis Ababa, continue to lag behind the other regions which offer longer provision of MTM. Students in SNNPR, where six years of MTM have been reduced to four, have results slightly ahead of those in MTM 6 cities and remain ahead of those in regions with six years of L2 Amharic MoI (Afar and Benishangul Gumuz), despite SNNPR's earlier introduction of English as MoI in grade 5. The relative success of SNNPR with MTM 4 in comparison with the two city-states with MTM 6 might be explained in several ways. First, SNNPR is offering four years of schooling in at least twelve of the region's nationality languages and also L2 MoI in Amharic for possibly up to 50% of students who have languages other than these twelve.

These twelve languages continue to be taught as subjects to the end of grade 8, offering some continued MT support and development. Just as Amharic is the L2 for approximately 50% of students in SNNPR,[4] so is it in Addis Ababa and Dire Dawa (the latter having experienced severe flooding and extended school closures in recent years). Thus the classification of MTM 6 in these two city-states is only partially correct – it is in reality MTM 6 for only half of students. SNNPR has demonstrated significant interest in development of its languages for education; nine additional MTs have been piloted and introduced as subjects in early primary since our fieldwork in 2006, and rural communities are reportedly very committed to supporting their schools. In contrast, we found little interest in the city-states in developing languages other than Amharic and English.

Gambella, Afar and Somali have similarly difficult socio-economic conditions and geographic challenges which allow some comparison. Of these regions, Somali with MTM 8 outperforms Afar with six years of L2 Amharic education and Gambella with MTM 4.

10.2.2 The Shift Toward English Since 2004

Increasing pressure towards earlier use of English as MoI at the primary and teacher training levels has been noticeable throughout Ethiopia since 2004. Gebre Yohannes (2005) had noted the gap between the language of teacher education and the medium of instruction in schools and our attention was drawn to this continuing trend by senior, middle and junior education officials and teacher educators in interviews conducted in late 2006. We subsequently reported on the detrimental effect this would potentially have on the quality of teaching and learning (Heugh *et al.* 2007, and see also Smith 2008). As discussed in Chapter 1, the MoE made a significant investment in the English Language Improvement Programme (ELIP) between 2004 and 2006. Every teacher in the education system was obliged to participate in a costly in-service programme and the position of English was reinforced through the development of teacher education materials in English rather than Amharic, and sent from Addis Ababa to the regions. No instructions or guidelines were provided for translation into the regional or local languages. By 2009 the MoE was pursuing a policy of teacher education that would 'professionalise' the force by demanding a higher level of formal education and training conducted in English. By the end of this year all primary teacher education had shifted from MTM to English medium. While this would not have affected the 2008 assessment data, it indicates the trajectory of change since 2004.

10.3 Summary of What the Data Tell Us

The variation of implementation of the MTM policy amongst the semi-autonomous regions and city administrations allows us to make a number of observations in relation to national assessment data from 2000, 2004 and 2008. We do not claim that the MoI is the only relevant factor which explains differences in student achievement. The diverse sociolinguistic and economic conditions, unevenly distributed resources and environmental and political crises are part of the context and also help explain some anomalies in the data. Nevertheless, our data appear to point towards a positive relationship amongst first language (L1/MT) development, teaching, learning and student achievement in primary school education in Ethiopia.

10.3.1 Two-language vs. Three-language 'Models' with Relation to Student Achievement

Students using three languages in primary school appear to have higher achievement across the curriculum than those using two languages. Two languages (Amharic and English) are used as MoI with students in three regions – Amhara, Benishangul Gumuz and Afar – as well as all students in state education in Addis Ababa and many in Dire Dawa. Three languages, including the L1 of most students, are used in the other regions. None of the three sets of assessment data indicate that there is any disadvantage to students in the use of three languages for six to eight years; rather, students with six to eight years of MTM, plus Amharic, and plus English are performing significantly better across the curriculum than those using only two languages. Students in SNNPR, who have four years of MTM and learn L1 as a subject for eight years (plus Amharic plus English), do better than those using only two languages, but slightly less well than those using three languages for six or eight years. The Ethiopian data therefore indicate that trilingual education does not detract from overall achievement – on the contrary, it coincides with higher achievement. This finding indicates a promising area of further study in psycholinguistics and second or third language acquisition.[5]

10.3.2 Student Achievement in Different 'Models' of MTM Education

The variation in implementation has allowed us to observe possible benefits or disadvantages of conducting MTM education for eight, six plus eight, six or four years; or not at all. Ethiopian data offer considerable evidence that eight years of MTM is more beneficial to students than six or four. Six years plus some L1 use in grades 7–8 appear to be nearly as beneficial as eight years, which would make it worthwhile to conduct a longitudinal study exploring the cognitive relationship between language and learning across the curriculum with particular attention to the six- to eight-year period. We can say now that there is evidence that teaching science through English before grade 9 is ill-advised in Ethiopia. This contributes further clarification of time-related considerations for learning a second or foreign language as a subject to the level needed for it to be used as a medium of instruction.

10.3.3 How Much MT/L1 is Needed to Prepare Students for Enrolment and Retention in Secondary Education?

Are eight years of MTM with English as a subject enough to prepare students for English-only teaching and learning in secondary school? The Ethiopian assessment authority disaggregated the 2008 assessment data into three broad bands: proficient, basic and below basic (see Figure 10.1 below). Across the country, and across all subjects assessed, 62.1% of students performed at below basic levels, with only 13.9% regarded as proficient (GEQAEA 2008: 46–50).[6] This is a way of understanding the relative health of the education system. If students are to have a good chance of engaging with the secondary school curriculum, they need to exit primary school at the proficient level. If they cannot make sufficient sense of the primary school curriculum, how can they cope with an increasingly decontextualised secondary school curriculum, and one delivered through a language which has little functional use beyond the classroom? According to Lewin (2008), the gross enrolment rate in secondary school (GER2) in Ethiopia is 19% (i.e. only 19% of the secondary school-aged population is enrolled). This is partly a function of limited availability of classrooms and partly a function of primary school exit results. According to Lewin's analysis of data from sub-Saharan Africa, in countries with a GER2 of 20% or lower, fewer than 10% will reach the end of secondary successfully. Furthermore, the greatest gender disparity (i.e. fewest girls reaching end of secondary) occurs in those countries with low GER2 enrolment. Based on Lewin's analysis, we would expect a 10% completion rate for Ethiopians of secondary school age. However, given that only 14% of students reached the required proficiency level at the end of primary in 2008 (representing a decrease from 2000 and 2004), we could only expect that 7% exit secondary school successfully, of which most would be boys.

Referring again to Figure 10.1 below, if we were to suggest in an optimistic scenario that those students who achieved at the basic level at the end of grade 8 are able to participate in early secondary, then 38% of students who reach the end of grade 8[7] could enter secondary, and the remaining 62% could not. Looking at the distribution of achievement across regions, it can be seen that Tigray region has the highest levels of achievement, where approximately 60% of students reach at least the basic level (28.5% of them functioning at the proficient level). The next highest is Oromiya with 46.3% of students, which is not surprising given that both Tigray and Oromiya offer eight years of MTM (MTM 8) primary schooling. The Amhara region, with its mix of six and eight years of MTM (MTM 6+8) is next highest with 42.5%. None of the other regions has more than 40% of students achieving at the basic level or above.

If we combine proficient and basic levels of achievement, the regions with the best prognosis for primary student achievement are those implementing the longest MTM programmes, that is Tigray, Oromiya and Amhara. All other regions have failed to ensure that more than 40% of grade 8 graduates reach a basic level of

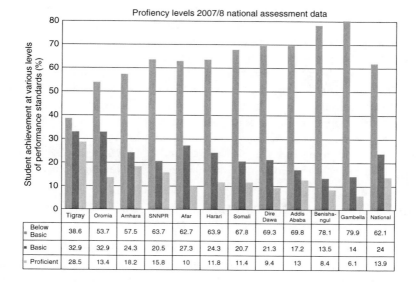

FIGURE 10.1 Student proficiency levels by region according to the 2008 assessment

Source: data from GEQAEA 2008: 50, table 19[8]

proficiency. Even Addis Ababa, the capital, essentially fails 70% of those students who have survived to grade 8.

It seems clear that any fewer than six years of MTM results in very low achievement that does not prepare students for secondary education or beyond. In a low-income country like Ethiopia, providing MTM 8 or MTM 6+8 thus facilitates access to secondary schooling for up to 28.5% of students (in Tigray), 18.2% in Amhara, 13.4% in Oromyia, 11.8% in Harari and 11.4% in Somali (with the most difficult socio-economic conditions). SNNPR, with MTM 4 plus eight years of L1 or L2 Amharic subject study, seems to be the third most efficient region at the proficient level with 15.8%; see above discussion regarding factors supportive of more successful education in SNNPR.

The data need to be read in relation to all three levels of achievement. Even if MTM 8 or MTM 6+8 are the most favourable for students, these models are clearly not adequate. While we might argue that six years of MTM are better than four, and eight are better than six, it is clear that insufficient numbers of students are progressing through primary school in Ethiopia.

To offer a comparison on the continent, in South Africa between 1955 and 1975, eight years of MTM prior to a switch to English (and/or Afrikaans) medium for secondary education did indeed facilitate student access to secondary schooling. In fact, the highest secondary student achievement in the country's history was recorded during this period, although this was under different circumstances than today (see Heugh 2003).[9] English was and is a de facto second language of South

Africa and used as one of the two languages of administration, legislation, civil service, education and the formal economy at every level from national to local until 1994, and as the primary language since then. English is also visible and audible in the media throughout the country, unlike in Ethiopia, where English has very little diffusion throughout the country, beyond its questionable use in the classroom.

The Ethiopian findings are consistent with both the South African experience and the frequently reported Six Year Primary Project in Nigeria (e.g. Bamgbose 2000) in that longer-term use of MTM is demonstrated to be beneficial to learners. We can see a clear trajectory of improvement from four to six to eight years of MTM, with some variation between six and eight. Using the 2008 data, we project throughput to secondary in the summary of the findings below.[10]

10.3.4 Summary of Findings Supporting Mother Tongue-based Bi/Multilingual Education (MLE)

Three sets of system-wide assessment data collected over a period of nine years show variations in relation to variations in MTM/MTE in the regions, and also offer a coherent picture of the overall health of a national mother tongue-based multilingual education (MLE) system. They offer Ethiopian, African and international researchers an opportunity to consider significant aspects of bilingual and multilingual education on a scale which has not previously been possible. Overall, we find clear evidence of the following:

• Students who receive eight years of MTM education, and whose teachers are correspondingly trained in the MT, achieve the highest scores across the curriculum, except where significant socio-economic deprivation applies.

• MTM 8 allows the highest percentage of students (28.5% of students in Tigray) to achieve at the proficient level that will allow them to enrol (and hopefully succeed) in secondary school. One implication is that the best results in a low-income, resource-poor education system are likely to come from maximum use and development of MTE.

• Students who receive MTM 6 +, i.e. six full years of MTM education plus some subjects taught through the L1 in grades 7–8 achieve the second highest scores overall (18.2% in Amhara achieve at the proficient level which gives them a reasonable chance of succeeding in secondary), but may have difficulty with science.

• Students who receive MTM 6, and whose teachers are trained in the MT at least for lower primary (grades 1–4), achieve the third highest category of scores across the curriculum, so fewer will be able to enrol in secondary school. (Of these, the highest ranked region is Addis Ababa where 13% of students reach proficient level at primary exit). The implication is that students with six years of MTM do not fare as well as those with eight, but one-third of them reach basic levels of proficiency in primary.

- Students who receive only four years of MTM education (MTM 4) show significant variation in achievement and the regions have to be discussed separately.

  - SNNPR, which has changed from MTM 6 to MTM 4, performs third best at the proficient level, but fifth out of 11 regions in overall achievement. In SNNPR, L1 development is supported and encouraged in increasing numbers of languages (from 12 in 2006 to 21 in 2009). Parent and community participation appear to be high, and the socio-economic conditions appear to be more favourable than in most other regions and these may contribute positively to student achievement.
  - Gambella, also with MTM 4, with less favourable socio-economic conditions (civil strife, lower community participation, sub-tropical illnesses), and using only three nationality languages, performs least well of all regions, with only 6% of students reaching the proficient level. The implication is that MTM 4 is not sufficient under such conditions.

- Students with six years of Amharic L2, despite its status as a national language (and its linguistic proximity to some MTs), do not succeed nearly as well as students with six or more years of MTM schooling. However, students with six years of Amharic L2-medium education as in Afar and Benishangul Gumuz have higher achievement than students in difficult MTM 4 contexts like Gambella. Surprisingly, marginalised Afar region with Amharic L2 has a modest incidence of below basic achievement compared with other regions, while Addis Ababa is one of the lowest achievers, coming ninth out of the eleven regions/city administrations. The implications of using a national language, like Amharic in Ethiopia, as a MoI thus require further investigation.

- Students who learn three languages during primary school do not achieve any less well than those who learn only two languages. In most instances, students with three languages especially in MTM 8 or MTM 6+8 programmes outperform those with two languages.

- Overall, more than 60% of students in regions offering fewer than eight years of MTM education have limited educational prospects beyond primary. Thus if the Ethiopian Ministry of Education were intending to increase the proportion of students who are well enough prepared for secondary school, it would appear that extending the use of MTM schooling is the way to go. However, we suggest that this measure on its own is not sufficient to meet what will inevitably become more pressing demands for secondary school enrolment.

10.4 Revisiting the Negative 'Washback Effect' of English in Ethiopian Education

As discussed above and in Chapter 1, there is significant pressure exerted towards earlier use of English as MoI in primary and teacher education. Although English was much admired in Ethiopia after the Second World War, earlier attempts to use English MoI in secondary were noted as problematic for precisely the same reasons found during and subsequent to our 2006 fieldwork (cf. McNab 1988). Smith (2008) also noted in her 2001 and 2003 fieldwork that civil society aspirations towards English might be in conflict with the language education policy. The change of medium to English in or before secondary gives English a gate-keeping function, which is exacerbated by the high-stakes school-exit examinations at the end of grades 10 and 12 (cf. Hussein 2010). Entry to teachers' colleges or university, subject to English language proficiency, is the point from which downward pressure has been exerted through the system (Heugh *et al.* 2007; Smith 2008; and Chapter 1, this volume). The negative impact is seen in the pressure for English MoI in grades 7 and 8, which has been resisted by Oromiya region but has caused policy reversals in other regions. In Amhara, MTM has been replaced by English in maths and sciences in grades 7–8, while in SNNPR English is introduced for all subjects beginning in grade 5. The negative washback effect is also evident in the 2009 discontinuation of L1-medium certificate training of lower primary teachers, and the requirement that all pre-service teachers undertake three-year diploma programmes through English. We view this total shift of MoI in teacher training as a particularly serious threat to what has, until recently, been a progressive and relatively successful implementation of a national mother tongue-based bi/multilingual primary school system.

Based on international experience (e.g. various authors in Mohanty *et al.* 2009, and chapters by McCarty and Pérez and Trapnell, this volume), and from our analysis of the Ethiopian assessment data, it is clear that longer-term use of the MT/L1 as MoI has positive outcomes for student language development and learning across the curriculum. Shortening of the MTM period to bring in English MoI earlier, while it may in theory expose learners to more English, is not likely to improve educational outcomes, nor is it likely to prepare students for entry to, and survival in, secondary education. While lower 2008 achievement levels across all subjects of the curriculum compared with the 2000 and 2004 data may be attributed to a number of factors, the decline does coincide with an earlier introduction of English medium in primary school and in teacher education in Ethiopia.

Is there any evidence that the ever-growing emphasis on English as MoI improves students' and teachers' English language proficiency? Our 2006 observations of classrooms where English was taught as a subject or used as MoI consistently showed that both teachers and students were struggling. In the 2007 report we pointed out that the presence of English as a subject from grade 1 is meaningless where teachers lack the proficiency needed to teach the language. If all of the interventions in support of English from late 2003 onwards (English language radio programmes for primary, plasma-TV lessons in English for secondary, ELIP participation of all teachers, earlier introduction of English MoI) have not yet shown any positive effect on student achievement, this should be great cause for concern. This is particularly since these interventions coincide with a decline in student learning outcomes. As shown in Table 10.1 above, the weighted mean achievement in English in 2000 was 39.57%; in 2004 it was up slightly at 41.43%; but in 2008 it was down to 38.70%. Since ELIP was conducted between 2005 and 2007, preceding the 2008 assessment, it is clear that the desired effect is not in evidence. While there is some relative improvement in English scores of students in Amhara and SNNPR, this success may be at the cost of overall achievement.

MTE based on three languages – the MTM for the first eight years, Amharic taught as L2, plus English (even though it is a foreign language/FL) for post-primary education – seemed logical at the time of national policy-making in 1994. However, the switch to English at grade 9 and use of this FL in continuing education was always going to be extremely challenging and unrealistic given teachers' limited exposure to the language and given the negligible functional use of English across Ethiopia. A recent study on education for pastoralists in Ethiopia draws attention to this situation in the following excerpt from an interview with a secondary teacher in Gambella:

> Do any of the teachers in your school speak the local language?
> No
> Do your students understand when the class is delivered in English?
> No
> How do your students follow the class?
> That is also my question.
>
> *(Pact Ethiopia 2008: 78).*

From another related perspective, Jeylan Hussein offers compelling autoethnographic reflections of how English disempowers students and teachers alike, 'based on the writer's own long experience as a learner and teacher of the English language and on the narrative experiences of his students' (Hussein 2010: 225–226). Through these reflections it becomes clear that English is both 'prized' and 'feared' in Ethiopia.

To illustrate the unattainable desire and expectation of English further, we turn to a relatively well-resourced South Africa, with approximately 9% L1 and 30% L2 speakers of English. Even though English has wider functional use in South Africa than in Ethiopia, education authorities have been unsuccessful in implementing a transition to English medium in fewer than eight years since a reduction of MTM 8 to MTM 4 followed civil unrest in 1976 (Heugh 2007). Given this scenario, one wonders how it could be possible to provide adequate access to education through English in Ethiopia, which is a country of fewer resources and where only 0.3% speak English as a first language (Wagaw 1999) and where it is a FL for 99% of citizens. Attempting to implement an earlier transition to English medium to achieve both educational success and desired proficiency in English is simply unrealistic and wasteful of educational resources.

As noted in Chapter 1 in this volume, our team wondered why greater use was not being made of Amharic as a national language in the Ethiopian school system, and why languages other than English – i.e. mother tongues and/or Amharic – were not being considered as MoI for secondary teaching and learning. Of course, Ethiopian languages are essential for teacher training as well. A decision to return to, or begin the use of, nationality languages in regional teacher education, or even a decision to give Amharic L2 a role as MoI in secondary and/or teacher education, would go a long way towards lessening the obsession with unattainable levels of English and promoting authentic communication in the classroom. One of our recommendations in 2007 was that the financial resources directed towards ELIP could be more fruitfully spent on MTM teacher education, further development of Ethiopian languages and producing relevant materials in these. While the MoE has not repositioned its English-focused trajectory, we note that in at least three regions, SNNPR, Benishangul Gumuz and Tigray, there has been further progress in developing additional languages at regional and local levels. This is a function of the regions' own dynamics rather than any policy directive from the federal government. As a whole, it is our view that reverse planning towards English has contributed to an erosion of some of the excellent progress made in MLE during a ten-year period between 1994 and 2003/4.

10.5 Conclusion

The timing of our study in 2006 permitted us access to ethnographic and classroom-based data during a period when regional implementation of MTE had reached a great degree of compliance with the national policy in Ethiopia. However, it also coincided with increasing emphasis of English which then showed signs of compromising the national MTE/MLE policy. We were able to observe how educators, officials, communities and language development agencies were endeavouring to make education function for as many students as possible, and on shoestring budgets. At the same time, we found evidence of a negative washback effect of English-medium secondary and higher education, and the inopportune diversion of human and technical resources from implementing the strong mother tongue-based primary programmes called for by the 1994 national policy. The current situation places at risk one of the most progressive multilingual education policies on the continent and, indeed, in the developing world: a policy which offers the best chance of high quality education for all. Educators and advisors at all levels would do well to take note of the Ethiopian case and also to consider the consequences of decisions to adopt apparently 'common sense' (Western) ideas – especially when they focus on one international language in low-income, linguistically diverse countries.

Lest there remain some who argue that MTM/MTE prevents access to the international language, whether this is English, French or Arabic, amongst others, Hussein has the following to say:

The view that education through mother tongue and political elevation of mother tongues is detrimental to the promotion of English is either mere linguistic chauvinism or linguistic self-denial founded on irrational theory about language, education and cognition.

(Hussein 2010: 236)

We remain hopeful that the strong MTM/MTE/MLE policy will remain, and that regions across Ethiopia will continue to strengthen their models based on the eight-year policy. Despite the current challenges, system-wide implementation of multilingual education across a large, poor country has been achieved with remarkable efficiency within a relatively short period of time. Ethiopia has gained a great deal of experience and expertise during this process and the country has contributed significantly to the body of data from which we may advance bi/multilingual education theory and practice in Africa and beyond.

Notes

1 This chapter is located at the end of the volume rather than immediately after Chapter 1, because we believe that the assessment data findings are potentially the most significant international data on bi/trilingual education to date because Ethiopia is the only country currently implementing MTM/MTE across an entire education system (editors' note).

2 Tigray, Oromiya (both MTM 8) and Benishangul Gumuz (Amharic L2 6) have the second best English as a subject scores. Afar (remote desert conditions and Amharic L2 6) and Gambella (MTM 4) have the lowest scores for English, along with Amhara region (MTM 8). The comparatively low English language scores in Amhara and comparatively high English scores in Benishangul Gumuz appear to be anomalies which disappear in subsequent assessment datasets.

3 We acknowledge with thanks, Mesfin Derash, who made these available to us for analysis.

4 It is more likely that a lower percentage of students in SNNPR have Amharic L2 medium and higher than 50% have MTM.

5 During the data collection in the field we took particular interest in whether or not students or teachers reported difficulty with the teaching and learning of two scripts, Ethiopic and Latin, for written text. We found no evidence that this posed difficulties for students.

6 The term proficient here is the term used in the assessment documentation and does not refer to language proficiency.

7 Up to 50% of those who started have already fallen out of the system by this point.

8 We are indebted to Jamie Mazraeh of the Research Centre for Languages and Cultures at the University of South Australia for assembling Figure 10.1.

9 MTM 8 in South Africa was implemented during a political process involving separate and unequal treatment of different ethnolinguistic groups. For this reason, the policy was rejected by civil society and it was only after its replacement by a MTM 4 programme followed by switch to English, accompanied by declining levels of achievement across the system, that the advantages of the earlier MTM 8 were noted (Heugh 1999).

10 These data are within the broad parameters of the 13 country study of student achievement, Southern and Eastern Africa Consortium for Monitoring Education Quality (SACMEQ) II study (Mothibeli 2005); and also several system-wide studies conducted in South Africa (see our Report, Heugh *et al.* 2007).

References

Alidou, Hassana, Boly, Aliou, Brock-Utne, Birgit, Diallo, Yaya Satina, Heugh, Kathleen and Wolff, H. Ekkehard (2006). *Optimizing Learning and Education in Africa – the Language Factor.* A Stock-taking Research on Mother Tongue and Bilingual Education in Sub-Saharan Africa. Association for the Development of Education in Africa (ADEA). (http://www.adeanet.org/adeaPortal/adea/biennial-2006/doc/document/B3_1_MTBLE_en.pdf).

Bamgbose, Ayo (2000). *Language and Exclusion. The Consequences of Language Policies in Africa.* Hamburg: Lit Verlag.

Benson, Carol (2005). *Girls, Educational Equity and Mother Tongue-based Teaching.* Bangkok: UNESCO. (http://www.ungei.org/resources/files/unesco_Girls_Edu_mother_tongue.pdf).

Benson, Carol (2009). Designing effective schooling in multilingual contexts: The strengths and limitations of bilingual 'models'. In Mohanty, Ajit, Panda, Minati, Phillipson, Robert and Skutnabb-Kangas, Tove (eds), *Multilingual Education for Social Justice: Globalising the Local.* New Delhi: Orient BlackSwan, 60–76.

Cummins, Jim (2009). Fundamental psychological and sociological principles underlying educational success for linguistic minority students. In Mohanty, Ajit, Panda, Minati, Phillipson, Robert and Skutnabb-Kangas, Tove (eds), *Multilingual Education for Social Justice: Globalising the Local.* New Delhi: Orient BlackSwan, 21–36.

García, Ofelia and Baker, Colin (2007). *Bilingual Education. An Introductory Reader.* Clevedon: Multilingual Matters.

Gebre Yohannes, Mekonnen Alemu (2005). *Socio-cultural and educational implications of using mother tongues as languages of instruction in Ethiopia.* Unpublished Master's thesis, University of Oslo.

Gebre Yohannes, Mekonnen Alemu (2009). Implications of the use of mother tongues versus English as languages of instruction for academic achievement in Ethiopia. In Brock-Utne, Birgit and Skattum, Ingse (eds), *Languages and Education in Africa: A Comparative and Transdisciplinary Analysis.* Oxford: Symposium Books, 189–199.

GEQAEA (General Education Quality Assurance and Examinations Agency) (2008). *Ethiopian Third National Learning Assessment of Grade Eight Students.* USAID/EQUIP II project. Addis Ababa: GEQAEA.

Heugh, Kathleen (1999). Languages, development and reconstructing education in South Africa. *International Journal of Educational Development*, 19, 301–313.

Heugh, Kathleen (2003). A re-take on bilingual education in and for South Africa. In Fraurud, Kari and Hyltenstam, Kenneth (eds), *Multilingualism in Global and Local Perspectives. Selected papers from the 8th Nordic Conference on bilingualism, November 1–3, 2001.* Stockholm: Centre for Research on Bilingualism, Stockholm University and Rinkeby Institute of Multilingual Research, 47–62.

Heugh, Kathleen (2006a). Theory and practice – language education models in Africa: research, design, decision-making, and outcomes. In Alidou *et al.*, 56–84. (http://www.ade.org/adeaPortal/adea/biennial-2006/doc/document/B3_1_MTBLE_en.pdf).

Heugh, Kathleen (2006b). Cost implications of the provision of mother tongue and strong bilingual models of education in Africa. In Alidou *et al.*, 138–156. (http://www.adeanet.org/adeaPortal/adea/biennial-2006/doc/document/B3_1_MTBLE_en.pdf).

Heugh, Kathleen (2007). Language and literacy issues in South Africa. In Rassool, Naz (ed.), *Global Issues in Language, Education, and Development: Perspectives from Postcolonial Countries.* Clevedon: Multilingual Matters, 187–218.

Heugh, Kathleen (2009). Into the cauldron: an interplay of indigenous and globalised knowledge with strong and weak notions of literacy and language education in Ethiopia and South Africa. *Language Matters. Studies in the languages of Africa*, 166–189.

Heugh, Kathleen, Benson, Carol, Bogale, Berhanu and Gebre Yohannes, Mekonnen Alemu (2007). *Final Report: Study on Medium of Instruction in Primary Schools in Ethiopia*. Research report commissioned by the Ministry of Education, Addis Ababa, September to December 2006.

Hussein, Jeylan Wolyie (2010). English supremacy in Ethiopia – autoethnographic reflections. In Heugh, Kathleen and Skutnabb-Kangas, Tove (eds), *Multilingual Education Works: From the Periphery to the Centre*. New Delhi: Orient BlackSwan, 224–238.

Lewin, Keith (2008). *Strategies for Sustainable Financing of Secondary Education in Sub-Saharan Africa*. World Bank Working Paper No. 136. Africa Human Development Series. Washington: World Bank.

McNab, Christine (1988). *Language policy and language practice: Implementation dilemma in Ethiopian education*. Unpublished Ph.D. dissertation in International Education. University of Stockholm, Institute of International Education.

MoE (Ministry of Education)/NOE (National Organization for Examinations) (April 2001). *Ethiopian National Baseline Assessment on Grade Eight Students' Achievement*. Addis Ababa: MoE.

MoE (Ministry of Education)/NOE (National Organization for Examinations). (December 2004). *Ethiopian Second National Learning Assessment of Grade 8 Students*. Addis Ababa: MoE.

Mohanty, Ajit, Panda, Minati, Phillipson, Robert and Skutnabb-Kangas, Tove (eds) (2009). *Multilingual Education for Social Justice: Globalising the Local*. New Delhi: Orient BlackSwan.

Mothibeli, Agnes (2005). Cross-Country achievement results from the SACMEQ 11 Project – 2000 to 2002. A quantitative analysis of education systems in Southern and Eastern Africa. *Edusource Data News*. No. 49. October. Johannesburg: The Education Foundation Trust.

Obanya, Pai (2002). *Revitalizing Education in Africa*. Ibadan: Stirling-Horden Publishers (Nig.) Ltd.

Ouane, Adama (2003). Introduction: the view from inside the linguistic jail. In Ouane, Adama (ed.), *Towards a Multilingual Culture of Education*. Hamburg: UNESCO Institute for Education, 1–22.

Pact Ethiopia (2008). Education for Pastoralists: Flexible Approaches, Workable Models. USAID. (http://www.pactworld.org/galleries/ethiopia/Education%20for%20Pastoralists-A4.pdf).

Skutnabb-Kangas, Tove (in press). Mother tongue medium education. In *The Encyclopedia of Applied Linguistics*. General editor Carol A. Chapelle; part *Bilingual Education*, Area editors Jasone Cenoz and Durk Gorter. Oxford: Wiley-Blackwell.

Smith, Lahra (2008). The politics of contemporary language policy in Ethiopia. *Journal of Developing Societies* 24(2), 207–243. (http://jds.sagepub.com/cgi/reprint/24/2/207).

Terefe, Gemechu Dereje (2010). *The implementation of a multilingual education policy in Ethiopia: The case of Afaan Oromoo in primary schools of Oromia Regional State*. Ph.D. dissertation in Social and Public Policy. University of Jyväskylä, Finland.

Thomas, Wayne P. and Collier, Virginia P. (2002). *A National Study of School Effectiveness for Language Minority Students' Long Term Academic Achievement*. George Mason University,

CREDE (Center for Research on Education, Diversity & Excellence). (http://www.crede.ucsc.edu/research/llaa/1.1_final.html).

Wagaw, Teshome (1999). *Conflict of Ethnic Identity and the Language of Education Policy in Contemporary Ethiopia. Northeast African Studies.* (New Series). 6(3), 75–88. (http://muse.jhu.edu/journals/northeast_african_studies/v006/6.3wagaw.pdf).

11

'PERIPHERIES' TAKE CENTRE STAGE

Reinterpreted Multilingual Education Works

Kathleen Heugh and Tove Skutnabb-Kangas

11.1 Introduction: What Works Well?

The expansion of primary education from the late 1800s, and subsequently, of secondary education since the end of the Second World War, is a fairly recent phenomenon in Western countries. Education systems in other parts of the world, however, go back millennia, to the early writing systems of China, India and Africa. It is therefore odd that Western perceptions have been based on incorrect historical accounts which have overlooked the long history and value of education in more diverse-rich parts of the world.

Optimistic assumptions about the contribution of formal education to the building of modern nations are questionable. Formal education in Africa and Asia in its present form tends to impede economic growth and promote political instability; in short, *education in Africa and Asia today is an obstacle to development* – and this has been known for a long time: 'that people's languages are not used either for literacy or for primary education' has been seen as one major reason for 'illiteracy' (Hanf *et al.* 1975: 68).

If it is the case that 'education in Africa and Asia today is an obstacle to development' *because* 'people's languages are not used either for literacy or for primary education', we may have been measuring students from settings with ancient educational and literary traditions against those of more recently developed Western countries.

This book is about what and how multilingual education works and how existing, indigenous resources are further developed in contemporary times. The studies and settings range in scope from NGO and community-based initiatives, to those initiated within regional education administrations, and to one that applies across an entire country. Each setting offers unique contributions to the field of bilingual and multilingual education either from a theoretical perspective and/or practical hands-on challenges and solutions.

As mentioned in our introductory chapter, MLE is practised in different ways, largely determined by a number of contextual factors including socio-economic, political, geographic, climatic and demographic conditions. The authors of this volume have highlighted the very palpable contextual features particular to their settings in order to show local and indigenous responses to the task of designing and implementing multilingual education. The message is that there is a number of basic principles which underpin successful education in general, and more specifically in situations where students require one or more additional language/s in order to participate in contemporary life.

MLE students are clearly shown to learn and deal with the curriculum more effectively; their self-confidence and pride are nurtured and allowed to grow; there are improved prospects of remaining in the school system for longer; and parents and other community members participate in and claim a stake in the education of their youth. These characteristics are usually missing from Western models of monolingual education for these groups of children.

MLE, furthermore, provides the environmental conditions to strengthen the use and further development of local, Indigenous, heritage and regional languages in written texts. These do not have any more intrinsic value than spoken texts, but they do make a considerable difference in terms of the power relations among communities on the fringes and those which inhabit the urban centres of economic and political power. It is all too simple to ignore the demands of people on the fringes when both their voice and their written word are inaudible and invisible. This has to do with the interconnectedness of issues of equality, participation, citizenship.

Written texts in ITM languages establish and develop a solid continuum of literacy practices, from early narrative, all the way through to decontextualised academic discourse required by the school curriculum (Panda and Mohanty 2009). They also facilitate the best opportunities for successful second/third language acquisition. This gives school students the best possible chance to participate in local, regional and even international activities. The chapters point towards fruitful practices and discoveries, mutually enriching in the South, but also important for contemporary concerns of recent migration and urbanisation in the West/North.

We finish this introductory section with a summary of what the studies here contribute to our understanding of bilingual and multilingual education in relation to student learning and achievement where the target language is a *foreign* (not second) language. The case-studies here show that there are considerable educational benefits of using the MT as a medium for as long as possible. This assists not only content learning in the various subjects but also the development of additional languages, including a dominant language that may become the medium of education later. It confirms the last 250 years of hypotheses (from the Seneca Chief Handsome Lake in the mid-1700s, through the USA Board of Indian Commissioners in 1880,[1] to Viceroy Curzon in India in 1904).[2] Likewise, it confirms the more than 60 years of scientific literature, starting from Malherbe (1946) to literally thousands of studies today. Bilingual education is possible in every setting. Trilingual and sometimes quadrilingual education is also possible to implement in resource-poor contexts.

The new data and evidence from the Ethiopian countrywide study about the consequences of using the MT as a medium in varying degrees from four to eight years, prior to a switch to English (foreign language) medium are of great significance for the international field.

- Students who receive MTM education to grade 8, and whose teachers are trained in the MT achieve the highest scores across the curriculum (unless socio-economic conditions are particularly unfavourable).
- Students who receive MTM education to grade 6 plus partial MTM education to grade 8, achieve the next highest scores overall, but appear to have difficulty with science.
- Students who receive MTM education to grade 6, and whose teachers are trained through the medium of the MT at least for the first four years of primary, achieve the third highest scores across the curriculum. These students are likely to have difficulty with mathematics and science and few would be expected to be retained to the end of secondary.
- Students who receive MTM education to grade 4, plus an additional four or more years of learning the MT as a subject in a trilingual programme and multilingually supportive environment achieve nearly as well as those in MTM 6 bilingual programmes. Students who have MTM education to grade 4 in poorly resourced and difficult social settings, achieve the lowest scores across the curriculum. These students experience greatest difficulty with mathematics and science and very few will be retained to the end of secondary.
- Students who receive a regional/local second language-medium education do not succeed as well as students with six or more years of MTM education. However, they achieve higher results than students with 4 years of MTM education in difficult contexts, but less well than those students who have 4 years of MTM schooling in more socio-economically stable contexts. Secondary school students from these programmes struggle with mathematics and science.
- Primary school students who learn three languages (even with two scripts) do not achieve less well than those who learn two languages. In fact, students with three languages usually outperform those with two, especially in programmes with 8 or a mix of 6&8 years of MTM education.
- Between 60 and 80% of students in the regions which do not offer MTM 8 have limited educational prospects beyond primary school.

Development economists agree that UNESCO's Education for All goals have to extend from universal primary education (where significant progress is being made) to increased secondary school enrolment. While systemic assessment in Ethiopia demonstrates that the *overall* average achievement of students retained to grade 8 is less than 40%, the minimum requirement for enrolling in secondary, this benchmark had been reached in six of eleven regions in 2000. This happened within six years of setting out and implementing a bold MLE policy across the country, demonstrating considerable progress over a short timeframe in a very poor country. Other studies in this book support this trend even where the programmes are not yet offering 8 years of MTM education. All the contexts presented in this volume also demonstrate various risks. We draw attention to some risks that may challenge, undermine, undo or prevent progress in MLE.

11.2 Risks

11.2.1 The Relationship between Scientific Knowledge about MLE and its Implementation

Decisions may be taken in the absence of scientific evidence, or despite strong scientific evidence which contradicts the decisions. Ignorance about MLE among people responsible for educational decisions about diverse students is widespread in many countries. Implementation of positive decisions may never happen or they happen grudgingly, or so partially that the expected positive outcomes do not materialise. Thus the sustainability of good programmes is compromised. Political apathy among decision-makers is common. Deliberate use of education to disempower people and attempts at making them complicit in their own subordination abound (e.g. Heugh 2010).

Despite the need to contextualise, research results are clear about the negative consequences of subtractive education through the medium of a dominant/foreign language while the positive results of mainly mother tongue-medium education for ITM children are solid and consistent. The few persistent counterarguments are political/ideological, not scientific.

But does this research knowledge translate into educational action? There seem to be three main trends, here presented from the most to least negative.

1   *Research results are completely ignored.* Denmark is an example of this: despite authorities having had considerable evidence, there are not even early-exit transitional programmes for immigrant minority children; most mother tongue as a subject teaching has been terminated, and the Minister of Education allows schools to forbid the speaking of minority languages during breaks (e.g. Arabic in November 2009, see http://politiken.dk/indland/article846430.ece).

2   *Research results are to some extent acknowledged,* in conference resolutions and by educational authorities, and government officials make promises, *but little or*

no implementation follows. There is a lot of well-intentioned hot air: '[W]e are not making any progress at all' (Alexander 2006: 9); 'most conference resolutions were no more than a recycling exercise' (Bamgbose 2001, quoted in Alexander 2006: 10); 'these propositions had been enunciated in one conference after another since the early 1980s' (Alexander 2006: 11). This has led to 'the palpable failure of virtually all post-colonial educational systems on the continent' (Alexander 2006: 16). Similar pronouncements abound on other continents. In both Nepal and India, the right to mother tongue-medium education has been in the constitutions for several decades, but implementation has not followed.

3   *Experimental projects, with early- or late-exit transitional programmes, are started.* However, when the project (and money) ends, *the project model is not continued or spread more widely, despite positive results.* After a few years the experience exists only in research papers. The Ile-Ife Six-Year Primary project in Nigeria, with Yoruba as the medium of education (Afolayan 1976) is one example, the Iloilo project in the Philippines is another.

Very little has changed in regard to strengthening the medium of education in Ethiopia since the Ministry of Education in Ethiopia commissioned the report on medium of instruction and received its findings and recommendations in 2007. Instead, English is steadily encroaching on MT time and space in the curriculum. The ADEA-UIE Report (Alidou *et al.* 2006) recommended a minimum of six years of MTM education. Although well-received by the Ministers of Education at the time, it has not yet been acted upon. Although it was followed by a public commitment to MTM 6 by the South African Minister of Education in 2006, most children continue to be subjected to early-exit bilingual education. As Nikièma and Ilboudo (this volume) illustrate, Ministers of Education in 'francophone' Africa are more concerned that the position of French, rather than African languages, is strengthened in education.

A particular characteristic of centralised national policy and planning is the taking of decisions which are not intended for implementation. The central authority exerts influence over the agency responsible for change and thus circumvents change. The Moroccan study (Kabel) gives us a salutary lesson on the complexities of overt language policy activity in the hands of the ruling authority. In this study, language development activities appear to move forwards, yet they are in reverse gear, undoing existing multilingual practices. Kabel discusses the need to be cautious about 'language development'. When wrested from community control/participation and used for ethnic cleansing purposes it may result in undemocratic and artful use of political power to marginalise and increase divisions amongst the underclasses. Kabel offers compelling evidence of the need for strong civil society organisations and their participation in language planning.

Decentralised language planning and community participation offer opportunities for forward planning which may counter or hold in check some straight-jacketing tendencies in the centre. Decentralised planning is particularly in evidence in this volume's case-studies on Peru (Pérez and Trapnell), Burkina Faso (Nikièma and Ilboudo), Nepal (Nurmela *et al.*, Taylor), India (Mohanty), South Asia (Benson and Kosonen), Ethiopia (Benson *et al.*) and in Native American bilingual programmes (McCarty).

Mother tongue-based MLE and its interrelatedness with socio-economic and political development requires thorough long-term planning and implementation which is sustained. Short-term plans and projects linked to the vagaries of political terms of office (typically five- to seven-year timeslots) are not suitable for education and socio-economic planning for future generations.

11.2.2 Ethics of Interventions and Research

There is in most chapters an undercurrent of *concerns about the ethics of interventions and of external consultants. These include advisors involved in curricula and pedagogies; in materials' production, especially for international languages; a merging of several roles, with economic and/or neo-colonial interests (e.g. British Council) (see Phillipson 2009a, b, c; Phillipson and Skutnabb-Kangas 2009) or religious interests (e.g. 'selling' Christianity under the guise of teaching English (see Wong and Canagarajah 2009) or organising bilingual early-exit programmes which are often inadequate). Likewise, there are concerns about external scholarship, knowledge and experience garnered in other contexts that are brought to bear on education in low-income, diverse settings in other parts of the world (e.g. Heugh 2006).* Many of these concerns are difficult to discuss because useful knowledge and well-intentioned people may be involved. It is often difficult to separate individuals from their organisational roles. Our reservations include a sense that local knowledge is either partially or wholly ignored while the views of (external) advisors and consultants are often privileged in new policy and plans. External advisors on second language pedagogy, training programmes and publishing have influenced (and continue to influence) countries of the South (e.g. Widin (2010), on Australian ESL interests in Asia). Often these have been glitzy early-exit models, claimed to transport children from their mother tongue to an international language in anything from a few months to two years. By the time early-exit programmes have ended and students' progress has been tracked over 5–6 years, the consultants have gone elsewhere. Any evaluation which identifies risks is simply too late. Alternatively, new consultants arrive with pre-formulated evaluation templates into which generic solutions are pasted. Inevitably, local publishers, experts and trainers are positioned as 'out of date' and redundant, and subsequently undermined and abandoned. Iina Nurmela (forthcoming), writes about ethical concerns with development cooperation specifically in relation to MLE:

> Graham Hancock (1991) writes about the many problems in development cooperation ranging from the excessive use of foreign experts (even for jobs that could be done by nationals of the countries concerned) and their

disregard for local knowledge of the marginalised, to the short-term planning, hurried appraisal, and absence of proper fieldwork in the development projects which often lead to harmful mistakes and irrelevant outcomes for the 'beneficiaries'.

Development projects are often constructed around technical assistance with most funds going towards salaries and other expenses of foreign advisors. Foreign staff may not understand the need to include local knowledge and to capture the views of local stakeholders via their own languages. Usually foreign experts leave before learning the language/s needed for real contact with the communities who are to receive the advice and recommendations (e.g. Hancock 1991: 118–119, 125).

The foreign experts may also run the risk of importing inappropriate advice while ignoring local initiatives and creativity. If models of teaching MLE are imposed from the outside, without local teacher participation in their development there is a risk of MLE becoming both at content and pedagogical levels a mere set of routines. Teachers may follow these without understanding the underlying theory and without the confidence to develop or adjust the model to their or the students' specific needs (Panda and Mohanty 2009: 299). Simultaneously with a rapid turn-over of external assistance, there is often an accompanying change of direction in the advice (model/routine). This serves to increase dependency on the outside rather than a building of internal capacity and expertise (Hancock 1991: 114, 189).

It is clear that the ethical burden on the shoulders of foreign experts weighs heavily because:

> it is outsiders like these [prosperous, propertied, healthy, educated and influential foreign experts and local and central government officials] who shape the ways in which the poor [or ITM peoples] are seen, define their problems, and formulate all the policies, projects and programmes intended to alleviate their poverty (Hancock 1991: 119).

> And, when invited, we may also participate in the struggle 'from within' the indigenous communities. In so doing, however, we must understand that we are always the guest (the manuhiri) (Hough and Skutnabb-Kangas 2005: 2).

And 'guests' always have much to learn. We need a code of ethics for the so-called language experts in this kind of work.

11.2.3 The Pressure Towards the Dominant/Majority or Global Language

Reverse planning or the washback effect of high-stakes assessment and gate-keeping in a particular language is noticeable in several countries, with some to-ing and fro-ing between more MT-medium and more English-medium (e.g. Malaysia, Tanzania and Madagascar). The Ethiopian case shows the most promising contemporary example of a system-wide education policy geared towards meeting linguistically diverse needs of students. Increasing emphasis on English, as an international language and the language of higher education from 2002 onwards, however, has resulted in a change in focus from the delivery of mass (quality) school education to the provision of higher education in English for a small elite (Chapters 1, 10). The negative washback effect, of an increased focus on English-medium school education from 2004 onwards has rapidly undermined excellent progress in MLE (1994–2004). An over-emphasis on English as the symbolic panacea of change (see Phillipson 2009c) mirrors closely the changes which took place in South Africa after a 20-year MT/bilingual/trilingual system based on eight years of MTM education was reduced to four years after 1976. The rapidity of the decline in student achievement was noticeable within five years, the point at which the first affected cohort of students reached the secondary school exit examinations. The change there was accompanied by the undoing of the expertise and resources established in MLE in terms of textbook production, teacher training, translation, lexicography, terminology development and multilingual assessment. The earlier experience of South Africa does not bode well for Ethiopia unless the current cycle of reverse planning is turned forwards.

Reverse planning occurs when policy or implementation is introduced to undermine or reverse the direction of an earlier positive policy. Far from achieving the hoped-for symbolic capital in English (or French or Spanish), the change of direction in fact makes access to the ILWC (Wolff 2006) more elusive (as evident in each of the chapters herein). The phenomenon relates to regionally dominant languages like Arabic, Hindi, Kiswahili and Amharic, illustrated in most chapters in this book. However, it is particularly noticeable in the overselling of false promises of employment and economic success through English. The phenomenon is connected with misleading and theoretically unsound language learning methods (early start, maximum exposure, etc.; see Cummins 2009).

The pressure towards the dominant/majority/global language is often so acute that even parents, teachers or decision-makers who understand the arguments may succumb, unless they see quick results from MLE in the students' dominant language competence (Skutnabb-Kangas, Phillipson, Mohanty and Panda 2009). Hearing children in English-medium education chattering away confidently at the point when their own MTM educated children can hardly formulate a sentence in English may break the confidence of even the most knowledgeable parents. As Hussein (2010) powerfully shows, many social, economic and pedagogical factors (including lack of quality MLE) prevented his and his informants' fluency in English. However, these factors are often forgotten in emotionally stressful situations. Even where there is minimal horizontal use of English, there is a prevailing belief that maximum exposure to the dominant language in school will deliver high-level proficiency in English. Where students experience a gap between their own proficiency in a dominant language and that of others, this is accompanied by loss of confidence and self-esteem. People often feel ashamed of their mother tongues and ashamed of not knowing the language/s of power well enough (Hussein 2010).[3] Because parents do not want their children to suffer as they did, the common-sense solution is often to send children to a dominant language-medium school. Thus the cycle of exclusion continues.

11.2.4 Unfounded Claims about the 'Impossibility' of Organising MLE Under Various Conditions, and about Allegedly 'Damaging' Consequences of MLE

It is often claimed that urban environments with hundreds of languages make MLE impossible. There are also claims that MLE leads to ghettoisation and segregation, to communalism, or to the disintegration of a state, as MLE-educated indigenous and tribal peoples, with more knowledge and self-confidence, begin demanding more rights, including to land and water. As minorities with MLE, they may reproduce themselves as minorities and 'demand' minority rights rather than assimilate into the dominant culture within three generations, as expected). These are nightmares for many neoliberal politicians (and some researchers).

When we interrogate MLE, we need to think of contemporary and future multiethnic and multilingual societies. Why is it that MLE is seen as appropriate in the peripheries, but not in the centre/s? Post Second World War patterns of migration to wealthier Western countries have been escalating in response to multiple sites of social upheaval around the world. New highly diverse, urbanised and globalised communities characterise Europe and North America while policy-makers and power-brokers are flummoxed. Earlier assimilationist policies are impossible when more than 50% of the world's population lives in highly diverse cities. Debates on (super)diversity often stagnate at the level of listing facts about difference and heterogeneity of urban environments, followed by multicultural but not multilingual rhetoric. But the formulation of appropriate accommodation and conclusions about necessary action, particularly in terms of education, are insubstantial, wasteful of human resources and often premised on fear.

The neoliberal tendency is towards homogenisation, a centripetal force (e.g. Lo Bianco 2010). Homogenisation reduces or eliminates cultural and linguistic diversity; diversity is seen as preventing integration and leading to a 'clash of civilisations'. Simultaneously, the tendency is to keep and promote the unthreatening aspects of cultural (but not linguistic) diversity. Education authorities often work with similar perceptions: if children were to be taught through the medium of their mother tongues, they would be segregated from each other, they would not learn to know each other or to live together, and they could not learn each other's languages and cultures. This would inevitably lead to conflict. Debi Pattanayak captured these unfounded misconceptions thus:

> While Weinstein, an eminent political scientist looking at the American structure asks 'how much diversity can this structure tolerate?', a person in

a Third World country must ask 'how much uniformity can that structure tolerate?' . . . The Western view is linear and binary, whereas the Eastern is cyclical and spiral. However, the westernized eastern elites, who are in charge of planning, follow essentially the Western worldview.

(Pattanayak 1991: 31)

Political scientists in the developing Third World, tutored in the theory and methodology of the social science of the West, also join the chorus and repeat ad nauseam that plurality is a threat to the stability of the fragile State. They forget that in these countries freedom is more fragile than the State . . . . It is inconceivable that there was a single language for all human beings at any time since human societies were formed. Multiplicity and diversity are the characteristics of nature.

(Pattanayak 1981: 3, vii)

Other arguments list the practical difficulties and the cost of organising this kind of education.

MLE is seen as possible in relatively homogeneous rural societies – but how about diverse cities? It seems that opposition towards organising MLE everywhere is mostly ideological; it is mostly about unfounded fears about the disintegration of a state. Even when peace and conflict researchers can demonstrate that a lack of language-related rights (including MTM education) is an important causal factor in conflicts that are *labelled* 'ethnic', opponents of MLE cling to arguments which result in the denial of these rights. Once the will to admit this is there, many of the practical challenges can be tackled, as experiences all over the world (cf. this volume) show. MLE is by no means unproblematic (see, e.g., Taylor, this volume) but examples in section 11.3 suggest solutions.

11.3 How does Multilingual Education Work?

11.3.1 What do MLE Participants Recommend?

Education officials in Ethiopia know exactly how MLE works and how it can work better. They are also able to articulate this in ways that are helpful elsewhere. The system-wide assessments in Ethiopia also collect data on the perceptions of students, parents, teachers, teacher education and regional education authorities about the state of the system and relevant concerns. The *second systemic assessment report* (MoE/NoE 2004), prior to the negative encroachment of English, includes the following recommendations:

- Teacher quality and working conditions need improvement.
- The quality and supply of curriculum materials have to be improved.
- Instructional practices and instructional support have to be strengthened . . . enabling students to understand their lessons.

- There is a need to shift to local languages from English in order to attain better achievements of students. Grade 8 results indicate that learning through local languages related very strongly with better achievements. Since there are only very few nationality languages used for classroom instruction . . . a lot remains to be done to enable all students to learn in these nationality languages instead of English.
- The alignment of home and school language has to be enhanced. The alignment of home and school language was found to have strong positive relationship with achievement of students at this level.
- Community participation and support is essential to the development of schools.

(Ibid.: 111–113)

These recommendations also emerge thematically from the other case-studies in this volume. All those who have tried early-exit models, are trying to extend them to higher grades and those who have late-exit models make similar recommendations.

11.3.2 Walk the Talk: the Need for Implementation[4]

We argue in section 11.2 that research results on the benefits of 6–8-year MTM education need to be acknowledged. Experience shows, though, that there are certain conditions under which MLE is successful. These include effective policy and planning mechanisms which are honoured by the state. There are many examples of ITMs that demand implementation of MLE-related rights through courts (e.g. in the Nordic countries, or in the USA), or that turn to various monitoring bodies for regional or international human rights instruments, some with success, cf. our Introduction). Anchoring decisions about MLE also legally is positive. On the other hand, often despite strong legal protection implementation is avoided (e.g. South Africa).

Mother tongue-based MLE requires ongoing implementation in all diverse contexts. In some of these, the educational debates coincide with rights-based debates regarding the rights of communities to use their languages in education, not only in short-term projects but on a broad basis (see above). In Iraqi Kurdistan, for example, the former Minister of Education, Abdul-Aziz Taib, said: 'Every child in the world has the right to education through the medium of their mother tongue' (interview 15 March 2006 with TSK). Kurdistan is trying: in addition to Kurdish-speakers, also Assyrian-, Turkoman-, and Arabic-speaking children are taught through their MTs; Assyrian/Syriac, Armenian, Chaldean, Turkoman and Arabic are taught as mother tongues, and also as elective subjects to those who want to learn them. Minorities have their own Departments in the Ministry of Education, each with their own Director General (DG). There are obviously also critical voices (for Assyrian education, see Odisho 2004). Everybody learns obligatory Kurdish (as MT or L2) and English (Skutnabb-Kangas and Fernandes 2008; Taylor and Skutnabb-Kangas 2009).

In Nepal, the government promised that the MLE programme (Nurmela *et al.* this volume) that officially ended in December 2009 would continue and be extended both horizontally (more languages and schools) and vertically (more years mainly through the mother tongue). The person who conceptualised the project, Lava Deo Awasthi (who experienced subtractive education himself in school and was 'pushed out' of school) was appointed DG of the Department of Education in September 2010, and is determined that MLE should succeed.

11.3.3 Teacher Education and Placement

The issue of teacher education has received considerable attention in the UNESCO frameworks for education and focus on quality across and within systems and it is highlighted in every chapter in this book. The importance of high quality pre- and in-service education for teachers in MLE theories and methods is crucial (see each case-study in this volume). Many teachers who have been trained through the medium of a dominant language rather than their ITM mother tongue experience difficulty with knowledge of terminology and its development. This may foster the misperception that mother tongues cannot be used for teaching, especially after primary school (e.g. Hussein 2010). Teacher education through the medium of the local, regional and national languages used in the classroom is entirely possible and preferable, as shown recently in Ethiopia, but earlier in South Africa and Namibia between 1955 and 1975. Most teachers need in-service training for MTM education. In-service teachers in an MLE programme in South Africa, initially sceptical of writing university assignments in Xhosa, found that they could explain, question and analyse theory and methodology in Xhosa. This was more satisfying than earlier experiences in which they felt constrained to borrow highbrow English discourse from the readings.[5]

Where most teachers are speakers of local, regional and national languages, the costs of training teachers to use MTs efficiently are considerably less than the rather futile attempt to have every teacher develop sufficiently high levels of proficiency in a foreign target language (Heugh 2006, and Chapters 1 and 10 in this volume). In general, the costs of using minority languages in education are surprisingly low, as François Grin has shown in several studies.[6] Within five years, the economic returns on investing in MTM education are evident in: lower attrition (especially for girls), lower repeater-rates, higher through-put to secondary, and the potential of a more highly educated citizenry. Enhanced teacher qualifications seem, not surprisingly, to be closely related to teacher salaries and status, and all of these are reflected in the consistently superior achievement of Finnish students in the internationally benchmarked PISA tests (http://www.pisa.oecd.org/).[7] Just as in some other professions, high-level skills, e.g. multilingualism, should also be rewarded in teacher salaries. Training of teacher trainers to support teachers, and in materials development, needs to be prioritised (e.g. Taylor, this volume). An experimental training of trainers (and education officials) programme in multilingual education, developed and trialled at the University of Cape Town between 2002 and 2005, supported initiatives of the *African Academy of Languages* (ACALAN) and was intended to be adapted by universities across the region. So this is possible, has been done, and it works. It simply requires institutional will to extend its reach. One of the most innovative programmes on the continent is a bilingual undergraduate degree offered at the University of Limpopo, where an African language is used as a medium of instruction in the *Contemporary English Language Studies (CELS) and Multilingual Studies (MUST)*, Bachelor of Arts Degree (Ramani and Joseph 2002).

Often governments decide where to place new teachers, and where to move experienced teachers. Elsewhere, regional or local authorities or schools hire the teachers. It is always vitally important that the mother tongues and linguistic competencies of teachers match those of the students. Often decisions are made without linguistic matching, or ITM teachers may be prevented from teaching in schools where students and teachers have the same mother tongue. This is a consequence of a misperception that forcing students to speak the dominant language of the teacher 'helps' the students to learn the dominant language. We have frequently encountered teachers who do not even know the MTs of their students (cf. also Plüddemann, Mati and Mahlalela-Thusi 2000). Iina Nurmela's table (adapted as Table 7.1 in Taylor, this volume), shows that teachers in some schools in the MLE project in Nepal do not always have the required linguistic competencies. On the other hand, both central and local authorities and many teachers themselves in Nepal are now aware of the issue, and there have been attempts to solve the problems, by moving teachers or hiring new teachers with better matching competencies (see Nurmela *et al.*, and Taylor, both this volume).

11.3.4 Language Policy and Planning for Education

In those settings where government takes a clear, unequivocal stance supportive of multilingualism, steps are quickly put in place to make it work. This was indeed the case in the first ten years of the Ethiopian MLE policy. It is important though, for responsible government stakeholders to distinguish between party-politicking and the long-term interests of the country. Unfortunately, a change of political leadership, a new Minister of Education, and the need for political posturing contributed towards a shift in focus from what would best serve students, even as identified in the system's national assessment report (see above). So a good policy that works, is being undone. Kabel's chapter on Morocco, also points towards other political motivations for (mis)using language policy and planning as an opportunity to engage in ethnic cleansing activities. Nikièma and Ilboudo point to political reluctance to let go of the privileged status of the language of power. Benson and Kosonen similarly point towards the constraints of overly centralised control of policy in South-East Asia, and strategies whereby dominant languages are promoted above non-dominant ones, even when there are tacit policy statements supportive of MTM education. Overly centralised power is dangerous for education and particularly MLE. Decentralisation of implementation and expanded community stakeholder participation offer more satisfactory alternatives (see Benson *et al.* Chapter 1, McCarty, Pérez and Trapnell, and Mohanty, this volume). This is significantly more limited in the South-East Asian countries.

A combination of strong government support and enabling decentralisation leads to the empowering of regional and local authorities and communities in relation to: language development activities, translation, writing of school textbooks, translation, and printing and publishing. This encourages and develops local expertise and industry, democratises education, and contributes to local economies. While we do not suggest that local communities would be able to produce all of the materials necessary for secondary and higher education, they are certainly able to do this for primary education, and also to get the books into the hands of students. In South Africa where school text book production has been directed towards large publishing houses in the metropolitan centres, expensive books seldom actually get into the hands of children in rural areas. Also in Nepal, there were stacks of centrally produced materials in the mother tongues lying around in central administration offices – now they have in fact reached the villages.

11.3.5 Developing Participatory Support Structures and Networks, with Community Involvement

Much of the literature on multilingual education has focused on the medium of education. Initiatives in MLE in several different countries/continents (among Native American Indian programmes in Peru and the USA, in India and Nepal among tribal and minority communities) point towards the intrinsic value of intercultural education as fundamental to inviting and drawing in the participation of and consequently the 'buy-in' of local communities. Pérez and Trapnell offer a compelling case of why and how intercultural education is deeply connected to bilingual education in Peru, and McCarty does this in her wide-ranging discussion of several programmes across North America. Often the communities themselves initiate the programmes.

Community engagement with the schools has long been recognised as a pillar of successful education everywhere. It is easily purchased in middle-class and elite education, but countless studies show that it is very difficult to involve communities in education when parents and students experience alienation from the institution and/or live in poverty. All the authors of this volume have experienced at first hand the sterile, forlorn face of schools from which the community is distanced, whether by virtue of language, culture or social class.

Schools in communities where diversity of languages and cultures is acknowledged and valued have a different energy about them. Community participation is evident no matter how poor parents might be (see chapters by Mohanty, and Nurmela *et al.*). In one example, at a rural primary school along the Rift Valley in Ethiopia, parents tend mango orchards and return the profits to the school, which in turn builds a community centre providing access, through a TV monitor, for the entire village to major sporting events, including the Soccer World or Africa Cup series and the Olympic Games at which Ethiopian athletes feature prominently. This in turn connects the school, its community, the region, the Ethiopian nation, and the wider global community. In another example, in the Palpa district in Nepal, half the village came to meet us researchers on the steep mountain path leading to the village, with flowers, and most of the villagers, from grandparents to babies only a few weeks old, stayed the whole day at a meeting discussing the plans for their children's education. Parents and grandparents told us how happy they were, being able for the first time to support their children in a school where their knowledge and skills were valued and used as part of the curriculum, in their own language.

There are examples in most chapters in this volume about civil society networks being developed to support MLE and to cooperate with other stakeholders. Students, teachers, elders, parents, teacher trainers, universities, researchers, development agencies and government agencies can cooperate to plan and implement MLE projects (see the chapter about Nepal; see also Panda and Mohanty 2009). They can collect traditional ecological knowledge (TEK) and indigenous knowledge (IK) in general, to be used in teaching and in materials development (see also Hough *et al.* 2009; Panda and Mohanty 2009). As examples, in the Orissa project, the MLE coordinator, Mahendra Kumar Mishra (a former school principal and folklorist) has collected tens of thousands of student essays among tribal students, and TEK and IK have been collected and used on many of their MLE teacher training courses.

In Nepal, the university MLE master's degree has been planned in close cooperation with the MLE programme (described in Nurmela *et al.* in this volume). Yogendra Yadava, the originator of the degree and chair of the Department of Linguistics at Tribhuvan University (and of the Linguistic Survey of Nepal), was very actively involved in the MLE project in several capacities.

Sharing the information and experience gathered in various countries in a South–South dialogue is today much easier than before electronic communication. Earlier, information collected in the South, travelled North. When researchers in an African country needed information from their neighbouring country, they had to go via London. Even today, prices of books prevent most South researchers from keeping up. This book itself is an example of South–South dialogue. Seeing and talking is often better than 'just' reading. The Nepali and Indian projects have, at several levels (teachers, administrators) visited each other and exchanged information and materials – including primary teaching materials and videos about the projects – and some of the Nepali project members have seen films from Peru. Many of the authors in this book have cooperated, exchanged information and materials and, importantly, established contact among the various projects (cf. chapters in Mohanty *et al.* 2009). Benson and Kosonen (this volume) specifically suggest that this kind of networking may encourage bolder steps towards the use of non-dominant languages in South-East Asia. Mazrui (2002) identified this kind of co-operative sharing of expertise and engagement in South–South dialogue as a key strategy to address the education crisis in much of Africa.

The establishment of the really ambitious *National Multilingual Education Resource Consortium* (NMRC) in India, directed by Ajit Mohanty and Minati Panda at Jawaharlal Nehru University, Delhi, (see their Objectives at http://www.nmrc-jnu.org/), is an example of building an optimal networking platform. Over time it will become an international research hub in MLE which also demonstrates co-operative practices at work. The NMRC website gives the most ambitious description we have seen on how to spread awareness, knowledge and practices of MLE. MLE is firmly on the Indian education map; its implementation is being concretised (both in schools and in the form of the centre), and the attachment to one of the most prestigious universities on the subcontinent undergirds the legitimacy of MLE. The vision statement states:

> The NMRC will work towards realizing a broader vision of an inclusive education for equity and excellence that maximizes development of linguistic human resources, respects linguistic human rights, and fosters positive cultural-linguistic identity through development of multilingual proficiency based on a strong foundation of mother tongue development.

The Association for the Development of Education in Africa (ADEA) and the UNESCO Institute of Lifelong Learning collaborate to bring new education research to the attention of the Ministers of Education in Africa every two years. While the Ministers may be slow to take action, the meetings serve a second purpose of strengthening research networks across African countries. One of these, the *African Academy of Languages* (ACALAN, www.acalan.org), with its headquarters in Mali, was until 2010 headed by former Minister of Education in Mali, Adama Samassekou, who was responsible for the implementation of the early-exit bilingual education model, *Pédagogie Convergente*, in Mali. Having noted the research on the benefits of longer term bilingual education he is now actively engaged in persuading governments of the benefits of longer term use of MTE. One of the Board members, Beban Sammy Chumbow from Cameroon is suggesting, after having been a panellist at an *International Hearing on the Harm Done in Schools by the Suppression of the Mother Tongue* (20–24 October 2009, Port Louis, Mauritius, organised by an NGO, *Ledikasyon Pu Travayer*), that ACALAN organise similar hearings all over Africa (for the Findings and Recommendations of the hearing, see www.lalitmauritius.org, 27 Oct. 2009, Documents). These are just a few examples of various kinds of possible support structures and networks.

11.4 To Conclude

Among the recurrent themes emerging from the chapters, we highlight the following. Firstly, we know that successful education of children everywhere requires the MT or the language of the immediate community to be the main language of teaching and learning for many years, and that this is possible even under resource-poor conditions. Secondly, we find that for children in low-income countries, particular attention needs to be paid to quality teacher education where the languages of the teacher and the students are matched. Thirdly, it is now even more clear that children need at least six years of MTM education, preferably longer, and that the longer the MTM schooling the better their prospects of reaching the end of secondary education. Fourthly, materials have to be locally, culturally and contextually anchored; this presupposes mainly local (rather than international 'one size fits all') production of materials, also in dominant languages as subjects. Fifthly, local participation and involvement is key to successful and sustainable bilingual and multilingual education. Sixthly, intercultural education has been found to be essential in both the Peruvian and North American contexts and would add considerable value to other settings. Finally, overly centralised control over education is likely to limit the nurturing of diversity, whereas a combination of both central and decentralised control offers considerable advantage.

What does the future hold? As we write, the face of English is undergoing rapid change. China's entry to the World Trade Organization in 2001 and its subsequent focus on the teaching of English as a foreign language bring unprecedented implications for the role and scale of Englishes in the future. Similar trends in Korea and Japan mean that new varieties of English are emerging rapidly ('Chinglish', 'Japlish', 'Konglish' and so on). Globalisation of English/es advances at an astounding pace. These recent changes (including phenomena like the 'call-centre' industry in India) are resulting in what some observers believe to be an appropriation of English by the East in ways that will advance towards the West (e.g. Lo Bianco 2010). This is a new phenomenon, which requires considerable attention, not explored here; we only want to point towards an implication it has for education in South Asia and Africa. It is no longer 'necessary' for organisations like the British Council to invest in the global expansion of English. This is happening not because of, but despite their efforts.

It is time really to look at the quality and appropriacy of dominant language programmes, particularly English, as these are introduced into school education. The programmes simply can no longer be based on subtractive or early-exit bilingual education: these do not work. They are in conflict with the findings of at least sixty years of research on language acquisition theory and bi/multilingual education. They are also in conflict with the right to mother tongue-medium education. For both of these reasons they are entirely unethical.

In the rapidly diversifying global world, the studies in this volume contribute towards understanding of, working with and working within diversity. Even where the administrative and political apparatuses of power impose serious constraints, dedicated and imaginative people are starting to transform formerly early-exit models into path-breaking longer-term language maintenance programmes, in Burkina Faso and Nepal, truly some of the poorest countries of the world.

The accommodation of diversity through creative responses to contextual challenges is nothing short of remarkable. The MLE initiatives included in this volume are by no means the only ones. We acknowledge the many other important contributions that are made all over the world.

An explicit message of this book is that there are considerable human resources, experience and expertise which reside in those parts of the world often regarded as poor, and largely dysfunctional. We show that the peripheries have something to offer the centre, particularly in the current period of unprecedented change on all fronts. Significant advances in MLE have in fact been made in Africa, South Asia, Latin America, and within marginalised communities in North America and Europe. Each of these contexts separately and collectively demonstrates that the centre of expertise for MLE lies in a new location, which is East and South.

Notes

1 There are many indications that Indigenous peoples (e.g. Handsome Lake, Seneca from the USA, in the mid-1700s, see Thomas 2001) knew the devastating results of submersion programmes. So did churches and educational authorities. There are many examples from the Nordic countries (e.g., in Skutnabb-Kangas and Phillipson 1989). The USA Board of Indian Commissioners also admitted in 1880 that students with MTM teaching were better in English after 3–4 years than those who had had everything in English (see Francis and Reyhner 2002).

2 An Indian government resolution, 1904, when Curzon was Viceroy, expressed serious dissatisfaction with the organisation of education in India, emphasising that English should not be taught as a subject to a child 'until he has made some progress in the primary stages of instruction and has received a thorough grounding in his mother-tongue' and should 'not be prematurely employed as the medium of instruction in other subjects . . . The line of division between the use of the vernacular and of English as a medium of instruction should, broadly speaking, be drawn at a minimum age of 13' (Curzon, cited in Evans 2002: 277–278).

3 There are well-documented examples (e.g. Crawhall 1998) of the kind of shame that speakers of Khoe and San languages, noted for their clicks, are made to feel. They live in the Kalahari desert regions of Southern Africa.

4 See Horton and Freire 1990.

5 In the Further Diploma in Multilingual Education (later, the Advanced Certificate of Education) run by the Project for the Study of Alternative Education in South Africa for the University of Cape Town in the late 1990s.

6 See http://www.unige.ch/eti/recherches/ecole/organisation/departements/dfr/dfr-corps-enseignant/pages-personnelles/francois-grin.html.

7 PISA is 'A three-yearly . . . global assessment that examines the performance of

15-year-olds in key subject areas as well as a wider range of educational outcomes, including students' attitudes to learning and their learning behaviour; collects contextual data from students, parents, schools and systems in order to identify policy levers. Coverage: Representative samples of between 3,500 and 50,000 15-year-old students drawn in each country . . . PISA covers roughly 90% of the world economy'. (http://www.pisa.oecd.org/document/22/0,3343,en_32252351_32236191_42466966_1_1_1_1,00.html#Presentation_of_findings, Presentation).

References

Afolayan, Abebisi (1976). The six-year primary project in Nigeria. In Bamgbose, Ayo (ed.), *Mother Tongue Education: the West African Experience*. Paris: UNESCO Press, 113–134.

Alexander, Neville (2006). Introduction. In *Intergovernmental Conference on Language Policies in Africa. Harare, Zimbabwe, 17–21 March 1997. Final Report*. Paris: UNESCO, Intangible Heritage Section, 9–16.

Alidou, Hassana, Boly, Aliou, Brock-Utne, Birgit, Diallo, Yaya Satina, Heugh, Kathleen and Wolff, H. Ekkehard (2006). *Optimizing Learning and Education in Africa – the Language Factor*. A Stock-taking Research on Mother Tongue and Bilingual Education in Sub-Saharan Africa. Association for the Development of Education in Africa (ADEA). (http://www.adeanet.org/adeaPortal/adea/biennial-2006/doc/document/B3_1_MTBLE_en.pdf).

Crawhall, Nigel (1998). Still invisible: San and Khoe in the new South Africa. *Southern Africa Report Archive*, 13: 3 (http://www.africafiles.org/article.asp?ID=3803).

Cummins, Jim (2009). Fundamental psychological and sociological principles underlying educational success for linguistic minority students. In Skutnabb-Kangas, Tove, Phillipson, Robert, Mohanty, Ajit and Panda, Minati (eds), *Social Justice through Multilingual Education*. Bristol: Multilingual Matters, 19–35.

Evans, Stephen (2002). Macaulay's Minute revisited: Colonial language policy in nineteenth-century India. *Journal of Multilingual and Multicultural Development* 23: 4, 260–281.

Francis, Norbert and Reyhner, Jon (2002). *Language and Literacy Teaching for Indigenous Education. A Bilingual Approach*. Clevedon, UK: Multilingual Matters.

Hancock, Graham (1991). *The Lords of Poverty*. London: Mandarin.

Hanf, Theodor, Amman, Karl, Dias, Patrick V., Fremerey, Michael and Weiland, Heribert (1975). Education: an obstacle to development? Some remarks about the political functions of education in Asia and Africa. *Comparative Education Review*, 19, 68–87.

Heugh, Kathleen (2006). 'Theory and Practice – Language Education Models in Africa: research, design, decision-making, and outcomes'. In Alidou *et al.*, 56–84.

Heugh, Katheen (2010). When a school principal does not believe in the impossible: From multilingual explorations to system-wide assessment. In Cuvelier, Pol, du Plessis, Theo, Meeuwis, Michael, Vanderkerckhove, Reinhild and Webb, Vic (eds), *Multilingualism from Below*. Pretoria: Van Schaik, 117–133.

Horton, Myles and Freire, Paulo (1990). *We Make the Road by Walking*. Philadelphia: Temple University Press.

Hough, David A. and Skutnabb-Kangas, Tove (2005). Beyond good intentions – combating linguistic genocide in education. In *AlterNative – an International Journal of Indigenous Scholarship* 1, 114–135.

Hough, David, Thapa Magar, Ram Bahadur and Yonjan-Tamang, Amrit (2009). Privileging Indigenous Knowledges: Empowering MLE in Nepal. In Mohanty, Ajit, Minati,

Panda, Phillipson, Robert and Skutnabb-Kangas, Tove (eds), *Multilingual Education for Social Justice: Globalising the Local*. New Delhi: Orient Longman, 146–161.

Hussein, Jeylan Wolyie (2010). English supremacy in Ethiopia – autoethnographic reflections. In Heugh, Kathleen and Skutnabb-Kangas, Tove (eds), *Multilingual Education Works. From the Periphery to the Centre*. Hyderabad: Orient BlackSwan, 224–238.

Lo Bianco, Joseph (2010). The struggle to retain diversity in language education. In Liddicoat, Anthony J. and Scarino, Angela (eds), *Languages in Australian Education: Problems, Prospects and Future Directions*. Newcastle, UK: Cambridge Scholars Publishing, 97–108.

Malherbe, E. G. (1946). *The Bilingual School: A Study of Bilingualism in South Africa*. London: Longmans.

Mazrui, Alamin M. (2002). The English language in African education: dependency and decolonization. In Tollefson, James W. (ed.), *Language Policies in Education. Critical Issues*. Mahwah, NJ: Lawrence Erlbaum, 267–281.

MoE (Ministry of Education)/NoE (National Organization for Examinations) (December 2004). *Ethiopian Second National Learning Assessment of Grade 8 Students*. Addis Ababa: MoE.

Mohanty, Ajit, Minati, Panda, Phillipson, Robert and Skutnabb-Kangas, Tove (eds) (2009). *Multilingual Education for Social Justice: Globalising the Local*. New Delhi: Orient Longman.

Nurmela, Iina (forthcoming). Omakielinen opetus monikielisissä kouluissa Nepalissa [Mother tongue-medium teaching in multilingual schools in Nepal].

Odisho, Edward Y. (2004). Assyrian (Aramaic): a recent model for its maintenance and revitalization. In Panaino, A. and Piras, A. (eds), *Melammu Symposia IV*. Milano, 183–196. [ISBN 88-88483-206-3].

Panda, Minati and Mohanty, Ajit (2009). Language matters, so does culture: beyond the rhetoric of culture in Multilingual Education. In Skutnabb-Kangas, Tove, Phillipson, Robert, Mohanty, Ajit and Panda, Minati (eds), *Social Justice through Multilingual Education*. Bristol: Multilingual Matters, 301–319.

Pattanayak, Debi Prasanna (1981). *Multilingualism and Mother-Tongue Education*. Delhi: Oxford University Press.

Pattanayak, Debi Prasanna (1991). *Language, Education and Culture*. Mysore: Central Institute of Indian Languages.

Phillipson, Robert (2009a). Disciplines of English and disciplining by English. *Asian EFL Journal* (electronic). December 2009. (http://www.asian-efl-journal.com/December_2009_rp.php).

Phillipson, Robert (2009b). The tension between linguistic diversity and dominant English. In Skutnabb-Kangas, Tove, Phillipson, Robert, Mohanty, Ajit and Panda, Minati (eds), *Social Justice through Multilingual Education*. Bristol: Multilingual Matters, 85–102.

Phillipson, Robert (2009c). *Linguistic Imperialism Continued*. Delhi: Orient BlackSwan, and New York: Routledge.

Phillipson, Robert and Skutnabb-Kangas, Tove (2009). The politics and policies of language and language teaching. In Long, Mike and Doughty, Catherine (eds), *The Handbook of Language Teaching*. Malden, MA and Oxford, UK: Wiley-Blackwell, 26–41.

Plüddemann, Peter, Mati, Xola and Mahlalela-Thusi, Babazile (2000). *Problems and Possibilities in Multilingual Classrooms in the Western Cape*. PRAESA Occasional Papers No. 2. Cape Town: PRAESA, University of Cape Town.

Ramani, Esther and Joseph, Michael (2002). Breaking new ground: Introducing an African language as medium of instruction at the University of the North. *Perspectives in Education*, 20:1, 233–240.

Skutnabb-Kangas, Tove (2000). *Linguistic Genocide in Education – or Worldwide Diversity and Human Rights?* Mahwah, NJ and London, UK: Lawrence Erlbaum Associates. [also 2008, New Delhi: Orient BlackSwan].

Skutnabb-Kangas, Tove and Fernandes, Desmond (2008). Kurds in Turkey and in (Iraqi) Kurdistan: A comparison of Kurdish educational language policy in two situations of occupation. *Genocide Studies and Prevention* 3:1, 43–73.

Skutnabb-Kangas, Tove and Phillipson, Robert (1989). *Wanted! Linguistic Human Rights*, ROLIG-papir 44. Roskilde: Roskilde University Centre. [Also available on microfiche from ERIC Clearinghouse on Languages and Linguistics, Center for Applied Linguistics, Washington, DC.]

Skutnabb-Kangas, Tove, Phillipson, Robert, Mohanty, Ajit and Panda, Minati (2009). MLE concepts, goals, needs and expense: English for all or achieving justice? In Mohanty, Ajit, Panda, Minati, Phillipson, Robert and Skutnabb-Kangas, Tove (eds), *Multilingual Education for Social Justice: Globalising the Local*. New Delhi: Orient Black-Swan, 313–334.

Taylor, Shelley and Skutnabb-Kangas, Tove (2009). The educational language rights of Kurdish children in Turkey, Denmark and Kurdistan (Iraq). In Ayers, William, Quinn, Teresa and Stovall, David (eds), *Handbook for Social Justice in Education. Section Three, Race and Ethnicity and Seeking Social Justice in Education*, ed. Annette Henry, 171–190.

Thomas, Jacob (Chief), with Terry Boyle (2001) [1994]. *Teachings from the Longhouse*. Toronto: Stoddart.

Widin, Jacqueline (2010). *Illegitimate Practices. Global English Language Education*. Bristol: Multilingual Matters.

Wolff, H. Ekkehard (2006). Background and history – language politics and planning in Africa. In Alidou *et al.*, 26–55.

Wong, Mary Shepard and Canagarajah, Suresh A. (eds) (2009). *Christian and Critical English Language Educators in Dialogue*. New York: Routledge/Taylor & Francis.

ABOUT THE AUTHORS

Lava Deo Awasthi, born in 1959 in the district of Baitadi in the mountain region of Nepal, gained primary education through a non-native tongue, Nepali. He was a dropout in grade 6 and rejoined school after a three-year break. His mother tongue is *Pahadi*, a language with oral tradition, spoken widely in the far west region of Nepal. English is his fourth language in sequence and competence. He has his B.Ed. from Tribhuvan University, Kathmandu, and an MA in Applied Linguistics and TESOL from the University of Leicester, UK and a Ph.D. in language policy and multilingual education from the Danish University of Education, Copenhagen, Denmark. He started his career as a school teacher from his home village. He has worked in different capacities in the Social Welfare Council, District Education Office, Curriculum Development Centre, Higher Secondary Education Board, Primary Teacher Training Centre, Basic and Primary Education Project in the Ministry of Education system. He is a visiting faculty in Kathmandu University and Tribhuvan University. In September 2010, he was appointed Director General, The Department of Education. He has authored a number of books and a dozen articles in language and pedagogy; medium of instruction; education and development; research methodologies; local cosmologies; ethnic studies and indigenizing of knowledge systems. lava.awasthi@gmail.com

Carol Benson is a lecturer and researcher at Stockholm University in Sweden as well as an independent consultant in educational development, specifically on implementation and evaluation of mother tongue-based multilingual education. She holds a Ph.D. in Social Sciences and Comparative Education from the University of California, Los Angeles with specialisations in bilingual education and linguistic anthropology. For the past 25 years she has been involved in educational language policy and practice in Latin America (Bolivia, Guatemala and Mexico), Asia (Laos and Vietnam) and Africa (Angola, Ethiopia, Guinea-Bissau, Mozambique, Niger, Nigeria and South Africa). She is also interested in regional and minority languages in Europe, and has worked in the Spanish Basque Country. Carol's research interests include bridging the gap between research and practice in multilingual education, and analysing connections between language, gender, power and education. carol.benson@upc.su.se

Berhanu Bogale. I was born in 1964 in Ethiopia. I got my first and second degrees from Addis Ababa University. I got my Ph.D. in TEFL from the University of Lancaster (UK) and Addis Ababa University. I have worked as Chairman of the Department of Foreign Languages and Literature, Addis Ababa University, for four years. I have also worked as coordinator of various programmes and as Director of the Continuing Education Programme of Addis Ababa University. Over the past 15 years I have taught various courses at both graduate and undergraduate levels. I have developed three Ph.D. curricula (Applied Linguistics and Development, Applied Linguistics and Communication, and Applied Linguistics and the Teaching of Ethiopian Languages) in which more than 80 Ph.D. candidates are currently enrolled. I have presented papers on different issues and participated in national and international workshops. My research interests include language and development, the role of local languages in education, and group dynamics. bbogale@gmail.com

Mekonnen Alemu Gebre Yohannes (first name: Mekonnen) is an Assistant Professor in Language and Education at Mekelle University in Ethiopia. He graduated with an M.Phil. in Comparative and International Education, from the University of Oslo, Norway. His research interests primarily lie in language in education and development, with a particular focus on understanding how language of instruction can empower or disenfranchise students in multilingual contexts. He has further worked as a national consultant for a study on Medium of instruction in Ethiopia. mekoalegb@yahoo.com

Kathleen Heugh has worked in post-colonial language policy and planning research in African countries, particularly South Africa, since the 1980s. She is a language teacher and researcher who is passionate about effective education with marginalised children. She co-ordinated the National Language Project and edited the *Language Projects' Review* in the late 1980s and joined the Project for the Study of Alternative Education in South Africa at the University of Cape Town from 1993 to 2004. During this time she worked on proposals for multilingual education in South Africa; and in teacher education and training of teacher educators for multilingual education. She participated in various post-apartheid ministerial committees and task groups and was appointed to the first Pan South African Language Board (1996–2001). In 2005 she joined the Human Sciences

Research Council to conduct large-scale research on language education and literacy in sub-Saharan Africa. Between 2005 and 2007 she led several system-wide studies including one in Ethiopia. The focus of all of her work has been the relationship amongst linguistic diversity, language policy and access to equitable educational opportunity. She looks at this nexus through the lenses of school children, classroom teachers, resources, policy, global trends, pressures and the political economy. Kathleen.heugh@unisa.edu.au; http://www.unisanet.unisa.edu.au/staff/homepage.asp?Name=Kathleen.Heugh

Paul Taryam Ilboudo was born in 1949; he holds two DEA (Masters) degrees, one in education and another in linguistics, and is preparing a Ph.D. in linguistics. He started his career as a primary school teacher and then became a second-ary school teacher and later a researcher in applied linguistics and in andragogy. Ilboudo authored and co-authored several publications in adult literacy and in applied linguistics. He conceived and conducted the experimentation of the 48-day intensive adult literacy training strategy and of centres for the continuing edu-cation of neoliterates in the national languages of Burkina Faso. He is a member of the team that conceived and experimented the ALFAA method (a method for the teaching/learning of the French language taking into consideration the com-petence of learners as literates in the national languages), and later he participated actively in the conception, experimentation and implementation of the mother tongue-medium education model in Burkina Faso. Paul Taryam Ilboudo is the representative of OSEO, the Swiss Labour Assistance in Burkina Faso since 1991. paultaryam@yahoo.fr

Ahmed Kabel teaches at the Center for Academic Development at Al Akhwayn University in Ifrane, Morocco. His work is largely in the area of English applied linguistics and language policy. He has published articles on the cultural politics of the global spread of English, native-speakerism, and stereotyping, racism and ideology in English applied linguistics. Additionally, his research interests also include language and educational policy in Morocco and the Maghreb, which is the focus of his work in progress. a.kabel@aui.ma; Ahmedkabel@gmail.com

Kimmo Kosonen is a consultant for multilingual education with SIL Interna-tional as well as a lecturer and researcher at Payap University in Thailand. He has been based in Chiang Mai, Thailand since 2003. He holds a Ph.D. in Education from University of Joensuu, Finland, with a specialisation on basic education in low-income countries. He has conducted research in South-East and South Asia, as well as taught in universities in Thailand and Finland. Kimmo is also con-sulted by agencies such as SEAMEO, UNESCO and UNICEF on language-in-education issues and advocacy for multilingual education. His research interests include multilingual and non-formal education in low-income countries, lan-guage planning, language policy, and minority language development. He has

also published articles, book chapters and monographs on these topics. kimmo_
kosonen@sil.org

Teresa L. McCarty is the Alice Wiley Snell Professor of Education Policy Studies
and Professor of Applied Linguistics at Arizona State University. She has worked
for 30 years with Indigenous communities throughout North America. Her
recent books include *A Place To Be Navajo – Rough Rock and the Struggle for Self-
Determination in Indigenous Schooling* (2002); *Language, Literacy, and Power in Schooling* (2005); *One Voice, Many Voices – Recreating Indigenous Language Communities*
(with O. Zepeda, 2006); *'To Remain an Indian': Lessons in Democracy from a Century of Native American Education* (with K. T. Lomawaima, 2006), and *Ethnography
and Language Policy* (2011). She lives in Phoenix, Arizona with her husband, John
Martin, and has two young grandchildren. Teresa.McCarty@asu.edu

Ajit Mohanty is a Professor of Psychology (and former Chairperson) at the Zakir
Husain Centre for Educational Studies, Jawaharlal Nehru University, New Delhi.
He has published over 100 papers in the areas of psycholinguistics, multilingual-
ism and multilingual education focusing on education, poverty and disadvantage
among linguistic minorities. He was a Fulbright Visiting Professor in Columbia
University, New York, Fulbright Senior Scholar (University of Wisconsin), Kil-
lam Scholar (University of Alberta), Senior Fellow (Central Institute of Indian
Languages) and Visiting Scholar (Universities of Geneva and Chicago). His recent
book *Multilingual Education for Social Justice* (Mohanty, Panda, Phillipson and
Skutnabb-Kangas: editors) was published by Orient BlackSwan (also an international edition by Multilingual Matters, UK). His other books include *Bilingualism
in a Multilingual Society, Psychology of Poverty and Disadvantage* and *Perspectives on
Indigenous Psychology* (co-editor: G. Misra). He teaches M.Phil. level courses on
Multilingualism and Education in India in his Centre and the Centre for Linguistics
and directs two International Projects – *From Mother Tongue to Other Tongue* and
the *National Multilingual Education Resource Consortium* (www.nmrc-jnu.org) – at
JNU. In 2009 he was an International Consultant to Governments of Finland and
Nepal developing a Multilingual Education Policy and Strategy document for
Nepal (along with Tove Skutnabb-Kangas). ajitmohanty@gmail.com

Norbert Nikièma is Professor of linguistics at the University of Ouagadougou,
Burkina Faso, where he got a B.A. in English before getting an M.A. and a Ph.D.
in linguistics, respectively, from Ohio University, Athens, and Indiana University, Bloomington, USA. Besides descriptive linguistics (focusing on Mòoré
among the Gur languages), he has been actively involved in workshops, seminars,
consultancy and publication on language-in-education issues (the use of African
languages in non-formal and formal education, mother tongue and multilingual
education), the empowerment of languages for new functions (writing dictionaries and practical grammars, the development of orthographies, the creation of

neologisms) and the creation of synergy between adult literacy, non-formal and formal education. The focus of his research and applications in education has been on Burkina Faso among the so-called francophone countries. norbert.nikiema@ univ-ouaga.bf; nikiema.norbert@gmail.com

Iina Nurmela started her career working with second language teaching and newly arrived immigrant children in Finland. She worked for two years in Nepal to support the development of mother tongue-based multilingual education in the Multilingual Education Programme. Currently she is working as a primary school teacher in European schooling. Iina has an M.Ed. in International Education from the University of Oulu, Finland. iina.nurmela@gmail.com

Adama Ouane is Director of the UNESCO Institute for Lifelong Learning (UIL) in Hamburg. He was the Director of the UNESCO Institute for Education (UIE) in Hamburg from 2000 until its closure in June 2006 and transformation into the UIL. 1995–1999 he was Senior Programme Specialist as well as leading specialist responsible for literacy, adult education, non-formal and basic education at UNESCO Headquarters in Paris. 1977–1982 he was Deputy National Director-General for Literacy, Adult Education and Applied Linguistics in Mali, Professor at the École Normale Supérieure in Bamako and Consultant to UNICEF, UNDP, the Agence de la Francophonie and The World Bank. Dr Ouane has been the main author of a number of major education papers and reports prepared by UNESCO and has published many books and papers dealing with literacy, post-literacy and continuing education, adult and lifelong learning, mother tongue and multilingual education. He was Executive Editor of the world's longest-running, international journal of comparative education, the *International Review of Education* 1985–1987. He coordinated the UNESCO NGO/Civil Society Consultation on Literacy and Adult Education and has organised major events around the world to promote adult education at policy and professional levels. In 2008 he was admitted as Member of the Hall of Fame for International Adult and Continuing Education. Having been one of the key organisers of the Fifth International Conference on Adult Education (CONFINTEA V) he had full responsibility for preparing and conducting CONFINTEA VI. a.ouane@unesco.org

Susanne Pérez Jacobsen worked for several years in Peru where she trained Indigenous teachers in Intercultural Bilingual Education and also learnt to speak and write the Indigenous language Quechua. Lately she has worked in Denmark in the Copenhagen Resource Centre for bilingualism and interculturality which trains teachers and does research on immigrants in the Danish education system. Currently she is teaching young immigrants and refugees in a Danish secondary school and developing second language educational materials for natural sciences subjects. Her research and teaching focus on the relationship between formal education and cultural and linguistic minority groups: Keywords: bilingual education, multicultural education, intercultural pedagogy, intercultural state policies, minority rights, indigenous cosmologies. She has written articles about Intercultural Bilingual Education in Peru and about immigrant pupils in the Danish school system. Susanne has an MA in Education and Intercultural Studies from Roskilde University, Denmark. As a member of the Danish minority in Germany, she grew up with Danish and German as her mother tongues. Spanish has become her third home language which she speaks with her husband and children. susanneperez@gmail.com

Tove Skutnabb-Kangas has been actively involved with minorities' struggles for language rights for the last five decades. Main research interests: linguistic human rights, linguistic genocide, linguicism, multilingual education, the subtractive spread of English, the relationship between linguistic and cultural diversity and biodiversity. Her books and articles have appeared in 46 languages. Some books in English: *Bilingualism or Not – the Education of Minorities* (1984); *Minority Education: from Shame to Struggle*, ed. with Jim Cummins (1988); *Linguistic Human Rights. Overcoming Linguistic Discrimination*, ed. with Robert Phillipson (1994); *Language: A Right and a Resource. Approaching Linguistic Human Rights*, ed. with Miklós Kontra, R. P. and Tibor Várady (1999); *Linguistic Genocide in Education – or Worldwide Diversity and Human Rights?* (2000); *Sharing a World of Difference. The Earth's Linguistic, Cultural, and Biological Diversity* (with Luisa Maffi and David Harmon, 2003), *Imagining Multilingual Schools: Language in Education and Glocalization*, ed. with Ofelia García and María Torres-Guzmán (2006), *Social Justice Through Multilingual Education* (2009), ed. with R. P., Ajit Mohanty and Minati Panda, and *Indigenous Children's Education as Linguistic Genocide and a Crime Against Humanity? A Global View* (2010, with Robert Dunbar). Tove lives on a small ecological/organic farm in Denmark with husband Robert Phillipson. For more, see www.Tove-Skutnabb-Kangas.org; skutnabbkangas@gmail.com

Shelley K. Taylor is an Associate Professor of Applied Linguistics in the Faculty of Education at the University of Western Ontario, Canada. She has extensive second language research and teaching experience, and is herself multilingual. Her research has focused on child tri-/multilinguals in bilingual education programmes designed with other target populations in mind; programmes that have not made the changes necessary to support the growing linguistic diversity within them. These studies have involved ethnic Kurdish children schooled in Denmark, and aboriginal and immigrant (allophone) children enrolled in French immersion programmes in various Canadian provinces. More recently, she conducted consultancies in Nepal related to national efforts to introduce L1-based instruction in all Indigenous and minority children's L1s in accordance with Nepal's constitution. As such, her work has long focused on how language policy and planning plays out in the education of children from (relatively) powerless groups. She recently co-edited a Special Issue of the *International Journal of Bilingual Education* *and Bilingualism* on the topic of overcoming (macro/micro) constraints in the development of multilingualism. tayshelley@gmail.com

Lucy Trapnell Forero became interested in school education in indigenous contexts while developing her Anthropology thesis in Ashaninka communities in the Central Amazon. This led her to study education and to become actively involved in the design, application and evaluation of teacher training intercultural bilingual programmes. She was one of the founders of the FORMABIAP Teacher Training Programme for Intercultural Bilingual Education in the Amazon Basin which the indigenous confederation AIDESEP and the Loreto state teacher training college develop since 1988. She has also been an active promoter of the Decentralized Teacher Training Programme that the Universidad Nacional Mayor de San Marcos develops with the Regional Organisation of Indigenous People of the Central Amazon, where she currently works as a Professor. Trapnell has been involved in various research initiatives regarding intercultural bilingual education in elementary and primary education and has written extensively about intercultural bilingual education in Peru. She has also coauthored educational materials for bilingual schools with Indigenous teachers and elders. Trapnell's research interests include examining curriculum issues and intercultural approaches in Indigenous school contexts. She is presently involved in the RINEIB International Network for Research in Intercultural and Intercultural Bilingual Education. Her most recent book is *Interculturalism, Knowledge and Power.* tsirapa@hotmail.com

INDEX

Abbi, A. 179
access to education 22, 52, 69, 93
Addis Ababa 40–1, 50, 56, 240, 242, 244–55
additive language learning xvi–xvii, 15, 69–71, 77, 165, 181, 202, 209, 265
Adivasi Janajati 174n^{18}
adult literacy 20–1, 128, 131, 198–9
Afan Oromo 34, 40–4, 54, 56–7, 126, 131, 241
Afar 38, 42–3, 51, 56–7, 241, 24–7, 249, 250–51, 255
African Academy of Languages (ACALAN), Mali 275, 278
Alaska Natives 64–5
Alidou, H. 193
Amazigh/Berber 217–26, 228, 234, 235n^1; attitudes towards education in 234; implementation of 232–3; standardisation of 227–31
Amazonas Regional Education Project 100–2
Amazonian Indigenous languages 87–9, 95
Amazonian Kichwa 94
American Indians 64–5
Amhara 38, 41, 47, 50, 56, 240, 242, 244–5, 247–9, 251–3, 257
Amharic: as a national language 44–5, 140, 241, 248, 258; as a second language 32, 48, 57–8, 248–50
Anaya, J. 161
Anderson, B. 222

Andhra Pradesh 145–6, 148
Anguak 42, 44
Annamalai, E. 179
Arabic 217–20, 222, 235, 273; as medium of instruction, 223–4
Arabisation 220–5
Ashaninka 87, 89, 94
assessment: in Nepal, 164; language of 164, 209; system-wide, in Ethiopia 33, 39–4, 56–9 239, 242–50, 254–59
assimilation 16, 66, 89, 123
Association for the Development of Education in Africa (ADEA) 6, 38, 278
Association Tin Tua 201, 210
Athapaharia Rai1 59, 186
attitudes towards mother tongue-medium education; dominant language, negative effects of 52–4, 126, 169, 171–3; feelings of shame or inadequacyof mother tongue 223, 234, 271; scepticism 37, 43 200; Soviet influence 131; by teachers 63, 188, 275; see also mathematics subjects; misconceptions about languages and learning; power relationships among languages and people; science subjects
attrition rates: effect of MLE on 187, 192, 274; as indicator of failed policies 70; see also drop out rates; repeater rates; retention rates

Awajun 87, 89
Awasthi, L. D. 155, 274
Ayacucho 100–2
Aymara 86, 87, 89, 94–5

Baetens Beardsmore, H. 179
Baker, C. 78
Bangladesh 140
Banma nuara 1 (CBN1) formulas 210
Basic Interpersonal Communication Skills
  (BICS) 105, 182, 193n^5
Beaulieu, D. 76
Bengali 140, 164
Benishangul 245, 247
Benishangul Gumuz 40, 42–4, 56–7, 240,
  248–9, 251, 255, 258
Benson, C. 128, 181
Berber *see* Amazigh/Berber
Berber Decree 226–7
Berbers 219, 227, 229
Berdouzi, M. 225
Bhutan 140
bilingual-bicultural education, 68–70,
  76–7
bi/multilingualism 2, 13–14, 154, 179–82
bi/multilingual education 23, 182,
  193; and bilingual teachers 92; and
  educationalachievement 69, 73, 182,
  210, 251; basis for learning other
  languages 54, 74, 76, 157, 264; *see also*
  language-learning models; medium
  of instruction (MOI); mother tongue
  medium (MTM) education; non-
  formal education
bi/multilingualism 5, 89, 181 attitudes
  towards 4, 13, 23, 271; additive
  69–70, 77; 209, subtractive 78; *see also*
  multiculturalism
Bogale, B. 4
Boukous, A. 228
Buckner, E. 232
Burkina Faso: *Alphabétisation-Formation
  Intensive pour le Développement*
  (AFI-D) 207; Constitution 198;
  Laws of Orientation of Education
  (LOE) 1996 and 2007, 200, 210;
  linguistic diversity 97; ministries
  ofeducation 200, 203, 211–12; non-
  formal education 198, 207; *Office
  National pour l'Éducation Permanente et
  l'Alphabétisation Fonctionnelle et Sélective*
  (ONEPAFS)199; Upper-Volta–
  UNESCO project 198

Cognitive Academic Language Proficiency
  (CALP) 191, 193
Cambodia 113, 115, 121; Education
  Law (2007) 128; Highland Children's
  Education Project 129; linguistic
  diversity 12, 113; ministries of
  education 121, 129
CARE International 121, 129
Castagno, A. 76
Catholic Church in Burkina Faso 203,
  213
centralisation of decision-making and
  policy implementation 121, 126;
  231–2, 234, 267
Cham 128
Chumbow, B. S. 278
citizenship, participatory 1, 24, 67, 264
civil society organisations 267, 277
classrooms: homogenisation of 184–6, 191
  interaction in 43; sizes 187–8, 233;
Classical Arabic 217–18
Cognitive Academic Language Proficiency
  (CALP) 105, 182
colonisation and subjugation 80n^1;
  in Africa 54–5; legacy 220, 267;
  in Morocco235$n^{2, 4}$; in North
  America 66, 75; in Peru 85, 87, 97
Commission Nationale des Langues
  Voltaïques 198
communicative language teaching 46
communism 114–15
community participation 15, 102,128,
  202, 255; in curriculum 125, 129; in
  decision-making 76, 129, 130–1, 203,
  267; in intercultural education 276–7,
  in Nepal 165–6; in the United
  States 74, 79; *see also* decentralisation
completion rates 208; primary school 2,
  199; secondary school 21, 252; *see also*
  drop out rates
Conference of Ministers in charge of
  education in 'Francophone Africa'
  (CONFEMEN) 209
constitutions: Burkina Faso 198; Ethiopia
  ix, 22, 34–5, 91; India 22, 142, 267;
  Lao 119; Morocco 220; Nepal 9, 15,
  155–6, 181, 183, 267; South Africa 22;
  United States 67; Vietnam 120; *see
  also* legislation
contextual factors 21, 75, 104, 131, 178,
  181, 264; in Ethiopia 241–2, 246; in
  Nepal 192; in Peru 105–6; for success
  of mother tongue medium 254–5

Continuous Assessment System
(CAS) 164
Cooper, R. L. 229
coordinate bilingual instruction 68
critical indigenous pedagogy 183, 188–9
culturally based education 76, 79; *see also*
intercultural bilingual education (IBE)
Cummins J. 105, 182, 191
curriculum: development of, in mother
tongue 73, 90, 101–2, 125, 129,
156,162, 168–9, 202–3, 231–3
Cusco Regional Education Project 100–2

Dakar Framework for Action 152
Dalit 152
Dalle, I. 223
Davies, A. 173n^{14}
decentralisation 98–103, 124–30, 267–8,
276; benefits of 50, 56, 234–5; in
Ethiopia 33, 36, 49–51, 56, 58, 124,
126, 240; and local participation 198;
and materials development 50–1;
risks 50, 56, 125–7
Demmert, W. G. 79
Dergue 35
Dhankuta 159, 186
dialects 114, 116, 226–8, 244
diglossia 224, 229, 231
Dire Dawa 41, 56, 242, 244, 245, 247,
249–50, 251
dominant languages 13, 78, 139, 183;
competence in 129; and loss of
languages 16, 114, 154–5; negative
effects on school achievement 35, 114–
15, 122, 142, 146, 183, 199; pressure
towards 104, 269–70; *see also* medium
of instruction; power relationships
among languages and people
Dravidian languages 151
drop out rates 19, 173n^8; in Burkina
Faso 198–9, 206, 208; among
indigenous youth 23; among Native
American Indian students 65, 79; in
Nepal 144, 155, 187
Dutcher, N. 71

early exit transitional bilingual model
89–90, 146, 201, 210, 212n^4, 278;
inadequacy of 172, 267–8, 273, 279
Economic Commission for Latin America
and the Caribbean (ECLAC) 21
economic viabilityof mother tongue
education 4, 56–8, 160, 191, 203,

212n^3, 188, 274
Educated Moroccan Arabic 224
Education for All (EFA) (2004–2009) *vii,*
152, 156, 207, 266; in Laos 119; in
Nepal, 152, 156–7, 171
Edwards, V. 105
EFA National Plan of Action (2001),
Nepal 152, 156
Elbiad, M. 224
endangered and extinct languages 14,
16, 62, 65–7, 86, 101, 151; *see also*
revitalization of ancestral languages
English: attitudes towards 256–7; as a
dominant language 75, 78, 139–41,
143, 148, 246, 254; in Ethiopia 34–5,
37–8, 42, 48, 52, 57, 122, 247, 252,
256; as a global language 33, 54–5,
47, 58, 66, 122, 139, 141, 270, 279; as
medium of instruction 37–8, 130, 270;
negative effects of 37, 42, 47–8, 52–9,
66, 248, 256–7; pressure towards 54–6;
proficiency in proficiency 73–9, 119,
122, 141, 173n^{14}; 256; as a second
language 54, 57, 72, 74; as a subject 33,
58, 141, 160; in teacher education 46;
unrealistic expectations of 53–5, 144
English Language Improvement
Programme (ELIP) 38, 46, 55, 122,
244, 250, 256–8
Ennaji, M. 224, 225
enrolment rates 19–21; in Ethiopia 36,
252; in primary school 35–36, 156; in
secondary school 20
Eritrea 49
Errihani, M. 231, 234
ethics of intervention 268–9
Ethiopia; Constitution ix, 22, 34–5,
91; Dergue 35; Education and
Training Policy 63; English Language
Improvement Programme (ELIP)
38, 46, 55, 122, 244, 250, 256–8;
Languages Resource Centre (ELRC)
51; language policies 119, 129–30,
266, 275; linguistic diversity 62; major
languages 32–4, 45, 122, 143; Ministry
of Education 36, 38–9, 53 122, 240,
245, 250, 255, 267, 272; People's
Revolutionary Democratic Front
(EPRDF) 35; Regional Education
Bureaus 36, 49–51, 246; relationship
with Britain 37–8; systemic
assessment 243, 247–8, 266, 272;
Transitional Government 35

Ethiopian Languages Resource Centre
(ELRC) 51
ethnolinguistic classification, 113–15;
Soviet system 131
European School MLE model 179, 181,
185

Fardon, R. 14
Fettes, M. 62
Fillerup, M. 74
Finland 183, 188
FoKn approach 189–90
formal education 11, 18, 127–9, 199–201,
207–8, 263; see also non-formal
education
four-language formula 13, 143, 179–80
Freinet, C. 189–90
French1 98–201, 207,209–10, 217, 220–5
funds of knowledge (FoKn) approach to
MLE teaching, 188

Gambella 40, 42, 44–5, 47, 56, 244–5,
247, 249–50, 255
Gamo 34, 50
García, O. 180
Gebre Yohannes, M. A. 4, 46,242, 250
gender disparities in education 20, 36,
198, 241, 252; and instruction in
unfamiliar language 55, 59, 230
George, E. 37
globalisation 1, 66, 225; languages of 33,
47, 55, 66, 141, 224, 270
Grin, F. 274
Gulmancema 201, 210
Gumuz 43, 245, 247
Gurung, O. 173n^4

Halaoui, N. 213
Hammoud 223–4
Hancock, G. 268–9
Harari 39, 44–7, 49–51, 56, 242, 244–9,
253
Harmon, D. 12
Hartley, E. 70–1
Hawaii 72–3
heritage language revitalization 2, 68,
71–7, 97, 101, 166
heterogeneous vs homogenous classrooms:
in Navajo schools 95; in Nepal 185,
187, 192; single- vs multi-grade
classrooms, 192
Heugh, K. 63, 69, 79, 119, 122, 124,
126, 141, 144, 182; contextual factors

in MLE 75–6; economic viability
of MLE 4, 33, 148, 178, 180, 188;
negative effect of English 122, 126,
141
Hill, R. 76
Hindi 13, 139, 140–3, 148
Hinton, L. 72
HIV-AIDS 18, 20
Holm, A. 68–9
Holm, W. 68–9, 74, 80
Hough, D. A. 183, 189, 269
Human Development Index 15–21
human rights 22, 26–7n^{15}, 153–4, 161,
273; access to quality education 21–2;
linguistic 24, 138, 182–3, 187, 272–3;
see also language rights
Hussein, J.W. 257, 258–9, 270

identity: and culture 73, 97, 102, 225;
and language 139–41, 220, 222, 225,
227, 229
ideologies 13, 115, 154, 226, 272
Ilboudo, P.T. 206
Ile-Ife Six-Year Primary project,
Nigeria 267
Iloilo project, Philippines 267
immersion programmes xvi–xvii, 70–9:
teacher education Hawaii 72–3, 79
implementation and planning see policy
implementation and planning
Index of Linguistic Diversity 12
India: Anthropological Survey 148;
Constitution 142; language-in-
education policy, lack of 139;
Language and Indigenous Resource
Centres 174n^{17}; National Knowledge
Commission 142; National
Multilingual Education Resource
Consortium (NMRC), in India 146,
174n^{17}; 278; Right of Children to
Free and Compulsory Education
Act 2009, 143; three-language
formula 179, 141–3, 148n^2
indigenous peoples xv, 21, 23, 25n^7,
85, 90–1, 93, 97; 103–4, 144, 148n^1,
153; access to education 174n^{18};
completion of secondary education 21;
knowledge 9–8, 145, 159, 165–6,
188–90, 277; languages 141, 143, 166,
169, rights 23; sovereignty 80n^1, 85,
97; ways of learning and teaching
105–6; see also country names and
languages, minorities

inequality: within countries 16–19, 21
Institut Royal de la Culture Amazighe (IRCAM) 226–7, 231–2
Interamerican Development Bank 98
intercultural bilingual education (IBE) 73–75, 90–91, 102–5
intercultural education 90–2, 102, 276
International Cooperation for Cambodia (ICC) 121
International Hearing on the Harm Done in Schools by the Suppression of the Mother Tongue 173 n^{11}, 278
International Labour Organisation, *Convention No. 169 on Indigenous and Tribal Peoples* 27n^{15}, 91, 153, 173n^4
international languages, pressure towards 15, 46–7, 63, 122, 224, 248, 251, 256, 269–71

Jagat Sundar Bhownekuthi school 171
J'rai 120, 128
Jessner's model of multilingualism 181–2
Jhapa 159, 162, 164, 184, 186
Johnson, F.T. 74
Jula 198, 200, 205, 212n^1

Kabyle activists 226–7
Kahuawaiola Indigenous Teacher Education Program 79
Kanchanpu 159, 164, 186
Kano, H. 208
Kendriya Vidyalaya (Central School) system 142
Khmer 113, 115–16, 120, 128
Kinh 114–15
Korgho, A. 203
Kosonen, K. 122
Kui 13, 145
Kurdistan 273

language acquisition 5; first (L1) 112, 120, 180–1 (*see also* language recovery); second (L2) 5, 54, 130, 148n^4, 180–1, 265; third 130, 148n^4; *see also* language-learning models
language development: 9; Burkina Faso 198–9; in Ethiopia 43–4, 48–51, 58, 122, 140, 240, 258; in Morocco 226–31; in Southeast Asia 115; *see also* curriculum development; materials development; standardisation of languages; writing systems

language-learning models viii, 23, 40, 118, 181, 201, 254–5, 273, 278; additive xvi–xvii, 15, 69–71, 77, 165, 181, 202, 209, 265; *Banmanuara* 1 (CBN1) 210; early exit 172, 201, 210, 212, 273; effectiveness of 6, 251; Ethiopia 4, 33, 240–1, 251, 254–5; European Schools MLE model 179, 181, 185; external imposition 268; immersion 74; intercultural 97; late-exit 148, 273; maintenace 77, 90, 93; MEBA-OSEO formula 197, 203, 205, 210–11; MLE 146, 158–62, 171–2, 173n^{15}, 185–8; subtractive xvii, 4, 77, 146, 170, 266, 279; three language formula 13, 141n^2, 142–3, 148, 179, 148n^2; *see also name of programme*
language planning 33; Amazigh/Berber 231; decentralised 267–8; in Ethiopia 33, 244, 248, 256; inMorocco 223, 226, 228, 230–1; in Native North America 62; in Nepal 161; in Peru 90, 160; local 33, 79, 80, 172; local and regional, in Peru 93, 99–100, 102; national 33; *see also* reverse planning
language policies: for assimilation 66, 271; in Burkina Faso 7–9; and decentralisation 49; in Ethiopia 48–50, 91, 244, 256; in India, 141; and maintenance of linguistic diversity 138; in Nepal 152–6; in Peru 90–1, 93, 98–102, 104; in Thailand 121; in the United States 66–8, 75, 80n^2; in Vietnam 130
language recovery 2, 62, 68, 71–7, 76, 97, 101, 166
language rights 26–7n^{15}, 63, 130, 143
languages of wider communication 6, 45, 54, 62–3, 224, 234, 241, 270
Lao 112, 116, 119
Laos 113, 115, 125–6; Constitution, 119; Education for All (EFA) plan, 119; National Socio-Economic Development Plan (NESDP) 119; People's Revolutionary Party, 120
late-exit model of language learning; success of 144, 148, 273
legislation: Burkino Faso, 210; Cambodia 128; India 143; international 25n^7, 143; United States: Hawaii Apology Act 1993 80$n^{1, 2}$; Peru: 90–1

Lewin, K. 252
Lewis, G. E. 233
Lewis, M. P. 113
lingua francas 14, 25n^8; Arabic 218;
    Afrikaans 45; Amharic 32, 34, 44;
    English 166; Jula, 198; Quecha 87;
    Russian 114
linguistic diversity 12–13, 16, 26n^{10}, 138;
    in Burkina Faso 97; in Cambodia 12,
    113; endangered languages 14, 16,
    62, 67, 86, 138; in Ethiopia 12;
    in India 12–13; in Morocco 12;
    in Native North America 62; in
    Nepal 13, 151, 154, 164, 184; in
    Papua New Guinea 127; in Peru 12,
    86–9; in Southeast Asia 113–14; see
    also language recovery, standardisation
    of languages
linguistic human rights 24, 138, 182–3,
    187, 272–3
literacy 19–21, 35, 58; 71, 152, 167–8,
    207; bi-literacy 69, 76–7; medium
    of instruction 263–4; non-formal
    education programmes for 198–9, 207;
    in mother tongue 94–5, 199, 264; in
    Nepal1 51–2, 166, 168–9; transfer
    across writing systems 116–17; in Viet
    Nam 152; see also under oracy
literary tradition: effect on culture 168
longitudinal evaluation of mother tongue
    medium education: in Ethiopia,
    240–55, 259n^1; in Navajo children 70
Lopez, L. E. 96, 105
Loreto Regional Education Project 100–2

Magar 166
Mahidol University 121: Research
    Institute for Languages and Cultures of
    Asia, Bangkok 115
maintenance-cum-development model of
    language learning 90, 93, 97
Maithili 162, 186
Manokotak 70–1
materials development 276; and
    decentralisation 56, 159; in
    Ethiopia 50–1, 250; in Nepal 159–60,
    162, 165, 169, 172, 184, 188–90, 192;
    in North America 68, 71; in Peru
    94–5, 105; use of indigenous
    knowledge in 159–60, 277; in
    Vietnam 115
mathematics subjects: expression of
    concepts in mother tongue 44, 69, 94,

104; international language, 46, 50,
    256; language for 37, 40–1, 43–4, 52–
    3, 104, 210, 243–4, 246–8, 251, 254,
    256; and years of MTM education 40,
    50, 104, 244, 246–8, 254, 265
May, S. 76
Mazrui, A. M. 4, 278
McCarty, T. L. 63, 75
MEBA-OSEO formula 197, 203, 205,
    210–11
models of teacher training: in-service 38;
    immersion 79; see also name of model
Moll, L. C. 188–9
medium of instruction (MOI); and
    communication in the classroom 94,
    155, 258; dominant language, negative
    effects on non-native speakers 155;
    foreign language 246; mother
    tongue 193n^4; teachers' language
    proficiency 44–6; for teacher
    education 40–1, 46, 53, 57, 250,
    274; see also nameoflanguage; attitudes;
    transition to dominant language
metalinguistic awareness 72, 148, 181
Ministry of Educationseeunder country name
minorities 25n^7, 148n^1; access to
    education 155; literacy rates 152; as
    mother tongue teachers 92–3, 97, 104,
    129, 145; submersion education 145;
    see also indigenous peoples
minority languages: see endangered and
    extinct languages; non-dominant
    languages
misconceptions about languages and
    learning 53–4, 104–5, 122–3, 126,
    157, 178
Mishra, M. K. 277
models of language learning; seelanguage-
    learning models
Modern Standard Arabic 217–18
Mohanty, A. K. 140, 144, 174n^{17}
Molle Molle community (Cusco) 93
Moll, L. C. 188, 189
monoculturalism 78, 99
monolingual policies and practices 155
monolingual vs multilingual
    classrooms 184–5, 186, 191
Mòoré 200–2, 205
Moroccan Arabic 217–220, 223–4
Morocco: Charter for Educational
    Reform, 221–2, 224;
    Constitution 220; curriculum
    development 231; *Institut Royal de la*

Culture Amazighe (IRCAM) 222; King Hassan II, 226; King Mohammed VI, 226; medium of instruction 224; Ministry of Education 223, 226, 231–2; national languages 220–1

mother tongue vii, xvi, 71–2; as academic language 41, 44, 57, 69, 104, 169; attitudes towards 43–4, 94, 199–200, 209, 233, 271, 274; and identity 14, 24, 72, 74, 64, 141; and literacy 116; oracy skills in 191; as a second language 71, as a subject xvi, 71–2, 76, 78, 90, 146, 170; at university level 170

mother tongue-based multilingual education (MLE) xv–xvi, 2–5, 22, 265; and access to education 145; awareness raising 162–3; benefits of 43, 69, 71, 274; conditions for success 182, 265, 273, 276, 279; and culture 159; and diversity 271–2; economic viability 4, 56–8, 160, 188, 191, 203, 212n³, 274; effect on attrition rates 192; as a human right 21–24; misconceptions about 122–3, 157, 178; multi- vs single-gradeclassrooms 186, 191; success of 266, 171; *see also* language-learning models; mother tongue medium (MTM) education; pedagogy

mother tongue medium (MTM) education 15, 22: benefits of 43, 69, 71, 274; conditions forsuccess 182, 265, 273, 276, 279; duration as first language of instruction 40–1, 76, 241–55, 257, 259n⁹, 265; and educational achievement 69, 71, 74, 85, 130, 203, 207, 249, 251–6; evidence for success 254–5; Soviet approachto 114; support for learning other languages 54, 74, 76, 119, 157, 264; teacher speakers of mother tongues 44, 160, 162, 164; *see also name of language, specific subject*

multilingual education: principles for 51, 126, 181–2, 264; *see also* language-learning models; mother tongue-based multilingual education (MLE)

multilingualism 24, 35, 154, 179–81: attitudes towards13

multilingual-multicultural education 72, 73

Myanmar 115

national/nationality languages: choice of script 116–17, 198–9; effects on linguistic minorities 183; and identity 140, 222; in multilingual education 3, 205; as medium of instruction 207, 255; instead of mother tongue 247, 249–50

Native American languages 62, 64–6, 71–7

Navajo 66, 68–9

Navajo Bureau of Indian Affairs (BIA) schools 68

Nāwahīokalaniʻōpuʻu Laboratory School 72

Nepal 139, 151, 274–5, 277; Education for All 2004–2009 Sector Program 156, 157; EFA National Plan of Action (2001–15), 156; ethnic, social and linguistic diversity 151–2, 170, 184; governments 183; Interim Constitution 2007, 9, 152, 155–6, 183, 267; Jagat Sundar Bhownekuthi school 171; MLE Implementation Guidelines 162–3; Multilingual Education Programme 2006–2009, 158–9; National Centre for Educational Development (NCED) 162–3, 184, 192; National Curriculum Framework 156; National Language Policy Recommendation Commission, Nepal 155

Nepali: as dominant language 139–40, 154–5, 160, 162, 170, 183; as a second language 169–70

New Zealand 76

Nigeria: Ile-Ife Six-Year Primary project 42, 44–5, 49, 254

non-dominant languages 112, 119–21, 123–5; 127–8

non-formal education (NFE) in mother tongue 127–8, 131, 198–9

Nurmela, I. 268, 275

oracy: and oral traditions 27, 67, 78, 166–9, 170, 191, 202; skills of 191

Orissa 144–6, 148

Oriya 13, 141, 145–6

Oromiya 38, 40–1, 44–5, 48, 51, 53–4, 56–7, 126, 240, 242, 244–5, 247, 249, 252–3, 256

orthographic development 116–17, 121, 131, 226; in Burkina Faso 198–9, in Cambodia 128; in Morocco 226; *see also* scripts

Oeuvre Suisse d'entraide ouvrière (Swiss Labour Assistance) (OSEO) 197, 201, 203, 205, 210–12
Orwell, G. 235
OSEO 203

Pakistan 139, 140
Panda, M. 141, 143, 146
Papua New Guinea 14, 16, 17, 127–8, 208
parental involvement 74–6, 95, 202, 208; see also community participation
participatory pedagogy 188
Patani Malay 117, 121, 125
Pattanayak, D. P. 13, 14, 271–2
Payap University, Linguistics Institute 115
pedagogy 264; hegemonic discourseof 98; indigenising of 145, 172, 183, 188–9; of language teaching 96; linguistically/culturally responsive 181–3, 190–1; of MTM education 51, 178, 181–2; participatory 188; vocabularyand MTM education 52, 170
Pédagogie Convergente, Mali 278
Peru: Juan Velasco Alvarado 89, Fujimori 98; General Education Law (GEL) 2003 90–1; intercultural bilingual education (IBE) 90–2, 96–100; linguistic diversity 12, 86–9; Ministry of Education 99–100; mother tongue instruction 93–6; National Bilingual Education Policy 1972, 90; Regional Education Projects (REPs) 99–103; teaching of Spanish 96–7; Toledo government 99
Philippines: Iloilo project 267
Phillipson, R. 154, 268, 270
policy see language policies
policy planning and implementation ix, 22, 52 124, 126, 198, 200, 235, 266–8; in Bhutan 140; in Burkina Faso 198; in Ethiopia 32–3, 35–6, 40–1, 44, 48, 50, 52, 55–6, 58–9, 63, 103–4, 118–19, 124, 130, 143, 250, 256, 258–9, 275; in India 141–2; in Morocco 220–1, 223–5, 231–4, 267; in Nepal 155–165, 169; in Peru 89–93, 99–101 in Southeast Asia 115, 120–1, 125, 130; see also decentralisation
political mobilisation of indigenous peoples 91, 103, 157, 173n^4
political parties andregimes: Dergue, Ethiopia 35; Fujimori, Peru, 98; Juan Velasco Alvarado, Peru, 89; Lao

People's Revolutionary Party, 120; Maoist government, Nepal 183; Vietnamese National Front for Liberation 115
political pressure on language education policy 92, 208, 211
power relationships among languages and people: hierarchy of 139–42, 144, 154, 157, 167, 199, 220, 223–7, 229, 231, 233–5, 264, 266–7, 275–6
primary education 263
principles for bi/multilingual education 51, 126, 181–2, 264
proficiency in dominant language 96, 270
Programa de Formación de Maestros Bilingües de la Amazonia Peruana (FORMABIAP) 94–5
progression: to secondary school 252–3, 274; to tertiary education 79
Puente de Hózhó Trilingual School, USA 74–5
Pukllasunchis IBE programme 93
Pūnana Leo (Hawaiian 'language nest') movement 72–3
Punjabi 139–40
push-outsee drop-out rates

Quechua 87, 89, 93, 94–5, 100

Rajbangsi 159, 162, 164, 186
Ramanathan, V. 140
Rana (Tharu) 159, 164, 186
Rau, C. 80
Reagan, T. 168
regional languages 139, 141, 244
religion, influence of 115
Remain-Kinda, Emma 208, 212
repeaterrates 199, 206, 274
resources for mother tongue education 51, 119, 161, 244, 245, 257
retention: in primary school, 265; rates 19, 73, 79, 156, 166, 187, 199, 213
reverse planning 258, 269–70, 275
Rosier, P. 69
Rough Rock English-Navajo Language Arts Program (RRENLAP) 68–9
Rough Rock–KEEP collaboration 69

Saib, J. 232
Samassekou, A. 278
Sen, A. 2
Santhali 149n^5, 159, 164
Save the Children 120, 201

science subjects, language for 37, 43–43, 47, 52, 68, 94, 210, 220–1, 224, 243–4, 246, 265
scripts 116, 145, 149n^5, 199: Arabic 226; Amazigh/Berber 226; effect on culture 168; Ethiopic 45, 259n^5; Khmer 117; Latin 45, 226–7, 259n^5; and national identity 227; Roman 116, 131; Sabean/Ethiopic 131; Tifinagh 219, 226–7
SEAMEO 119
Serrano, J. 94, 95
shift away from MTM education: negative effects of 248–50, 256–7, 259n^9, 267, 270
Shipibo 87, 89
Sindhi 139–40
Sirles, C. A. 223
Skutnabb-Kangas, T. 24, 72, 188; linguistic human rights 21–2, 182–83; medium of instruction 155; mother tongue 72, 112, principles of multilingual education 179–82, 191; oracy 167–8, 188
Smith, L. 256
Somali 34, 39–41, 44, 47–8, 50, 54, 56, 126, 241, 244–7, 249–50, 253
South Africa 22, 49–50, 253, 257, 259n^9, 270
Southern Nations, Nationalities and Peoples Region (SNNPR), Ethiopia 39, 42–43, 46, 50–1, 54, 56–7, 240, 242, 244–5, 248–51, 253, 255, 258
South–South dialogue x, 6, 132, 277–8
Spanish: as a second language 96–7; as dominant language 89, as medium of instruction 93–4, 104
Stairs, A. 97
standardisation of languages 170, 227–31, 236 n^5
Stoddart, J. 37
submersion education *xvi*, 78, 97; negative effects of 142, 145–8, 187, 280n^1
subtractive models of language learning xvii, 4, 78, 146, 170, 266, 279; *see also* submersion education
Summer Institute of Linguistics 89, 94–5
Sunsari 159, 162, 164, 186
sustainability of MLE, 26–7

Taib, A.-A. 273

Tamazight 217, 219
Tamil 140–1
Tarifit 217, 219
Tashelhit 217, 219
teacher education 79, 160, 274; in-service 203, 274; intercultural bilingual education (IBE) 96–8; language and culture 77–79; 94–8, 101, 188; medium of instruction 40–1, 52–3, 94–6, 162, 169–70, 232–3, 250, 256, 258; in mother tongue 258, 274; readiness 192; training of trainers 211, 274–5, 184–5
teachers: competence in minority language 180; recruitment and placement 44
teaching materials, 14, 33, 43–4, 50–3; lack of 45
Telugu 141, 145, 146
Terai 164
Terai/Madhesh 158
Thai 113, 116
Thailand 113, 115, 121, 127
Thomas, W. P. 76
Tharu 162, 186
Tharu/Maithili 159, 164
three language formula 13, 141n^2, 142–3, 148, 179
Tibeto-Burman languages 151
Tigray region 34, 39, 40–1, 44, 46, 48, 50, 53, 56, 126, 244, 245, 247–9, 252–3, 258
Tigrinya 45–6, 52, 126
Toe-Sidibé, S. 213
Tomaševski, K. 22
transition to dominant language 63, 145, 148, 172, 241, 244, 256–7: best time for 242–3, 245–6
Trapnell, L. 94, 99, 100, 106
tribal peoples *see* indigenous peoples
Tribhuvan University 277
trilingual formula 207, 251
Tséhootsooí Diné Bi'ólta' (Fort Defiance Navajo Immersion School) 73–4
Tuareg 219
Tubino, F. 92, 106
Tuhiwai Smith, L. 166
Turkoman 273

Uka, N. 168
UNESCO 36, 103, 274; Convention for the Safeguarding of the Intangible Cultural Heritage, 2006 vii;

UNESCO (*cont.*)
Convention on the Protection and Promotion of the Diversity of Cultural Expressions, 2005 vii; Declaration on Cultural Diversity, 2001 vii; Education for AllFramework vii, 156, 207, 266, 157; Institute for Education (UIE) 6, 38; Institute of Lifelong Learning 278; Upper-Volta–UNESCO project 198
UNICEF 120, 124, 201; universal primary education (UPE) 36
UN International Covenant on Economic, Social and Cultural Rights (ICESCR) 154
United Nations: Committee on the Rights of the Child 23, 153–4; *Convention on the Rights of the Child* (CRC) 1989, 22, 27n[15], 153; *Declaration on the Rights of Indigenous Peoples* (UNDRIP) 22, 27–8n[15], 153, 189; The International Covenant on Economic, Social and Cultural Rights (ICESCR) 27n[15]; International Labour Organisation, *Convention No. 169 on Indigenous and Tribal Peoples* 27n[15], 91, 153, 173n[4]; Millennium Development Goals 2, 161; Permanent Forum on Indigenous Issues 21; *Report on the situation of indigenous peoples in Nepal* 161; The Universal Declaration of Human Rights 26–7n[15]
universal primary education (UPE) 36
University of Cape Town 275
University of Limpopo 275
Uranw 159, 162, 164, 166
Urdu 139–40
United States of America: Constitution 67; Esther Martinez

Native American Languages Protection Act 2006, 80; Hawaii Apology Act 1993, 80n[1]; Kahuawaiola Indigenous Teacher Education Program; Native American Languages Act 1990/1992, 80n[2]

Vernacular–Other language divide, 141
Vietnam 113–15, 120, 125–6; constitutions 120; Department of Ethnic Minority Education 123; National Front for Liberation 115; National Institute of Linguistics, Hanoi 115
Vietnamese: as dominant language 114–15, 123; as non-dominant language 128
Vigil, N. 96
Vu, T. T. H. 120

Wagaw, Teshome, 240
Watson-Gegeo, Karen, 5
'washback effect' of prioritisation of English 54–6, 58, 141, 255, 258, 270
Wilson, W. H. 72–3, 76, 79
Yadava, Y. P. 155, 277
writing systems, development of 67, 114–16, 128, 198, 226
written language: effect on culture 168

Xhosa 274

Yassine, N. 225
Yonjan-Tamang, A. 151, 189
Yoruba, 49, 267
Yup'ik 70–1

Zavala, V. 92